Reading the Saints

Biblio Resource Publications, Inc.
Bessemer, Michigan

Reading the Saints

Lists of Catholic Books for Children Plus Book Collecting Tips for the Home and School Library
Second Edition

Janet P. McKenzie

A RACE for Heaven Product

Biblio Resource Publications, Inc.
Bessemer, Michigan

© 2007 by Janet P. McKenzie (previously ©2003 as *Saintly Resources*)

This second edition © 2013 by Janet P. McKenzie contains updated availiability information for out-of-print books as well as new books printed into 2013.

All rights reserved. No part of this book may be reproduced, stored in a retrieval system, or transmitted, in any form or by any means, electronic, mechanical, photocopying, recording, or otherwise, without the written permission of the author.

Published by
Biblio Resource Publications, Inc.
108 ½ South Moore Street
Bessemer, MI 49911
info@BiblioResource.com
www.BiblioResource.com

ISBN: 978-1-934185-45-2

Library of Congress Control Number: 2013905057

Cover photo of St. James © Martin Mullen - Fotolia.com

A **R**ead **A**loud **C**urriculum Enrichment Product
RACEforHeaven.com

Printed in the United States of America

Table of Contents

Introduction .... i-ii
A Note about Spiritual Read-Aloud .... iii-vi
Catholic Out-of-Print Series Books 1-37
    Caldecott Award Books 1
    Kid Scripts 2
    Dorcy Biographies 3
    Faith and Freedom Readers 4-5
    Dujarie Press Biographies 6-15
    Along the Paths of the Gospels Saint Series 16
    Catherine Beebe Biographies 17
    Newbery Award Books 18
    Patron Saint Books 19
    Windeatt Saint Series 20
    Banner Books 21
    Junior Vision Books 22
    Clarion Books 23-24
    Encounter Books 25-26
    Holy Cross Press 27
    Vision Books 28-30
    Weaver Books 31
    American Background Books 32-33
    Catholic Treasury Books 34-35
    Hawthorn Junior Biographies/Catholic Digest Junior Books Shelf/Credo 36-37
Favorite Catholic Books for Various Ages 38
Catholic Series Books in Print 39-66
    Tomie de Paola 39-40
    Father Francis Coloring Books 41
    Mary Fabyan Windeatt Coloring Books 42
    Saint Joseph Bible Story Books 43
    Saint Joseph Picture Books 44-47
    Little Book of Saints Series 48
    Aquinas Kids Lives of the Saints 49
    Dujarie Press Biography Reprints 50
    In the Footsteps of the Saints 51-54
    Catholic Stories for Boys and Girls 55
    Glory of America Series 56
    Easy Reading Books of Saints and Friendly Beasts 57
    Windeatt Saint Biography Series 58-59
    Claire Jordan Mohan Biographies 60
    Encounter the Saints 61-62
    Vision Books 63

    Catholic Children's Library Text-Picture Books 64
    Forbes Biographies 65
    Louis de Wohl Historical Fiction 66

Author Bibliography **67-84**
    Abodaher—Cullen 67-70
    Daley—Francis 70-73
    Gardiner—Kyle 73-76
    Lamers—Ryan 76-80
    Salesians—Wiseman 80-84

Catholic Publishers, Authors, and Poets **85-86**
    Major and Minor Catholic Publishers of Children's Books 85-86
    Favorite Authors and Poets for Catholic Children 86

Saint Series Books by Geographical Setting **87-158**

Saint Series Books in Chronological Order **159-244**

A Bibliomaniac's Guide to Collecting Books **245-251**
    Books about Books 245-247
        Books with Reading Lists 245-246
        Books about Collecting Books 246
        Books that Discuss Books 246-247
        Books about Displaying Book Collections 247
    Book Collecting Basics 247-251
        General Information 247-248
        Used Catholic Children's Books 248
        Library Discards 248-249
        Identification of First Editions 249-250
        Book Club Editions 250
        Reprint Publishers 250-251
        Remainders 251

Care and Storage of Books **252-258**
    Care of Used Books 252-256
        Introduction 252
        Cleaning Books 252-253
        Removal of Stickers, Labels, and Tape Marks 253
        Rolled or Cocked Spines and Broken or Loose Hinges 253
        Elimination of Odors and Insects 254
        Book Covers 254-255
        Yellowing, Toning, Browning, and Foxing 255
        Handling and Shelving Books 255-256
    Book Storage and Retrieval 257-258
        Shelves 257
        Temperature, Humidity, and Sunlight 257
        Creating a System for Retrieving Books in Your Library 258

Other Resources by Janet P. McKenzie **259-264**

Introduction

Every attempt has been made to ensure that the book lists included below are accurate and complete. If any errors or omissions are found in any of these lists, please contact the publisher. Any and all corrections and suggestions for additions are appreciated. Note that no distinction has been made between biography and historical fiction. In the case of the Newbery and Caldecott Award books, many of the selections are fictional books with Catholic and/or Christian content.

While some of the out-of-print series books described in *Reading the Saints* are back in print, many are not. This means that they are not currently being published; new copies may no longer be available. However, this does not mean that the book cannot be purchased. In fact, many of the out-of-print hardbacks are less expensive to purchase than the paperback editions that are currently in print. (See "Book Collecting Basics" beginning on page 247 for more information.) To assist in purchasing, the following symbols are used to indicate the relative availability of each out-of-print book within the series' listings:

* * In print and readily available
* ® Out of print, rare, usually priced over $15.00
* § Out of print, scarce, usually priced over $30.00 with limited copies available

No symbol beside a book indicates that it is readily available for $15.00 or less.

In this new edition, it is necessary to note the proliferation of print-on-demand publishing companies who produce out-of-print books. Beware that often these books are low quality and may be overpriced. While the availability of these books by companies such as Kessinger or Literary Licensing LLC is noted by the initials "POD" and the year, note that many print-on-demand books are scanned copies that are mass-produced and come replete with typos, missing pages, and generic covers. While you may obtain a book you have long been seeking, you may be disappointed in both the quality and the price. To avoid these types of books, it is important to check the name of the book's publisher before you purchase.

Whenever possible, space is provided at the end of each series listing for personal notes. Consider your copy of *Reading the Saints* to be your workbook to keep a record of your family's favorite books on Catholc saints. Use it as a reading diary for your children, noting the dates of completion beside each book. Utilize the databases to incorporate a study of our Catholic saints into your history and religious curriculum, or evening read-aloud program. Make your own list of best-loved books to recommend to others, your most wanted books to purchase, and your own finds of favorite Catholic books for children (See page 84.).

The books listed within each series are in chronological or alphabetical order. The order in which each series is introduced is based upon the reading level of the series; those series with books geared to the youngest readers are listed first in both the "Catholic Out-of-Print Series Books" and "Catholic Series Books in Print" sections.

While this volume is an attempt to list traditional Catholic series books about saints, no attempt has been made to include other types of resources. Below are other possible options:

† In addition to the Fr. Francis and Windeatt series of saint coloring books, many other Catholic coloring book options are available. If your artists enjoy coloring books, check the many options available from your favorite Catholic publisher or vendor.

† Some of the books listed in *Reading the Saints* have also been produced in audio format. For example, under the "Favorite Catholic Books for Various Ages" section on page 38, *The King of the Golden City, The Outlaws of Ravenhurst,* and many of the books published by Bethlehem Books and Ignatius Press are also available as audio books; Catholic Audio Children's Saint Series has begun to record the Mary Fabyan Windeatt saint series books. The Holy Heroes website (www.HolyHeroes.com) offers a variety of audio saint resources including Glory Stories, a series of (currently) twelve audio CD's each containing the stories of two Catholic saints. These are but a few of the audio options available.

† It is increasing popular and, in fact, routine for many publishers to produce their traditional books as e-books in downloadable PDF format. If you or your children prefer this format, consult the publisher's website to see which books are available in this format.

† In addition to the audio Glory Stories series, Holy Heroes also offers various movies in DVD format on the lives of the saints for children. Ignatius Press sells the saint series from CCC of America that includes nine saints as well as many family-appropriate videos on saints' lives. Vision Video also has an excellent selection of Catholic videos including the *My Catholic Family* series that uses the lives of various saints to help teach virtues. If you prefer to rent videos, check out PiusMedia.com. Explore the Internet for many other video options. Viewing a movie about a saint often prompts an increased interest in reading a full-length saint biography.

† Many comicbook-type books that focus on the lives of the saints (such as Comicolor Saints by Pauline Media) are available. If this is your child's interest, please search the World Wide Web for these resources.

† Another valuable saint biography resource is children's saint anthology books. Try the Sisters of Notre Dame's *Saints and Feast Days: A Resource and Activity Book* (2006) or *Illustrated Lives of the Saints* by Rev. Hugo Hoever for daily saint readings. Options are plentiful in this category whether you want daily readings or short stories on specific saints. Again, check with your favorite Catholic publisher or vendor for suggestions.

† And last but not least, consider a phone app on the saints to educate, entertain, and inspire your children. Pauline Media's "Little Ap of Saints" and "Little Ap of More Saints" are available for $.99 each. Designed for children aged 5-11, this ap provides a jigsaw puzzle on various saints with the choice of three levels of difficulty. After the puzzle is solved, a gift is opened that contains a short first-person audio narration of the saint's life (or a song) as well as an application to daily life. Check around for other children's saint aps.

May *Reading the Saints* be a blessing to you and your family as you learn from Holy Mother Church's vast selection of saintly personalities how each of us is called to uniquely serve and praise our loving God.

Janet P. McKenzie
April 7, 2013
Feast of Divine Mercy

Be as careful of the books you read, as of the company you keep, for your habits and character will be as much influenced by the former as the latter.
—Paxton Hood

A Note about Spiritual Read-Aloud

Spiritual Reading

In *My Daily Bread, A Summary of the Spiritual Life* by Father Anthony Paone, S.J., Christ tells us: "My Child, reading and reflecting are a great help to your spiritual life. My doctrine is explained in many books. . . . Some of these books are written simply, and some are very profound and learned. Choose those which will help you most toward a greater understanding and appreciation of My Truth. Do not read to impress others but rather to be impressed yourself. Read so that you may learn My way of thinking and of doing things."

In her book, *Saint Dominic, Preacher of the Rosary and Founder of the Dominican Order*, Mary Fabyan Windeatt quotes St. Dominic as saying, "A little good reading, much prayer and meditation . . . and God will do the rest." Father Peter-Thomas Rohrbach, O.C.D., states that spiritual reading is the "third essential asset for mediation" (after detachment and recollection). The great value he places on the habit of spiritual reading is expressed in his book *Conversation with Christ, An Introduction to Mental Prayer*:

> We live in a world devoid, in great part, of a Christian spirit, in an atmosphere and culture estranged from God. Living in such a non-theological environment makes it difficult for us to remain in contact with the person of Christ and the true purpose of life itself. We must, if we are to remain realistically attached to Christ, combat this atmosphere and surround ourselves with a new one. Constant spiritual reading fills our minds with Christ and His doctrine—it creates this new climate for us.
>
> In former ages, spiritual reading was not as essential for one's prayer life. People lived in a Christian world and culture which was reflected in their laws, customs, amusements, and their very outlook on life. This situation has radically altered in the last two hundred years, and men must now compensate for this deficit through other media, principally reading. And as the de-Christianization of our world continues, the necessity for spiritual reading simultaneously increases. We stand in need of something to bridge the gap between our pagan surroundings and our conversation with Christ—spiritual reading fills this need.
>
> There is today in our country an alarming decline in general reading of all types. It has been estimated that in 1955 an astonishing forty-eight percent of the American adult population reads *no books at all*, and only eighteen percent read from one to four books. The decline in reading is naturally reflected in religious reading as well. And, while the lack of secular reading will occasion a decrease in culture life, the decline in religious reading will have repercussions of a more serious nature—severe detriment to one's spiritual life. Any serious attempt to better one's life spiritually should, therefore, include the resolution to engage in more spiritual reading.
>
> If we confine our reading to non-Catholic books, magazines and newspapers, we almost automatically exclude ourselves from full development in our prayer life. The maxims and philosophy of life expressed in these avenues of communication slowly begin to seep into our lives until eventually they occupy a ruling position. We will not

have surrounded ourselves with a new climate; rather, the non-Catholic climate will have engulfed us.

As all of the above quotations were written over fifty years ago, one can safely surmise that the necessity of cultivating the habit of spiritual reading has only grown in the past several decades.

Spiritual Read Aloud

As supported above, spiritual reading is an essential element of every Christian's life. However, as demonstrated by the ancient practice within monasteries of spiritual read-aloud, this habit is a powerful tool for shared community growth in the spiritual life. For Catholic families, the practice of reading spiritual books aloud produces four desirable effects:

I. It reinforces the habit of spiritual reading for each member of the family and allows each member to practice this habit regardless of age.
II. It reinforces the habit of spiritual conversation if the reading results in even a general discussion of the values and virtues being portrayed in the story.
III. It strengthens the family as the domestic Church where members exist to learn and live the Faith together for the support and enrichment of all family members.
IV. It allows the discussion and demonstration of the practical application of the Faith for all age levels.

The Habit of Spiritual Reading

As outlined above, establishing the habit of daily spiritual reading is essential to our spiritual growth. Through read-aloud, children can be taught at an early age that daily spiritual reading is a fun, rewarding exercise. Make this time together pleasant by allowing the children to do crafts, draw, play quietly with puzzles, toys, etc. As long as their attention is not divided and they can participate in a discussion of the reading afterwards, allow quiet activity. One cannot expect children to sit piously with hands clasped prayerfully throughout the read-aloud session! As the children get older, encourage them to read other spiritual books, including the Bible, during a quiet time of their own. Model this habit by allowing them to observe your habit of daily spiritual reading as well. Although the family read-aloud sessions may average around thirty minutes, private spiritual reading times may be considerably shorter (or longer) depending on the habits and temperament of each child.

The Habit of Spiritual Conversation

This habit, for many families, may begin with spiritual read-aloud. When each member of the family participates in a spiritual discussion of a religious book, the practice of discussing matters of faith and Christ-like living begins to form. If the formation of holy habits and the imitation of the saints is the goal, these discussions will become commonplace in the home as each member checks the others on their actions and words. As family members become more comfortable and open about spiritual matters, this practice will soon spread into other areas of their lives. Spiritual discussions with friends and other relatives will become more natural and, in fact, become an important and vital spiritual habit. Sharing one's own spirituality and encouraging others to become more open and vocal about matters of faith will then become an integral pattern of living.

A Note about Spiritual Read-Aloud

Strengthening the Domestic Church
As we read more about the saints and their lives and begin to share our faith more openly with others, we realize the importance of holy companionship—living with others who share our faith ideas and supporting each other in our attempts to become more like Christ. Families begin to grow together in their knowledge of the Catholic faith and become more willing—even enthused—to support each other throughout the ups and downs of community living. We begin to "bear one another's burdens with peace and harmony and unselfishness." Just as Christ has His Church to help bring salvation to all, we—as family members—have each other to provide mutual support and encouragement in our efforts to enter the narrow gate. Within our families, we will begin to create the Catholic culture that is missing from our world's culture.

The Practical Application of the Faith for All Age Levels
When stories about the saints' lives are read aloud in the family setting, all aged children can participate in a discussion of the imitation of the saint's virtues and holy habits. Each member can help others understand how to apply the lessons the saints teach us on a practical level. All family members can help choose a particular habit or virtue upon which to focus. A reward system can be established for virtuous behavior. A family "plan of attack" on non-virtuous habits and attitudes can be developed, implemented, checked, and revised. All members can be encouraged and taught to imitate Christ by the imitation of His saints.

Summary
Regular family read-loud sessions that center around the lives of the saints will benefit the family with an increased interest in reading—especially saintly literature—a growth in vocabulary, and an improved sense of family unity. Additionally, family members will be encouraged to develop the habit of spiritual reading on their own, will become more comfortable and experienced with spiritual conversation, and be able to apply the Truths of the Catholic faith, on a practical level, to all aspects of their lives—no matter what their age. The customs, habits, and attitudes of the family will more and more reflect those of a Catholic culture. Perseverance in this simple daily ritual will help to "bridge the gap between our pagan surroundings and our conversation with Christ." May *Reading the Saints* be an asset to you and your family as you strive to develop the necessary habit of daily spiritual read-aloud.

When Mother Reads Aloud

When Mother reads aloud the past
Seems real as every day;
I hear the tramp of armies vast,
I see the spears and lances cast,
I join the thrilling fray;
Brave knights and ladies fair and proud
I meet when Mother reads aloud.

When Mother reads aloud, far lands
Seem very near and true;
I cross the desert's gleaming sands,
Or hunt the jungle's prowling bands,
Or sail the ocean blue;
Far heights, whose peaks the cold mists shroud,
I scale, when Mother reads aloud.

When Mother reads aloud I long
For noble deeds to do—
To help the right, redress the wrong,
It seems so easy to be strong, so simple
to be true,
O, thick and fast the visions crowd
When Mother reads aloud.
—*Anonymous*

The Reading Mother

I had a mother who read to me
Sagas of pirates who scoured the sea,
Cutlasses clenched in their yellow teeth,
"Blackbirds" stowed in the hold beneath.

I had a mother who read me plays
Of ancient and gallant and golden days
Stories of Marmion and Ivanhoe,
Which every boy has a right to know.

I had a mother who read me tales
Of Gelert, the hound of the hills of Wales,
True to his trust till his tragic death,
Faithfulness blest with his final breath.

I had a mother who read me things
That wholesome life to the boy-heart brings—
Stories that stir with an upward touch,
O, that each mother of boys was such.

You may have tangible wealth untold,
Caskets of jewels and coffers of gold.
Richer than I you can never be—
I had a mother who read to me.
—*Strickland Gullilan*

> **When I read, it will not be to satisfy my curiosity or natural desire of the spirit to know things, nor for the purpose of remembering beautiful things, but only for tasting and savoring divine things, to nourish my soul with this taste, because these tastes of divine things are the marrow that nourishes and fattens the soul. The words and the thoughts are like the dregs and the lees which one rejects once one has experienced the marrow and the substance.**
> —John Cassian

Catholic Out-of-Print Series Books

Caldecott Award Books

The following books are those that have won the Caldecott Medal or have been recognized as Caldecott Honor books. The Caldecott Medal was named in honor of the nineteenth-century English illustrator Randolph Caldecott. Since 1938, this award has been presented each year by the Association for Library Service to Children—a division of the American Library Association—to the "artist of the most distinguished American picture book for children." While the books listed below are not strictly about saints, the books listed contain Catholic and/or Christian content. Independent reading level on most of these books is around age eight, but these picture books can be enjoyed by all ages. (Later books in this series are still in print.)

> **Children are made readers on the laps of their parents.**
> —Emilie Buchwald

Ages: 4 and up

1. §Ageless Story by Lauren Ford, with antiphons pictured by the author (1939) – the story of Christ's birth with Gregorian chant notations
2. *Baboushka and the Three Kings by Ruth Robbins, illustrated by Nicolas Sidjakov (1960) – a Russian tale of the Epiphany
3. ®Christmas Anna Angel by Ruth Sawyer, illustrated by Kate Seredy (1944) – a Hungarian Christmas of long ago
4. *Juanita by Leo Politi, illustrated by the author (1948) – traditional Mexican blessing of the animals on the day before Easter
5. Nine Days to Christmas, A Story of Mexico by Marie Hall Ets and Aurora Labastida, illustrated by Marie Hall Ets (1959) – *posadas* and *pinatas* for Christmas
6. *Noah's Ark by Jerry Pinkney, illustrated by author (2003) – story of the Flood
7. *Noah's Ark by Peter Spier, illustrated by the author (1977) – wordless story of the Flood
8. *Pedro, the Angel of Olvera Street by Leo Politi, illustrated by the author (1946) – *posadas* and *pinatas* for Christmas
9. *Saint George and the Dragon by Margaret Hodges, illustrated by Trina Schart Hyman (1984) – the legend of St. George
10. *Song of the Swallows by Leo Politi, illustrated by the author (1948) – swallows' annual return to the Mission of San Juan Capistrano on St. Joseph's Day

> **Everything we read stimulates our mind to think, and what we think determines what we desire, and desires are the seedbed of our actions.**
> —Fr. John Hardon

Kid Scripts

These newer publications were written for ages four through eight to introduce them to the Old Testament characters. Written by Katy Keck Arnsteen, each paperback is twenty-four pages in length. Unfortunately, all of the titles are currently out of print. Some copies can be obtained through used book vendors at reasonable prices. (The titles in this series are not numbered.)

Name of Publisher: Pauline Books and Media

Ages: 4-8

Date of Publication: 1997

1. Abraham and Isaac
2. Deborah
3. Jonah, the Whale, and the Vine
4. Joseph and the Dream
5. Joshua, God's General
6. Moses
7. Naomi and Ruth
8. ®Queen Esther

> **God be thanked for books! They are the voices of the distant and the dead, and make us heirs of the spiritual life of past ages.**
> —W.E. Channing

Notes:

_____
_____
_____
_____
_____
_____
_____
_____
_____

> **Books are the quietest and most constant of friends: they are the most accessible and wisest of counsellors, and the most patient of teachers.**
> —Charles W. Eliot

Dorcy Biographies

The Dominican sister, Mary Jean Dorcy, is well known for her silhouette scissor paper cuttings as well as her books on saints—especially Dominican saints. These are written on varied reading levels. Some of Sr. Dorcy's saint books have been reprinted, but many have recently gone out of print again. Pick up these treasures when you can find them!

Ages: 5 and up

1. ®Mary, My Mother: A Mary-book for Little Boys and Girls (1944)
2. ®Our Lady's Feasts (1945, 1954, 1999)
3. ®A Crown for Joanna (Joanna of Portugal, 1946)
4. §Army in Battle Array, Dominican Saints and Blessed (Pius V, John of Gorkum, James of Ulm, Catherine de Ricci, Peter Geremia, Rose of Lima, Margaret of Castello, Martin de Porres, Alphonsus Navarrette, and Louis de Montfort; 1947)
5. *Truth Was Their Star (Albert the Great, Thomas Aquinas, Agnes of Montepulciano, Vincent Ferrer, Antonimus, Imelda Lambertini, Blessed Joanna of Portugal, Catherine of Siena, Louis Bertrand, and John Masias; 1947; 1999 by New Hope Publications)
6. ®Hunters of Souls, Dominican Saints and Blesseds, (Dominic, Peter Martyr of Verona, Hyacinth, Zedislava of Bohemia, Raymond of Pennafort, Margaret of Hungary, James of Voragine, Albert of Bergamo, Catherine of Racconigi, Sadoc and Martyrs of Sandomir; 1949; 1999 by The Neumann Press)
7. Our Lady of Springtime – poetry (1953; 2000 by The Neumann Press)
8. ®Master Albert, The Story of Saint Albert the Great (1955)
9. *Fount of Our Joy, Madonna Legends for Dramatization (1955, 2011 by POD)
10. ®Shrines of Our Lady (1956)
11. §Our Lady of the Fields (1957)
12. *Saint Dominic (1959; 1982 and 2009 by Tan Books/St. Benedict Press)
13. *St. Dominic's Family (over 300 saint stories, 1964; 1983, 1999, and 2009 by Tan Books/St. Benedict Press)

Notes:

_____

_____

_____

_____

_____

_____

I have always imagined that paradise will be a kind of library. —Jorge Luis Borges

Faith and Freedom Readers

Although Seton Press has reprinted the revised editions of the Faith and Freedom readers in paperback (*), all of these readers are out of print in the hardcover edition by Ginn and Company. These books were published in the original edition (1940's), as well as new (1950's) and revised (1960's) editions—all containing different stories. In addition, several different titles were published in Canada. Remember when searching for these books that although the newer editions are more reasonably priced and easier to find, the Catholic content decreases with each republished edition. The first availability code for each reader denotes the Seton reprint while the second code refers to the hardcover book—in any edition. (The following series list may be incomplete, especially concerning the Canadian editions.)

Name of Publisher: Ginn and Company

Ages: 5 and up

> To learn to read is to light a fire; every syllable that is spelled out is a spark. —Victor Hugo

Primers
  §On the Road to Reading (pre-reader)
  *§Here We Come (first pre-primer)
  *§This Is Our Home (second pre-primer – original softcover and hardback)
  *§Here We Are Again (third pre-primer)
  *This Is Our Family (primer)
Grade 1
  *These Are Our Friends
Grade 2
  *These Are Our Neighbors (Grade 2.1)
  *®This Is Our Parish (Grade 2.2)
  *§A Book of Sanctity (literary reader)
Grade 3
  *®This Is Our Town (Grade 3.1)
  *This Is Our Valley (Grade 3.2)
  *®The Story Tree (Grade 3.3)
  §A Book of Joy (literary reader for teachers)
Grade 4
  *®This Is Our Land
  *§Book of Gladness (literary reader)
  *§Book of Gratitude (literary reader)
Grade 5
  *®These Are Our People
  §These Are Our Stories (Canada)
  ®A Book of Kindness (literary reader)

Grade 6
    *®This Is Our Heritage
    *§A Book of Valor (literary reader)

Grade 7
    *These Are Our Freedoms
    *§A Book of Fortitude (literary reader)

Grade 8
    *®These Are Our Horizons
    *®A Book of Friendliness (literary reader)

Notes:

_____
_____
_____
_____
_____
_____
_____
_____
_____
_____
_____

_____
_____
_____
_____
_____
_____
_____

> **MY BOOK! I did it! I did it!**
> **Come and look at what I've done!**
> **I read a book!**
> **When someone wrote it long ago**
> **For me to read how did he know**
> **That this was the book**
> **I'd take from the shelf**
> **And lie on the floor**
> **And read by myself?**
> **I really read it! Just like that!**
> **Word by word, from first to last!**
> **I'm sleeping with this book in bed,**
> **This first FIRST book**
> **I've ever read!** —David L. Harrison

Dujarie Press Biographies

No list of children's out-of-print Catholic biographies would be complete without mentioning the Dujarie Press books. Written by the brothers of the Holy Cross Congregation (C.S.C.), these books were published from the 1940's through the 1960's. Brother Ernest (Ryan) founded Dujarie Press in 1940. By 1943, Brother Ernest had written four novels; and by 1960, he had authored 124 books. Brother Ernest died on March 4, 1963; but by 1964, Dujarie Press had published almost four hundred fictionalized biographies of Catholic artists, saints, scientists, explorers, and musicians. For many years, these books remained out of print, scarce, and expensive. However beginning in March of 2005, The Neumann Press began republishing books from this series. After five books, they discontinued in 2009 when Mary's Books Publishing began, with the permission of Brother Roberto of the Holy Cross Congregation, to reprint this series in its entirety. To date, Mary's Books Publishing has reprinted over 70 books from this series with more slated for 2013 and 2014. (See "In the Footsteps of the Saints" below.)

Listed below are 370 Dujarie Press biographies—hopefully a complete, or at least nearly complete, list of those published. The books are organized by author and, due to scarcity, not included on the chronological and geographical data bases in this book.

Publisher's Description: "Dujarie Press specializes in books for young readers from the first grade on up through high school. Our books are produced on four rather distinct levels: primary (first through third grades), intermediate (fourth through sixth grades), upper class (seventh and eighth grades), and high school books."

Ages: 6 and up

Look for these books at thrift shops, yard sales, and Catholic library discard sales. Watch especially for the more common authors in this series: Brother Ernest, Brother Roberto (Brother Gerald Francis Muller), and Brother Flavius. Any hardcover book from this series—in any condition—that can be found for less than $15.00 is a bargain and, if possible, should be rescued and read. See "Dujarie Press Biography Reprints" and "In the Footsteps of the Saints" in the "Catholic Series Books in Print" section below for a current listing of republications from this series.

Brother Anthony Blasi
Jeremy, A Story of Jeremiah the Prophet

Brother Bernard Donahoe
Fold it Gently, A Story of Fr. Abram J. Ryan
Patriot in Purple, A Story of Archbishop John Carroll
Stars on My Shoulders, A Story of General Philip Sheridan
Up from the Sidewalks, A Story of Alfred Emmanuel Smith
Voice that Shook the Windows, A Story of Prince Gallitzin
Where Roams the River, A Story of Father Marquette

Brother Bernardine Mosier
Saint of the Impossible, A Story of St. Rita

Brother Daniel Bengert
King of Coaches, A Story of Knute Rockne

Brother Donald Pelous
Angel of Peace, A Story of St. Elizabeth of Hungary
Dream Come True (A), A Story of Saint Isaac Jogues
I Am a Beggar, A Story of Benedict Joseph Labre
Saint Who Forgot Herself (The), A Story of St. Collette

Brother Donan Johnroe
Gold Tried by Fire, A Story of St. Jean De Brebeuf

Brother Dunstan Bowles
Poor Rich Man (A), A Story of St. Thomas of Villanova

Brother Edward Overstreet
From the Lion's Mouth, A Story of Daniel the Prophet
Ink in His Blood, A Story of Monsignor Ronald Knox
Ox Was an Angel (The), A Story of St. Thomas Aquinas

Brother Edwin Reggio
Microbe Detective, A Story of Louis Pasteur
Saint in the Kitchen (A), A Story of St. Zita

Brother Ernest (Ryan)
Angel of the Poor, A Story of Mother Emmelie Gamelin
Archer Saint (The), A Story of Saint Hubert
Black Saint (The), A Story of St. Benedict the Negro
Boy Who Saw the World (The), A Story of St. Francis Xavier
Boy Who Threw Away His Gold (The), A Story of St. Francis of Assisi
Boy Who Worked Wonders (The), A Story of St. Anthony of Padua
Captain Johnny Ford
Children's Bishop (The), A Story of Bishop James A. Healy
Come to Bethlehem, A Story of Jesus Christ
Dragon Killer (The), A Story of St. George
Flames Against the Sky, A Story of St. Joan of Arc
Giant Saint (The), A Story of St. Christopher
Happy Heart (A), A Story of Mother Pauline Von Mallickrodt
He's a Man, A Story of St. Gerard Majella
Hound of God (The), A Story of St. Dominic
Just for Today, A Story of Mother Leonie
Just One of Us, A Story of Saint Gabriel Possemti
King of Giants (The), A Story of Michaelangelo
Little Brother Martin, A Story of Saint Martin de Porres
Little Flower (The), A Story of St. Therese Martin

> **No man can be called friendless who has God and the companionship of good books.**
> —Elizabeth Barrett Browning

Man under the Stairs (The), A Story of St. Alexis
Miracle Man of Muro (The), A Story of St. Gerard Majella
Monogram Saint (The), A Story of St. Bernard of Siena
Our Lady Comes to Banneux (Belgium 1933)
Our Lady Comes to Beuraing (Belgium 1932)
Our Lady Comes to Fatima
Our Lady Comes to Guadalupe
Our Lady Comes to LaSalette
Our Lady Comes to Lourdes
Our Lady Comes to Newenham, A Story of St. Simon Stock and the Scapular
Our Lady Comes to Paris, A Story of St. Catherine Laboure
Our Lady Comes to Pontmain
Our Lady's Portrait Painter, A Story of Raphael
Prisoner of the Vatican (A), A Story of Pope Pius IX
Red Cross Saint (The), A Story of St. Camillus de Lellis
Saint of Little Things, A Story of St. Bovaventure
Saint of the Eucharist, A Story of St. Paschal Baylon
Saint of the Fighting Irish, A Story of St. Patrick
So Shines the Lamp, A Story of St. Lawrence of Brindisi
Son of Thunder, A Story of St. John
Star for All Eternity (A), A Story of Brother Adain O'Reilly, C.S.C.
Star Forever (A), A Story of St. Tarcisus

Story of Beethoven, A
Story of Blessed Imelda, A
Story of Blessed Julie Billiart, A
Story of Blessed Margaret D'Youville, A
Story of Charles Gounod, A
Story of Columbus, A
Story of Diego Mendez, A
Story of Doctor Tom Dooley, A
Story of Dvorak, A
Story of Father Damien, A
Story of Franz Haydn , A
Story of Franz Schubert, A
Story of John XXIII, A
Story of Louis Braille, A
Story of Louis Pasteur, A
Story of Michelangelo, A
Story of Millet, A
Story of Mother Catherine McAuley , A
Story of Mother Clare Fey, A
Story of Mother Elizabeth Seton, A
Story of Mother Pauline von Mallinkrodt

Story of Mozart, A
Story of Our Lady Comes to Banneaux
Story of Our Lady of Fatima, A
Story of Our Lady of Guadalupe, A
Story of Our Lady of LaSallete, A
Story of Prince Father Gallitzin, A
Story of Rubens, A
Story of St. Agatha, A
Story of St. Agnes, A
Story of St. Aloysius Gonzaga, A
Story of St. Andrew, A
Story of St. Angela Merici, A
Story of St. Anthony of Padua, A
Story of St. Benedict, A
Story of St. Benedict the Negro, A
Story of St. Bernadette, A
Story of St. Bonaventure, A
Story of St. Boniface, A
Story of St. Bridget, A
Story of St. Camillus, A
Story of St. Catharine Laboure, A

Story of St. Catherine of Sienna, A
Story of St. Cecilia, A
Story of St. Charles, A
Story of St. Christopher, A
Story of St. Clare, A
Story of St. Cyprian, A
Story of St. Dominic, A
Story of St. Dominic Savio, A
Story of St. Dorothy, A
Story of St. Elizabeth of Hungary, A
Story of St. Frances of Rome. A
Story of St. Frances Xavier Cabrini, A
Story of St. Francis of Assisi, A
Story of St. Francis Xavier, A
Story of St. Gabriel Possenti, A
Story of St. Gemma, A
Story of St. George, A
Story of St. Gerard Majella, A
Story of St. Germaine, A
Story of St. Hyacinth, A
Story of St. Ignatius Loyola, A
Story of St. Issac Jogues, A
Story of St. James, A
Story of St. Jane Frances de Chantal, A
Story of St. Joan of Arc, A
Story of St. John, A
Story of St. John Berchmans, A
Story of St. John Bosco, A
Story of St. John Gaulbert, A
Story of St. John Vianney, A
Story of St. Joseph, A
Story of St. Jude, A
Story of St. Louis, A
Story of St. Louise de Marillac, A
Story of St. Lucy, A
Story of St. Margaret Mary Alacoque, A
Story of St. Margaret of Hungary, A
Story of St. Margaret of Scotland, A
Story of St. Mark, A
Story of St. Martin de Porres, A
Story of St. Matthew, A
Story of St. Meinrad, A
Story of St. Paschal Baylon, A
Story of St. Patrick, A
Story of St. Paul, A
Story of St. Peregrine, A
Story of St. Perpetua, A
Story of St. Peter, A
Story of St. Peter of Verona, A
Story of St. Phillip, A
Story of St. Pius X, A
Story of St. Raphael, A
Story of St. Raymond, A
Story of St. Rita, A
Story of St. Rose of Lima, A
Story of St. Sebastian, A
Story of St. Simon Stock, A
Story of St. Stanislaus Kostka, A
Story of St. Stephen, A
Story of St. Tarcisius, A
Story of St. Therese, A
Story of St. Thomas Aquinas, A
Story of St. Thomas More, A
Story of St. Vincent de Paul, A
Story of St. Wenceslaus, A
Story of St. Zita, A
Story of the Infant Jesus of Prague, A
Story of Verdi, A
St. Joseph's Little Brother, A Story of Brother Andre
That Boy! A Story of St. Gabriel Possenti
These Two Hearts, A Story of Brother Columba O'Neil
Through the Dark Night, A Story of Matt Talbot
To the End of Time, A Story of St. Angela Merci
When All Ships Fall, A Story of St. Raymond of Pennafort
When the Going Gets Tough, A Story of St. Jude

Young Prince Gonzaga, A Story of St. Aloysius
Your Mother and Mine, Blessed Mother of God

Brother Evan Schmid
Cardinal from Oxford, A Story of John Henry Cardinal Newman
Dante and His Journey
David, A Story of the King of Israel
Eagle of Avila (The), A Story of Saint Teresa of Avila
Giant in Mind, A Story of Leonardo Da Vinci
Great Saint Augustine (The), A Story of St. Augustine of Hippo
Master Mozart
Merry Saint (The), A Story of St. Thomas More
Mighty Bernard (The), A Story of St. Bernard of Clairvaux

Brother Flavius (Ellison)
Apostle in Michigan (An), A Story of Father Gabriel Richard
Come on In! A Story of St. John Bosco
Father of the American Cavalry, A Story of Brigadier General Casimir Pulaski
Father of the American Navy, A Story of Captain John Barry
House on Logan Square (The), A Story of Blessed John Neumann
In Virtue's Cause, A Story of John F. Kennedy
Melody in Their Hearts, A Story of St. Benedict and St. Scholastica
Miracle for the Bride, A Story of St. Bridget
No Stranger in Paradise, A Story of Blessed Mother Julie Billiart
Pride of Our Nation (The), A Story of Chief Justice Roger Brooke Taney
Proudly We Hail, A Story of St. Francis de Sales
Star in the East (A), A Story of St. Catherine of Alexandria
Stepping Stones to Heaven, A Story of St. Gaspar del Bufalo
Story of St. Agnes of Assisi, A
Story of St. Catherine of Alexandria, A

Brother Franciscus Willett
Fisherman Saint (The), A Story of St. Peter
Merry Music Maker, A Story of Franz Schubert
Story of St. Germaine, A
Tentmaker from Tarsus, A Story of St. Paul

Brother Franklin Cullen
Song of the Sword (The), A Story of St. Martin of Tours
Story of St. Blaise, A
Story of St. Roch, A
Victory on Pambar Hill (A), A Story of St. John de Britto

Brother Genard Greene
Above the Wind's Roar, A Story of St. Francis Solano
All on Fire, A Story of St. Gemma Galgani
Behind Shuttered Windows, A Story of St. Catherine of Sienna

> **When you reread a classic, you do not see more in the book than you did before; you see more in you than there was before.**
> —Cliff Fadiman

Cry in the Wilderness, A Story of St. John the Baptist
Hour of the Dragon, A Story of Theophane Venard
Runaway Saint (The), A Story of St. John of God
Saint of the Slaves, A Story of St. Peter Claver
Song in Her Heart (A), A Story of St. Cecilia
To the Ends of the Earth, A Story of St. Frances Xavier Cabrini
Watchdog on the Rhine, A Story of Saint Peter Canisius

Brother Gerard Hagemann
Child of Many Wonders, A Story of the Divine Infant Jesus of Prague
Crossbearer to the Savages, A Story of Fra Junipero Serra
Hero of the Gallows, A Story of Blessed Edmund Campion
Man on the Bench, A Story of Chief Justice Edward White
Show Us Your Face, A Story of Leo DuPont
Sword that Sings to Mary, A Story of St. Alphonsus Ligouri

Brother Germain Faddoul
Angel for His Guide (An), A Story of Tobit and Tobias
Knight Without Armor, A Story of St. Thomas Aquinas

Brother Gerontius McCarthy
Who Is Like God, A Story of St. Pius V

Brother John Boyle
Behold this Heart, A Story of Margaret Mary Alacoque
Fire on Earth, A Story of St. Vincent De Paul
Little One (The), A Story of St. Therese of the Child Jesus
Princess of Poverty, A Story of St. Clare

Brother Joseph Dispenza
Forgotten Patriot, A Story of Father Pierre Gibault

Brother Lawrence Emge
Story of St. Lawrence, A

Brother Lawrence Fitch
Song of the Shoemaker's Son (The), A Story of Saint Pius X
World and the White Prince (The), A Story of Pope Pius XII

Brother Louis Gazagne
Saint on Horseback (The), A Story of St. Louis IX King of France

Brother Marco Daly
Boy from Cheapside (The), A Story of St. Thomas Of Canterbury
Magic Brush (The), A Story of Giotto
Queen of the Poor, A Story of St. Elizabeth of Hungary
Saint Who Asked Why (The), A Story of St. Albert the Great
Secret Service, A Story of Venerable Robert Southwell, S.J.
Wool Merchant's Son (The), A Story of St. Alfonso Rodriguez

> **Read the best books first or you may not have a chance to read them at all.**
> —Henry David Thoreau

Brother Paulus McCory
Saint of the Countryside (The), A Story of St. John Vianney

Brother Raymond Fleck
Angel in the Streets (An), A Story of Blessed Martin de Porres
Christ Comes to Molokai, A Story of Father Damien
Good St. Joseph, A Story of St. Joseph

Brother Raymond Papenfuss
Christ Comes to the Indians, A Story of St. Louis Bertnard
Cortez Rides Again, A Story of Hernando Cortez
God's Warrior, A Story of St. Peter Damian

Brother Richard Shea
At the Bottom of My Class, A Story of Gilbert Keith Chesterton
In the Palm of His Hand, A Story of John McCormick

Brother Roberto (Muller)
And the Thunder Roared, A Story of St. Norbert
And Thor Was Silent, A Story of St. Boniface of Germany
Angel of the Ragpickers, A Story of Fr. Jean Lamay
Ax Must Fall (The), A Story of St. John Fisher
Blue Angels with White Hats, A Story of St. Louise de Marillac
Boy in a Hurry, A Story of St. Dominic Savio
Boys and Brothers, A Story of St. John Baptist de Lasalle
Brave Never Die (The), A Story of Frederick Ozanam
Break Down the Doors, A Story of Pope Pius VII
Bring Me an Ax! A Story of St. Boniface of Germany
Broken Lamp (The), A Story of Edith Stein
Catherine of Mercy, A Story of Mother Catherine McAuley
Crown for the Butcher's Wife (A), A Story of Blessed Margaret Clitherow
Crown for the Schoolboy (A), A Story of St. John Berchmans
Cry Mutiny! A Story of Ferdinand Magellan
Dawn Brings Glory, A Story of Father Pro
Death Beneath the Trees, A Story of Joyce Kilmer
Diamond in the Dust, A Story of Blessed Therese Couderc
Don't Push! A Story of Cesar Franck
Don't Turn Back, A Story of St. Ignatius Loyola
Drop the Dagger! A Story of St. Anthony Claret
Face in the Flames (The), A Story of St. Bridget of Sweden
Family that Never Died (The), A Story of St. Felicitas and Her Seven Sons
Flame Still Burns (The), A Story of St. Margaret of Cortona
Flames for the Bride, A Story of St. Agnes
Follow the Setting Sun, A Story of Christopher Columbus
Forgotten Madonna, A Story of Our Lady of Prompt Succor
Girl in the Grotto (The), A Story of St. Bernadette of Lourdes

Girl Who Laughed at Satan (The), A Story of St. Rose of Lima
Girl Who Worked Wonders (The), A Story of St. Philomena
Golden Gift (The), A Story of Peter Paul Rubens
Great Mistake (The), A Story of John Cabot
He Sings with Kings, A Story of Gioacchino Rossini
Heart in the Desert, A Story of Charles De Foucald
Hide the Children! A Story of St. Bernard of Clairvaux
Hide this Treasure, A Story of Blessed Therese Couderc
I Come to Conquer, A Story of Francisco Pizarro
I Fight for Freedom, A Story of Thaddeus Kosciuszko
I Paint with Fire, A Story of Delacrovix
I Saw an Angel, A Story of St. Frances of Rome
I Serve the King, A Story of St. Francis Borgia
I Walk with Giants, A Story of Sandro Botticelli
Killer Comes! (The), A Story of St. Anthony Claret
King of Colors (The), A Story of Fra Angelica
King without a Crown (The), A Story of St. Wenceslaus
King's Trumpeter (The), A Story of St. Vincent Ferrer
Kitty! Come Quickly, A Story of Mother Catherine McAuley
Lead My Sheep, A Story of Pope John XXIII
Let Edward Be King! A Story of St. Edward the Confessor
Let Him Live, A Story of St. John Gualbert
Let Them Sing, A Story of Charles Gounod
Let There Be Radio! A Story of Guglielmo Marconi
Light on the Mountain, A Story of St. Paul of the Cross
Lion of Bethlehem (The), A Story of St. Jerome
Listen for His Laughter, A Story of Camille Corot
Man Who Limped to Heaven (The), A Story of St. Ignatius Loyola
Man Who Tamed a Monster (The), A Story of Andre Ampere
Man without Fear (The), A Story of Hernando De Soto
Martyr Who Laughed (The), A Story of Father Pro
Merry Watchmaker (The), A Story of Louis Martin
Miracles for the Asking, A Story of St. Germaine
More than Money Can Buy, A Story of Mother Katherine Drexel
Music for Millions, A Story of Ignace Paderewski
Music from the Hunger Pit, A Story of Father Maximilian Kolbe
My Friends, the Bandits! A Story of St. Paul of the Cross
No Jewels for Jane, A Story of St. Jane Frances de Chantal
No More Shall I Wander, A Story of Carl Von Weber
No Tears for the Bride, A Story of St. Perpetua
No Wings for Nine Angels, A Story of Zelie Martin
Now Comes the Hangman, A Story of Blessed Oliver Plunkett
Our Lady Comes to New Orleans

> **These are not books, lumps of lifeless paper, but minds alive on the shelves.**
> —Gilbert Highet

Out of the Darkness, A Story of Louis Martin
Peter Laughed at Pain, A Story of St. Peter of Alcantara
Please Bring the Children, A Story of St. Mother Elizabeth Seton
Prince on a Galloping Horse (The), A Story of St. Charles Borremeo
Rambling Rebel (The), A Story of Father John Banister Tabb
Roar from the Cave, A Story of St. Jerome
Rock Cannot be Moved (The), A Story of Pope Innocent XI
Rose for Rita (A), A Story of Saint Rita of Cascia
Saint Therese Martin
Sea Is My Highway (The), A Story of Vasco da Gama
Search for a Shepherd (A), A Story of Father Paul of Graymoor
Secrets of the Silent Tongue, A Story of St. John Nepomucene
So Much for So Many, A Story of St. Margaret of Scotland
Soldier Died Twice (The), A Story of St. Sebastian
Stairway to the Stars, A Story of St. Germaine
Tell My People, A Story of St. Bridget of Sweeden
There Are No Bad Boys, A Story of Father Flanagan of Boys Town
These Boys Will Not Grow Up, A Story of Cerregio
Throw Him to the Lions! A Story of St. Cyprian
Tomb for the Living, A Story of Father Maxmilian Kolbe
Torch in the Darkness (A), A Story of St. John Capistrano
Treasures at My Finger Tip, A Story of Louis Braille
Trial by Torture, A Story of St. John Nepomucene
We Sail at Dawn! A Story of Ferdinand Magellan
Who Will Believe Me?, A Story of Marco Polo
With Fire, Swords and Whips, A Story of St. Andrew Bobola

Brother Roy Nash
And the Angels Sang, A Story of G. Pl. Palestrina
Death Is My Parish, A Story of Blessed Henry Morse
I'll Bow Sadly, A Story of Guiseppe Verdi
Sing My Poor Heart, Sing, A Story of Franz Peter Schubert
Thundering Silence (The), A Story of Ludwig von Beethoven
Wandering Minstrel (The), A Story of Antonin Dvorak
With Flaming Heart, A Story of Saint Philip Neri

Brother Russell J. Huff
Come Build My Church, The Story of Our Lady of Guadalupe

Brother Sabinus
Maid of Corinaldo (The), A Story of St. Maria Goretti

Brother Sigismund
Lad Who Hiked to Heaven (The), A Story of St. Stanislaus Kostka

Brother Theodore Latour
Schoolboy Saint (The), A Story of St. Dominic Savio

> **Far more seemly were it for thee to have thy study full of books, than thy purse full of money.** —John Lyly

Brother Thomas Balthazor
Apostle in the Rockies (An), A Story of Father de Smet
Grant, Chet
Fumblestumble Sandy, The True Story of Sandy Sanders
Sister Joseph Eleanor
Call to Courage, A Story of Mother Theodore Guerin
Sister Mary Henrica
Christmas Forever, A Story of Mother Clare Fey
Sister Mary Thomas
Not Words but Deeds, A Story of Nano Nagle

Notes:

Along the Paths of the Gospel Saint Series

Publisher's Description: "This . . . series introduces children to some special friends whose stories will help them remember that God lives in every person they meet. As children learn to love and respect everyone, they will follow the way of the Gospel—just as the saints did. Full color illustrations on every page, a prayer and glossary encourage children to interact with the story." This hardback series is colorfully illustrated for primary children. Other editions of these books—some in paperback format—are also available. These books are rapidly becoming scarce and expensive; if you find one at a reasonable price, it would be wise to purchase it. (The titles in this series are not numbered and may be incomplete.)

Name of Publisher: Pauline Books and Media

Ages: 7 and up

Date of Publication: 1997-2002

1. ®Saint John Bosco: The Friend of Children and Young People by Carole Monmarché (1997)
2. §Saint Colette: In the Footsteps of Saint Francis and Saint Clare by the Poor Clares of Poligny and Sister Elisabeth (1998)
3. Saint Francis of Assisi: God's Gentle Knight by Francoise Vintrou (1998)
4. ®Saint Anthony of Padua: Proclaimer of the Good News by Marie Baudouin-Croix (1999)
5. ®Saint Thérèse of Lisieux: And the "Little Way" of Love by Marie Baudouin-Croix (1999)
6. §Saint Vincent de Paul: Servant of Charity by Sister Catherine Ethievant (1999)
7. §Saint Angela Merici: Leading People to God by Sister Maryellen Keefe (2000)
8. §Saint Catherine Laboure: Mary's Messenger by Sister Marie-Genevieve Roux and Sister Elisabeth Charpy (2000)

The following books follow the format of the above series books but were not published by Pauline Books and Media. All are currently out of print.

1. §Saint Dominic de Guzman by Emilio Diez Ordonez (2000)
2. §St. Margaret Mary: Apostle of the Sacred Heart by Francoise Vintrou (2000)
3. ®Saint Louise de Marillac by Sister Marie-Genevieve Roux and Sister Elisabeth Charpy (2001)
4. §Maria Domenica Mazzarello by Catherino Fino (2002)

Notes:

_____

_____

_____

_____

Catherine Beebe Biographies

Catherine Beebe has authored many children's books including several in the Vision series and an anthology book of saints, *Saints for Boys and Girls* (1959). Her husband, Robb Beebe, illustrated many of her books. Mrs. Beebe also co-authored the Faith and Freedom reader, *This Is Our Parish*. Included below are the children's books she has written on saints, excluding her three Vision series books. These books were published by various publishers. While all of these books are out of print, their availability has been noted.

Ages: 8 and up

1. ®The Children's Saint Anthony (1939, 1943)
2. ®The Children's Saint Francis (1941, 1946)
3. The Story of Jesus for Boys and Girls (1945)
4. *®Little Patron of Gardeners: The Good Saint Fiacre (1948, 2012 by POD)
5. §Days of Praise for Mary Our Mother (large-print book on Marian feasts days, 1949)
6. ®The Story of Mary, The Mother of Jesus (1950)
7. *®Saint Christopher for Boys and Girls (1955, 2012 by POD)
8. ®The Apostles of the Lord (1958)
9. ®Saints for Boys and Girls (1959)
10. ®The Christmas Story According to the Holy Gospel (ages five through eight, 1963)
11. §David, The Shepherd King (1966)
12. ®Saint Patrick: Apostle of Ireland (40 pages, 1968)

Notes:

> **The books we read should be chosen with great care, that they may be, as an Egyptian king wrote over his library, "The medicines of the soul."**
> —Paxton Hood

Newbery Award Books

The John Newbery Award has been awarded annually by the Association for Library Service to Children since 1922. Named after an eighteenth-century bookseller, this annual award is bestowed upon "the author of the most distinguished contribution to American literature for children." Additionally, each year several books—the number varies each year—are recognized as Newbery Honor Books. The following Newbery books are not saint biographies; some fall under the genre of historical fiction and the rest are purely fictional. Note the absence of Newbery winners published since the 1960's that contain Catholic content (*I, Juan de Pareja* by Elizabeth Barton de Trevino in 1965, *And Now Miguel* by Joseph Krumgold in 1984, *Adam of the Road* by Elizabeth Janet Gray in 1987, and *Crispin, The Cross of Lead* by Avi in 2002) as well as *The Trumpter of Krakow* by Eric P. Kelly in 1928 as these books contain certain errors regarding Cathilic culture and history; they are, therefore, not recommended. Use this list cautiously to broaden your Catholic reading, but keep in mind that most were not written specifically as Catholic literature. [**Editor's Note:** A special "thank-you" to Barbara Huet de Guerville for her thoughtful input to this list.]

Ages: 8 and up

1. §A Daughter of the Seine, A Life of Madame Roland by Jeannette Eaton (1929)
2. §Apprentice of Florence by Ann Kyle (1933)
3. §Big Tree of Bunlahy, Stories of My Own Countryside by Padraic Colum (1933)
4. *§Cedric the Forester by Bernard Marshall (1921, 2012 by POD)
5. ®Dobry by Monica Shannon (1935)
6. §Mountains Are Free by Julie Davis Adams (1930)
7. Nino by Valenti Angelo (1938)
8. Pancakes-Paris by Claire Huchet Bishop (1947)
9. *The Apple and the Arrow by Mary and Conrad Buff (1959)
10. The Black Fox of Lorne by Marguerite de Angeli (1956)
11. §The Boy Who Was by Grace Hallock (1928)
12. *The Door in the Wall by Marguerite de Angeli (1949)
13. §The Golden Basket (introduction of Madeleine) by Ludwig Bemelmans (1936)
14. *The Hidden Treasure of Glaston by Eleanore M. Jewett (1946, 2000 by Bethlehem Books)
15. §Truce of the Wolf and Other Tales of Old Italy by Mary Gould Davis (1931)

> **A book is like a garden carried in the pocket.**
> —Chinese proverb

Notes:

_____

_____

_____

_____

Patron Saint Books

Designed to familiarize children with saints who have their Christian name, these books are shorter in length and have many full-page illustrations. Patron Saint Books are written at the third- or fourth-grade reading level. Almost all of these books are out of print. Unfortunately, many are scarce and expensive. (The following series list may be incomplete.)

Name of Publisher: Sheed and Ward

Ages: 8 and up

Date of Publication: 1958-1964

> **It is a great thing to start life with a small number of really good books which are your very own.**
> —Sir Arthur Conan Doyle

1. ®Joseph by Wilfrid Sheed (1958)
2. ®Mary by Sister Mary Jean Dorcy (1958)
3. §Barbara by M.K. Richardson (1959)
4. §Francis by Mary Francis (1959)
5. *Margaret by Sister M. Juliana (1959, 2007 by The Neumann Press)
6. Richard by M.K. Richardson (1959)
7. §Anne by M.K. Richardson (1960)
8. Bernard by Norah Smaridge (1960)
9. ®David by Eva K. Betz (1960)
10. §Linda by M.K. Richardson (1960)
11. ®Elizabeth by Mary Harris (1961)
12. ®Robert by M.K. Richardson (1961)
13. §Helena by Mary Harris (1964)
14. §Patrick by Marigold Hunt (1964)

Notes:

_____

_____

_____

_____

_____

_____

_____

> **Books let us into their souls and lay open to us the secrets of our own.** —William Hazlitt

Windeatt Saint Series

Mary Fabyan Windeatt became known as the "storyteller of the saints" due to her many saint biographies—a series of twenty-one full-length books, at least twenty-four saint biographies formatted as coloring books, and several saint biographies formatted as comic books. All of these books, with the exception of *The Children of La Salette*, were republished in paperback by Tan Books and Publishers [now an imprint of St. Benedict Press] in the 1990's, although under different titles—see "Windeatt Saint Series" in "Catholic Series Books in Print" section below. The books in this series are not numbered. (The biography of St. Benedict is also included in the Vision series, and the book on Blessed Marie of New France was published as an American Background series book.) If you can find a copy, her book of poetry *Sing Joyfully, A Book of Verse* (1942) is also enjoyable!

Name of Publisher: Sheed & Ward, St. Anthony Guild Press, and Grail Publications

Ages: 8 and up

Date of Publication: 1941-1958

> **We read to know we are not alone.** —C.S. Lewis

1. *Saints in the Sky, The Story of St. Catherine of Siena for Children (1941, 2013 by POD)
2. Lad of Lima, The Story of Blessed Martin de Porres (1942)
3. ®My Name Is Thomas, The Story of St. Thomas Aquinas, Patron of Catholic Schools (1943)
4. Hero of the Hills, The Story of St. Benedict (1943)
5. *®Angel of the Andes, The Story of Saint Rose of Lima (1943, 2012 by POD)
6. ®Little Queen, The Story of Saint Therese of the Child Jesus (1944)
7. *®Little Sister, The Story of Blessed Imelda, Patroness for First Communicants (1944, 2011 by POD)
8. Warrior in White, The Story of Blessed John Masias (1944)
9. *Children of Fatima (1945, 2012 by POD)
10. ®Northern Lights, The Story of St. Hyacinth of Poland and His Companions (1945)
11. *Song in the South, The Story of St. Francis Solano, Apostle of Argentina and Peru (1946, 2012 by POD)
12. *David and His Songs, A Story of the Psalms (1947, 2012 by POD)
13. *The Parish Priest of Ars, St. John Marie Vianney (1947, 2012 by POD)
14. ®St. Dominic (1948)
15. The Man on Fire, The Story of St. Paul (1949)
16. *§The Medal, The Story of St. Catherine Labouré (1949, 2012 by POD)
17. ®The Children of La Salette (1951) – *Please read this book prior to having your children read it unsupervised.*
18. Pennies for Pauline, The Story of Marie Pauline Jaricot, Foundress of the Society for the Propagation of the Faith (1952)
19. ®Mission for Margaret, The Story of the First Fridays (1953)
20. Our Lady's Slave, The Story of St. Louis Mary Grignion de Montfort (1957)
21. Mère Marie of New France (1958)

Banner Books

Publisher's Description: "For readers from nine to the teens, Banner books present the stories of men and women who contributed to the growth of our country and to the spread of the Catholic Faith in the new world. Based on historical facts, the stories stress the inspirational and adventurous elements in the lives of the persons treated. The books give rich background material on the customs and way of life in each historical period . . . an outstanding series that will . . . inculcate high religious and patriotic ideals." (Titles in this series are not numbered.)

Name of Publisher: Benziger Brothers, Inc.

Ages: 9 and up

Date of Publication: 1958-1960

> It is what you read when you don't have to that determines what you will be when you can't help it. —Oscar Wilde

1. *Friar among Savages, Father Luis Cancer by Brother Kurt and Brother Antoninus (1958, 2011 by POD)
2. *Crusaders of the Great River, Marquette and Joliet by Rev. William Doty (1958, 2011 by POD)
3. *Star of the Mohawk, Kateri Tekakwitha by Francis MacDonald (1958, 2011 POD)
4. Frontier Priest and Congressman, Father Gabriel Richard by Brother Alois (1958)
5. *Giant of the Western Trail, Father Peter de Smet by Rev. Michael McHugh (1958, 2003 by The Neumann Press)
6. *The Forty-Ninth Star, Alaska by Alma Savage (1959, 2011 by POD)
7. *Light in the Early West, Berenice Chouteau by Rev. James Schlafly (1959, 2011 by POD)
8. *Father of the American Navy, Captain John Barry by Floyd Anderson (1959, 2011 by POD)
9. Armorer of the Confederacy, Secretary Mallory by Rev. Joseph T. Durkin (1960)
10. Mother Alfred and the Doctors Mayo by James P. Richardson (1959)
11. *The Long Trail, The Story of Buffalo Bill by Frank Kolars (1960, 2011 by POD)
12. *Priest, Patriot and Leader, The Story of Archbishop Carroll by Eva K. Betz (1960, 2011 by POD)
13. *®Hands of Mercy, The Story of Sister-Nurses in the Civil War by Norah Smaridge (1960, 2011 by POD)

Notes:

_____

_____

_____

_____

Junior Vision Books

At least nine of the Vision titles were also published in a larger format with full-page illustrations and abridged text. Guild Press published these Junior Vision Books for readers aged nine to eleven. These books are getting very difficult to find. Grab them if you see them! (The following series list may be incomplete. Titles in this series are not numbered.)

Name of Publisher: Guild Press

Ages: 9 -11

Date of Publication: 1962-1963

1. §Father Marquette and the Great Rivers by August Derleth (1962)
2. §St. Francis and the Seven Seas by Albert J. Nevins (1963)
3. ®St. Pius X, the Farm Boy Who Became Pope by Walter Diethelm (1963)
4. §Francis and Clare, Saints of Assisi by Helen Walker Homan (1962)
5. §St. Joan, The Girl Soldier by Louis de Wohl (1962)
6. ®Mother Seton and the Sisters of Charity by Alma Power-Waters (1963)
7. ®Father Damien and the Bells by Arthur and Elizabeth Sheehan (1962)
8. §St. Anthony and the Christ Child by Helen Walker Homan (1963)
9. ®St. Elizabeth's Three Crowns by Blanche Jennings Thompson (1962)

Notes:

A truly great book should be read in youth, again in maturity and once more in old age, as a fine building should be seen by morning light, at noon, and by moonlight.
— Robertson Davies

Clarion Books

Publisher's Description: ". . . a new fiction series by outstanding authors featuring exciting events in Catholic world history told in fast-paced adventure stories bringing the past to life—designed to appeal to boys and girls of today."

Name of Publisher: Doubleday & Company Publishers

Ages: 9 and up

Date of Publication: 1959-1966 (Several different publishers have begun to reprint titles in this series including Bethlehem Books/Ignatius Press, Hillside Education, and Lepanto Press)

This historical fiction series, intended for ages nine and up, began as the Clarion series with the trumpet as its symbol. Later, Doubleday changed the symbol to an anchor with two fish imposed over the top and began to refer to the series as the "Adventures from History for Young People" series. Doubleday later secularized that fish and anchor logo and continued to use it for general juvenile books into at least the mid 1970's. (The following series list may be incomplete. Titles in this series are not numbered.)

1. *Son of Charlemagne (8th and 9th centuries) by Barbara Willard (1959; 1998 by Bethlehem Books, an imprint of Ignatius Press)
2. *Where Valor Lies (Seventh Crusade—12th century) by Adèle and Cateau de Leeuw (1959, 2007 by Lepanto Press)
3. *Blood Red Crescent (16th century, Europe) by Henry Garnett (1960, 2004 by Lepanto Press, 2007 by Sophia Press Institute)
4. *Blue Gonfalon (First Crusade, 11th century) by Margaret Hubbard (1960, 2004 by Lepanto Press)
5. *Ship's Boy with Magellan (16th century) by Milton Lomask (1960, 2010 by Hillside Education)
6. *Sword of Clontarf (11th century, Iceland and Ireland) by Charles A. Brady (1960, 2006 by Hillside Education)
7. *Cross Among the Tomahawks (17th century, North America) by Milton Lomask (1961, 2011 by Hillside Education)
8. *Fingal's Quest (6th century, France) by Madeleine Polland (1961, 1997 by Clairview, and 2003 by Yorke-Smith Press)
9. *If All the Swords in England (Thomas Becket and Henry II) by Barbara Willard (1961, 2000 by Bethlehem Books)
10. *King's Thane (Edwin and Beorn, 7th century, England) by Charles A. Brady (1961, 2009 by Hillside Education)
11. Two Trumpeters of Vienna, The (17th century, Italy) by Hertha Pauli (1961)
12. *Chuiraquimba and the Black Robes (17th century, Paraguay) by Madeleine Polland (1962, 2010 by Hillside Education)

13. The King's Men, A Story of St. Olaf of Norway (11th century, Norway) by Alan Boucher (1962)
14. A Trumpet Sounds (16th century, England) by Henry Garnett (1962)
15. *Augustine Came to Kent (6th and 7th century, England) by Barbara Willard (1963, 1996 by Bethlehem Books)
16. *City of the Golden House (1st century, Rome) by Madeleine Polland (1963, 2005 by Hillside Education)
17. Locked Crowns, The (6th century, England and Denmark by Marion Garthwaite (1963)
18. Road to the King's Mountain, The (18th century, Junipero Serra) by Margaret Ann Hubbard (1963)
19. *Flame over Tara (5th century, Ireland) by Madeleine Polland (1964, 2004 by Sonlight Curriculum)
20. Knights Besieged (16th century, Turkey) by Nancy Faulkner (1964)
21. Red Bonnet, The (18th century, France) by Henry Garnett (1964, 1974 by White Lion Publishers)
22. *Mission to Cathay (16th century, China) by Madeleine Polland (1965, 1997 by Sonlight Curriculum)
23. Assignment to the Council (Second Vatican Council) by Milton Lomask (1966)

Notes:

_____
_____
_____
_____
_____
_____
_____
_____
_____
_____
_____
_____
_____

Encounter Books

Publisher's Description: "For story lovers from 9 to 90. Encounter Books are a goldmine of enjoyable reading and wholesome inspiration, written in an engaging, smooth-flowing style. Great heroes and saints of God come alive with all the dynamism of their noble ideals. Dramatically illustrated." (The following list may be incomplete. Titles in this series are not numbered.)

Editor's Note: If I could only collect one out-of-print Catholic series for children of various ages, this would be it. The books are relatively short, great read-alouds, and full of various spiritual and doctrinal teachings.

Name of Publisher: Daughters of St. Paul

Ages: 9 and up

Date of Publication: 1963-1987

> In a library we are surrounded by many hundreds of dear friends imprisoned by an enchanter in paper and leathern boxes. —Ralph Waldo Emerson

This series was first published in the 1960's with some new titles added in the 1970's and 1980's along with the republication of several of the 1960's titles. While all titles were published in cloth hardcover, some books were also published in a paperback edition. Currently, the Daughters of St. Paul are reintroducing this series in paperback. (See Encounter the Saints below.)

1. African Triumph, The Life of Charles Lwanga by Charles Dollen (1967, 1978)
2. Ahead of the Crowd, The Story of St. Dominic Savio by the Daughters of St. Paul (1970)
3. Bells of Conquest, The Life of St. Bernard of Clairvaux by the Daughters of St. Paul (1968, 1987)
4. Boy with a Mission, The Life of Francis Marto of Fatima by the Daughters of St. Paul (1967, 1981)
5. §Came the Dawn: Mary of Nazareth, God's Mother and Ours by the Daughters of St. Paul (1982)
6. Catherine of Siena by Father Raimondo Sorgia (1975)
7. Cheerful Warrior, The Life of St. Charles Garnier by Charles Dollen (1967)
8. Conscience Game, The Story of St. Thomas More by the Daughters of Saint Paul (1966, 1967, 1981)
9. Country Road Home, The: The Story of St. John Vianney, Cure of Ars by the Daughters of St. Paul (1966, 1987)
10. Fisher Prince, The Life of St. Peter Apostle by the Daughters of St. Paul (1966, 1984)
11. Flame in the Night, The Life of St. Francis Xavier by the Daughters of St. Paul (1967, 1981)
12. §Footsteps of a Giant, Life of St. Charles Borromeo by the Daughters of St. Paul (1970)
13. §For the Greater Glory of God, St. Ignatius of Loyola by Patrick Kelly
14. ®Gamble for God (A), St. Camillus de Lellis by the Daughters of St. Paul (1983)
15. ®Gentle Revolutionary, The Life of St. Francis of Assisi by the Daughters of St. Paul (1978)
16. §Girl in the Stable (The), The Life of St. Germaine by Louise Bellucci Cantoni (1967)

17. ®God's Secret Agent, The Life of Father Michael Augustine Pro, S.J. by the Daughters of St. Paul (1967)
18. Great Hero, St. Paul the Apostle by the Daughters of St. Paul (1963)
19. Her Dream Came True, The Life of Blessed Imelda Lambertini by the Daughters of St. Paul (1967)
20. Journeys with Mary, Apparitions of the Blessed Mother by Zerlina de Santis (1981, 1982)
21. ®Leaving Matters to God, The Life of St. Teresa of Avila by Louise B. Cantoni (1982, 1984)
22. Light in the Grotto, The Life of St. Bernadette by the Daughters of St. Paul (1967, 1978)
23. ®Love as Strong as Death, The Story of St. Thecla by Rev. Paul Panunzi (1966)
24. Mademoiselle Louise, The Life of Louise de Marillac by Charles Dollen (1967)
25. §Mary's Pilgrim, The Life of St. Peregrine by the Daughters of St. Paul (1972)
26. More Than a Knight, The True Story of St. Maximilian Kolbe by the Daughters of St. Paul (1982)
27. Music Master, The Story of Herman Cohen by Amedeo Rodino (1968)
28. §No Greater Love, The Life of Father Damien of Molokai by the Daughters of St. Paul (1979)
29. ®No Place for Defeat, Life of St. Pius V by the Daughters of St. Paul (1970, 1987)
30. §Noble Lady, The Life of St. Helen by the Daughters of St. Paul (1966)
31. ®Pillar in the Twilight, The Life of St. Thomas Aquinas by the Daughters of St. Paul (1967, 1978)
32. §Trailblazer for the Sacred Heart, Father Mateo Crawley-Boevey (Globe-Trotter for the Sacred Heart) by Pat Balskus (1976)
33. Wind and Shadows, The Story of Joan of Arc by the Daughters of St. Paul (1968)
34. ®Woman Who Loved (A), Louise de Marillac by Charles Dollen (1987)
35. ®Yes Is Forever! Mother Thecla Merlo, The First Daughter of St. Paul by the Daughters of St. Paul (1981)

The following books are similar to the Encounter Books but are not designated as such:
1. Great Black Robe, Father de Smet by Jean Pitrone (1964, 1965, 1981)
2. I Lay Down My Life, Biography of Joyce Kilmer by Harry Cargas (1964)
3. §St. Germaine and Her Guardian Angel by Louise Cantoni (1964)
4. Mother Seton: Wife, Mother, Educator, Foundress, Saint by the Daughters of St. Paul (1975)
5. §St. Tarcisius by Mary R. Bernadi

Notes:

_____

_____

_____

_____

Holy Cross Press

Written by the brothers of the Holy Cross Congregation (C.S.C.) and well-known Catholic authors, this series is similar to the Dujarie Press books. Many of these titles are from the "Saints Who Changed History" series. Holy Cross Press also published a series in the 1960's entitled "Holy Cross Bible Series" with titles such as *St. Matthew and His Gospel*, *The Glorious Maccabees*, and *Our Christian Beginnings: The Acts of the Apostles*. With large type and black-line drawings, these 70-130 paged books are excellent reading material for elementary-aged children. (The following list may be incomplete.)

Name of Publisher: Holy Cross Press

Ages: 9 and up

Date of Publication: late 1950's and 1960's

1. Athletes of God: Lives of the Saints for Every Day in the Year by Shirley Hughson (1930, 1940, 1957)
2. Apostle of the Ice and Snow: A Life of Bishop Charles Seghers by Eva Betz (1964)
3. ®The Cardinal Said No! The Story of St. John Fisher by Brother Jeremy Premont (1964)
4. §Figs from Thistles: St. John Baptist de la Salle by Brother Gerald Robbins (1964)
5. Fire Is His Name: A Life of St. Vincent de Paul by Brother Robert Lomupo (1964)
6. Stout Hearts and Gentle Hands: The Life of Mother Angela of the Sisters of the Holy Cross by Eva Betz (1964)
7. §The Thunder of Silence: The Life of St. Bernard of Clairvaux by Brother Franciscus Willett (1964)
8. ®The Eagle of God: A Life of St. John the Evangelist by Brother Jeremy Premont (1965)
9. ®A Mountain for St. Joseph: The Life of Brother Andre, Miracle Man of Montreal by Ian Bond (1965)
10. The Mountain of God: A Life of St. Benedict by Brother Franciscus Willett (Orrin Primm) (1965)
11. §David, the Shepherd King by Catherine Beebe (1966)
12. §I Charge Each of You: The Story of Dr. Thomas Dooley by Sister Mary Celine O'Brien (1966)
13. §The Promise to Angela: A Life of St. Angela Merici by Pat McKern (1966)
14. ®Champion of the Apostolate: The Life of St. Vincent Pallotti by Brother Ellis Greene (1967)

Notes:

Vision Books

Publisher's Description: ". . . rich collection of biographies for Catholic youngsters from 9 to 15. Written by well-known authors in sparkling, lively language, Vision Books are based upon careful research and historical fact." Note that many of the Vision books were also published in a Catholic Youth Book Club edition. The original editions—not book club—can be identified by the Vision Book logos on the front and back end pages—the pages attached to the covers.

Name of Publisher: Farrar, Straus & Cudahy, Inc.

Ages: 9 and up

Date of Publication: 1955-1967

> **A bookstore is one of the only pieces of evidence we have that people are still thinking.**
> —Jerry Seinfield

Most of the original hardbacks are readily available in used bookstores for $4.00 or less. Some of these titles (*) have been reprinted in paperback by Ignatius Press; see "Vision Books" in the "Catholic Series Books in Print" section below.

1. *St. John Bosco and the Children's Saint, Dominic Savio by Catherine Beebe (1955)
2. *St. Therese and the Roses by Helen Walker Homan (1955)
3. *Father Marquette and the Great Rivers by August Derleth (1955)
4. *St. Francis of the Seven Seas by Albert J. Nevins (1955)
5. *Bernadette and the Lady by Hertha Pauli (1956)
6. *St. Isaac and the Indians by Milton Lomask (1956)
7. Fighting Father Duffy by Jim and Virginia Lee Bishop (1956)
8. *St. Pius X, the Farm Boy Who Became Pope by Walter Diethelm (1956)
9. *St. Ignatius and the Company of Jesus by August Derleth (1956)
10. John Carroll: Bishop and Patriot by Milton Lomask (1956)
11. *St. Dominic and the Rosary by Catherine Beebe (1956)
12. The Cross in the West by Mark Boesch (1956)
13. My Eskimos: A Priest in the Arctic by Roger P. Buliard (1956)
14. Champions in Sports and Spirit by Ed Fitzgerald (1956)
15. *Francis and Clare, Saints of Assisi by Helen Walker Homan (1956)
16. *®Christmas and the Saints by Hertha Pauli (1956, 2010 POD)
17. *Edmund Campion, Hero of God's Underground by Harold C. Gardiner (1957)
18. Modern Crusaders by John Travers Moore and Rosemarian Staudacher (1957)
19. *Our Lady Came to Fatima by Ruth Fox Hume (1957)
20. The Bible Story, The Promised Lord and His Coming by Catherine Beebe (1957)
21. St. Augustine and His Search for Faith by Milton Lomask (1957)
22. *St. Joan, The Girl Soldier by Louis de Wohl (1957)
23. *St. Thomas More of London by Elizabeth M. Ince (1957)
24. *Mother Seton and the Sisters of Charity by Alma Power-Waters (1957)
25. *St. Thomas Aquinas and the Preaching Beggars by Brendan Larnen and Milton Lomask (1957)

26. *Father Damien and the Bells by Arthur and Elizabeth Sheehan (1957)
27. Columbus and the New World by August Derleth (1957)
28. *St. Philip of the Joyous Heart by Francis X. Connolly (1957)
29. ®Lydia Longley, the First American Nun by Helen A. McCarthy (1958)
30. *St. Anthony and the Christ Child by Helen Walker Homan (1958)
31. *St. Elizabeth's Three Crowns by Blanche Jennings Thompson (1958)
32. *Katharine Drexel, Friend of the Neglected by Ellen Tarry (1958)
33. *§St. Louis and the Last Crusade by Margaret Ann Hubbard (1958)
34. *Kateri Tekakwitha, Mohawk Maid by Evelyn M. Brown (1958)
35. *St. Benedict, Hero of the Hills by Mary Fabyan Windeatt (1958)
36. *The Cure of Ars, The Priest Who Outtalked the Devil by Milton Lomask (1958)
37. ®Catholic Campuses, Stories of American Catholic Colleges by Rosemarian Staudacher (1958)
38. *§St. Helena and the True Cross by Louis de Wohl (1959)
39. Governor Al Smith by James Farley and James Conniff (1959)
40. Kit Carson of the Old West by Mark Boesch (1959)
41. Rose Hawthorne: The Pilgramage of Nathaniel's Daughter by Arthur and Elizabeth Sheehan (1959)
42. The Ursulines, Nuns of Adventure by Harnett T. Kane (1959)
43. *Mother Cabrini, Missionary to the World by Frances Parkinson Keyes (1959)
44. More Champions in Sports and Spirit by Ed Fitzgerald (1959)
45. St. Margaret Mary, Apostle of the Sacred Heart by Ruth Fox Hume (1960)
46. When Saints Were Young by Blanche Jennings Thompson (1960)
47. Frances Warde and the First Sisters of Mercy by Sr. Marie Christopher (1960)
48. *Vincent de Paul, Saint of Charity by Margaret Ann Hubbard (1960)
49. *Florence Nightingale's Nuns by Emmeline Garnett (1961)
50. §Pope Pius XII, the World's Shepherd by Louis de Wohl (1961)
51. St. Jerome and the Bible by George Sanderlin (1961)
52. Saints of the Byzantine World by Blanche Jennings Thompson (1961)
53. Chaplains in Action by Rosemarian Staudacher (1962)
54. *St. Catherine Laboure and the Miraculous Medal by Alma Power-Waters (1962)
55. Mother Barat's Vineyard by Margaret Ann Hubbard (1962)
56. Charles de Foucauld, Adventurer of the Desert by Emmeline Garnett (1962)
57. Martin de Porres, Saint of the New World by Ellen Tarry (1963)
58. Marguerite Bourgeoys, Pioneer Teacher by Sister Mary Genevieve (1963)
59. §Father Kino, Priest to the Pimas by Ann Nolan Clark (1963)
60. ®Children Welcome: Villages for Boys and Girls by Rosemarian Staudacher (1963)
61. St. Gregory the Great, Consul of God by George Sanderlin (1964)
62. Peter and Paul: The Rock and the Sword by Blanche Jennings Thompson (1964)
63. Irish Saints by Robert T. Reilly (1964, 1981, 2002 by Gramercy)
64. Dear Philippine: Mission of Mother Duchesne by Margaret Ann Hubbard (1964)
65. Peter Claver, Saint Among Slaves by Ann Roos (1965)
66. John Neumann, The Children's Bishop by Elizabeth Odell Sheehan (1965)

67. St. Francis de Sales by Blanche Jennings Thompson (1965)
68. Sarah Peter: The Dream and the Harvest by Alma Power-Waters (1965)
69. Good Pope John by Elizabeth Odell Sheehan (1966)
70. In American Vineyards, Religious Orders in the United States by Rosemarian Staudacher (1966)
71. §Brother Andre of Montreal by Ann Nolan Clark (1967)
72. ®Edel Quinn: Beneath the Southern Cross by Evelyn Brown (1967)

Notes:

You may have tangible wealth untold;
Caskets of jewels and coffers of gold.
Richer than I you can never be—
I had a mother who read to me.
—Strickland Gillilan

Weaver Books

Publisher's Description: "True stories of ordinary people who used the 'threads' God gave them—happy or sad experiences, blessings, inspirations, and even challenges—to weave with the Lord a wonderful gift of life and love."

Name of Publisher: Pauline Books and Media

Ages: 9 and up

Date of Publication: 1996-2000

Each of these paperback booklets is approximately sixty-four pages long. Intended for ages nine through twelve, these short biographies help children understand the saints as ordinary people.

1. ®Beyond the Clouds: The Story of Christa McAuliffe by David R. Collins (1996)
2. §Got a Penny? The Story of Dorothy Day by David R. Collins (1996)
3. ®You're Never Alone: The Story of Thomas Merton by David R. Collins (1996)
4. Magnificent Failure: The Story of Father Solanus Casey by David R. Collins (1999)
5. §Rich in Love: The Story of Padre Pio of Pietrelcina by Eileen Dunn Bertanzetti (1999)
  [This book was republished in 2002 as an Encounter the Saints book.]
6. §Servant to the Slaves: The Story of Henriette Delille by David R. Collins (2000)

Notes:

**Let books be your dining table,
And you shall be full of delights.
Let them be your mattress
And you shall sleep restful nights.**
—Author Unknown

American Background Books

Publisher's Description: ". . . for readers [ages] ten to fifteen dealing with . . . Catholic men and women who have played an important role in the history of our Continent. Although most [books] concern those whose contributions were made to the discovery, exploration and development of the United States, the series also introduces . . . the heroes and heroines of Canada and other countries of North America. Great explorers, colonizers, war heroes, pioneer women, missionaries, and persons of achievement in various fields . . . light up the pages of these books." Note that many of the American Background books were also published in a Catholic Youth Book Club edition. The original editions—not book club —can be identified by the American Background logos on the front and back end pages—the pages attached to the covers. Except for the last few books in the series, most of these titles are plentiful and reasonably priced.

Name of Publisher: P. J. Kenedy & Sons

Ages: 10 and up

Date of Publication: 1957-1969

> **I cannot live without books.**
> —Thomas Jefferson

1. Cavalry Hero, Casimir Pulaski by Dorothy Adams (1957)
2. Colonial Governor, Thomas Dongan of New York by J. G. E. Hopkins (1957)
3. The Friar and the Knight, Padre Olmedo and Cortez by Flora Strousse (1957)
4. Adventurous Lady, Margaret Brent of Maryland by Dorothy Fremont Grant (1957)
5. Sidewalk Statesman, Alfred E. Smith by William G. Schofield (1958)
6. Chaplain in Gray, Abram Ryan: Poet-Priest of the Confederacy by H. J. Heagney (1958)
7. Mère Marie of New France by Mary Fabyan Windeatt (1958)
8. ®Black Robe Peacemaker, Pierre de Smet by J. G. E. Hopkins (1958)
9. Charles Carroll and the American Revolution by Milton Lomask (1959)
10. *Simon Bruté and the Western Adventure by Elizabeth Bartelme (1959, 2012 by Hillside Education)
11. General Phil Sheridan and the Union Cavalry by Milton Lomask (1959)
12. De Tonti of the Iron Hand and the Exploration of the Mississippi by Anne Heagney (1959)
13. Mathew Carey, Pamphleter for Freedom by Jane F. Hindman (1960)
14. Padre Kino and the Trail to the Pacific by Jack Steffan (1960)
15. Knute Rockne, Football Wizard of Notre Dame by Arthur Daley (1960)
16. Charles John Seghers, Pioneer in Alaska by Antoinette Bosco (1960)
17. Margaret Haughery, Bread Woman of New Orleans by Flora Strousse (1961)
18. John Hughes, Eagle of the Church by Doran Hurley (1961)
19. Joseph the Huron by Antoinette Bosco (1961)
20. ®Rose Greenhow, Confederate Secret Agent by Dorothy Fremont Grant (1961)
21. Fanny Allen, Green Mountain Rebel by Eva K. Betz (1962)
22. ®Lucrezia Bori of the Metropolitan Opera by John Francis Marion (1962)

23. Padre Pro, Mexican Hero by Fanchón Royer (1963)
24. Pierre Toussaint, Pioneer in Brotherhood by Arthur and Elizabeth Odell Sheehan (1963)
25. Virgil Barber, New England Pied Piper by Eva K. Betz (1963)
26. Don Diego de Vargas, The Peaceful Conquistador by Rosemary Buchanan (1963)
27. §William Gaston, Fighter for Justice by Eva K. Betz (1964)
28. John Fitzgerald Kennedy, Man of Courage by Flora Strousse (1964)
29. Rochambeau and Our French Allies by Milton Lomask (1965)
30. Raphael Semmes, Confederate Admiral by Robert W. Daly (1965)
31. Daniel Duluth, Explorer of the Northlands by David J. Abodaher (1966)
32. Commandant Paul and the Founding of Montreal (Paul de Maisonneuve) by Charles Morrow Wilson (1966)
33. John LaFarge, Gentle Jesuit by Flora Strousse (1967)
34. §Father Flanagan, Builder of Boys by Clifford J. Stevens (1967)
35. §Princess Isabel of Brazil and the Glittering Pen by Mildred Houghton Comfort (1969)
36. §Pedro Menéndez de Avilés and the Founding of St. Augustine by Elaine Murray Stone (1969)

Notes:

> **Books had instant replay long before televised sports.** —Bern Williams

> **Books constitute capital. A library book lasts as long as a house, for hundreds of years. It is not, then, an article of mere consumption but fairly of capital, and often in the case of professional men setting out in life, it is their only capital.** —Thomas Jefferson

Catholic Treasury Books

Publisher's Description: ". . . a series of book planned for readers ten years of age and older. Taken from the great wealth of Catholic history, the books include true-to-life biographies and dramatic stories of persons and events which will make the reader proud of his Catholic heritage." Some of these titles were also published in paperback. (The following list may be incomplete. Titles in this series are not numbered.)

Name of Publisher: Bruce Publishing Company

Ages: 10 and up

Date of Publication: 1955-1963

> He fed his spirit with the bread of books.
> —Edwin Markham

1. Boy of Philadelphia: A Story about the Continental Congress by Frank Morriss (1955)
2. §Candle for Our Lady (16th century, England) by Regina Victoria Hunt (1955)
3. *®Hand Raised at Gettysburg (Irish Brigade) by Grace and Harold Johnson (1955, 2012 by POD)
4. Simon o' the Stock (12th century, England) by Anne Heagney (1955)
5. Bright Banners (17th century, England, Claude de la Colombière) by Regina Victoria Hunt (1956)
6. §Charcoal Faces (19th century, Canada) by Mabel Otis Robinson (1956)
7. ®Last Apostle (St. Paul) by Mother Mary Eleanor (1956)
8. Medicine for Wildcat: A Life Story about Samuel Charles Mazzuchelli, O.P. (19th century, United States) by Robert Riordan (1956)
9. Bishop's Boy (18th century, United States, John Carroll) by Floyd Anderson (1957)
10. Marc's Choice: A Story of the Time of Diocletian (3rd and 4th centuries, Rome) by Sister Mary Cornelius (1957)
11. Adventures of Broken Hand (19th century, United States) by Frank Morriss (1957)
12. Marylanders: A Story of the Puritan Revolt in Lord Baltimore's Colony (17th century, United States) by Anne Heagney (1957)
13. *Red Hugh, Prince of Donegal (16th century, Ireland) by Robert T. Reilly (1957, 1997 by Bethlehem Books/Ignatius Press)
14. ®Wires West (telegraph, 19th century, United States) by Leo Vincent Jacks (1957)
15. Amazing John Tabb (United States civil war) by Eva K. Betz (1958)
16. Brother Dutton of Molokai (19th-20th centuries, Hawaii) by Howard E. Crouch (1958, 1998 by Damien-Dutton Society)
17. Courageous Catherine: Mother Mary Catherine McAuley, The First Sister of Mercy (19th century, Ireland) by Sister Raymond Marie (1958)
18. ®Alfred of Wessex: The King Who Saved His Country (9th century, England) by Frank Morriss (1959)
19. Desert Padre: Eusebio Francisco Kino (17th century, North America) by John Thayer (1959)

20. *Frontier Bishop: Simon Gabriel Bruté (19th century, United States) by Riley Hughes (1959, 2012 by POD)
21. Thunder Maker: General Thomas Meagher (19th century, Ireland and United States) by William M. Lamers (1959)
22. Massacre at Ash Hollow (19th century, United States) by Robert T. Reilly (1960)
23. §Turquoise Rosary (19th century, United States) by Leo Vincent Jacks (1960)
24. Charity Goes to War (United States Civil War/Sisters of Charity) by Anne Heagney (1961)
25. *®Submarine Pioneer: John Philip Holland (19th and 20th centuries, United States) by Frank Morriss (1961, 2012 by POD)
26. *Gold Rush Bishop (Patrick Manogue, 19th century, United States) by Floyd Anderson (1962, 2012 by POD)
27. Golden Caravel (Christopher Columbus) by Margaret Bemister (1962)
28. Quiet Flame: Mother Marianne of Molokai (19th century, Hawaii) by Eva K. Betz (1963)

The following books, published by Bruce Publishing Company, are uniform with the Catholic Treasury books, but are not designated as such. On most of the dust jackets, the Catholic Treasury series books are advertised.

1. God and the General's Daughter (Ethan Allen's daughter) by Anne Heagney (1953)
2. Lady and the Pirate, The (Battle of New Orleans in 1814) by Robert Riordan (1957)
3. Prairie Venture (19th-century homesteading in Colorado) by Leo Vincent Jacks (1959)
4. Johann of the Trembling Hand: A Story Set in Oberammergau (Passion play) by Theodora Koob (1960)
5. Prisoner of Lost Island (20th century, Chile) by Frank Kolars (1961)
6. Web Begun, The (United States civil war novel) by Eva K. Betz (1961)
7. *Rebels in the Shadows (Pennsylvania coal mines in the 1870's) by Robert T. Reilly (1962, 1979 by University of Pittsburgh Press)
8. First Sioux Nun, Sister Marie-Josephine Nebraska (1859-1894) by Sister Mary Ione Hilger (1963)
9. Spaldings of Old Kentucky, The (19th century, United States) by Anne Heagney (1964)
10. §Hong Kong Altar Boy (20th century, Hong Kong) by Joseph E. Hanson (1965)

Notes:

_____

_____

_____

_____

_____

_____

Hawthorn Junior Biographies
Catholic Digest Junior Book Shelf
Credo Books

Publisher's Description: Intended for ages eleven and up, this is "an important new series of biographies that will appeal to both boys and girls. The subjects of these biographies are Catholic, but their stories are not of their faith so much as how that faith helped them to lead remarkable lives. Past and present will be represented here. . . . Heroes are made by the greatness of the human spirit and all the figures to be portrayed in Credo Books were great in spirit, courage and effort, no matter what task they took upon themselves."

Name of Publisher: Hawthorn Books, Inc.

Ages: 11 and up

Date of Publication: 1962-1967

> You don't have to burn books to destroy a culture. Just get people to stop reading them.
> —Ray Bradbury

This series by Hawthorn Books was printed under three different series names: Catholic Digest Junior Book Shelf, Hawthorn Junior Biography, and Credo Books. While the subjects remain constant, slight title variations occur within these series. Although each of these books is a Hawthorn Junior Biography, it is uncertain whether each book was reprinted under each of the three series. Note that the numbers correspond to the numbering of the Credo and Hawthorn Junior Biography book series. These Catholic biographies are the most widely-available and reasonably priced of all the Catholic out-of-print series books. (The following list may be incomplete.)

1. Operation Escape: The Adventure of Father O'Flaherty by Daniel Madden (1962)
2. To Far Places: The Story of Francis X. Ford by Eva K. Betz (1962)
3. *Lion of Poland: The Story of Paderewski by Ruth and Paul Hume (1962, 2012 by POD)
4. §Conscience Game: The Story of Thomas More by Margaret Stanley-Wrench (1962) (Credo title. Conscience of a King, is widely available.)
5. Pen and Bayonet: The Story of Joyce Kilmer by Norah Smaridge (1962)
6. Man Who Found Out Why: The Story of Gregor Mendel by Gary Webster (1963)
7. Tall American: The Story of Gary Cooper by Richard Gehman (1963)
8. Wings of an Eagle: The Story of Michelangelo by Anne Merriman Peck (1963)
9. Door of Hope: The Story of Katharine Drexel by Katherine Burton (1963)
10. Fire of Freedom: The Story of Colonel Carlos Castillo Armas by Jack Steffan (1963)
11. Doctor America: The Story of Tom Dooley by Terry Morris (1963)
12. Sea Tiger: The Story of Pedro Menéndez by Frank Kolars (1963)
13. First Californian: The Story of Fray Junípero Serra by Donald Demarest (1963)
14. Wilderness Explorer: The Story of Samuel de Champlain by Charles Morrow Wilson (1963)
15. Forked Lightning: The Story of General Philip H. Sheridan by Albert Orbaan (1964)
16. ®Hammer of Gaul: The Story of Charles Martel by Shane Miller (1964)

17. Dawn from the West: The Story of Genevieve Caulfield by Margaret Rau (1964)
18. Journey into Light: The Story of Louis Braille by Gary Webster (1964)
19. §Monuments to Glory: The Story of Antonio Barluzzi, Architect of the Holy Land by Daniel M. Madden (1964)
20. Crusader: The Story of Richard the Lion-Heart (Richard I) by Alma Power-Waters (1964)
21. Fighting Irishman: The Story of "Wild Bill" Donovan by Maria Wilhelm (1964)
22. ®Anvil Chorus: The Story of Giuseppe Verdi by Helen L. Kaufman (1964)
23. King of Song: The Story of John McCormack by Ruth and Paul Hume (1964)
24. Teller of Tales: The Story of Geoffrey Chaucer by Margaret Stanley-Wrench (1965)
25. Light Within: The Story of Maria Montessori by Norah Smaridge (1965)
26. Under Three Flags: The Story of Gabriel Richard by David J. Abodaher (1965) (Hawthorn Junior Biography)
27. *®Young People's Book of Saints: Sixty-Three Saints of the Western Church from the First to the Twentieth Centuries by Hugh Ross Williamson (CDJBS only) (1963, 2009 by Sophia Press Institute under the title of *Young People's Book of Saints*)
28. Apostle of Peace: The Story of Pope Pius XII by Alden Hatch (1965) (Hawthorn Junior Biography)
29. Miracle in Mexico: The Story of Juan Diego by Lon Tinkle (1965) (Hawthorn Junior Biography)
30. Island Hero: The Story of Ramon Magsaysay by Marvin M. Gray (1965) (Hawthorn Junior Biography)
31. Silver King: Edward the Confessor, the Last Great Anglo-Saxon Ruler by Margaret Stanley-Wrench (1966) (Hawthorn Junior Biography)
32. Man Who Could Read Stones: Champollion and the Rosetta Stone by Alan Honour (1966) (Hawthorn Junior Biography)
33. Master Mariner: The Adventurous Life of Joseph Conrad by Norah Smaridge (1966) (Hawthorn Junior Biography)
34. Desert Fighter: The Story of General Yigael Yadin and the Dead Sea Scrolls by Shane Miller (1967) (Hawthorn Junior Biography)

Notes:
_____
_____
_____
_____
_____
_____
_____

Favorite Catholic Books for Various Ages
(Not All about Saints but All Great Books)

1. *A Child's Rule of Life* by Robert Hugh Benson (1912, 1992) [picture book, poetry]
2. ®*The Angel's Alphabet* by Hilda van Stockum (1948, 1996) [picture book, poetry]
3. §*The Child on His Knees* by Mary Dixon Thayer (1926, 2006) [poetry]
4. **The Weight of the Mass, A Tale of Faith* by Josephine Nobisso (2002) [picture book]
5. *The Little Friar Who Flew* by Patricia Lee Gauch (1980) [picture book, biography of St. Joseph of Copertino]
6. ®*This Is What I Pray Today, The Divine Hours for Children* by Phyllis Tickle (2007) [picture book with short prayers for morning and evening for each day of the week]
7. **The Monk Who Grew Prayer* by Claire Brandenburg (2003) [picture book about praying constantly from Orthodox perspective, beautifully done]
8. §*Sing a Song of Holy Things* by Sister Mary Josita (1945) [poetry]
9. ®*A Candle Burns for France* by Blanche Jennings Thompson (1946) [fictional story that tells about seven French saints; see also this author's excellent anthology of Catolic children's poems, *With Harp and Lute* (1935)]
10. *The Latsch Valley Farm series by Anna Pellowski – *First Farm in the Valley: Anna's Story, Winding Valley Farm: Annie's Story, Stairstep Farm: Anna Rose's Story*, and *Willow Wind Farm: Betsy's Story* (1981-1982) [a Catholic generational Little House on the Prairie series]
11. **The King of the Golden City Study Edition, An Allegory for Children* by Mother Mary Loyola (1921, 2007) [story of a young girl's deepening relationship with Jesus]
12. ®*A Lovely Gate Set Wide, A Book of Catholic Verse for Young Readers* by Sister Margaret Patrice (1946) [poetry]
13. **Olivia and the Little Way* (2008) and *Olivia's Gift* (2010) by Nancy Carabio Belanger [Catholic fiction about St. Therese of Lisieux for upper elementary]
14. **The Winged Watchman* by Hilda Van Stockum (1962, 1997) [WWII adventure with Catholic elements including the Sacrament of Reconciliation]
15. **Outlaws of Ravenhurst Study Edition* by Sister M. Imelda Wallace (1950, 2009) [Catholic adventure set in twelfth-century Scotland]
16. **A Philadelphia Catholic in King James's Court* by Martin de Porres Kennedy (1999, with optional study guide) [contemporary Catholic apologetical story for teens]
17. **The Story of Rolf and the Viking Bow* by Allen French (1924, 1995) [not a Catholic book but a better book on friendship you will not find, exciting adventure]
18. Saint books by Joan Windham – *Six O'Clock Saints* series (1934-1945), *Saints for Boys* (1948), and *Saints for Girls* (1962) [less traditional stories of saints]
19. **Story of a Soul* by St. Therese of Lisieux (1898, etc.) [autobiography for teens and up]
20. **Divine Mercy in My Soul, The Diary of Saint Maria Faustina Kowalska* (2000) [teen and adult spiritual reading]

Catholic Series Books in Print

> **The worst thing about new books is that they keep us from reading the old ones.** —Joseph Joubert

Tomie de Paola

Tomie de Paola has been publishing books since 1965. He has written and/or illustrated over two hundred books for children. Most of Tomie de Paola's books are intended for ages four through eight but appeal to all ages. While some books are currently out of print, most are available (*) in inexpensive paperbacks. Although not included in this listing, several of his books are also available in Spanish. (Some of his books deal with magic and witches, especially his *Strega Nona* titles. Many of his Christmas titles are more about Santa than Jesus so preview before purchasing.)

Ages: 2 (board books) and up

Biography:
- Christopher, The Holy Giant (1994)
- §David and Goliath (1984)
- ®Francis, The Poor Man of Assisi (also covers St. Clare; 1982, 1990)
- *Holy Twins, The (St. Benedict and St. Scholastica, paperback, 2001)
- ®Mary, Mother of Jesus (1995)
- ®Noah and the Ark (1983)
- §Our Lady of Guadalupe (1980)
- *Pascual and the Kitchen Angels (St. Pascal Baylon, patron saint of cooks and the kitchen, paperback, 2006)
- *Patrick, Patron Saint of Ireland (1994)
- ®Queen Esther (1986)
- Song of Francis (hardcover, 2009)

Christmas Season—books for an Advent/Christmas/Epiphany unit study:
- Baby's First Christmas (board book, 1988)
- *Birds of Bethlehem, The (hardcover, 2012)
- Christmas Pageant (story from St. Matthew and St. Luke, 1978)
- *Christmas Remembered (more adult content, 2006)
- *Clown of God, The (a juggler offers his talent to the Christ Child; 1978, 1989)
- Country Angel Christmas (Saint Nicholas, 1995)
- Early American Christmas (decorating the house for Christmas, 1987)
- Family Christmas Tree Book (origins of the Christmas tree, 1980)
- §First Christmas, The (pop-up book, birth of Jesus, 1984)
- *Friendly Beasts, An Old English Christmas Carol (1998)
- ®Hark, A Christmas Sampler—text by Jane Yolen, illustrated by de Paola (Christmas stories, poems, and songs, 1991)

Jingle, the Christmas Clown (Christmas Eve, 1998)

*Joy to the World, Tomie's Christmas Stories (contains *The Night of Las Posadas*, *The Story of the Three Wise Kings*, and *The Legend of the Poinsettia* as well as two other stories plus illustrated Christmas carols and hymns from his *Book of Christmas Carols*, 2010)

*Legend of Old Befana, The (Epiphany, 1989)

*Legend of the Poinsettia, The (Christmas procession in Mexico, 1997)

*Merry Christmas, Strega Nona (Christmas Eve feast, 1991)

*My First Bible Stories (board book adapted from his *Book of Bible Stories*, 2010)

*My First Christmas (board book, 2008)

*My First Christmas Carols (board book adapted from his *Book of Christmas Carols*, 2010

*Night of Las Posadas, The (Mary and Joseph arrive in Bethlehem, 2001)

®Story of the Three Wise Kings, The (Epiphany, 1983)

Tomie de Paola's Book of Christmas Carols (1987)

Tomie's Little Christmas Pageant (board book, ages 2-5, 2002)

Other titles of religious nature:

*Angels, Angels Everywhere (hardcover, 2005)

Book of the Old Testament (1995)

*Let the Whole Earth Sing Praise (hardcover, 2011)

*Miracles of Jesus (hardcover and paperback, 2008)

*My First Angels (board book adapted from his *Angels, Angels Everywhere*, 2011)

*My First Easter (board book, 2008)

*My First Chanukah (board book, 2008)

*My First Passover (board book, 2008)

*My First Thanksgiving (board book, 2008)

*Mysterious Giant of Barletta (myth of an eleventh century Italian statue that saves the town, paperback, 1988)

Parables of Jesus (1995)

*Tomie de Paola's Book of Bible Stories: New International Version (2002)

*Tomie's Little Book of Love (board book with 28 verses about love, 2007)

Notes:

_____

_____

_____

_____

_____

_____

**The more that you read,
the more things you will know.
The more that you learn,
the more places you'll go.**
—Dr. Seuss

Father Francis Coloring Books

These 8½″ by 11″ coloring books are thirty-two pages each. They have one page of text followed by a full-page line drawing suitable for coloring. Published by Seraphice Press in the 1950's, some have been republished by Our Lady of the Rosary School. Below are the saint titles by Father Francis. He also has other titles that deal with the doctrines of our faith. These books are readily available from various Catholic vendors. (The titles in this series are not numbered.)

Date of Publication: 1951-1959

Ages: 4 and up

1. Jesus Our Savior: The Life of Jesus for the Very Young – Book 1: His Early Life (1954)
2. Jesus Our Savior: The Life of Jesus for the Very Young – Book 2: His Public Life (1954)
3. Saints of the Eucharist: Tarcisius, Imelda, Pius X, and Maria Goretti (1958)
4. More Saints of the Eucharist: Paschal Baylon, Therese of the Child Jesus, Gerard Majella, and Gemma Galgani (1959)
5. Our Mother Mary (1959)
6. Mary, Full of Grace (1954, 1997)
7. They Became Saints (poems and pictures about Christopher, Tarcisius, Agnes, Francis, Louis, Imelda, Joan of Arc, Aloysius, Martin de Porres, Kateri Tekakwitha, Dominic Savio, Bernadette, Therese of the Child Jesus, and Mary Goretti – 1951)

Notes:

_____
_____
_____
_____
_____
_____
_____
_____

Books are the treasured wealth of the world and the fit inheritance of generations and nations.
—Henry David Thoreau

Mary Fabyan Windeatt Coloring Books

In addition to her full-length biographies, Ms. Windeatt wrote a series of saint biographies that were published by Grail Publications in the 1950's and formatted as coloring books. These have been republished by Tan Books and Publishers, Inc. Each book has thirty-two pages with sixteen pictures to color and sixteen pages of large-print text. Although some have gone out of print, most are readily available from the publisher as well as numerous Catholic vendors. (The titles in this series are not numbered.)

Ages: 4 and up

1. §Blessed Kateri Tekakwitha (1955, 1989)
2. §The Brown Scapular (1956, 1989)
3. *Our Lady of Banneux [1933, Belgium] (1954, 1989)
4. *Our Lady of Beauraing [1932-33, Belgium] (1954, 1989)
5. *Our Lady of Fatima [1917, Portugal] (1954, 1989)
6. ®Our Lady of Guadalupe [1531, Mexico] (1954, 1989)
7. §Our Lady of Knock [1879, Ireland] (1954, 1989)
8. *Our Lady of La Salette [1846, France] (1954, 1989)
9. ®Our Lady of Lourdes [1858, France] (1954, 1989)
10. *Our Lady of Pellevoisin [1875, France] (1954, 1989)
11. *Our Lady of Pontmain [1870, France] (1954, 1989)
12. *Our Lady of the Miraculous Medal [1830, France] (1954, 1989)
13. ®The Rosary (1955, 1989)
14. *Saint Anthony of Padua (1955, 1989)
15. §Saint Christopher (1955, 1989)
16. *Saint Dominic Savio (1955, 1989)
17. *Saint Frances Cabrini (1956, 1989)
18. *Saint Francis of Assisi (1956, 1989)
19. ®Saint Joan of Arc (1955, 1989)
20. *Saint Maria Goretti (1955, 1989)
21. *Saint Meinrad (1954, 1989)
22. ®Saint Philomena (1955, 1989)
23. *Saint Pius X (1955, 1989)
24. *Saint Teresa of Avila (1955, 1989)

> **Wear the old coat and buy the new book.**
> —Austin Phelps

Notes:

_____

_____

_____

Saint Joseph Bible Story Books

These inexpensive books that relate the lives of several Old Testament characters are intended for younger children; each book is about thirty-two pages long. The author of this series is Father Jude Winkler, who also wrote several of the books in the St. Joesph Picture Book series. It appears that most of these titles have been published in both hardcover and paperback editions. However, most of the titles are already out of print. The one remaining title in print as of April 2013 is indicated with an asterisk (*). (The titles in this series are not numbered.)

> **It is our duty to live among books; especially to live by one book, and a very old one.**
> —Cardinal Newman

Name of Publisher: Catholic Book Publishing Company

Ages: 5 and up

Date of Publication: 1988-2004

1. The Story of Abraham by Rev. Jude Winkler (1988, 1994)
2. The Story of Moses by Rev. Jude Winkler (1988, 1994)
3. The Story of Isaac and Jacob by Rev. Jude Winkler (1988, 1994)
4. ®The Story of Joseph and His Brothers by Rev. Jude Winkler (1988, 1994)
5. The Story of Ruth by Rev. Jude Winkler (1988)
6. ®The Story of Joshua by Rev. Jude Winkler (1988)
7. The Story of Noah and the Flood by Rev. Jude Winkler (1989, 1991, 2004)
8. *The Story of the Birth of Jesus by Rev. Jude Winkler (1989)

Notes:
___
___
___
___
___
___
___
___

Saint Joseph Picture Books

Name of Publisher: Catholic Book Publishing Company

Ages: 5 and up

Date of Publication: 1970's-Current

Written by Father Lawrence Lovasik SVD, with later titles by Father Jude Winkler OFM, these smaller (5½" by 7½") paperback books have thirty-two pages, are simply written, and beautifully illustrated. This series has been published since the 1970's by The Catholic Book Publishing Company, who continues to add new titles. Some books in this series, especially those that replicate topics, are being phased out or reformatted. Books still in print are indicated with an asterick (*). Most of the books in this series continue to be readily available in both new and used conditions, including several titles that have been published in Spanish.

- *Angels, The
- §Apostles' Creed
- *Apostles of Jesus
- *Book of Saints, Part 1
- *Book of Saints, Part 2
- *Book of Saints, Part 3
- *Book of Saints, Part 4
- *Book of Saints, Part 5
- *Book of Saints, Part 6
- *Book of Saints, Part 7
- *Book of Saints, Part 8
- *Book of Saints, Part 9
- *Book of Saints, Part 10
- *Book of Saints, Part 11
- *Book of Saints, Part 12
- *Catholic ABC Book
- *Catholic Book of Prayers for Children, The
- *Celebrating Advent with the Jesse Tree
- *Celebrating Christmas
- *Celebrating Lent
- §Children's Prayers
- *Children's Prayers for All Occasions
- *Child's Prayers in Verse
- *Children's Prayers to Mary
- §Christmas Traditions
- *Church Year for Children, The
- *Commandments of God, The
- *Easter Story, The
- *Eight Beatitudes, The
- §Favorite Prayers for Children
- *Feasts of Jesus
- *Following Jesus
- *Gifts of the Holy Spirit
- *God Loves Us All
- *God the Father
- *Going to Confession
- *Good Saint Joseph
- *Great Men of the New Testament
- *Great Men of the Old Testament
- *Great Women of the Bible
- §Hail Mary
- §Holy Communion
- *Holy Eucharist, The
- *Holy Family, The
- *Holy Rosary, The
- *Holy Spirit, The
- *Holy Trinity, The
- *I Believe in God
- *I Love My Pet
- *Immaculate Conception, The
- *Joy of Being a Catholic Child, The
- §Life of Jesus
- §Life of Mary
- §Lives of the Saints for Boys
- §Lives of the Saints for Girls
- *Mary, My Mother
- *Mass for Children, The
- *Miracles of the Bible
- *Miracles of Jesus, The
- *Mother Teresa
- *My Day with Jesus
- *My First Catechism
- §My First Missal
- *My First Catholic Picture Dictionary
- *My First Prayer Book
- *My First Prayers
- *My Friend Jesus
- *My Life with God
- §My Mass Book

*My Novena to the Holy Spirit
*My Picture Missal
§Our Father
*Our Father and Hail Mary, The
*Our Lady of Fatima
*Our Lady of Guadalupe
*Our Lady of Lourdes
*Our Parish Church
*Padre Pio
*Parables of Jesus, The
*Pope John Paul II
*Pray Always
§Prayers and Beliefs for Children
*Prayers for Every Day
*Prayers to My Favorite Saints, Part 1
*Prayers to My Favorite Saints, Part 2
*Prayers to the Boy Jesus
*Praying to My Guardian Angel
*Precepts of the Church
*Promises of the Sacred Heart, The
*Psalms, The
*Receiving Holy Communion
§Rosary for Children
*Sacrament of Reconciliation, The
*Sacramentals of the Church, The
*Sacraments, The
*Saint Anthony of Padua
*Saint Elizabeth Ann Seton
*Saint Francis of Assisi
*Saint Francis of Paola
*Saint Joseph Book of Prayers for Children
*Saint Kateri Tekakwitha
*Saint Martin de Porres
*Saint Patrick
*Saint Paul the Apostle
*Saint Peter the Apostle
*Saint Therese of the Child Jesus
*Saints of the Americas
*Scriptural Rosary for Children
*Seven Sacraments, The
*Stations of the Cross
*Teachings of Jesus, The
*Ten Commandments
*Twelve Apostles, The
*Way of the Cross for Children, The
*Works of Mercy, The

Each of the following saint anthology books has thirty-two pages. These books were published between 1981 and 1999. Written by Father Lawrence Lovask SVD, each volume contains a brief biography of fifteen well-known "Super-Heroes of God." These inexpensive booklets are excellent introductory saint books for young children.

Book of Saints, Part 1 (1981)
1. St. Elizabeth Ann Seton
2. St. John Bosco
3. St. Patrick
4. St. John Baptist de La Salle
5. St. Anthony of Padua
6. St. Thomas More
7. St. Anne
8. St. Lawrence
9. St. Pius X
10. St. Peter Claver
11. St. Vincent de Paul
12. St. Teresa of Avila
13. St. Margaret Mary Alacoque
14. St. Isaac Jogues
15. St. Stephen

Book of Saints, Part 2 (1981)
1. St. Agnes
2. St. Bernadette
3. St. Dominic Savio
4. St. Dymphna
5. St. Joan of Arc
6. St. Aloysius Gonzaga
7. St. Maria Goretti
8. St. John Berchmans
9. St. Tarcisius
10. St. Rose of Lima
11. St. Therese of the Child Jesus
12. St. Gerard Majella
13. St. Stanislaus Kostka
14. St. Lucy
15. Blessed Kateri Tekakwitha

Book of Saints, Part 3 (1982)
1. St. Francis de Sales
2. St. Thomas Aquinas
3. St. Isidore
4. St. John the Baptist
5. St. Benedict
6. St. Clare
7. St. Bernard
8. St. Augustine
9. St. Charles Borromeo
10. St. Frances Cabrini
11. St. Elizabeth
12. St. Cecilia
13. St. Catherine Laboure
14. St. Francis Xavier
15. St. John of the Cross
16. Our Lady, Queen

Book of Saints, Part 5 (1985)
1. St. Basil the Great
2. St. Anthony the Abbot
3. St. Isidore of Seville
4. St. Vincent Ferrer
5. St. Gemma Galgani
6. St. Philip Neri
7. St. Camillus of Lellis
8. St. Christopher
9. St. Ignatius of Loyola
10. St. John Eudes
11. St. Gregory the Great
12. St. Robert Bellarmine
13. St. Paul of the Cross
14. St. Leo the Great
15. St. Peter Canisius

Book of Saints, Part 7 (1993)
1. St. Blasé
2. St. Valentine
3. St. Margaret of Cortona
4. St. George
5. St. Zita
6. St. Peregrine
7. St. Lawrence of Brindisi

Book of Saints, Part 4 (1982)
1. St. Sebastian
2. St. John of God
3. St. Angela Merici
4. Sts. Cyril and Methodius
5. St. Louise de Marillac
6. St. John Nepomucene
7. St. Rita
8. St. Joachim
9. St. Boniface
10. St. Alphonsus Liguori
11. St. John Vianney
12. St. Dominic
13. St. Helen
14. St. Barbara
15. St. Nicholas
16. The Saints in Heaven

Book of Saints, Part 6 (1985)
1. St. Edward
2. St. John Neumann
3. St. Benedict Labré
4. St. Catherine of Siena
5. St. Madeleine Sophie Barat
6. St. Bonaventure
7. St. Maximilian Kolbe
8. St. Gabriel the Archangel
9. St. Jerome
10. St. Francis of Assisi
11. St. Ignatius of Antioch
12. St. Anthony Mary Claret
13. St. Pius V
14. St. Martin of Tours
15. St. Ambrose

8. St. Bridget
9. St Jane Frances de Chantal
10. St. John Chrysostom
11. Sts. Cosmas and Damian
12. St. Michael the Archangel
13. St. Martin de Porres
14. St. Gertrude
15. St. Catherine of Alexandria

Book of Saints, Part 8 (1993)
1. St. Joseph
2. St. Mark
3. Sts. Philip and James
4. St. Matthias
5. St. Peter
6. St. Paul
7. St. Thomas
8. St. James the Greater
9. St. Bartholomew
10. St. Matthew
11. St. Luke
12. St. Jude Thaddeus
13. St. Simon
14. St. Andrew
15. St. John

Book of Saints, Part 9 (1996)
1. St. Fulgentius of Ruspe
2. St. Hildegund
3. St. Miguel Cordero
4. St. Cuthbert
5. St. Benedict the Black
6. St. Louis de Montfort
7. St. Mariana of Quito
8. St. Juliana Falconieri
9. St. Olga
10. Bl. Titus Brandsma
11. St. Peter Julian Eymard
12. Bl. Teresa (Edith Stein)
13. St. Hildegard of Bingen
14. St. Galla
15. St. Agnes of Assisi

Book of Saints, Part 10 (1997)
1. St. Ermengild
2. St. John Ogilvie
3. St. Zozimus
4. St. George the Younger
5. St. Fructuosus of Braga
6. Blessed Helen of Udine
7. St. Eugene de Mazenod
8. St. Monegundis
9. St. Mildred
10. St. Justin de Jacobis
11. St. Moses the Black
12. St. Beatrice Da Silva
13. St. Catherine of Genoa
14. St. Gerard Sagredo
15. St. Mary Soledad

Book of Saints, Part 11 (1997)
1. St. Alberic
2. St. Mutien Marie Wiaux
3. St. Margaret of Cortona
4. Bl. Angela Guerrero
5. St. Clement Mary Hofbauer
6. St. Hermenegild
7. St. Wiborada
8. St. Epiphanius of Salamis
9. St. Madeleine Sophie Barat
10. St. John of Sahagún
11. Bl. Osanna of Mantua
12. St. Macrina the Younger
13. St. Grimonia
14. St. Eulalia of Mérida
15. Bl. Jutta of Diessenberg

Book of Saints, Part 12 (1999)
1. St. Rosalina
2. St. Teresa Margaret Redi
3. St. Lucy Filippini
4. St. Mary Mazzarello
5. St. Simeon the Younger
6. St. William of York
7. St. Bertrand of Le Mans
8. St. Philip Benizi
9. St. Mary Soledad
10. St. Bertrand of Comminges
11. St. Peter of Alcantara
12. St. Winifred
13. St. Andrew Avellino
14. Bl. Mary Fontanella
15. St. Anthony of Lérins

Little Book of Saints Series

These books are similar to the Saint Joseph Picture Books in that each saint has a two-page spread—a large picture and some explanatory text. More simply done with less text per saint, the illustrations are softer—more muted— when compared to the bright pages of the Saint Joseph Picture Books. Each book is 24 pages long and contains the biographical information, feast days, pictures and virtues to imitate for ten saints. As of April 2013, all six volumes of this series are in print. (Due to the limited scope of these books, this series is not included on the chronological and geographical databases.)

Publisher's Description: "Large 8½" x 6½" size format, sewn signatures, quality 60 lb. cream paper, 30 pages, illustrated, beautiful laminated hardcover."

Name of Publisher: Pauline Books and Media

Ages: 5-7

Date of Republication: 2005-2010

1. Little Book of Saints, Volume I by Kathleen M. Muldoon (Blessed Virgin Mary, St. Joseph, St. Francis of Assisi, St. Joan of Arc, St. Bernadette Soubirous, St. Paul, St. Nicholas, St. Bakhita, St. Faustina Kowalska, and St. Juan Diego)
2. Little Book of Saints, Volume II by Kathleen M. Muldoon (St. Patrick, St. Thérèse of Lisieux, St. Anthony, St. Elizabeth Ann Seton, St. Michael the Archangel, St. Catherine of Siena, St. Monica, St. Martin de Porres, St. Agnes, and St. Maximilian Kolbe)
3. Little Book of Saints, Volume III by Susan Helen Wallace (St. Peter Claver, St. Brigid of Ireland, Bl. Damien of Molokai, St. Elizabeth of Hungary, St. Dominic Savio, Sts. Anne and Joachim, St. Paul Miki, Bl. Kateri Tekakwitha, St. Alberto Hurtado Cruchaga, and Bl. Teresa of Calcutta)
4. Little Book of Saints, Volume IV by Susan Helen Wallace (Bl. André Bessette, St. Teresa of Ávila, Bl. Miguel Pro, St. Katharine Drexel, St. Moses the Black, St. Rose of Lima, St. Francis Xavier, St. Gianna Molla, St. John Neumann, and Blesseds Jacinta Marto and Francisco Marto)
5. Little Book of Saints, Volume V by Susan Helen Wallace (Bl. Marie of the Incarnation Guyard, St. Thecla, St. Bridget of Sweden, St. Teresa of the Andes, St. Clare of Assisi, St. Sharbel Makhlouf, St. Lorenzo Ruiz, Bl. Charles de Foucauld, Bl. Junipero Serra, and St. Benedict)
6. Little Book of Saints, Volume VI by Susan Helen Wallace (St. Margaret of Scotland, St. Frances Xavier Cabrini, St. Germaine, St. Marguérite d'Youville, St. Edith Stein, St. Benedict the Moor, St. Peter the Apostle, St. Stanislaus Kostka, St. Thomas More, and St. Pedro de San José Betancur)

There is no substitute for books in the life of a child.
—Mary Ellen Chase

Aquinas Kids – Lives of the Saints

Publisher's Description: "What is a saint? A saint is someone who goes all out for God! God's dream is for each of His sons and daughters to become a saint—fully human and fully holy. Portrayer in [each of these] books are 15 of the best-known saints from [four periods of history].... these stories will take the reader on a grand adventure throught the lives and missions of our heroes..."

Name of Publisher: Aquinas Kids

Ages: 05 and up

Date of Publication: 2010-current

Written by Bart Tesoriero with illustrations by Michael Adams, these books are similar in size and content to the St. Joseph picture books. They are very inexpensive with striking illustrations.

1. Lives of the Saints: The Early Church (St. Michael the Archangel, St. Gabriel the Archangel, St. Anne, St. Joseph, The Blessed Virgin Mary, St. Martha, St. Peter, St. Paul, St. Matthew, St. Veronica, St. Luke, St. John the Apostle, St. Cecilia, St. Christopher, and St. Lucy)
2. Lives of the Saints: The Monastic Era (St. Apollonia, St. Sebastian, St. Barbara, St. Adrian of Nicomedia, St. Florian, St. Catherine of Alexandria, St. Blaise, St. Nicolas, St. Augustine, St. Patrick, St. Benedict, St. Isidore of Seville, St. Dymphna, St. Isidore the Farmer, and St. Francis of Assisi)
3. Lives of the Saints: The Middle Ages (St. Anthony, St. Thomas Aquinas, St. Peregrine, St. Roch, St. Catherine of Siena, St. Vincent Ferrer, St. Bernadine of Siena, St. Rita, St. Joan of Arc, St. Thomas More, St. John of God, St. Ignatius of Loyola, St. Francis Xavier, St. Teresa of Avila, and St. Charles Borromeo)
4. Live of the Saints: Modern Saints (St. Francis de Sales, St. Rose of Lima, St. Martin de Porres, St. Vincent de Paul, St. Louise de Marillac, St. John Baptist de La Salle, St. Kateri Tekakwitha, St. Gerard, St. Elizabeth Ann Seton, St. John Vianney, St. John Neumann, St. Bernadette Soubirous, St. Therese of Lisieux, St. Maximilan Koble, and St. Pio of Pietrelcina)

Two companion books to this series include the following books written by Solveig Muus and Bart Teroriero:

1. Saints for Girls (St. Anne, The Blessed Virgin Mary, St. Lucy, St. Barbara, St. Catherine of Siena, St. Joan of Arc, St. Rita, St. Clare, St. Rose of Lima, St. Margaret Mary, St. Kateri Tekakwitha, St. Elizabeth Ann Seton, St. Francis Cabrini, St. Bernadette Soubirous, and St. Therese of Lisieux)
2. Saints for Boys (St. Joseph, St. John the Baptist, St. Peter, St. Jude, St. Paul, St. Christopher, St. Augustine, St. Patrick, St. Benedict, St. Francis of Assisi, St. Anthony, St. Thomas Aquinas, St. Ignatius of Loyola, St. Francis Xavier, and St. Martin de Porres)

Dujarie Press Biography Reprints

Publisher's Description: "Large 8½" x 6½" size format, sewn signatures, quality 60 lb. cream paper, 30 pages, illustrated, beautiful laminated hardcover."

Name of Publisher: The Neumann Press

Ages: 6-12

Date of Republication: 2005-2009

Neumann Press began republishing these wonderful biographies by the brothers of the Holy Cross Congregation (C.S.C.) in 2005, ceasing in 2009 after the complete series republication was begun by Mary's Books Publishing. In the 1950's and 1960's, Dujarie Press published almost four hundred biographies about Catholic scientists, saints, artists, explorers, and musicians on four different reading levels. See "Dujarie Press" in the "Out-of-Print Books" above for more information about this series as well as the current series, In the Footsteps of the Saints. (Note that the titles in this series are not numbered.)

1. *A Story of Beethoven by Brother Ernest (1960, 2005)
2. *A Story of Catherine of Alexandria by Brother Flavius (1965, 2005)
3. *A Story of John Bosco by Brother Ernest (1958, 2005)
4. *A Story of St. John Vianney by Brother Ernest (1959, 2008)
5. *A Story of Mother Elizabeth Seton by Brother Ernest (1960, 2008)
6. *A Story of St. Lawrence by Brother Lawrence Emge (1961, 2009)

Notes:

_____
_____
_____
_____
_____
_____
_____

> **A thousand lifetimes would be too short to read everything readable. Nor is everything in print worth reading. Common sense, not to say enlightened prudence, tells us we must be selective. The secret is to know what to read.** —Fr. John Hardon

In the Footsteps of the Saints Series

In 2008, Mary's Books Publishing began reprinting the Dujarie Press biography series. These books are excellent Catholic biographies, great for read aloud and reasonably priced at $6.95 for Level 1 books, $9.95 for Level 2 books, and $10.95 for Level 3 books. Level 1 books (grades one through three) are approximately 32 pages each while Level 2 books (grades fourth through sixth) are 90-96 pages each. Level 3 books are intended for grades seven and eight. The Level 1 paperback books are 6" by 8" and can be purchased in sets of ten. The titles listed below include books currently in print by level, then titles slated for printing in 2013 and 2014.

Name of Publisher: Mary's Books Publishing

Ages: 6 and up

Date of Republication: 2008-current

Level 1 books currently in print:

> **The man who is fond of books is usually a man of lofty thought, and of elevated opinions.**
> —Christopher Dawson

Set 1
A Story of St. Therese by Brother Ernest (Ryan) (1957, 2009)
A Story of St. Anthony by Brother Ernest (Ryan) (1960, 2009)
A Story of St. Cecilia by Brother Ernest (Ryan) (1959, 2009)
A Story of St. Charles by Brother Ernest (Ryan) (1962, 2009)
A Story of the Infant Jesus of Prague by Brother Ernest (Ryan) (1956, 2009)
A Story of St. Joan of Arc by Brother Ernest (Ryan) (1958, 2009)
A Story of St. Agatha by Brother Ernest (Ryan) (1960, 2009)
A Story of St. Margaret of Scotland by Brother Ernest (Ryan) (1957, 2009)
A Story of St. Elizabeth of Hungary by Brother Ernest (Ryan) (1960, 2009)
A Story of St. Bernadette by Brother Ernest (Ryan) (1958, 2009)

Set 2
A Story of St. Rita by Brother Ernest (Ryan) (1959, 2008)
A Story of St. Germaine by Brother Ernest (Ryan) (1956, 2008)
A Story of St. Dominic by Brother Ernest (Ryan) (1959, 2008)
A Story of St. Simon of Stock by Brother Ernest (Ryan) (1959, 2008)
A Story of St. Peregrine by Brother Ernest (Ryan) (1958, 2008)
A Story of St. Stephen by Brother Ernest (Ryan) (1962, 2008)
A Story of St. Wenceslaus by Brother Ernest (Ryan) (1961, 2008)
A Story of St. Hyacinth by Brother Ernest (Ryan) (1960, 2008)
A Story of St. Bridget by Brother Ernest (Ryan) (1959, 2008)
A Story of Stanislaus Kostka by Brother Ernest (Ryan) (1958, 2008)

Set 3
A Story of St. Blaise by Brother Franklin Cullen (1958, 2010)
A Story of St. Louise de Marillac by Brother Ernest (Ryan) (1960, 2010)
A Story of St. Sebastian by Brother Ernest (Ryan) (1959, 2010)

Andrew the Apostle by S.E. Danielski (1966, 2010)
A Story of Our Lady of Fatima by Brother Ernest (Ryan) (1957, 2010)
A Story of St. Clare by Brother Ernest (Ryan) (1957, 2010)
A Story of Louis Braille by Brother Ernest (Ryan) (1962, 2010)
A Story of Bl. Pauline Von Mallinckrodt by Brother Ernest (Ryan) (1961, 2010)
A Story of Millet by Brother Ernest (Ryan) (1961, 2010)
A Story of St. Gemma by Brother Ernest (Ryan) (1957, 2010)

Set 4

A Story of St. John Bosco by Brother Ernest (Ryan) (1958, 2011)
A Story of St. Peter by Brother Ernest (Ryan) (1961, 2011)
A Story of St. Isaac Jogues by Brother Ernest (Ryan) (1958, 2011)
A Story of St. Patrick by Brother Ernest (Ryan) (1958, 2011)
A Story of St. Joseph by Brother Ernest (Ryan) (1957, 2011)
A Story of St. Dominic Savio by Brother Ernest (Ryan) (1957, 2011)
A Story of St. Paschal Baylon by Brother Ernest (Ryan) (1960, 2011)
A Story of Schubert by Brother Ernest (Ryan) (1961, 2011)
A Story of Venerable Catherine McAuley by Brother Ernest (Ryan) (1959, 2011)
A Story of St. Angela Merici by Brother Ernest (Ryan) (1960, 2011)

Set 5

A Story of St. Cyprian by Brother Ernest (Ryan) (1960, 2012)
A Story of St. Lucy by Brother Ernest (Ryan) (1957, 2012)
A Story of St. Camillus by Brother Ernest (Ryan) (1959, 2012)
A Story of Michaelangelo by Brother Ernest (Ryan) (1961, 2012)
A Story of St. Benedict by Brother Ernest (Ryan) (1958, 2012)
A Story of St. Lawrence by Brother Lawrence Emge (1961, 2012)
A Story of Our Lady of Guadalupe by Brother Ernest (Ryan) (1957, 2012)
A Story of St. Catherine of Alexandria by Brother Flavius (Ellison) (1965, 2012)
A Story of Captain John Barry by Brother Flavius (Ellison) (1965, 2012)
A Story of St. Christopher by Brother Ernest (Ryan) (1959, 2012)

Level 2 books currently in print:

Set 1

No Tears for the Bride, A Story of St. Perpetua by Brother Roberto (Muller) (1958, 2008)
Stairway to the Stars, A Story of St. Germaine Cousin by Brother Roberto (Muller) (1958, 2008)
Music from the Hunger Pit, A Story of St. Maximillian Kolbe by Brother Roberto (Muller) (1954, 2008)
The Girl Who Laughed at Satan, A Story of St. Rose of Lima by Brother Roberto (Muller) (1956, 2008)
Bring Me an Axe, A Story of St. Boniface of Germany by Brother Roberto (Muller) (1964, 2008)

Set 2

The Archer Saint, A Story of St. Hubert by Brother Ernest (Ryan) (1950, 2009)

Queen of the Poor, A Story of St. Elizabeth of Hungary by Brother Marco Daly (1961, 2009)

The Saint on Horseback: A Story of St. Louis IX, King of France by Brother Louis Gazagne (1953, 2009)

Our Lady Comes to Paris, A Story of St. Catherine Laboure by Brother Ernest (Ryan) (1953, 2009)

To the Ends of the Earth, A Story of St. Frances Xavier Cabrini by Brother Genard Greene (1955, 2009)

Set 3

King of Colors, A Story of Fra Angelico by Brother Roberto (Muller) (1962, 2010)

Just for Today, A Story of Blessed Marie Leonie by Brother Ernest (Ryan) (1955, 2010)

I Serve the King, A Story of St. Francis Borgia by Brother Roberto (Muller) (1954, 2010)

The Wandering Minstrel, A Story of Antonin Dvorak by Brother Roy Nash (1955, 2010)

Our Lady Comes to Pontmain by Brother Ernest (Ryan) (1959, 2010)

Set 4

A Torch in the Darkness, A Story of St. John of Capistrano by Brother Roberto (Muller) (1956, 2010)

Fold It Gently, A Story of Fr. Abram Ryan by Brother Bernard Donahoe (1960, 2010)

Stepping Stones to Heaven, A Story of St. Gaspar del Bufalo by Brother Flavius (Ellison) (1964, 2010)

Hide the Children, A Story of St. Bernard of Clarivaux by Brother Roberto (Muller) (1962, 2010)

When All Ships Failed, A Story of St. Raymond of Pennafort by Brother Ernest (Ryan) (1953, 2010)

Set 5

Show Us Your Face, A Story of Venerable Leo Papin Dupont by Brother Gerard Hagemann (1962, 2011)

David, King of Israel by Brother Evan Schmid (1966, 2011)

The Face in the Flames, A Story of St. Bridget of Sweden by Brother Roberto (Muller) (1959, 2011)

The Miracle Man of Muro, A Story of St. Gerard Majella by Brother Ernest (Ryan) (1950, 2011)

A Search for a Shepherd, A Story of Fr. Paul of Graymoor by Brother Roberto (Muller) 1959, 2011)

Level 3 books currently in print:

Set 1

The Ox Was an Angel, A Story of St. Thomas Aquinas by Brother Edward Overstreet (1961, 2013)

Ink in His Blood, A Story of Monsignor Ronald Knox by Brother Edward Overstreet (1960, 2013)

Don't Turn Back, A Story of St. Ignatius Loyola by Brother Roberto (Muller) (1958, 2013)
Dawn Brings Glory, A Story of Blessed Miguel Pro by Brother Roberto (Muller) (1956, 2013)
Dante and His Journey by Brother Evan Schmid (1961, 2011 by POD, 2013)

Upcoming Books: (These books have not been included on the geographical and chronological databases in this book.)

Level 1

A Story of St. Francis of Assisi by Brother Ernest (Ryan)
A Story of St. Ignatius Loyola by Brother Ernest (Ryan)
A Story of St. Francis Xavier by Brother Ernest (Ryan)
A Story of St. Martin de Porresby Brother Ernest (Ryan)
A Story of St. Marguerite D'Youville by Brother Ernest (Ryan)
A Story of Diego Mendez by Brother Ernest (Ryan)
A Story of St. John by Brother Ernest (Ryan)
A Story of St. Meinrad by Brother Ernest (Ryan)
A Story of St. Margaret Mary of Alacoque by Brother Ernest (Ryan)
A Story of St. Agnes of Assisi by Brother Flavius (Ellison)

Level 2

The Boy from Cheapside, A Story of St. Thomas Beckett by Brother Marco Daly
The Magic Brush, A Story of Giotto by Brother Marco Daly
The Great Saint Augustine by Brother Evan Schmid
Our Lady's Portrait Painter, A Story of Raphael by Brother Ernest (Ryan)
The Boy Who Saw the World, A Story of St. Francis Xavier by Brother Ernest (Ryan)
Our Lady Comes to New Orleans by Brother Roberto (Muller)
The Girl Who Worked Wonders, A Story of St. Philomena by Brother Roberto (Muller)
The Man Who Limped to Heaven, A Story of St. Ignatius Loyola by Brother Roberto (Muller)
Child of Many Wonders, A Story of the Infant Jesus by Brother Gerard Hagemann
Proudly We Hail, A Story of St. Francis de Sales by Brother Flavius (Ellison)

Notes:

_____
_____
_____
_____
_____
_____

Catholic Stories for Boys and Girls

This four-volume series, reprinted by Neumann Press from the Daughters of Charity's *Medal Stories* series, is written for second- or third-grade readers. Each book of 140 pages has stories about saints as well as other Catholic stories, simply written and illustrated. These stories originally were published in two formats—a series of seven books and a series of four books. While the original *Medal Stories* series is out of print and quite scarce, the reprinted *Catholic Stories for Boys and Girls* series is widely available from a variety of Catholic vendors.

Name of Publisher: The Neumann Press

Ages: 7-10

Date of Republication: 1987-2000

*Catholic Stories for Boys and Girls, Volume I: (§The Blue Book of Medal Stories)
 - The Best Deed (fiction story about a Confirmation class)
 - The Wreath of Flowers (fiction story about the rosary)
 - Pedro of the Water Jars (Christopher Columbus)
 - The Little Dove of Our Lady (St. Catherine Laboure)
 - The Great Gift of Our Lady (St. Catherine Laboure & the Miraculous Medal)
 - Black Robe (St. Isaac Jogues)

*Catholic Stories for Boys and Girls, Volume II: (§The Gold Book of Medal Stories)
 - Ottawanta (Our Lady of the Fields)
 - Elizabeth Bayley Seton
 - Anina (daughter of St. Elizabeth Seton)
 - Silver Wings (a Catholic fiction story)
 - John Philip (fiction story about the Feast of the Assumption)

*Catholic Stories for Boys and Girls, Volume III: (§The Rose Book of Medal Stories)
 - Begga's Bracelet (St. Begga, an Irish princess)
 - In the Tower of London (St. Edmund Campion)
 - Joseph (foster father of Jesus)
 - Louise (St. Louise de Marillac)

*Catholic Stories for Boys and Girls, Volume IV: (§The Violet Book of Medal Stories)
 - The Dawn of Spring (a Catholic fiction story about a grandfather's death)
 - The Land of Erin (St. Patrick)
 - The Flowery Kingdom (John Gabriel in China)
 - The Lion Tamer (early Christian martyr Martina)
 - A Shepherd and His Sheep (St. Vincent and the Sisters of Charity)

Notes:

Glory of America Series

Publisher's Description: "Discover Catholic America with the Glory of America Series for ages 7-12. These historical fiction stories introduce the reader to American saints through the eyes of the girls and boys who meet them. Using extensive historical and genealogical research, the true-to-life characters of the Glory of America Series come alive! A great way to learn history while challenging children to embrace their American Catholic heritage with enthusiasm! Each book covers a period of nineteenth-century America from a distinctly Catholic perspective. The unit studies in each book make the learning experience complete." Some of these titles are also available as electionic books. (The titles in this series are not numbered.)

Name of Publisher: Ecce Homo Press

Ages: 7-12

Date of Publication: 1999-Current

1. *The Orphans Find a Home, A St. Frances Xavier Cabrini Story by Joan Stromberg (1998)
2. *Kat Finds a Friend, A St. Elizabeth Ann Seton Story by Joan Stromberg (1999)
3. *Thomas Finds a Treasure, A St. John Neumann Story by Joan Stromberg (2001)
4. *Jose Finds the King, A Blessed Miguel Pro Story by Ann Ball (2002)
5. *Willy Finds Victory, A Blessed Francis Seelos Story by Joan Stromberg (2004)

Notes:

> **The man who doesn't read good books has no advantage over the man who can't read them.** —Mark Twain

Easy Reading Books of Saints and Friendly Beasts

Publisher's Description: "As the name implies, this set of books is about particular saints and their relation to the animal world. All children will love these books, and their educational and spiritual value is priceless. Each book has a full-color illustrated cover and the text inside has been re-typeset to correspond with the beautiful illustrations by Charles Vukovich and Russell Peterson which appear on each page." Reprinted from the original St. Anthony Guild Press editions from the 1960's, these books are intended for middle elementary readers. The original copyright is noted as well as the availability of the original hardbacks. (The titles in this series are not numbered.)

Name of Publisher: The Neumann Press

Ages: 8 and up

Date of Republication: 2003-2004

1. ®*Blessed Sebastian and the Oxen by Eva K. Betz (1961, 2003)
2. ®*Saint Colum and the Crane by Eva K. Betz (1961, 2003)
3. ®*Saint Germaine and the Sheep by Eva K. Betz (1961, 2004)
4. ®*Saint Martin de Porres and the Mice by Eva K. Betz (1963, 2003)
5. ®*Saint Brigid and the Cows by Eva K. Betz (1964, 2004)

Notes:

"Tell me what you read and I'll tell you who you are" is true enough, but I'd know you better if you told me what you reread. —Francois Muriac

Windeatt Saint Biography Series

Twenty of the full-length saint biographies written by Mary Fabyan Windeatt were republished in paperback by Tan Books and Publishers in the 1990's. The name of the Tan biography is listed first followed by the book's original name and publication date. These paperback books are all readily available from the publisher and other Catholic vendors. (Books are listed approximately from the easiest to the most difficult.)

Name of Publisher: Tan Books and Publishers, Inc.

Ages: 8 and up

Date of Republication: 1991-1994

1. Saint Thomas Aquinas, The Story of "The Dumb Ox" (1993) – My Name Is Thomas, 1943
2. Saint Martin de Porres, The Story of the Little Doctor of Lima, Peru (1993) – Lad of Lima, 1942
3. Saint Rose of Lima, The Story of the First Canonized Saint of the Americas (1993) – Angel of the Andes, 1943
4. Patron Saint of First Communicants, The Story of Blessed Imelda Lambertini (1991) – Little Sister, 1944
5. Saint John Masias, Marvelous Dominican Gatekeeper of Lima, Peru (1993) – Warrior in White, 1944
6. King David and His Songs, A Story of the Psalms (1993) – David and His Songs, 1947
7. Saint Catherine of Siena, The Story of the Girl Who Saw Saints in the Sky (1993) – Saints in the Sky, 1941
8. Saint Benedict, The Story of the Father of the Western Monks (1993) – Benedict, Hero of the Hills, 1943
9. Children of Fatima and Our Lady's Message to the World (1991) – The Children of Fatima, 1945
10. Blessed Marie of New France, The Story of the First Missionary Sisters in Canada (1994) – Mère Marie of New France, 1958 (published as an American Background edition only)
11. Saint Dominic, Preacher of the Rosary and Founder of the Dominican Order (1993) – Saint Dominic, 1948)
12. Saint Hyacinth, The Story of the Apostle of the North (1993) – Northern Lights, 1945
13. The Curé of Ars, The Story of Saint John Vianney, Patron Saint of Parish Priests (1991) – The Parish Priest of Ars, 1947
14. The Miraculous Medal, The Story of Our Lady's Appearances to Saint Catherine Labouré (1991) – The Medal, 1949
15. Saint Francis Solano, Wonderworker of the New World and Apostle of Argentina and Peru (1994) – Song in the South, 1946
16. Saint Paul the Apostle, The Story of the Apostle to the Gentiles (1993) – The Man on Fire, 1949
17. The Little Flower, The Story of Saint Therese of the Child Jesus (1991) – Little Queen, 1944

18. Pauline Jaricot, Foundress of the Living Rosary and the Society for the Propagation of the Faith (1993) – Pennies for Pauline, 1952
19. Saint Louis de Montfort, The Story of Our Lady's Slave (1991) – Our Lady's Slave, 1957
20. Saint Margaret Mary and the Promises of the Sacred Heart of Jesus (1994) – Mission for Margaret, 1953

Notes:

There are books so alive that you're always afraid that while you weren't reading, the book has gone and changed, has shifted like a river; while you went on living, it went on living too, and like a river moved on and moved away. No one has stepped twice into the same river. But did anyone ever step twice into the same book? —Marina Tsvetaeva

Claire Jordan Mohan Biographies

These biographies, suitable for ages nine through twelve, have between sixty and one hundred pages. Most books in this series include an index, chronology, map, glossary, and references for further reading. Many of these books have unfortunately gone out of print and are hard to find. (The titles in this series are not numbered.)

Name of Publisher: Young Sparrow Press (except as indicated)

Ages: 9 and up

Date of Publication: 1989-2007

1. §A Red Rose for Frania: A Story of the Young Life of Francis Siedliska (1989)
2. *Mother Teresa's Someday: The Young Life of Mother Teresa of Calcutta (1990)
3. ®Kaze's True Home: The Young Life of a Modern-day Saint, Mother Maria Kaupas (1992)
4. *The Young Life of Pope John Paul II (1995, 2005 by New Hope Publications)
5. The Young Life of Mother Teresa of Calcutta (1996)
6. St. Maximilian Kolbe: The Story of Two Crowns (1999)
7. ®The Young Life of Sister Faustina (2000 by Marian Press)
8. Katie: The Young Life of Mother Katharine Drexel (2000)
9. The Young Life of Saint Maria Faustina (2000 by Marian Press)
10. §The Way of the Cross: A Story of Padre Pio (2002)
11. §Joseph from Germany: The Life of Pope Benedict XVI for Children (2007 by Pauline Media)
12. *The Story of Pope Benedict XVI for Children (2007 by New Hope Publications)

Notes:

_____
_____
_____
_____
_____
_____
_____

Everywhere I have sought rest and not found it, except sitting in a corner by myself with a little book.
—Thomas à Kempis

Encounter the Saints

This series was first published as the "Encounter Books" series in the 1960's with some new titles added in the 1980's along with the republication of several of the 1960's titles. Pauline Media has reintroducied this series as "Encounter the Saints." The new editions have updated language and illustrations, and have added a prayer and a glossary of terms. New titles continue to be written and published. (Note that as of June 2007, *Saint Julie Billiart* is out of print and has been replaced as #11 in the series by *Saint John Vianney*.)

Name of Publisher: Pauline Media & Books

Ages: 9 and up

Date of Publication: 1999-Current

> **My library was dukedom large enough.** —William Shakespeare (*The Tempest*)

1. Saint Anthony of Padua: Fire and Light by Margaret Charles Kerry, F.S.P. and Mary Elizabeth Tebo, F.S.P. (1999)
2. Saint Bernadette Soubirous: Light in the Grotto by Anne Eileen Heffernan (1999)
3. Saint Elizabeth Ann Seton: Daughter of America by Jeanne Marie Grunwell and Mari Goering (1999)
4. Saint Francis of Assisi: Gentle Revolutionary by Mary Emmanuel Alves, F.S.P. (1999)
5. Saint Edith Stein: Blessed by the Cross by Mary Lea Hill, F.S.P. (1999)
6. Blessed Jacinta and Francisco Marto: Shepherds of Fatima by Anne Eileen Heffernan, F.S.P., and Patricia E. Jablonski, F.S.P. (2000)
7. Saint Joan of Arc: God's Soldier by Susan Helen Wallace (2002)
8. Saint Ignatius of Loyola: For the Greater Glory of God by Donna Giaimo, F.S.P. and Patricia Edward Jablonski, F.S.P. (2000)
9. Journeys with Mary: Apparitions of Our Lady by Zerlina de Santis (2001, 2002)
10. Saint Maximiliam Kolbe: Mary's Knight by Patricia Edward Jablonski, F.S.P. (2001)
11. §Saint Julie Billiart: The Smiling Saint by Mary Kathleen Glavich, SND (2002)
11. Saint John Vianney: A Priest for all People by Elizabeth Marie DeDomenico (2008)
12. Saint Isaac Jogues: With Burning Heart by Christine Virginia Orfeo, F.S.P. and Mary E. Tebo, F.S.P. (2002)
13. Saint Pio of Pietrelcina: Rich in Love by Eileen Dunn Bertanzetti (2002)
14. Saint Juan Diego: And Our Lady of Guadalupe by Josephine Nobisso (2002)
15. Saint Katherine Drexel: The Total Gift by Susan Helen Wallace (2003)
16. Saint Thérèse of Lisieux: The Way of Love by Mary Kathleen Glavich, SND (2003)
17. Blessed Teresa of Calcutta: Missionary of Charity by Mary Kathleen Glavich (2003)
18. Blessed Pier Giorgio Frassati: Journey to the Summit by Ana Maria Vazquez and Jennings Dean (2004)
19. Saint Martin de Porres: Humble Healer by Elizabeth Marie DeDomenico (2005)
20. Saint Frances Xavier Cabrini: Cecchina's Dream by Victoria Dority and Mary Lou Andes (2005)
21. Saint Bakhita of Sudan: Forever Free by Susan Helen Wallace (2006)
22. Saint Paul: The Thirteenth Apostle by Mary Lea Hill (2007)

23. Saint Faustina Kowalska: Messenger of Mercy by Susan Helen Wallace (2007)
24. Saint Teresa of Avila: Joyful in the Lord by Susan Helen Wallace (2008)
25. Saint Damien of Molokai: Hero of Hawaii by Virginia Helen Richards (2009)
26. Saint Clare of Assisi: A Light for the World by Marianne Lorraine Trouvé (2009)
27. Saint André Bessette: Miracles in Montreal by **Patricia Edward Jablonski (2010)**
28. **Blessed John Paul II: Be Not Afriad by Susan Helen Wallace (2011)**
29. Saint Gianna Beretta Molla: The Gift of Life by Susan Helen Wallace (2012)
30. Saint Catherine Laboure: And Our Lady of the Miraculous Medal by Marianne Lorraine Trouvé (2112)
31. Saint Kateri Tekakwitha: Courageous Faith by Lillian Fisher (2012)

Notes:

_____
_____
_____
_____
_____
_____
_____
_____
_____
_____
_____
_____
_____
_____
_____
_____
_____
_____

Vision Books

These classic saint biographies, written in the 1950's and 1960's by a variety of beloved Catholic authors, provide excellent reading material for children aged nine through fifteen. Not only do these books offer a studied glimpse into the everyday life of the saints but also into the times in which they each lived. Note that some of these books have been published as e-books. (See "Vision Books" above in the "Out-of-Print Books" section.)

Name of Publisher: Ignatius Press

Ages: 9 and up

Date of Republication: 1991-Current

1. Kateri Tekakwitha, Mohawk Maid by Evelyn M. Brown (1991)
2. St. Isaac and the Indians by Milton Lomask (1991)
3. Edmund Campion, Hero of God's Underground by Harold C. Gardiner (1992)
4. St. John Bosco and the Children's Saint, Dominic Savio by Catherine Beebe (1992)
5. St. Philip of the Joyous Heart by Francis X. Connolly (1993)
6. Francis and Clare, Saints of Assisi by Helen Walker Homan (1994)
7. St. Pius X, the Farm Boy Who Became Pope by Walter Diethelm (1994)
8. St. Francis and the Seven Seas by Albert J. Nevins (1995)
9. St. Therese and the Roses by Helen Walker Homan (1995)
10. St. Dominic and the Rosary by Catherine Beebe (1996)
11. St. Elizabeth's Three Crowns by Blanche Jennings Thompson (1996)
12. Mother Cabrini, Missionary to the World by Frances Parkinson Keyes (1997)
13. St. Anthony and the Christ Child by Helen Walker Homan (1997)
14. The Cure of Ars, The Priest Who Outtalked the Devil by Milton Lomask (1998)
15. Father Marquette and the Great Rivers by August Derleth (1998)
16. Bernadette and the Lady by Hertha Pauli (1999)
17. St. Ignatius and the Company of Jesus by August Derleth (1999)
18. Katharine Drexel, Friend of the Neglected by Ellen Tarry (2000)
19. Mother Seton and the Sisters of Charity by Alma Power-Waters (2000)
20. St. Catherine Laboure and the Miraculous Medal by Alma Power-Waters (2000)
21. St. Benedict, Hero of the Hills by Mary Fabyan Windeatt (2001)
22. St. Joan, The Girl Soldier by Louis de Wohl (2002)
23. Vincent de Paul, Saint of Charity by Margaret Ann Hubbard (2002)
24. St. Thomas More of London by Elizabeth M. Ince (2003)
25. Father Damien and the Bells by Arthur and Elizabeth Sheehan (2004)
26. St. Thomas Aquinas and the Preaching Beggars by Brendan Larnen and Milton Lomask (2005)
27. Our Lady Came to Fatima by Ruth Fox Hume (2005)
28. Florence Nightingale's Nuns by Emmeline Garnett (2009)
29. St. Helena and the True Cross by Louis de Wohl (2012)
30. St. Louis and the Last Crusade by Margaret Ann Hubbard (2013)

> **Beware of the man of one book.**
> —St. Thomas Aquinas

Catholic Children's Library Text-Picture Books

This series of books was originally published by Regina Press. The interior illustrations are black and white with each page presenting four numbered pictures with explanatory text beneath.

Publisher's Description: ". . . an outstanding collection of inspirational stories to instruct, to delight, to increase the Faith and devotion of the young reader. These books have a delightful combination of text and pictures that will hold the interest and add to reading pleasure. Four pictures and text on each page. Each book has 48 large 7" x 11" pages with a beautiful full color laminated cover."

Name of Publisher: The Neumann Press

Ages: 10 and up

Date of Republication: 2012

1. Kateri Tekakwitha, The Little Iroquois Girl by Agnes Richomme (1965, 2012)
2. Joan of Arc by Agnes Richomme (1950, 2112)
3. Our Lady of Fatima by Agnes Richomme (1965 ,2012)
4. The Uganda Martyrs by Fr. Paul Bouin (1964 , 2012)
5. Saint Francis Xavier by Fr. Norbert Marchand (1965, 2012)

Notes:
_____
_____
_____
_____
_____
_____
_____
_____

> **If one cannot enjoy reading a book over and over again, there is no use in reading it at all.** —Oscar Wilde

Forbes Biographies

Mother Frances Alice Monica Forbes (F. A. Forbes) was born in Scotland in 1869. She became a Catholic in 1900 and joined the order of the Society of the Sacred Heart. Mother Forbes wrote a series of short lives of the saints that were published as the *Standard Bearers of the Faith: A Series of Lives of the Saints for Young and Old*. Tan Books and Publishers have republished eight of these biographies. These books are shorter biographies—90 to 110 pages each—suitable for ages twelve and up. (List may be incomplete. The titles in this series are not numbered.)

Name of Publisher: Tan Books and Publishers, Inc.

Ages: 12 and up

Date of Republication: 1987-1998

1. *Pope St. Pius X (1918, 1987)
2. *§Saint Athanasius, The Father of Orthodoxy (1919, 1998)
3. *§Saint Catherine of Siena (1913, 1998)
4. *§Saint Ignatius Loyola, Founder of the Jesuits (1913, 2008 by POD)
5. *Saint John Bosco, The Friend of Youth (1935, 1941, 2000)
6. *§Saint Monica, Model of Christian Mothers (1915, 1998, 2008 by POD)
7. *®Saint Teresa of Avila, Reformer of Carmel (1917, 1998)
8. *Saint Vincent de Paul (1919, 1998)
9. §Saint Benedict (1921, 2009 by POD, 2012 by POD)

> **My fondness for good books was my salvation.**
> —St. Teresa of Avila

Notes:

Louis de Wohl Historical Fiction

Louis de Wohl has written several wonderfully informative books on Catholic saints including several in the Vision series. The following books were written on a high school or adult level, and are classified as historical fiction rather than strict biography. While several of these books are currently out of print, Ignatius Press has reprinted most of these titles in paperback (*). Additionally, many of these books are now available as an electronic book. The older, hardback editions are getting harder to find. (The titles in this series are not numbered.)

Name of Publisher: Ignatius Press

Ages: 15 and up

Date of Republication: 1991-2002

> **The books that help you the most are those which make you think the most.** —Theodore Parker

1. *The Living Wood, A Novel of Saint Helena (1947)
2. *The Quiet Light, A Novel of Saint Thomas Aquinas (1950, 1996)
3. §*The Restless Flame, A Novel of Saint Augustine (1951, 1997)
4. ®*The Golden Thread, A Novel of Saint Ignatius Loyola (1952, 2002)
5. *Set All Afire, A Novel of Saint Francis Xavier (1953, 1991)
6. *The Spear, A Novel of the Crucifixion (1955, 1998) (Be aware that there is one sexual scene in this book.)
7. §The Glorious Folly, A Novel of the Time of Saint Paul (1957)
8. *The Joyful Beggar, A Novel of Saint Francis of Assisi (1958, 2001)
9. *Citadel of God, A Novel of Saint Benedict (1959, 1994)
10. ®*Lay Siege to Heaven, A Novel of Saint Catherine of Siena (1960, 1991)
11. §Founded on a Rock, A History of the Catholic Church (1961, 1981)
12. David of Jerusalem (1963)

Notes:

_____

_____

_____

_____

_____

_____

_____

Author Bibliography

A-C

Abodaher, Daniel
- Daniel Duluth: Explorer of the Northlands (American Background)
- Under Three Flags: The Story of Gabriel Richard (Hawthorn Junior Biography)

Adams, Dorothy – Cavalry Hero: Casimir Pulaski (American Background)

Adams, Julie Davis – Mountains Are Free (Newbery)

Alois, Brother – Frontier Priest and Congressman: Father Gabriel Richard (Banner Books)

Alves, Mary Emmanuel – Saint Francis of Assisi: Gentle Revolutionary (Encounter the Saints)

Anderson, Floyd
- Bishop's Boy (Catholic Treasury)
- Father of the American Navy: Captain John Barry (Banner Books)
- Gold Rush Bishop (Catholic Treasury)

Andes, Mary Lou and Victoria Dority – Saint Frances Xavier Cabrini: Cecchina's Dream (Encounter the Saints)

Angelo, Valenti – Nino (Newbery)

Antoninus, Brother and Brother Kurt – Friar among Savages: Father Luis Cancer (Banner Books)

Arnsteen, Katy Keck (Kid Scripts)
- Abraham and Isaac
- Deborah
- Jonah: The Whale and the Vine
- Joseph and the Dreams
- Joshua: God's General
- Moses
- Naomi and Ruth
- Queen Esther

Ball, Ann – Jose Finds the King, A Blessed Miguel Pro Story (Glory of America)

Balskus, Pat – Trailblazer for the Sacred Heart: Father Mateo Crawley-Boevey, Globe-Trotter for the Sacred Heart (Encounter Books)

Bartelme, Elizabeth – Simon Bruté and the Western Adventure (American Background)

Baudouin-Croix, Marie (Along the Paths of the Gospel)
- Saint Anthony of Padua: Proclaimer of the Good News
- Saint Therese of Lisieux: And the "Little Way" of Love

Beebe, Catherine
- Apostles of the Lord, The (Beebe Biography)
- Bible Story (The), The Promised Lord and His Coming (Vision Books)
- Children's Saint Anthony, The (Beebe Biography)
- Children's Saint Francis, The (Beebe Biography)
- Christmas Story According to the Holy Gospel, The (Beebe Biography)
- David, the Shepherd King (Beebe Biography and Holy Cross Press)

> **The closest we will ever come to an orderly universe is a good library.**
> —Ashleigh Brilliant

    Days of Praise for Mary Our Mother (Beebe Biography)
    Little Patron of Gardeners: The Good Saint Fiacre (Beebe Biography)
    Christopher for Boys and Girls (Beebe Biography)
    Saint Dominic and the Rosary (Vision Books)
    Saint John Bosco and the Children's Saint: Dominic Savio (Vision Books)
    Saint Patrick: Apostle of Ireland (Beebe Biography)
    Saints for Boys and Girls (Beebe Biography)
    Story of Jesus for Boys and Girls, The (Beebe Biography)
    Story of Mary (The): The Mother of Jesus (Beebe Biography)

Belanger, Nancy Carabio (Favorite Catholic Books)
    Olivia and the Little Way
    Olivia's Gift

Bemelmans, Ludwig – The Golden Basket (Newbery)

Bemister, Margaret – Golden Caravel (Catholic Treasury)

Benson, Robert Hugh – A Child's Rule of Life (Favorite Catholic Books)

Bernadi, Mary R. – St. Tarcisius (Similar to Encounter Books)

Bertanzetti, Eileen Dunn
    Rich in Love: The Story of Padre Pio of Pietrelcina (Weaver Books)
    Saint Pio of Pietrelcina: Rich in Love (Encounter the Saints)

Betz, Eva K.
    Amazing John Tabb (Catholic Treasury)
    Apostle of Ice and Snow: A Life of Bishop Charles Seghers (Holy Cross Press)
    Blessed Sebastian and the Oxen (Saints and Friendly Beasts)
    David (Patron Saint Books)
    Fanny Allen: Green Mountain Rebel (American Background)
    Priest, Patriot and Leader: The Story of Archbishop Carroll (Banner Books)
    Quiet Flame: Mother Marianne of Molokai (Catholic Treasury)
    Saint Brigid and the Cows (Saints and Friendly Beasts)
    Saint Colum and the Crane (Saints and Friendly Beasts)
    Saint Germaine and the Sheep (Saints and Friendly Beasts)
    Saint Martin de Porres and the Mice (Saints and Friendly Beasts)
    Stout Hearts and Gentle Hands: The Life of Mother Angela of the Sisters of the Holy Cross (Holy Cross Press)
    To Far Places: The Story of Francis X. Ford (Hawthorn Junior Biography)
    Virgil Barber: New England Pied Piper (American Background)
    Web Begun, The (Similar to Catholic Treasury)
    William Gaston: Fighter for Justice (American Background)

Bishop, Claire Huchet – Pancakes-Paris (Newbery)

Bishop, Jim and Virginia Lee – Fighting Father Duffy (Vision Books)

Boesch, Mark (Vision Books)
    Cross in the West, The
    Kit Carson of the Old West

Author Bibliography

Bond, Ian – A Mountain for St. Joseph: The Life of Brother Andre, Miracle Man of Montreal (Holy Cross Press)
Bosco, Antoinette (American Background)
    Charles John Seghers: Pioneer in Alaska
    Joseph the Huron
Boucher, Alan – King's Men: A Story of St. Olaf of Norway (Clarion Books)
Bouin, Fr. Paul – Uganda Martyrs (Catholic Children's Library)
Brady, Charles A. (Clarion Books)
    King's Thane
    Sword of Clontarf
Brandenburg, Claire – The Monk Who Grew Prayer (Favorite Catholic Books)
Brown, Evelyn M. (Vision Books)
    Edel Quinn: Beneath the Southern Cross
    Kateri Tekakwitha: Mohawk Maid
Buchanan, Rosemary – Don Diego de Vargas (American Background)
Buff, Mary and Conrad – The Apple and the Arrow (Newbery)
Buliard, Roger P. – My Eskimos: A Priest in the Arctic (Vision Books)
Burton, Katherine – Door of Hope: The Story of Katharine Drexel (Hawthorn Junior Biography)
Cantoni, Louise Bellucci
    Girl in the Stable (The): The Life of St. Germaine (Encounter Books)
    Leaving Matters to God: The Life of St. Teresa of Avila (Encounter Books)
    Saint Germaine and Her Guardian Angel (Similar to Encounter Books)
Cargas, Harry – I Lay Down My Life: Biography of Joyce Kilmer (Similar to Encounter Books)
Charpy, Sister Elisabeth and Marie-Genevieve Roux – Saint Catherine Laboure: Mary's Messenger (Along the Paths of the Gospel)
Christopher, Sister Marie – Frances Warde and the First Sisters of Mercy (Vision Books)
Clark, Ann Nolan (Vision Books)
    Brother Andre of Montreal
    Father Kino: Priest to the Pimas
Collins, David R. (Weaver Books)
    Beyond the Clouds: The Story of Christa McAuliffe
    Got a Penny? The Story of Dorothy Day
    Magnificent Failure: The Story of Father Solanus Casey
    Servant to the Slaves: The Story of Henriette Delille
    You're Never Alone: The Story of Thomas Merton
Colum, Padraic – Big Tree of Bunlahy: Stories of My Own Countryside (Newbery)
Comfort, Mildred Houghton – Princess Isabel of Brazil and the Glittering Pen (American Background)
Conniff, James C. G. and James A. Farley – Governor Al Smith (Vision Books)
Connolly, Francis X. – Saint Philip of the Joyous Heart (Vision Books)

> **Read in order to live.**
> —Henry Fielding

Cornelius, Sister Mary – Marc's Choice: A Story of the Time of Diocletian (Catholic Treasury)
Crouch, Howard E. – Brother Dutton of Molokai (Catholic Treasury)
Cullen, Brother Franklin – A Story of St. Blaise (In the Footsteps of the Saints)

D-F

Daley, Arthur – Knute Rockne: Football Wizard of Notre Dame (American Background)
Daly, Brother Marco – Queen of the Poor, A Story of St. Elizabeth of Hungary (In theFootsteps of the Saints)
Daly, Robert W. – Raphael Semmes: Confederate Admiral (American Background)
Danielski, S.E. – A Story of Andrew the Apostle (In the Footsteps of the Saints)
Daughters of Charity – Catholic Stories for Boys and Girls, Volumes I-IV
Daughters of St. Paul
    Ahead of the Crowd: The Story of St. Dominic Savio (Encounter Books)
    Bells of Conquest: The Life of St. Bernard of Clairvaux (Encounter Books)
    Boy with a Mission: The Life of Francis Marto of Fatima (Encounter Books)
    Came the Dawn: Mary of Nazareth, God's Mother and Ours (Encounter Books)
    Conscience Game (The): The Story of St. Thomas More (Encounter Books)
    Country Road Home (The): The Story of St. John Vianney, Cure of Ars (Encounter Books)
    Fisher Prince (The): The Life of St. Peter, Apostle (Encounter Books)
    Flame in the Night: The Life of St. Francis Xavier (Encounter Books)
    Footsteps of A Giant: Life of St. Charles Borromeo (Encounter Books)
    Gamble for God (A): St. Camillus de Lellis (Encounter Books)
    Gentle Revolutionary (The): The Life of St. Francis of Assisi (Encounter Books)
    God's Secret Agent: The Life of Father Michael Augustine Pro, S.J. (Encounter Books)
    Great Hero (The): St. Paul the Apostle (Encounter Books)
    Her Dream Came True: The Life of Blessed Imelda Lambertini (Encounter Books)
    Light in the Grotto: The Life of St. Bernadette (Encounter Books)
    Mary's Pilgrim: The Life of St. Peregrine (Encounter Books)
    More Than a Knight: The True Story of St. Maximilian Kolbe (Encounter Books)
    Mother Seton: Wife, Mother, Educator, Foundress, Saint (Similar to Encounter Books)
    No Greater Love: The Life of Father Damien of Molokai (Encounter Books)
    No Place for Defeat: Life of St. Pius V (Encounter Books)
    Noble Lady: The Life of St. Helen (Encounter Books)
    Pillar in the Twilight: The Life of St. Thomas Aquinas (Encounter Books)
    Wind and Shadows: The Story of Joan of Arc (Encounter Books)
    Yes Is Forever! Mother Thecla Merlo: The First Daughter of St. Paul (Encounter Books)
Davis, Mary Gould – Truce of the Wolf and Other Tales of Old Italy (Newbery)
de Angeli, Marguerite (Newbery)
    Black Fox of Lorne, The
    Door in the Wall, The
de Leeau, Adele and Cateau – Where Valor Lies (Clarion Books)
de Paola, Tomie (See list of books in "Books in Print" for this author.)

de Santis, Zerlina
- Journeys with Mary: Apparitions of Our Lady (Encounter the Saints)
- Journeys with Mary: Apparitions of the Blessed Mother (Encounter Books)

de Wohl, Louis
- Citadel of God: A Novel of Saint Benedict (de Wohl Biography)
- David of Jerusalem (de Wohl Biography)
- Founded on a Rock: The History of the Catholic Church (de Wohl Biography)
- Glorious Folly (The): A Novel of the Time of Saint Paul (de Wohl Biography)
- Golden Thread (The): A Novel of Saint Ignatius Loyola (de Wohl Biography)
- Joyful Beggar (The): A Novel of Saint Francis of Assisi (de Wohl Biography)
- Lay Siege to Heaven: A Novel of Saint Catherine of Siena (de Wohl Biography)
- Living Wood (The): A Novel of Saint Helena (de Wohl Biography)
- Pope Pius XII: the World's Shepherd (Vision Books)
- Quiet Light (The): A Novel of Saint Thomas Aquinas (de Wohl Biography)
- Restless Flame (The): A Novel of Saint Augustine (de Wohl Biography)
- Saint Helena and the True Cross (Vision Books)
- Saint Joan: The Girl Soldier (Junior Vision)
- Saint Joan: The Girl Soldier (Vision Books)
- Set All Afire: A Novel of Saint Francis Xavier (de Wohl Biography)
- Spear (The): A Novel of the Crucifixion (de Wohl Biography)

Dean, Jennings and Ana Maria Vazquez – Blessed Pier Giorgio Frassati: Journey to the Summit (Encounter the Saints)

DeDomenico, Elizabeth Marie (Encounter the Saints)
- Saint John Vianney: Priest for all People
- Saint Martin de Porres: Humble Healer

Demarest, Donald – First Californian: The Story of Fray Junipero Serra (Hawthorn Junior Biography)

Derleth, August
- Columbus and the New World (Vision Books)
- Father Marquette and the Great Rivers (Junior Vision)
- Father Marquette and the Great Rivers (Vision Books)
- Saint Ignatius and the Company of Jesus (Vision Books)

Diethelm, Walter
- Saint Pius X: The Farm Boy Who Became Pope (Junior Vision)
- Saint Pius X: The Farm Boy Who Became Pope (Vision Books)

Dollen, Charles (Encounter Books)
- African Triumph: The Life of Charles Lwanga
- Cheerful Warrior (The): The Life of St. Charles Garnier
- Mademoiselle Louise: Life of Louise de Marillac
- Woman Who Loved (A): Louise de Marillac

Donahoe, Brother Bernard – Fold It Gently, A Story of Father Abram J. Ryan (In the Footsteps of the Saints)

Dorcy, Sister Mary Jean
- Army in Battle Array, An (Dorcy Biography)
- Crown for Joanna, A (Dorcy Biography)
- Fount of Our Joy, Madonna Legends for Dramatization (Dorcy Biography)
- Hunters of Souls (Dorcy Biography)
- Mary (Patron Saint Books)
- Mary, My Mother: A Mary-book for Little Boys and Girls (Dorcy Biography)
- Master Albert: The Story of Saint Albert the Great (Dorcy Biography)
- Our Lady of Springtime (Dorcy Biography)
- Our Lady's Feasts (Dorcy Biography)
- Saint Dominic (Dorcy Biography)
- Shrines of Our Lady (Dorcy Biography)
- St. Dominic's Family (Dorcy Biography)
- Truth Was Their Star (Dorcy Biography)

Dority, Victoria and Mary Lou Andes – Saint Frances Xavier Cabrini: Cecchina's Dream (Encounter the Saints)

Doty, Rev. William – Crusaders of the Great River: Marquette and Joliet (Banner Books)

Durkin, Rev. Joseph T. – Armorer of the Confederacy: Secretary Mallory (Banner Books)

Eaton, Jeannette – A Daughter of the Seine: A Life of Madame Roland (Newbery)

Eleanor, Mother Mary – The Last Apostle (Catholic Treasury)

Elizabeth, Sister and the Poor Clares of Poligny – Saint Colette: In the Footsteps of St. Francis and St. Clare (Along the Paths of the Gospel)

Ellison, Brother Flavius (In the Footsteps of the Saints)
- A Story of Captain John Barry
- A Story of St. Catherine of Alexandria
- Stepping Stones to Heaven, A Story of St. Gaspar del Bufalo

Emge, Brother Lawrence – A Story of St. Lawrence (Dujarie Press Reprint/In the Footsteps of the Saints)

Ernest, Brother (See Brother Ernest Ryan below.)

Ethievant, Sister Catherine – Saint Vincent de Paul: Servant of Charity (Along the Paths of the Gospel)

Ets, Marie Ets and Aurora Labastida – Nine Days to Christmas: A Story of Mexico (Caldecott)

Farley, James A. and James C. G. Conniff – Governor Al Smith (Vision Books)

Faulkner, Nancy – Knights Besieged (Clarion Books)

Fino, Catherine – Maria Domenica Mazzarello (Along the Paths of the Gospel)

Fisher, Lillian – Saint Kateri Tekakwitha: Courageous Faith (Encounter the Saints)

Fitzgerald, Ed (Vision Books)
- Champions in Sports and Spirit
- More Champions in Sports and Spirit

Flavius, Brother (See also Brother Flavius Ellison above.) – A Story of St. Catherine of Alexandria (Dujarie Press Reprint)

Forbes, F.A. (See list of books in "Books in Print" for this author.)

Ford, Lauren – Ageless Story (Caldecott)

> **Choose an author as you choose a friend.**
> —Sir Christopher Wren

Francis, Father (Father Francis Coloring Books)
- Jesus Our Savior: The Life of Jesus for the Very Young: Book 1, His Early Life
- Jesus Our Savior: The Life of Jesus for the Very Young: Book 2, His Public Life
- Mary, Full of Grace
- More Saints of the Eucharist
- Our Mother Mary
- Saints of the Eucharist
- They Became Saints

Francis, Mary – Saint Francis (Patron Saint Books)

French, Allen – The Story of Rolf and the Viking Bow (Favorite Catholic Books)

G-K

Gardiner, Harold C. – Edmund Campion: Hero of God's Underground (Vision Books)

Garnett, Emmeline (Vision Books)
- Charles de Foucauld: Adventurer of the Desert
- Florence Nightingale's Nuns

Garnett, Henry (Clarion Books)
- Blood Red Crescent
- Red Bonnet, The
- Trumpet Sounds, A

Garthwaite, Marion – The Locked Crowns (Clarion Books)

Gauch, Patricia Lee – The Little Friar Who Flew (Favorite Catholic Books)

Gazagne, Brother Louis – The Saint on Horseback: A Story of St. Louis IX, King of France (In the Footsteps of the Saints)

Gehman, Richard – Tall American: The Story of Gary Cooper (Hawthorn Junior Biography)

Genevieve, Sister St. Mary – Marguerite Bourgeoys: Pioneer Teacher (Vision Books)

Giaimo, Donna FSP and Patricia Edward Jablonski FSP – Saint Ignatius of Loyola: For the Greater Glory of God (Encounter the Saints)

Glavich, Mary Kathleen SND (Encounter the Saints)
- Blessed Teresa of Calcutta: Missionary of Charity
- Saint Therese of Lisieux: The Way of Love
- Saint Julie Billiart: The Smiling Saint

Goering, Mari and Jeanne Marie Grunwell – Saint Elizabeth Ann Seton: Daughter of America (Encounter the Saints)

Grant, Dorothy Fremont (American Background)
- Adventurous Lady: Margaret Brent of Maryland
- Rose Greenhow: Confederate Secret Agent

Gray, Marvin M. – Island Hero: The Story of Ramon Magsaysay (Hawthorn Junior Biography)

Greene, Brother Ellis – Champion of the Apostolate: The Life of St. Vincent Pallotti (Holy Cross Press)

Greene, Brother Genard – To the Ends of the Earth, A Story of St. Francis Xavier Cabrini (In the Footsteps of the Saints)

> My home is where my books are.
> —Ellen Thompson

Grunwell, Jeanne Marie and Mari Goering – Saint Elizabeth Ann Seton: Daughter of America (Encounter the Saints)

Hagemann, Brother Gerard – Show Us Your Face, A Story of Venerable Leo Papin Dupont (In the Footsteps of the Saints)

Hallock, Grace – The Boy Who Was (Newbery)

Hanson, Joseph E. – Hong Kong Altar Boy (Similar to Catholic Treasury)

Harris, Mary (Patron Saint Books)
- Elizabeth
- Helena

Hatch, Alden – Apostle of Peace: The Story of Pope Pius XII (Hawthorn Junior Biography)

Heagney, Anne
- Charity Goes to War (Catholic Treasury)
- De Tonti of the Iron Hand and the Exploration of the Mississippi (American Background)
- God and the General's Daughter (Similar to Catholic Treasury)
- Marylanders: A Story of the Puritan Revolt in Lord Baltimore's Colony (Catholic Treasury)
- Simon o'The Stock (Catholic Treasury)
- Spaldings of Old Kentucky, The (Similar to Catholic Treasury)

Heagney, H.J. – Chaplain in Gray: Abram Ryan (American Background)

Heffernan, Anne Eileen FSP (Encounter the Saints)
- Blessed Jacinta and Francisco Marto: Shepherds of Fatima (with author Patricia Edward Jablonski)
- Saint Bernadette Soubirous: Light in the Grotto

Hilger, Sister Mary Ione – First Sioux Nun: Sister Marie-Josephine Nebraska (Similar to Catholic Treasury)

Hill, Mary Lea FSP (Encounter the Saints)
- Blessed by the Cross: St. Edith Stein
- Saint Paul: The Thirteenth Apostle

Hindman, Jane F. – Mathew Carey: Pamphleter for Freedom (American Background)

Hodges, Margaret (adaptor) – Saint George and the Dragon: A Golden Legend (Caldecott)

Homan, Helen Walker
- Francis and Clare: Saints of Assisi (Junior Vision)
- Francis and Clare: Saints of Assisi (Vision Books)
- Saint Anthony and the Christ Child (Junior Vision)
- Saint Anthony and the Christ Child (Vision Books)
- Saint Therese and the Roses (Vision Books)

Honour, Alan – The Man Who Could Read Stones: Champollion and the Rosetta Stone (Hawthorn Junior Biography)

Hopkins, J.G.E. (American Background)
- Black Robe Peacemaker: Pierre de Smet
- Colonial Governor: Thomas Dongan of New York

Hubbard, Margaret
- Blue Gonfalon (Clarion Books)
- Dear Philippine: The Mission of Mother Duchesne (Vision Books)

Mother Barat's Vineyard (Vision Books)
Road to the King's Mountain, The (Clarion Books)
Saint Louis and the Last Crusade (Vision Books)
Vincent de Paul, Saint of Charity (Vision Books)

Hughes, Riley – Frontier Bishop: Simon Gabriel Bruté (Catholic Treasury)

Hughson, Shirley – Athletes of God: Lives of the Saints for Every Day in the Year (Holy Cross Press)

Hume, Ruth and Paul (Hawthorn Junior Biography)
King of Song: The Story of John McCormack
Lion of Poland: The Story of Paderewski

Hume, Ruth Fox (Vision Books)
Our Lady Came to Fatima
Saint Margaret Mary: Apostle of the Sacred Heart

Hunt, Marigold – Patrick (Patron Saint Books)

Hunt, Regina Victoria (Catholic Treasury)
Bright Banners
Candle for Our Lady

Hurley, Doran – John Hughes, Eagle of the Church (American Background)

Ince, Elizabeth M. – Saint Thomas More of London (Vision Books)

Jablonski, Patricia Edward FSP (Encounter the Saints)
Blessed Jacinta and Francisco Marto: Shepherds of Fatima (with author Anne Eileen Heffernan)
Saint André Bessette: Miracles in Montreal
Saint Ignatius of Loyola: For the Greater Glory of God (with author Donna Giaimo)
Saint Maximilian Kolbe: Mary's Knight

Jacks, Leo Vincent
Prairie Venture (Similar to Catholic Treasury)
Turquoise Rosary (Catholic Treasury)
Wires West (Catholic Treasury)

Jewett, Eleanor – The Hidden Treasure of Glaston (Newbery)

Johnson, Grace and Harold – Hand Raised at Gettysburg (Catholic Treasury)

Josita, Sister Mary – Sing a Song of Holy Things (Favorite Catholic Books)

Kane, Harnett T. – The Ursulines: Nuns of Adventure, The Story of the New Orleans Community (Vision Books)

Kaufman, Helen L. – Anvil Chorus: The Story of Giuseppe Verdi (Hawthorn Junior Biography)

Keefe, Sister Maryellen – Saint Angela Merici: Leading People to God (Along the Paths of the Gospel)

Kennedy, Martin de Porres – A Philadelphia Catholic in King James's Court (Favorite Catholic Books)

Kerry, Margaret Charles FSP. and Mary Elizabeth Tebo, FSP – Saint Anthony of Padua: Fire and Light (Encounter the Saints)

Keyes, Frances Parkinson – Mother Cabrini: Missionary to the World (Vision Books)

> **A house without books is like a room without windows.**
> —Heinrich Mann

Kolars, Frank
   Long Trail (The): The Story of Buffalo Bill (Banner Books)
   Prisoner of Lost Island (Similar to Catholic Treasury)
   Sea Tiger: The Story of Pedro Menendez (Hawthorn Junior Biography)

Koob, Theodora – Johann of the Trembling Hand: A Story Set in Oberammergau (Similar to Catholic Treasury)

Kowalska, Saint Maria Faustina – Divine Mercy in My Soul, The Diary of (Favorite Catholic Books)

Kurt, Brother and Brother Antoninus – Friar among Savages: Father Luis Cancer (Banner Books)

Kyle, Ann – Apprentice of Florence (Newbery)

L-R

Lamers, William M. – Thunder Maker: General Thomas Meagher (Catholic Treasury)

Larnen, Brendan and Milton Lomask – Saint Thomas Aquinas and the Preaching Beggars (Vision Books)

Lomask, Milton
   Assignment to the Council (Clarion Books)
   Charles Carroll and the American Revolution (American Background)
   Cross Among the Tomahawks (Clarion Books)
   Cure of Ars (The): The Priest Who Outtalked the Devil (Vision Books)
   General Phil Sheridan and the Union Cavalry (American Background)
   John Carroll: Bishop and Patriot (Vision Books)
   Rochambeau and Our French Allies (American Background)
   Saint Augustine and His Search for Faith (Vision Books)
   Saint Isaac and the Indians (Vision Books)
   Saint Thomas Aquinas and the Preaching Beggars (with author Brendan Larnen) (Vision Books)
   Ship's Boy with Magellan (Clarion Books)

Lomupo, Brother Robert – Fire Is His Name: A Life of St. Vincent de Paul (Holy Cross Press)

Lovasik, Father Lawrence (See list of books in "Books in Print, St. Joseph Picture Books" for this author.)

Loyola, Mother Mary – The King of the Golden City Study Edition, An Allegory for Children (Favorite Catholic Books)

MacDonald, Francis – Star of the Mohawk, Kateri Tekakwitha (Banner Books)

Madden, Daniel (Hawthorn Junior Biography)
   Operation Escape: The Adventure of Father O'Flaherty
   Monuments to Glory: The Story of Antonio Barluzzi, Architect of the Holy Land

Marchand, Fr. Norbert – Saint Francis Xavier (Catholic Children's Library)

Marie, Sister Raymond – Courageous Catherine: Mother Mary Catherine McAuley, The First Sister of Mercy (Catholic Treasury)

Marion, John Francis – Lucrezia Bori of the Metropolitan Opera (American Background)

Marshall, Bernard – Cedric the Forester (Newbery)
McCarthy, Helen A. – Lydia Longley: the First American Nun (Vision Books)
McHugh, Rev. Michael – Giant of the Western Trail: Father Peter de Smet (Banner Books)
McKern, Pat – The Promise to Angela: A Life of St. Angela Merici (Holy Cross Press)
Miller, Shane (Hawthorn Junior Biography)
    Desert Fighter: The Story of General Yigael Yadin and the Dead Sea Scrolls
    Hammer of Gaul: The Story of Charles Martel
Mohan, Claire Jordan (Claire Jordan Mohan Biographies)
    Joseph from Germany: The Life of Pope Benedict XVI for Children
    Katie: The Young Life of Mother Katharine Drexel
    Kaze's True Home: The Young Life of a Modern-day Saint, Mother Maria Kaupas
    Mother Teresa's Someday: The Young Life of Mother Teresa of Calcutta
    Red Rose for Frania (A): A Story of the Young Life of Francis Siedliska
    St. Maximilian Kolbe: The Story of Two Crowns
    Story of Pope Benedict XVI for Children, The
    Way of the Cross: A Story of Padre Pio, The
    Young Life of Mother Teresa of Calcutta, The
    Young Life of Pope John Paul II, The
    Young Life of Saint Maria Faustina, The
    Young Life of Sister Faustina, The
Monmarche, Carole and the Salesians of Don Bosco – Saint John Bosco: The Friend of Children and Young People (Along the Paths of the Gospel)
Moore, John Travers and Rosemarian Staudacher – Modern Crusaders (Vision Books)
Morris, Terry – Doctor America: The Story of Tom Dooley (Hawthorn Junior Biography)
Morriss, Frank (Catholic Treasury)
    Adventures of Broken Hand
    Alfred of Wessex: The King Who Saved His Country
    Boy of Philadelphia: A Story about the Continental Congress
    Submarine Pioneer: John Philip Holland
Muldoon, Kathleen M. – Little Book of Saints, Volumes I-II (Little Books of Saints Series)
Muller, Brother Roberto (In the Footsteps of the Saints)
    Bring Me an Ax, A Story of St. Boniface of Germany
    Dawn Brings Glory, A Story of Blessed Miguel Pro
    Don't Turn Back, A Story of St. Ignatius Loyola
    Face in the Flames (The), A Story of St. Bridget of Sweden
    Girl Who Laughed at Satan (The), A Story of St. Rose of Lima
    Girl Who Worked Wonders (The), A Story of St. Philomena
    Hide the Children, A Story of St. Bernard of Clarivaux
    I Serve the King, A Story of St. Francis Borgia
    King of Colors, A Story of Fra Angelico
    Man Who Limped to Heaven (The), A Story of St. Ignatius Loyola
    Music from the Hunger Pit, A Story of St. Maximillian Kolbe
    No Tears for the Bride, A Story of St. Perpetua

Our Lady Comes to New Orleans
   Search for a Shepherd (A), A Story of Fr. Paul of Graymoor
   Stairway to the Stars, A Story of St. Germaine Cousin
   Torch in the Darkness, (A) A Story of St. John Capistrano
Muus, Solveig (Aquinas Kids)
   Lives of the Saints for Boys (with Bart Tesoriero)
   Lives of the Saints for Girls (with Bart Tesoriero)
Nash, Brother Roy – The Wandering Minstrel, A Story of Antonin Dvorak (In the Footsteps of the Saints)
Nevins, Albert J.
   Saint Francis of the Seven Seas (Junior Vision)
   Saint Francis of the Seven Seas (Vision Books)
Nobisso, Josephine
   Saint Juan Diego and Our Lady of Guadalupe (Encounter the Saints)
   Weight of the Mass (The), A Tale of Faith (Favorite Catholic Books)
O'Brien, Sister Mary Celine – I Charge Each of You: The Story of Dr. Tom Dooley (Holy Cross Press)
Orbaan, Albert – Forked Lightning: The Story of Philip H. Sheridan (Hawthorn Junior Biography)
Orfeo, Christine Virginia FSP and Mary E. Tebo, FSP – Saint Isaac Jogues: With Burning Heart (Encounter the Saints)
Overstreet, Brother Edward (In the Footsteps of the Saints)
   Ink in His Blood, A Story of Monsignor Ronald Knox
   The Ox Was an Angel, A Story of St. Thomas Aquinas
Panunzi, Rev. Paul – Love as Strong as Death: The Story of St. Thecla (Encounter Books)
Patrice, Sister Margaret – A Lovely Gate Set Wide, A Book of Catholic Verse for Young Readers (Favorite Catholic Books)
Pauli, Hertha
   Bernadette and the Lady (Vision Books)
   Christmas and the Saints (Vision Books)
   Two Trumpters of Vienna, The (Clarion Books)
Peck, Anne Merriman – Wings of an Eagle: The Story of Michelangelo (Hawthorn Junior Biography)
Pellowski, Anna – Latsch Valley Farm series (Favorite Catholic Books)
Pickney, Jerry – Noah's Ark (Caldecott)
Pitrone, Jean Maddern – The Great Black Robe (Similar to Encounter Books)
Politi, Leo (Caldecott)
   Juanita
   Pedro, The Angel of Olvera Street
   Song of the Swallows
Polland, Madeleine (Clarion Books)
   Chuiraquimba and the Black Robes
   City of the Golden House

Fingal's Quest
Flame over Tara
Mission to Cathay

Poor Clares of Poligny and Sister Elisabeth – Saint Colette: In the Footsteps of St. Francis and St. Clare (Along the Paths of the Gospel)

Power-Waters, Alma
Crusader: The Story of Richard the Lion-Heart (Hawthorn Junior Biography)
Mother Seton and the Sisters of Charity (Junior Vision)
Mother Seton and the Sisters of Charity (Vision Books)
Saint Catherine Laboure and the Miraculous Medal (Vision Books)
Sarah Peter: The Dream and the Harvest (Vision Books)

Premont, Brother Jeremy (Holy Cross Press)
The Cardinal Said No! The Story of St. John Fisher
The Eagle of God: A Life of St. John the Evangelist

Primm, Orrin (See Brother Franciscus Willett below.)

Rau, Margaret – Dawn from the West: The Story of Genevieve Caulfield (Hawthorn Junior Biography)

Reilly, Robert T.
Irish Saints (Vision Books)
Massacre at Ash Hollow (Catholic Treasury)
Rebels in the Shadows (Similar to Catholic Treasury)
Red Hugh, Prince of Donegal (Catholic Treasury)

Richards, Virginia Helen– Saint Damien of Molokai: Hero of Hawaii (Encounter the Saints)

Richardson, James P. – Mother Alfred and the Doctors Mayo (Banner Books)

Richardson, M.K. (Patron Saint Books)
Anne
Barbara
Linda
Richard
Robert

Richomme, Agnes (Catholic Children's Library)
Joan of Arc
Kateri Tekakwitha, The Iroquois Girl
Our Lady of Fatima

Riordan, Robert
Lady and the Pirate, The (Similar to Catholic Treasury)
Medicine for Wildcat: A Life Story about Samuel Charles Mazzuchelli (Catholic Treasury)

Robbins, Brother Gerald – Figs from Thistles: St. John Baptist de la Salle (Holy Cross Press)

Robbins, Ruth – Baboushka and the Three Kings (Caldecott)

Roberto, Brother (See Brother Roberto Muller above.)

Robinson, Mabel Otis – Charcoal Faces (Catholic Treasury)

Rodino, Amedeo – Music Master: The Story of Herman Cohen (Encounter Books)

Roos, Ann – Peter Claver: Saint among Slaves (Vision Books)

Roux, Marie-Genevieve and Sister Elisabeth Charpy – Saint Catherine Laboure: Mary's Messenger (Along the Paths of the Gospel)

Royer, Fanchon – Padre Pro, Mexican Hero (American Background)

Ryan, Brother Ernest (Dujarie Press Reprint)
  Story of Beethoven, A
  Story of John Bosco, A
  Story of John Vianney, A
  Story of Mother Elizabeth Seton, A
  (See many more books by Brother Ernest in "In the Footsteps of the Saints Series.")

S-Z

Salesians of Don Bosco and Carole Monmarche – Saint John Bosco: The Friend of Children and Young People (Along the Paths of the Gospel)

Sanderlin, George (Vision Books)
  Saint Gregory the Great: Consul of God
  Saint Jerome and the Bible

Savage, Alma – The Forty-Ninth Star, Alaska (Banner Books)

Sawyer, Ruth – The Christmas Anna Angel (Caldecott)

Schlafy, Rev. James – Light in the Early West: Berenice Chouteau (Banner Books)

Schmid, Brother Evan (In the Footsteps of the Saints)
  David, King of Israel
  Dante and His Journey

Schofield, William G. – Sidewalk Statesman: Alfred E. Smith (American Background)

Shannon, Monica – Dobry (Newbery)

Sheed, Wilfrid – Joseph (Patron Saint Books)

Sheehan, Arthur and Elizabeth
  Father Damien and the Bells (Junior Vision)
  Father Damien and the Bells (Vision Books)
  Pierre Toussaint: Pioneer in Brotherhood (American Background)
  Rose Hawthorne: The Pilgrimage of Nathaniel's Daughter (Vision Books)

Sheehan, Elizabeth Odell (Vision Books)
  Good Pope John
  John Neumann: The Children's Bishop

Sister M. Juliana of Maryknoll – Margaret (Patron Saint Books)

Smaridge, Norah
  Bernard (Patron Saint Books)
  Hands of Mercy: The Story of Sister-Nurses in the Civil War (Banner Books)
  Light Within: The Story of Maria Montessori (Hawthorn Junior Biography)
  Master Mariner: The Adventurous Life of Joseph Conrad (Hawthorn Junior Biography)
  Pen and Bayonet: The Story of Joyce Kilmer (Hawthorn Junior Biography)

Sorgia, Father Raimondo – Catherine of Siena (Encounter Books)

Spier, Peter – Noah's Ark (Caldecott)

Stanley-Wrench, Margaret
    Conscience of a King (The), The Story of Thomas More (Hawthorn Junior Biography) [Catholic Junior Digest Book Shelf name: Conscience Game]
    Silver King: Edward the Confessor, The Last Great Anglo-Saxon Ruler (Hawthorn Junior Biography)
    Teller of Tales: The Story of Geoffrey Chaucer (Hawthorn Junior Biography)

Staudacher, Rosemarian (Vision Books)
    Catholic Campuse: Stories of American Catholic Colleges
    Chaplains in Action
    Children Welcome: Villages for Boys and Girls
    In American Vineyards: Religious Orders in the United States
    Modern Crusaders (with author John Travers Moore)

Steffan, Jack
    Fire of Freedom: Story of Colonel Carlos Castillo Armas (Hawthorn Junior Biography)
    Padre Kino and the Trail to the Pacific (American Background)

Stevens, Clifford J. – Father Flanagan: Builder of Boys (American Background)

Stone, Elaine Murray – Pedro Menendez de Aviles and the Founding of St. Augustine (American Background)

Stromberg, Joan (Glory of America)
    Kat Finds a Friend: A St. Elizabeth Ann Seton Story
    Orphans Find a Home (The): A St. Frances Xavier Cabrini Story
    Thomas Finds a Treasure: A St. John Neumann Story
    Willy Finds Victory: A Blessed Francis Seelos Story

Strousse, Flora (American Background)
    Friar and the Knight (The): Padre Olmedo and Cortez
    John Fitzgerald Kennedy: Man of Courage
    John LaFarge, Gentle Jesuit
    Margaret Haughery, Bread Woman of New Orleans

Tarry, Ellen (Vision Books)
    Katharine Drexel, Friend of the Neglected
    Martin de Porres, Saint of the New World

Tebo, Mary Elizabeth FSP (Encounter the Saints)
    Saint Anthony of Padua: Fire and Light (with author Margaret Charles Kerry FSP)
    Saint Isaac Jogues: With Burning Heart (with author Christine Virginia Orfeo FSP)

Tesoriero, Bart (Aquinas Kids)
    Lives of the Saints, Volumes I-IV (The Early Church, The Monastic Era, The Middle Ages, and Modern Saints)
    Lives of the Saints for Boys (with Solveig Muus)
    Lives of the Saints for Girls (with Solveig Muus)

Thayer, Jack – Desert Padre: Eusebio Francisco Kino (Catholic Treasury)

Thayer, Mary Dixon – The Child on His Knees (Favorite Catholic Books)

Therese, Saint of Lisieux – The Story of a Soul (Favorite Catholic Books)

Thompson, Blanche Jennings
- Candle Burns for France, A (Favorite Catholic Books)
- Peter and Paul: The Rock and the Sword (Vision Books)
- Saint Elizabeth's Three Crowns (Junior Vision)
- Saint Elizabeth's Three Crowns (Vision Books)
- Saint Francis de Sales (Vision Books)
- Saints of the Byzantine World (Vision Books)
- When Saints Were Young (Vision Books)

Tinkle, Lon – Miracle in Mexico: The Story of Juan Diego (Hawthorn Junior Biography)

Tinkle, Phyllis – This Is What I Pray Today, The Divine Hours for Children (Favorite Catholic Books)

Trouvé, Marianne Lorraine (Encounter the Saints)
- Saint Catherine Laboure: And Our Lady of the Miraculous Medal
- Saint Clare of Assisi, The Light for the World

van (von) Stockum, Hilda
- Angel's Alphabet, The (Favorite Catholic Books)
- Winged Watchman, The (Favorite Catholic Books)

Vazquez, Ana Maria and Jennings Dean – Blessed Pier Giorgio Frassati: Journey to the Summit (Encounter the Saints)

Vintrou, Francoise (Along the Paths of the Gospel)
- Saint Francis of Assisi: God's Gentle Knight
- Saint Margaret Mary: Apostle of the Sacred Heart

Wallace, Sister M. Imelda S. L. – Outlaws of Ravenhurst Study Edition (Favorite Catholic Books)

Wallace, Susan Helen
- Blessed John Paul II: Be Not Afriad (Encounter the Saints)
- Little Book of Saints, Volumes III-VI (Little Book of Saints Series)
- Saint Bakhita of Sudan: Forever Free (Encounter the Saints)
- Saint Faustina Kowalska: Messenger of Mercy (Encounter the Saints)
- Saint Gianna Beretta Molla: The Gift of Life (Encounter the Saints)
- Saint Joan of Arc: God's Soldier (Encounter the Saints)
- Saint Katharine Drexel: The Total Gift (Encounter the Saints)
- Saint Teresa of Avila: Joyful in the Lord (Encounter the Saints)

Webster, Gary (Hawthorn Junior Biography)
- Journey into Light: The Story of Louis Braille
- Man Who Found Out Why: The Story of Gregor Mendel

Wilhelm, Maria – Fighting Irishman: The Story of "Wild Bill" Donovan" (Hawthorn Junior Biography)

Willard, Barbara (Clarion Books)
- Augustine Came to Kent
- If All the Swords in England
- Son of Charlemagne

Willett, Brother Franciscus (Orrin Primm)
    The Mountain of God: A Life of St. Benedict (Holy Cross Press)
    The Thunder of Silence: The Life of St. Bernard of Claivaux (Holy Cross Press)
Williamson, Hugh Ross – Young People's Book of Saints, Sixty-Three Saints of the Western
    Church from the First to the Twentieth Centuries (Catholic Digest Junior Book Shelf)
Wilson, Charles Morrow
    Commandant Paul and the Founding of Montreal (American Background)
    Wilderness Explorer: The Story of Samuel de Champlain (Hawthorn Junior Biography)
Windeatt, Mary Fabyan (See also Windeatt Saint Series [out of print], and Mary Fabyan
    Windeatt Coloring Books and Windeatt Saint Biography Series [in print].)
    St. Benedict, Hero of the Hills (Vision Books)
    Mère Marie of New France (American Background)
Windham, Joan (Favorite Catholic Books)
    Saints for Boys
    Saints for Girls
    Six O'Clock Saints series
Winkler, Father Jude
    Great Men of the Bible: New Testament (St. Joseph Picture Books)
    Great Men of the Bible: Old Testament (St. Joseph Picture Books)
    Great Women of the Bible (St. Joseph Picture Books)
    Holy Family, The (St. Joseph Picture Books)
    Mother Teresa (St. Joseph Picture Books)
    Padre Pio (St. Joseph Picture Books)
    Pope John Paul II (St. Joseph Picture Books)
    Saint Therese of the Child Jesus (St. Joseph Picture Books)
    Saint Francis of Paola (St. Joseph Picture Books)
    Saints of the Americas (St. Joseph Picture Books)
    Story of Abraham, The (St. Joseph Bible Story Books)
    Story of Isaac and Jacob, The (St. Joseph Bible Story Books)
    Story of Joseph and His Brothers, The (St. Joseph Bible Story Books)
    Story of Joshua, The (St. Joseph Bible Story Books)
    Story of Moses, The (St. Joseph Bible Story Books)
    Story of Noah and the Flood, The (St. Joseph Bible Story Books)
    Story of Ruth, The (St. Joseph Bible Story Books)
    Story of the Birth of Jesus, The (St. Joseph Bible Story Books)

> **Books are not made for furniture, but there is nothing else that so beautifully furnishes a house.** —Henry Ward Beecher

Other Favorite Authors and Titles

Catholic Publishers, Authors, and Poets
Major Catholic Publishers of Children's Books
(* denotes current)

*Benziger Brothers—a Swiss publishing company that opened its publishing doors in the United States in 1853 as publishers of Catholic educational, theological, and liturgical works, as well as general interest trade books and magazines; acquired in 1968 by Crowell Collier Macmillan; merged with Glencoe Press and Bruce Publishing in 1971; now affiliated with Macmillan/McGraw-Hill, publishing Catholic catechetical materials

Bruce Publishing Company—founded by William George Bruce of Milwaukee, Wisconsin in 1891 to publish the *American School Board Journal*; additionally, the company published many religious works and high school textbooks; sold to Macmillan in 1968 by Willam G. Bruce's grandson, Robert

*Catholic Book Publishing Company—a family business started in 1911; publishes Catholic resources (Bibles, missals, prayerbooks, liturgical books and children's books) for parishes, homes, and schools; acquired Resurrection Press imprint in 2000

Dujarie Press—founded in Notre Dame, Indiana in 1940 by Brother Ernest (Ryan), a brother of the Holy Cross Congregation (C.S.C.), to publish fictionalized biographies of saints, musicians, scientists, and explorers for young readers; published over 350 inspiring novels and saint biographies before closing its doors in 1968

*Ignatius Press—under the encouragement of Frank Sheed, founded by Fr. Joseph Fessio in San Francisco in 1978 to publish little-known theological works; publishes Catholic literature, two catechetical series, four Catholic magazines; reprints Catholic classics; sells videos and audio materials; distributor of Bethlehem Books—quality reprints of exceptional historical fiction and nonfiction; see www.BethlehemBooks.com

*Neumann Press—started as a family business in 1981; publishes superior-quality, orthodox Catholic books, especially reprints of Roman Catholic classics

*Our Sunday Visitor Publishing House—established in 1912 by Fr. John Francis Noll to print a parish bulletin, *Our Sunday Visitor*, to counter the anti-Catholic literature of the times; now produces six periodicals in addition to books, tapes, software, educational materials, and offering envelopes

P.J. Kenedy & Sons—established by John Kenedy in 1826 in Baltimore; moved to New York in 1838, printing books on Catholic doctrine and Catholic biographies; succeeded by Patrick John Kenedy in 1866; "& Sons" added in 1903 after death of Patrick John and succession of his two sons, Arthur and Louis; merged with Macmillan Publishing Company

*Pauline Media and Books—Daughters of St. Paul founded in 1915 by Blessed James Alberione in Alba, Italy, to work with media and communications; established in the United States in 1932; Pauline Media and Books is now the publishing house of this religious order; specializes in Catholic books, videos, music, software, and cards

Sheed and Ward—founded by Francis John Sheed and his wife Maisie in London in 1926; established in New York in 1933 to introduce the works of contemporary Catholic authors; purchased in 1973 by Universal Press Syndicate (now Andrews and McMeel)

*****Sophia Press Institute**—established by John L. Barger in 1983 in Manchester, New Jersey, to re-introduce fine, vintage Catholic books to modern readers

*****Tan Books and Publishers**—established by and named after Thomas A. Nelson in 1967 to publish and distribute the best Catholic books; reprints traditional Catholic books; in 2008, became an imprint of St. Benedict Press of Charlotte, North Carolina

Minor Catholic Publishers of Children's Books

(These publishers reprint quality Catholic books that have gone out of print.)

Biblio Resource Publications – BiblioResource.com
Ecce Homo Press—eccehomopress.com
Hillside Education—hillsideeducation.com
Lepanto Press—olvs.org
Mary's Books Publishing – Marys-books.com
Neumann Press—Neumannpress.com
Refuge of Sinners – moscompany.com

Favorite Authors for Catholic Children

The following list includes favorite authors of Catholic juvenile literature not included in the author bibliography list above.

Anderson, Catherine Corley (author of the Sister Beatrice books)
Ball, Ann
Beckett, Sister Wendy
Boyton, Neil, S.J.
Brennan, Rev. Gerald T.
Buehrle, Marie Cecilia
Carr, Mary Jane
Criss, Mildred
Delamare, Henriette Eugénie
Doman, Regina
Eliot, Ethel Cook
Farjeon, Eleanor
Farnum, Mabel
Finn, Fr. Francis (Tom Playfair series)
Godden, Rumer
Maynard, Sara
McSwigan, Marie
Newcomb, Covelle
Repplier, Agnes
Scriven, Gerard F. (Wopsy series)
Spalding, Rev. Henry S.
Undset, Sigrid (adult)
Weber, Lenora Mattingly
White, Helen C.

Favorite Poets for Catholic Children

Belloc, Hillaire
Benson, Robert Hughes
Dorcy, Sr. Mary Jean
Farjeon, Eleanor
Feeney, Rev. Leonard
Hopkins, Gerard Manley
Kilmer, Joyce
Madeleva, Sister M.
Metcalfe, James J.
Morriss, Frank
Noyes, Alfred
Patrice, Sister Margaret
Ryan, Fr. Abram J.
Thayer, Mary Dixon

Saint Series Books by Geographical Setting

The following pages list the saint series books by geographical location. The reading level of each book as well as the series to which it belongs are also indicated. The "OOP" column indicates whether the book is currently out of print—as of April 2013.

Country	Cen.	Book Title	Author	Series	Year	OOP	Ages
Africa	03	Saint Christopher	Windeatt, Mary Fabyan	Windeatt Coloring	1955	YES	04 and up
Africa	03	Story of St. Cyprian, A	Ernest, Brother	Footsteps of the Saints	1960, 2012	NO	06-09
Africa	04	Monica, Model for Christian Mothers	Forbes, F.A.	Forbes Biography	1915, 1998	NO	12 and up
Africa	04 & 05	Lives of the Saints: The Monastic Era (St. Augustine)	Tesoriero, Bart	Aquinas Kids	2010	NO	05-09
Africa	04 & 05	Saints for Boys (St. Augustine of Hippo)	Muus, Solveig and Bart Tesoriero	Aquinas Kids	2012	NO	05-09
Africa	19	Book of Saints, Part 10 (St. Justin de Jacobis)	Lovasik, Fr. Lawrence	St. Joseph Picture	1997	NO	05 and up
Africa	20	Edel Quinn: Beneath the Southern Cross	Brown, Evelyn M.	Vision Books	1967	YES	09-15
Africa (Uganda)	19	African Triumph, The Life of Charles Lwanga	Dollen, Charles	Encounter Books	1967, 1978	YES	09 and up
Africa (Sudan)	19 & 20	Saint Bakhita of Sudan: Forever Free	Wallace, Susan Helen	Encounter the Saints	2006	NO	09 and up
Albania	20	Blessed Teresa of Calcutta: Missionary of Charity	Glavich, Mary Kathleen SND	Encounter the Saints	2003	NO	09 and up
Albania	20	Mother Teresa	Winkler, Father Jude	St. Joseph Picture	2002	NO	05 and up
Algeria	19 & 20	Charles de Foucauld, Adventurer of the Desert	Garnett, Emmeline	Vision Books	1962	YES	09-15
Arabia	01	Book of Saints, Part 8 (St. Bartholomew or Nathaniel)	Lovasik, Father Lawrence	St. Joseph Picture Books	1993	NO	05 and up
Armenia	01	Saints for Boys (St. Jude Thaddeus)	Muus, Solveig and Bart Tesoriero	Aquinas Kids	2012	NO	05-09
Armenia	04	Book of Saints, Part 7 (St. Blase)	Lovasik, Fr. Lawrence	St. Joseph Picture	1993	NO	05 and up
Armenia	04	Lives of the Saints: The Monastic Era (St. Blaise)	Tesoriero, Bart	Aquinas Kids	2010	NO	05-09
Armenia	04	Story of St. Blaise, A	Cullen, Brother Franlkin	In the Footsteps of the Saints	1958, 2010	NO	06-09

Assyria	B.C.	Jonah, the Whale and the Vine	Arnsteen, Katy Keck	Kid Scripts	1997	NO	04-08
Austria	17	Book of Saints, Part 7 (St. Lawrence of Brindisi)	Lovasik, Fr. Lawrence	St. Joseph Picture	1993	NO	05 and up
Austria	18	Story of Franz Schubert, A	Ernest, Brother	Footsteps of the Saints	1961, 2011	NO	06-09
Austria	20	Father Flanagan, Builder of Boys	Stevens, Clifford J.	American Background	1967	YES	10-15
Austria (Moravia)	18 & 19	Book of Saints, Part 11 (St. Clement Mary Hofbauer)	Lovasik, Father Lawrence	St. Joseph Picture Books	1997	NO	05 and up
Austria (Moravia)	19	Man Who Found Out Why: The Story of Gregor Mendel	Webster, Gary	Hawthorn Junior Biography	1963	YES	11 and up
Bavaria	20	Johann of the Trembling Hand: A Story Set in Oberammergau (Passion Play)	Koob, Theodora	Similar to Catholic Treasury	1960	YES	10 and up
Belgium	07	Book of Saints, Part 2 (St. Dymphna)	Lovasik, Fr. Lawrence	St. Joseph Picture	1981	NO	05 and up
Belgium	16	Robert	Richardson, M.K.	Patron Saint Books	1961	YES	08 and up
Belgium	16 & 17	Saints for Boys and Girls (St. John Berchmans)	Beebe, Catherine	Beebe Biography	1959	YES	09-14
Belgium	17	Book of Saints, Part 2 (St. John Berchmans)	Lovasik, Fr. Lawrence	St. Joseph Picture	1981	NO	05 and up
Belgium	17	Robert	Richardson, M.K.	Patron Saint Books	1961	YES	08 and up
Belgium	19	Apostle of Ice and Snow: A Life of Bishop Charles Seghers	Betz, Eva	Holy Cross Press	1964	YES	09 and up
Belgium	19	Black Robe Peacemaker, Pierre de Smet	Hopkins, J.G.E.	American Background	1958	YES	10-15
Belgium	19	Charles John Seghers, Pioneer in Alaska	Bosco, Antoinette	American Background	1960	YES	10-15
Belgium	19	Father Damien and the Bells	Sheehan, Arthur and Elizabeth	Junior Vision	1962	YES	09-11
Belgium	19	Father Damien and the Bells	Sheehan, Arthur and Elizabeth	Vision Books	1957, 2004	NO	09-15
Belgium	19	Great Black Robe, The (Father Peter de Smet)	Pitrone, Jean Maddern	Similar to Encounter Books	1964, 1965, 1981	YES	09 and up
Belgium	19	No Greater Love, Life of Father Damien of Molokai	Daughters of St. Paul	Encounter Books	1979	YES	09 and up
Belgium	19	Saint Damien of Molokai: Hero of Hawaii	Richards, Virginia Helen	Encounter the Saints	2009	NO	09 and up

Saint Series Books by Geographical Setting

Belgium	19	Story of Blessed Pauline von Mallinckrodt, A	Ernest, Brother	Footsteps of the Saints	1961, 2010	NO	06-09
Belgium	19 & 20	Book of Saints, Part 11 (St. Mutien Marie Wiaux)	Lovasik, Fr. Lawrence	St. Joseph Picture	1997	NO	05 and up
Belgium	20	Our Lady of Banneux	Windeatt, Mary Fabyan	Windeatt Coloring	1954	NO	04 and up
Belgium	20	Our Lady of Beauraing	Windeatt, Mary Fabyan	Windeatt Coloring	1954	NO	04 and up
Bohemia	10	Story of St. Wenceslaus, A	Ernest, Brother	Footsteps of the Saints	1961, 2008	NO	06-09
Bohemia	13	Hunters of Souls (Blessed Zedislava of Bohemia)	Dorcy, Sister Mary Jean	Dorcy Biography	1949, 1999	YES	10 and up
Bohemia	16 & 17	Story of the Infant Jesus of Prague, A	Ernest, Brother	Footsteps of the Saints	1956, 2009	NO	06-09
Bohemia	19	Book of Saints, Part 6 (St. John Neumann)	Lovasik, Fr. Lawrence	St. Joseph Picture	1985	NO	05 and up
Bohemia	19	John Neumann, The Children's Bishop	Sheehan, Elizabeth	Vision Books	1965	YES	09-15
Bohemia	19	Lives of the Saints: Modern Saints (St. John Neumann)	Tesoriero, Bart	Aquinas Kids	2012	NO	05-09
Bohemia	19	Saints of the Americas (St. John Neumann)	Winkler, Rev. Jude	St. Joseph Picture	2006	NO	05 and up
Bohemia	19	Wandering Minstrel (The), A Story of Antonin Dvorak	Nash, Brother Roy	In the Footsteps of the Saints	1955, 2010	NO	09-12
Brazil	19 & 20	Princess Isabel of Brazil and the Glittering Pen	Comfort, Mildred Houghton	American Background	1969	YES	10-15
Bulgaria	20	Dobry	Shannon, Monica	Newbery	1935	YES	10 and up
Canada	16 & 17	Wilderness Explorer: The Story of Samuel de Champlain	Wilson, Charles Morrow	Hawthorn Junior Biography	1963	YES	11 and up
Canada	17	Anne (shrine at Beaupre)	Richardson, M.K.	Patron Saint Books	1960	YES	08 and up
Canada	17	Black Robe (St. Isaac Jogues)	Daughters of Charity	Catholic Stories, Volume I	1987	NO	07-10
Canada	17	Blessed Kateri Tekakwitha	Windeatt, Mary Fabyan	Windeatt Coloring	1955	YES	04 and up
Canada	17	Blessed Kateri Tekakwitha, The Lily of the Mohawks	Lovasik, Fr. Lawrence	St. Joseph Picture	1981, 1996	YES	05 and up
Canada	17	Blessed Marie of New France, The Story of the First Missionary Sisters in Canada	Windeatt, Mary Fabyan	Windeatt Saint Series	1994	NO	10 and up

Canada	17	Book of Saints, Part 1 (St. Isaac Jogues)	Lovasik, Fr. Lawrence	St. Joseph Picture	1981	NO	05 and up
Canada	17	Book of Saints, Part 2 (Bld. Kateri Tekakwitha)	Lovasik, Fr. Lawrence	St. Joseph Picture	1981	NO	05 and up
Canada	17	Commandant Paul and the Founding of Montreal	Wilson, Charles	American Background	1966	YES	10-15
Canada	17	Cross Among the Tomahawks	Lomask, Milton	Clarion Books	1961, 2011	NO	09 and up
Canada	17	Crusaders of the Great River, Marquette and Joliet	Doty, Rev. William	Banner Books	1958, 2011	NO	09-15
Canada	17	Father Marquette and the Great Rivers	Derleth, August	Junior Vision	1962	YES	09-11
Canada	17	Father Marquette and the Great Rivers	Derleth, August	Vision Books	1955, 1998	NO	09-15
Canada	17	Joseph the Huron	Bosco, Antoinette	American Background	1961	YES	10-15
Canada	17	Kateri Tekakwitha, Mohawk Maid	Brown, Evelyn M.	Vision Books	1958, 1991	NO	09-15
Canada	17	Kateri Tekakwitha, The Little Iroquois Girl	Richomme, Agnes	Catholic Children's Library	1965, 2012	NO	10 and up
Canada	17	Lives of the Saints: Modern Saints (St. Kateri Tekakwitha)	Tesoriero, Bart	Aquinas Kids	2012	NO	05-09
Canada	17	Marguerite Bourgeoys, Pioneer Teacher	Genevieve, Sister St. Mary	Vision Books	1963	YES	09-15
Canada	17	Mère Marie of New France	Windeatt, Mary Fabyan	American Background	1958	YES	10-15
Canada	17	Saint Isaac and the Indians	Lomask, Milton	Vision Books	1956, 1991	NO	09-15
Canada	17	Saint Isaac Jogues: With Burning Heart	Orfeo, Christine and Mary E. Tebo	Encounter the Saints	2002	NO	09 and up
Canada	17	Saint Kateri Tekakwitha: Courgeous Faith	Fisher, Lillian	Encounter the Saints	2012	NO	09 and up
Canada	17	Saint Kateri Tekakwitha, The Lily of the Mohawks	Lovasik, Fr. Lawrence	St. Joseph Picture	2012	NO	05 and up
Canada	17	Saints for Girls (Blessed Kateri Tekakwitha)	Muus, Solveig and Bart Tesoriero	Aquinas Kids	2012	NO	05-09
Canada	17	Saints of the Americas (St. Isaac Jogues)	Winkler, Rev. Jude	St. Joseph Picture	2006	NO	05 and up
Canada	17	Saints of the Americas (Kateri Tekakwitha)	Winkler, Rev. Jude	St. Joseph Picture	2006	NO	05 and up
Canada	17	Star of the Mohawk, Kateri Tekakwitha	MacDonald, Francis	Banner Books	1958, 2011	NO	09-15

Saint Series Books by Geographical Setting

Canada	17	Story of St. Isaac Jogues, A	Ernest, Brother	Footsteps of the Saints	1958, 2011	NO	06-09
Canada	17	They Became Saints (Kateri Tekakwitha: "The Lily of the Mohawks")	Francis, Father	Father Francis Coloring	1951	NO	07 and up
Canada	17 & 18	Daniel Duluth, Explorer of the Northlands	Abodaher, Daniel	American Background	1966	YES	10-15
Canada	17 & 18	Lydia Longley, The First American Nun	McCarthy, Helen A.	Vision Books	1958	YES	09-15
Canada	19	Apostle of Ice and Snow: A Life of Bishop Charles Seghers	Betz, Eva	Holy Cross Press	1964	YES	09 and up
Canada	19	Charcoal Faces	Robinson, Mabel Otis	Catholic Treasury	1956	YES	10 and up
Canada	19	Charles John Seghers, Pioneer in Alaska	Bosco, Antoinette	American Background	1960	YES	10-15
Canada	19	Fighting Father Duffy	Bishop, Jim & Virginia Lee	Vision Books	1956	YES	09-15
Canada	19	First Sioux Nun, Sister Marie-Josephine Nebraska (1859-1894)	Hilger, Sister Mary Ione	Similar to Catholic Treasury	1963	YES	10 and up
Canada	19	Just for Today, A Story of Blessed Marie Leonie	Roberto, Brother	Footsteps of the Saints	1955, 2010	NO	09-12
Canada	19	Medicine for Wildcat: A Life Story about Samuel Charles Mazzuchelli	Riordan, Robert	Catholic Treasury	1956	YES	10 and up
Canada	19	Mountain for St. Joseph (A): Life of Brother Andre, Miracle Man of Montreal	Bond, Ian	Holy Cross Press	1965	YES	09 and up
Canada	19	Saint Andre Bessett: Miracles in Montreal	Jablonski, Patricia	Encounter the Saints	2010	NO	09 and up
Canada	19	Saints of the Americas (Bld. Marie Rose Durocher)	Winkler, Rev. Jude	St. Joseph Picture Books	2006	NO	05 and up
Canada	19 & 20	Brother Andre of Montreal	Clark, Ann Nolan	Vision Books	1967	YES	09-15
Canada	20	Champions in Sports and Spirit (Gil Hodges, Rocky Marciano, Yogi Berra, Bob Cousy, Terry Brennan, Maureen Connolly, and Maurice Richard)	Fitzgerald, Ed	Vision Books	1956	YES	09-15
Canada	20	More Champions in Sports and Spirit (Stan Musial, Carmen Basilio, Alex Olmedo, Ron Delany, Juan Manuel Fangio, Eddie Arcaro, Herb Score, and Jean Beliveau)	Fitzgerald, Ed	Vision Books	1959	YES	09-15

Canada	20	Mountain for St. Joseph (A): The Life of Brother Andre, Miracle Man of Montreal	Bond, Ian	Holy Cross Press	1965	YES	09 and up
Canada	20	My Eskimos: A Priest in the Arctic	Buliard, Roger P.	Vision Books	1956	YES	09-15
Canada	20	Saint Andre Bessett: Miracles in Montreal	Jablonski, Patricia Edward	Encounter the Saints	2010	NO	09 and up
Canary Islands	19	Book of Saints, Part 6 (St. Anthony Mary Claret)	Lovasik, Fr. Lawrence	St. Joseph Picture	1985	NO	05 and up
Central America	16	Friar and the Knight (The), Padre Olmedo and Cortez	Strousse, Flora	American Background	1957	YES	10-15
Chile	20	Prisoner of Lost Island (Catholic fiction)	Kolars, Frank	Similar to Catholic Treasury	1961	YES	10 and up
China	16	Lives of the Saints: The Middle Ages (St. Francis Xavier)	Tesoriero, Bart	Aquinas Kids	2010	NO	05-09
China	16	Mission to Cathay	Polland, Madeleine	Clarion Books	1965, 1997	NO	09 and up
China	16	Saints for Boys (St. Francis Xavier)	Muus, Solveig and Bart Tesoriero	Aquinas Kids	2012	NO	05-09
China	19	Flowery Kingdom, The (St. John Gabriel)	Daughters of Charity	Catholic Stories, Volume IV	1995	NO	07-10
China	19	Irish Saints (Bishop Edward J. Galvin)	Reilly, Robert T.	Vision Books	1964, 1981, 2002	YES	09-15
China	20	To Far Places: The Story of Francis X. Ford	Betz, Eva K.	Hawthorn Junior Biography	1962	YES	11 and up
Cuba	16	Friar and the Knight (The), Padre Olmedo and Cortez	Strousse, Flora	American Background	1957	YES	10-15
Cuba	19	Book of Saints, Part 6 (St. Anthony Mary Claret)	Lovasik, Fr. Lawrence	St. Joseph Picture	1985	NO	05 and up
Cyprus	12	Crusader: The Story of Richard the Lion-Heart (Richard I)	Power-Waters, Alma	Hawthorn Junior Biography	1964	YES	11 and up
Cyprus	13	Where Valor Lies (Seventh Crusade)	de Leeau, Adele and Cateau	Clarion Books	1959, 2007	NO	09 and up
Czech Republic	13	Hunters of Souls (Bld. Zedislava of Bohemia)	Dorcy, Sister Mary Jean	Dorcy Biography	1949, 1999	YES	10 and up
Czech Republic	16 & 17	Story of the Infant Jesus of Prague, A	Ernest, Brother	Footsteps of the Saints	1956, 2009	NO	06-09

Czecho-slovakia	14	Book of Saints, Part 4 (St. John Nepomucene)	Lovasik, Fr. Lawrence	St. Joseph Picture	1982	NO	05 and up
Czecho-slovakia	19	Man Who Found Out Why: The Story of Gregor Mendel	Webster, Gary	Hawthorn Junior Biography	1963	YES	11 and up
Czecho-slovakia	19	Wandering Minstrel (The), A Story of Antonin Dvorak	Nash, Brother Roy	In the Footsteps of the Saints	1955, 2010	NO	09-12
Denmark	06	Locked Crowns, The	Garthwaite, Marion	Clarion Books	1963	YES	09 and up
Ecuador	17	Book of Saints, Part 9 (St. Mariana of Quito)	Lovasik, Fr. Lawrence	St. Joseph Picture	1996	NO	05 and up
Ecuador	17	Saints of the Americas (St. Mariana of Quito)	Winkler, Rev. Jude	St. Joseph Picture	2006	NO	05 and up
Ecuador	19 & 20	Book of Saints, Part 9 (St. Miguel Cordero)	Lovasik, Fr. Lawrence	St. Joseph Picture	1996	NO	05 and up
Ecuador	19 & 20	Saints of the Americas (St. Miguel Cordero)	Winkler, Rev. Jude	St. Joseph Picture	2006	NO	05 and up
Egypt	B.C.	Joseph and the Dreams	Arnsteen, Katy Keck	Kid Scripts	1997	NO	04-08
Egypt	B.C.	Moses	Arnsteen, Katy Keck	Kid Scripts	1997	NO	04-08
Egypt	B.C.	Story of Joseph and His Brothers, The	Winkler, Rev. Jude	St. Joseph Bible Story	1988, 1994	YES	05-09
Egypt	B.C.	Story of Moses, The	Winkler, Rev. Jude	St. Joseph Bible Story	1988, 1994	YES	05-09
Egypt	02-03	Lives of the Saints: The Monastic Era (St. Catherine of Alexandria)	Tesoriero, Bart	Aquinas Kids	2010	NO	05-09
Egypt	03	Barbara	Richardson, M.K.	Patron Saint Books	1959	YES	08 and up
Egypt	03	Book of Saints, Part 4 (St. Barbara)	Lovasik, Fr. Lawrence	St. Joseph Picture	1982	NO	05 and up
Egypt	03	Book of Saints, Part 7 (St. Catherine of Alexandria)	Lovasik, Fr. Lawrence	St. Joseph Picture	1993	NO	05 and up
Egypt	03	Lives of the Saints: The Monastic Era (St. Apollonia)	Tesoriero, Bart	Aquinas Kids	2010	NO	05-09
Egypt	03	Lives of the Saints: The Monastic Era (St. Barbara)	Tesoriero, Bart	Aquinas Kids	2010	NO	05-09
Egypt	03	Saints for Boys and Girls (St. Barbara)	Beebe, Catherine	Beebe Biography	1959	YES	09-14
Egypt	03	Saints for Boys and Girls (St. Catherine Alexandria)	Beebe, Catherine	Beebe Biography	1959	YES	09-14
Egypt	03	Saints for Girls (St. Barbara)	Muus, Solveig and Bart Tesoriero	Aquinas Kids	2012	NO	05-09

Egypt	03	Story of St. Catherine of Alexandria, A	Flavius, Brother	Dujarie Reprint	1965, 2005	NO	06-09
Egypt	03	Story of St. Catherine of Alexandria, A	Flavius, Brother	Footsteps of the Saints	1965, 2012	NO	06-09
Egypt	03 & 04	Book of Saints, Part 5 (St. Anthony the Abbot)	Lovasik, Fr. Lawrence	St. Joseph Picture	1985	NO	05 and up
Egypt	03 & 04	Saints of the Byzantine World (St. Anthony of Egypt and St. Paul the Hermit)	Thompson, Blanche Jennings	Vision Books	1961	YES	09-15
Egypt	04	Book of Saints, Part 10 (St. Moses the Black)	Lovasik, Fr. Lawrence	St. Joseph Picture	1997	NO	05 and up
Egypt	04	Saint Athanasius, The Father of Orthodoxy	Forbes, F.A.	Forbes Biography	1919, 1998	NO	12 and up
Egypt	04	Saints of the Byzantine World (St. Athanasius)	Thompson, Blanche	Vision Books	1961	YES	09-15
Egypt	04	Saints of the Byzantine World (St. Hilarion)	Thompson, Blanche Jennings	Vision Books	1961	YES	09-15
Egypt	04	Saints of the Byzantine World (St. Pachomius)	Thompson, Blanche Jennings	Vision Books	1961	YES	09-15
Egypt	04 & 05	Saints of the Byzantine World (Saint Cyril of Alexandria)	Thompson, Blanche Jennings	Vision Books	1961	YES	09-15
Egypt	13	Where Valor Lies (Seventh Crusade)	de Leeau, Adele & Cateau	Clarion Books	1959, 2007	NO	09 and up
Egypt	18 & 19	Man Who Could Read Stones: Champollion and the Rosetta Stone	Honour, Alan	Hawthorn Junior Biography	1966	YES	11 and up
England	03	Book of Saints, Part 4 (St. Helen)	Lovasik, Fr. Lawrence	St. Joseph Picture	1982	NO	05 and up
England	03	Living Wood (The), A Novel of St. Helena	de Wohl, Louis	de Wohl Biography	1947	YES	15 and up
England	03	Noble Lady, The Life of St. Helen	Daughters of St. Paul	Encounter Books	1966	YES	09 and up
England	03	Saint Helena and the True Cross	de Wohl, Louis	Vision Books	1958, 2012	NO	09-15
England	03	Saints for Boys and Girls (St. Helen)	Beebe, Catherine	Beebe Biography	1959	YES	09-14
England	04	Living Wood (The), A Novel of Saint Helena	de Wohl, Louis	de Wohl Biography	1947	YES	15 and up
England	04	Saint George and the Dragon, A Golden Legend	Hodges, Margaret	Caldecott	1984	NO	04 and up
England	04	Saint Helena and the True Cross	de Wohl, Louis	Vision Books	1958, 2012	NO	09-15
England	04	Saints for Boys and Girls (St. Helen)	Beebe, Catherine	Beebe Biography	1959	YES	09-14

Saint Series Books by Geographical Setting

England	06	Locked Crowns, The	Garthwaite, Marion	Clarion Books	1963	YES	09 and up
England	07	Book of Saints, Part 4 (St. Boniface)	Lovasik, Fr. Lawrence	St. Joseph Picture	1982	NO	05 and up
England	07	Book of Saints, Part 10 (St. Ermengild)	Lovasik, Fr. Lawrence	St. Joseph Picture	1997	NO	05 and up
England	07	Book of Saints, Part 10 (St. Mildred)	Lovasik, Fr. Lawrence	St. Joseph Picture	1997	NO	05 and up
England	07	Bring Me an Ax, A Story of St. Boniface of Germany	Roberto, Brother	In the Footsteps of the Saints	1964, 2008	NO	09-12
England	07	King's Thane (Edwin and Beorn)	Brady, Charles A.	Clarion Books	1961, 2009	NO	09 and up
England	09	Alfred of Wessex: The King Who Saved His Country	Morriss, Frank	Catholic Treasury	1959	YES	10 and up
England	11	Book of Saints, Part 6 (St. Edward)	Lovasik, Fr. Lawrence	St. Joseph Picture	1985	NO	05 and up
England	11	Margaret (St. Margaret of Scotland)	Sister M. Juliana of Maryknoll	Patron Saint Books	1959	NO	08 and up
England	11	Saints for Boys and Girls (St. Edward the Confessor)	Beebe, Catherine	Beebe Biography	1959	YES	09-14
England	11	Silver King: Edward the Confessor, The Last Great Anglo-Saxon Ruler	Stanley-Wrench, Margaret	Hawthorn Junior Biography	1966	YES	11 and up
England	11	Story of St. Margaret of Scotland, A	Ernest, Brother	Footsteps of the Saints	1957, 2009	NO	06-09
England	11 & 12	Saints for Boys and Girls (St. Robert)	Beebe, Catherine	Beebe Biography	1959	YES	09-14
England	12	Book of Saints, Part 12 (St. William of York)	Lovasik, Fr. Lawrence	St. Joseph Picture Book	1999	NO	05 and up
England	12	Brown Scapular, The (St. Simon Stock)	Windeatt, Mary Fabyan	Windeatt Coloring	1956	YES	04 and up
England	12	Crusader: The Story of Richard the Lion-Heart (Richard I)	Power-Waters, Alma	Hawthorn Junior Biography	1964	YES	11 and up
England	12	If All the Swords in England	Willard, Barbara	Clarion	1961, 2000	NO	09 and up
England	12	Richard	Richardson, M.K.	Patron Saint Books	1959	YES	08 and up
England	12	Simon o' The Stock	Heagney, Anne	Catholic Treasury	1955	YES	10 and up
England	12	Story of St. Simon of Stock, A	Ernest, Brother	Footsteps of the Saints	1959, 2008	NO	06-09
England	12	When Saints Were Young (St. Thomas of Canterbury)	Thompson, Blanche Jennings	Vision Books	1960	YES	09-15

England	12 & 13	Saints for Boys and Girls (St. William of Rochester)	Beebe, Catherine	Beebe Biography	1959	YES	09-14
England	13	Brown Scapular, The (St. Simon Stock)	Windeatt, Mary Fabyan	Windeatt Coloring	1956	YES	04 and up
England	13	Cedric the Forester	Marshall, Bernard	Newbery	1921, 2012	NO	10 and up
England	13	Richard	Richardson, M.K.	Patron Saint Books	1959	YES	08 and up
England	13	Simon o' The Stock	Heagney, Anne	Catholic Treasury	1955	YES	10 and up
England	13	Story of St. Simon of Stock, A	Ernest, Brother	Footsteps of the Saints	1959, 2008	NO	06-09
England	14	Book of Saints, Part 5 (St. Vincent Ferrer)	Lovasik, Fr. Lawrence	St. Joseph Picture	1985	NO	05 and up
England	14	Door in the Wall, The	de Angeli, Marguerite	Newbery	1949	NO	09 and up
England	14	Teller of Tales: The Story of Geoffrey Chaucer	Stanley-Wrench, Margaret	Hawthorn Junior Biography	1965	YES	11 and up
England	15	Cardinal Said No! (The), The Story of St. John Fisher	Premont, Brother Jeremy	Holy Cross Press	1964	YES	09 and up
England	15 & 16	Book of Saints, Part 1 (St. Thomas More)	Lovasik, Fr. Lawrence	St. Joseph Picture	1981	NO	05 and up
England	15 & 16	Conscience of a King (The), The Story of Thomas More (also called The Conscience Game)	Stanley-Wrench, Margaret	Hawthorn Junior Biography	1962	YES	11 and up
England	15 & 16	Lives of the Saints: The Middle Ages (St. Thomas More)	Tesoriero, Bart	Aquinas Kids	2010	NO	05-09
England	15 & 16	Saint Thomas More of London	Ince, Elizabeth M.	Vision Books	1957, 2003	NO	09-15
England	16	Blood Red Crescent	Garnett, Henry	Clarion Books	1960, 2004, 2007	NO	09 and up
England	16	Candle for Our Lady (Shrine of Walsingham)	Hunt, Regina Victoria	Catholic Treasury	1955	YES	10 and up
England	16	Cardinal Said No! (The), The Story of St. John Fisher	Premont, Brother Jeremy	Holy Cross Press	1964	YES	09 and up
England	16	Conscience Game (The), The Story of St. Thomas More	Daughters of St. Paul	Encounter Books	1967, 1981	YES	09 and up
England	16	Edmund Campion, Hero of God's Underground	Gardiner, Harold C.	Vision Books	1957, 1992	NO	09-15
England	16	In the Tower of London (St. Edmund Campion)	Daughters of Charity	Catholic Stories, Volume III	1995	NO	07-10

Saint Series Books by Geographical Setting

Setting	Century	Title	Author	Publisher	Year	In Print	Ages
England	16	Red Hugh, Prince of Donegal	Reilly, Robert T.	Catholic Treasury	1957, 1997	NO	10 and up
England	16	Trumpet Sounds, A	Garnett, Henry	Clarion Books	1962	YES	09 and up
England	17	Adventurous Lady, Margaret Brent of Maryland	Grant, Dorothy	American Background	1957	YES	10-15
England	17	Bright Banners (St. Claude de la Colombiere)	Hunt, Regina Victoria	Catholic Treasury	1956	YES	10 and up
England	17	Saints for Boys and Girls (Blessed Richard Herst)	Beebe, Catherine	Beebe Biography	1959	YES	09-14
England	19	Florence Nightingale's Nuns	Garnett, Emmeline	Vision Books	1961, 2009	NO	09-15
England	19 & 20	Master Mariner: The Adventurous Life of Joseph Conrad	Smaridge, Norah	Hawthorn Junior Biography	1966	YES	11 and up
England	20	Golden Basket, The [the introduction of Madeleine]	Bemelmans, Ludwig	Newbery	1936	YES	08 and up
England	20	Ink in His Blood, A Story of Monsignor Ronald Knox	Overstreet, Brother Edward	In the Footsteps of the Saints	1960, 2013	NO	12-15
England	20	Lion of Poland: The Story of Paderewski	Hume, Ruth and Paul	Hawthorn Junior Bio.	1962, 2012	NO	11 and up
England	20	You're Never Alone: The Story of Thomas Merton	Collins, David R.	Weaver Books	1996	YES	09-12
Ethiopia	01	Book of Saints, Part 8 (St. Matthias)	Lovasik, Fr. Lawrence	St. Joseph Picture	1993	NO	05 and up
Ethiopia	04	Book of Saints, Part 10 (St. Moses the Black)	Lovasik, Fr. Lawrence	St. Joseph Picture	1997	NO	05 and up
Europe	01	Book of Saints, Part 8 (St. Simon)	Lovasik, Father Lawrence	St. Joseph Picture Books	1993	NO	05 and up
Europe	08 & 09	Son of Charlemagne	Willard, Barbara	Clarion	1959, 1998	NO	09 and up
Europe	11	Blue Gonfalon (First Crusade)	Hubbard, Margaret	Clarion Books	1960, 2004	NO	09 and up
Europe	20	Fighting Irishman: The Story of "Wild Bill" Donovan	Wilhelm, Maria	Hawthorn Junior Biography	1964	YES	11 and up
Europe	20	Lion of Poland: The Story of Paderewski	Hume, Ruth and Paul	Hawthorn Junior Biography	1962, 2012	NO	11 and up
Far East	18 & 19	Father of the American Navy, Captain John Barry	Anderson, Floyd	Banner Books	1959, 2011	NO	09-15
France	03	Saints for Boys and Girls (St. Dennis)	Beebe, Catherine	Beebe Biography	1959	YES	09-14

France	04	Book of Saints, Part 6 (St. Ambrose)	Lovasik, Father Lawrence	St. Joseph Picture Books	1985	NO	05 and up
France	04	Book of Saints, Part 6 (St. Martin of Tours)	Lovasik, Fr. Lawrence	St. Joseph Picture	1985	NO	05 and up
France	04	Book of Saints, Part 11 (St. Grimonia)	Lovasik, Father Lawrence	St. Joseph Picture Books	1997	NO	05 and up
France	05	Candle Burns for France, A (St. Genevieve)	Thompson, Blanche Jennings	Favorite Catholic Books	1946	YES	07 and up
France	05	Land of Erin, The (St. Patrick)	Daughters of Charity	Catholic Stories, Volume IV	1995	NO	07-10
France	05	Story of St. Patrick, A	Ernest, Brother	Footsteps of the Saints	1958, 2011	NO	06-09
France	05 & 06	Book of Saints, Part 12 (St. Anthony of Lerins)	Lovasik, Fr. Lawrence	St. Joseph Picture	1999	NO	05 and up
France	05 & 06	When Saints Were Young (St. Genevieve of Nanterre)	Thompson, Blanche Jennings	Vision Books	1960	YES	09-15
France	06	Book of Saints, Part 10 (St. Monegundis)	Lovasik, Fr. Lawrence	St. Joseph Picture	1997	NO	05 and up
France	06	Fingal's Quest	Polland, Madeleine	Clarion Books	1961, 2003	NO	09 and up
France	06 & 07	Book of Saints, Part 12 (St. Bertrand of Le Mans)	Lovasik, Fr. Lawrence	St. Joseph Picture	1999	NO	05 and up
France	06 & 07	Irish Saints (St. Columban)	Reilly, Robert T.	Vision Books	1964, 1981, 2002	YES	09-15
France	07	Little Patron of Gardeners: Good Saint Fiacre	Beebe, Catherine	Beebe Biography	1948, 2012	NO	08 and up
France	07 & 08	Archer Saint (The), A Story of St. Hubert	Ernest, Brother	Footsteps of the Saints	1950, 2009	NO	09-12
France	08	Hammer of Gaul: The Story of Charles Martel	Miller, Shane	Hawthorn Junior Bio.	1964	YES	11 and up
France	08 & 09	Son of Charlemagne	Willard, Barbara	Clarion	1959, 1998	NO	09 and up
France	10 & 11	Bernard (of Menthon)	Smaridge, Norah	Patron Saint Books	1960	YES	08 and up
France	11	Bells of Conquest, The Life of St. Bernard of Clairvaux	Daughters of St. Paul	Encounter Books	1968, 1987	YES	09 and up
France	11	Saints for Boys and Girls (St. Edward, Confessor)	Beebe, Catherine	Beebe Biography	1959	YES	09-14
France	11	Silver King: Edward the Confessor, The Last Great Anglo-Saxon Ruler	Stanley-Wrench, Margaret	Hawthorn Junior Biography	1966	YES	11 and up

Country	Century	Title	Author	Publisher	Year	In Print	Ages
France	11	Thunder of Silence (The), The Life of St. Bernard of Clairvaux	Willett, Brother Franciscus	Holy Cross Press	1964	YES	09 and up
France	11 & 12	Book of Saints, Part 11 (St. Alberic)	Lovasik, Fr. Lawrence	St. Joseph Picture	1997	NO	05 and up
France	11 & 12	Book of Saints, Part 12 (St. Bertrand of Comminges)	Lovasik, Father Lawrence	St. Joseph Picture Books	1999	NO	05 and up
France	11 & 12	Hide the Children, A Story of St. Bernard of Clairvaux	Roberto, Brother	In the Footsteps of the Saints	1962, 2010	NO	09-12
France	12	Bells of Conquest, The Life of St. Bernard of Clairvaux	Daughters of St. Paul	Encounter Books	1968, 1987	YES	09 and up
France	12	Book of Saints, Part 3 (St. Bernard)	Lovasik, Fr. Lawrence	St. Joseph Picture	1982	NO	05 and up
France	12	Crusader: The Story of Richard the Lion-Heart (Richard I)	Power-Waters, Alma	Hawthorn Junior Biography	1964	YES	11 and up
France	12	Hunters of Souls (St. Dominic)	Dorcy, Sister Mary Jean	Dorcy Biography	1949, 1999	YES	10 and up
France	12	If All the Swords in England	Willard, Barbara	Clarion	1961, 2000	NO	09 and up
France	12	Irish Saints (St. Laurence O'Toole)	Reilly, Robert T.	Vision Books	1964, 1981, 2002	YES	09-15
France	12	Saint Dominic and the Rosary	Beebe, Catherine	Vision Books	1956, 1996	NO	09-15
France	12	Thunder of Silence (The), The Life of St. Bernard of Clairvaux	Willett, Brother Franciscus	Holy Cross Press	1964	YES	09 and up
France	12 & 13	Saint Dominic de Guzman	Ordonez, Emilio	Along the Paths of the Gospel	2000	YES	07-10
France	12 & 13	Story of St. Dominic, A	Ernest, Brother	Footsteps of the Saints	1959, 2008	NO	06-09
France	12 & 13	Truce of the Wolf and Other Tales of Old Italy	Davis, Mary Gould	Newbery	1931	YES	10 and up
France	13	Book of Saints, Part 4 (St. Dominic)	Lovasik, Fr. Lawrence	St. Joseph Picture	1982	NO	05 and up
France	13	Saint Dominic	Dorcy, Sister Mary Jean	Dorcy Biography	1959, 1982	NO	14 and up
France	13	Saint Dominic, Preacher of the Rosary and Founder of the Dominican Order	Windeatt, Mary Fabyan	Windeatt Saint Series	1993	NO	09 and up
France	13	Saint Louis and the Last Crusade	Hubbard, Margaret Ann	Vision Books	1958, 2013	NO	09-15

France	13	Saint on Horseback (The): A Story of St. Louis, King of France	Gazagne, Brother Louis	In the Footsteps of the Saints	1953, 2009	NO	09-12
France	13	They Became Saints (St. Louis, King of France)	Francis, Father	Father Francis Coloring Books	1951	NO	07 and up
France	13	Where Valor Lies (Seventh Crusade)	de Leeau, Adele and Cateau	Clarion Books	1959, 2007	NO	09 and up
France	14	Book of Saints, Part 12 (St. Rosalina)	Lovasik, Father Lawrence	St. Joseph Picture Books	1999	NO	05 and up
France	14	Lives of the Saints: The Middle Ages (St. Roch)	Tesoriero, Bart	Aquinas Kids	2010	NO	05-09
France	14	Saint Colette: In the Footsteps of St. Francis and St. Clare	Poor Clares of Poligny and Sister Elizabeth	Along the Paths of the Gospel	1998	YES	07-10
France	15	Book of Saints, Part 2 (St. Joan of Arc)	Lovasik, Fr. Lawrence	St. Joseph Picture	1981	NO	05 and up
France	15	Book of Saints, Part 5 (St. Vincent Ferrer)	Lovasik, Fr. Lawrence	St. Joseph Picture	1985	NO	05 and up
France	15	Candle Burns for France, A (St. Jeanne d'Arc)	Thompson, Blanche Jennings	Favorite Catholic Books	1946	YES	07 and up
France	15	Joan of Arc	Richomme, Agnes	Catholic Children's Library	1950, 2012	NO	10 and up
France	15	Lives of the Saints: The Middle Ages (St. Joan of Arc)	Tesoriero, Bart	Aquinas Kids	2010	NO	05-09
France	15	Saint Colette: In the Footsteps of St. Francis and St. Clare	Poor Clares of Poligny and Sister Elisabeth	Along the Paths of the Gospel	1998	YES	07-10
France	15	Saint Joan of Arc	Windeatt, Mary Fabyan	Windeatt Coloring	1955	YES	04 and up
France	15	Saint Joan of Arc: God's Soldier	Wallace, Susan Helen	Encounter the Saints	2002	NO	09 and up
France	15	Saint Joan, The Girl Soldier	de Wohl, Louis	Junior Vision	1962	YES	09-11
France	15	Saint Joan, The Girl Soldier	de Wohl, Louis	Vision Books	1957, 2001	NO	09-15
France	15	Saints for Girls (St. Joan of Arc)	Muus, Solveig and Bart Tesoriero	Aquinas Kids	2012	NO	05-09
France	15	Story of St. Joan of Arc, A	Ernest, Brother	Footsteps of the Saints	1958, 2009	NO	06-09

France	15	They Became Saints (St. Joan of Arc: Patroness of France)	Francis, Father	Fr. Francis Coloring Books	1951	NO	07 and up
France	15	Wind and Shadows, The Story of Joan of Arc	Daughters of St. Paul	Encounter Books	1968	YES	09 and up
France	15 & 16	Saint Francis of Paola (Paula)	Winkler, Father Jude	St. Joseph Picture Books	2006	NO	05 and up
France	16	Candle Burns for France, A (St. Germaine)	Thompson, Blanche Jennings	Favorite Catholic Books	1946	YES	07 and up
France	16	Don't Turn Back, A Story of St. Ignatius Loyola	Roberto, Brother	Footsteps of the Saints	1958, 2013	NO	12-15
France	16	Girl in the Stable (The), The Life of St. Germaine (Cousin)	Cantoni, Louise Bellucci	Encounter Books	1967	YES	09 and up
France	16	Golden Thread (The), A Novel of Saint Ignatius Loyola	de Wohl, Louis	de Wohl Biography	1952, 2002	NO	15 and up
France	16	Lives of the Saints: The Middle Ages (St. Francis Xavier)	Tesoriero, Bart	Aquinas Kids	2010	NO	05-09
France	16	Robert	Richardson, M.K.	Patron Saint Books	1961	YES	08 and up
France	16	Saint Germaine (Cousin) and Her Guardian Angel	Cantoni, Louise Bellucci	Similar to Encounter Books	1964	YES	09 and up
France	16	Saint Germaine and the Sheep	Betz, Eva K.	Saints and Friendly Beasts	1961, 2004	NO	08 and up
France	16	Saint Ignatius and the Company of Jesus	Derleth, August	Vision Books	1956, 1999	NO	09-15
France	16	Saint Ignatius Loyola, Founder of the Jesuits	Forbes, F.A.	Forbes Biography	1913, 1998	NO	12 and up
France	16	Saint Ignatius of Loyola: For the Greater Glory of God	Giaimo, Donna and Patricia Jablonski	Encounter the Saints	2000	NO	09 and up
France	16	Saints for Boys (St. Francis Xavier)	Muus, Solveig and Bart Tesoriero	Aquinas Kids	2012	NO	05-09
France	16	Stairway to the Stars, A Story of St. Germaine Cousin	Roberto, Brother	In the Footsteps of the Saints	1958, 2008	NO	09-12
France	16	Story of St. Germaine, A	Ernest, Brother	Footsteps of the Saints	1956, 2009	NO	06-09
France	16 & 17	Book of Saints, Part 1 (St. Vincent de Paul)	Lovasik, Fr. Lawrence	St. Joseph Picture Books	1981	NO	05 and up

Country	Century	Title	Author	Publisher	Year	Illustrated	Ages
France	16 & 17	Book of Saints, Part 3 (St. Francis de Sales)	Lovasik, Fr. Lawrence	St. Joseph Picture	1982	NO	05 and up
France	16 & 17	Fire Is His Name: A Life of St. Vincent de Paul	Lomupo, Br. Robert	Holy Cross Press	1964	YES	09 and up
France	16 & 17	Lives of the Saints: Modern Saints (St. Francis de Sales)	Tesoriero, Bart	Aquinas Kids	2012	NO	05-09
France	16 & 17	Lives of the Saints: Modern Saints (St. Vincent de Paul)	Tesoriero, Bart	Aquinas Kids	2012	NO	05-09
France	16 & 17	Saint Francis de Sales	Thompson, Blanche	Vision Books	1965	YES	09-15
France	16 & 17	Saint Vincent de Paul	Forbes, F.A.	Forbes Biography	1919, 1998	NO	12 and up
France	16 & 17	Saint Vincent de Paul: Servant of Charity	Ethievant, Sister Catherine	Along the Paths of the Gospel	1999	YES	07-10
France	16 & 17	Shepherd and His Sheep, A (St. Vincent de Paul)	Daughters of Charity	Catholic Stories, Volume IV	1995	NO	07-10
France	16 & 17	Vincent de Paul, Saint of Charity	Hubbard, Margaret	Vision Books	1960, 2002	NO	09-15
France	16 & 17	Wilderness Explorer: The Story of Samuel de Champlain	Wilson, Charles Morrow	Hawthorn Junior Biography	1963	YES	11 and up
France	17	Anne (shrine at Auray)	Richardson, M.K.	Patron Saint Books	1960	YES	08 and up
France	17	Black Robe (St. Isaac Jogues)	Daughters of Charity	Catholic Stories, Volume I	1987	NO	07-10
France	17	Blessed Marie of New France, The Story of the First Missionary Sisters in Canada	Windeatt, Mary Fabyan	Windeatt Saint Series	1994	NO	10 and up
France	17	Book of Saints, Part 1 (St. Isaac Jogues)	Lovasik, Fr. Lawrence	St. Joseph Picture	1981	NO	05 and up
France	17	Book of Saints, Part 1 (St. Margaret Mary Alacoque)	Lovasik, Father Lawrence	St. Joseph Picture Books	1981	NO	05 and up
France	17	Book of Saints, Part 4 (St. Louise de Marillac)	Lovasik, Fr. Lawrence	St. Joseph Picture	1982	NO	05 and up
France	17	Book of Saints, Part 5 (St. John Eudes)	Lovasik, Fr. Lawrence	St. Joseph Picture	1985	NO	05 and up
France	17	Book of Saints, Part 7 (St. Jane Frances de Chantel)	Lovasik, Father Lawrence	St. Joseph Picture Books	1993	NO	05 and up
France	17	Cheerful Warrior (The), The Life of St. Charles Garnier	Dollen, Charles	Encounter Books	1967	YES	09 and up

Country	Century	Title	Author	Publisher	Year	In Print	Age
France	17	Commandant Paul and the Founding of Montreal	Wilson, Charles Morrow	American Background	1966	YES	10-15
France	17	Crusaders of the Great River, Marquette and Joliet	Doty, Rev. William	Banner Books	1958, 2011	NO	09-15
France	17	Father Marquette and the Great Rivers	Derleth, August	Junior Vision	1962	YES	09-11
France	17	Father Marquette and the Great Rivers	Derleth, August	Vision Books	1955, 1998	NO	09-15
France	17	Figs from Thistles: St. John Baptist de la Salle	Robbins, Br. Gerald	Holy Cross Press	1964	YES	09 and up
France	17	Lives of the Saints: Modern Saints (St. Louise de Marillac)	Tesoriero, Bart	Aquinas Kids	2012	NO	05-09
France	17	Louise (St. Louise de Marillac)	Daughters of Charity	Catholic Stories, Volume III	1995	NO	07-10
France	17	Mademoiselle Louise, Life of Louise de Marillac	Dollen, Charles	Encounter Books	1967	YES	09 and up
France	17	Marguerite Bourgeoys, Pioneer Teacher	Genevieve, Sister St. Mary	Vision Books	1963	YES	09-15
France	17	Mère Marie of New France	Windeatt, Mary Fabyan	American Background	1958	YES	10-15
France	17	Robert	Richardson, M.K.	Patron Saint Books	1961	YES	08 and up
France	17	Saint Isaac and the Indians	Lomask, Milton	Vision Books	1956, 1991	NO	09-15
France	17	Saint Isaac Jogues: With Burning Heart	Orfeo, Christine and Mary E. Tebo	Encounter the Saints	2002	NO	09 and up
France	17	Saint Louise de Marillac	Roux, Marie-Genevieve and Sr. Elisabeth Charpy	Along the Paths of the Gospel	2001	YES	07-10
France	17	Saint Margaret Mary and the Promises of the Sacred Heart of Jesus	Windeatt, Mary Fabyan	Windeatt Saint Series	1994	NO	11 and up
France	17	Saint Margaret Mary, Apostle of the Sacred Heart	Hume, Ruth Fox	Vision Books	1960	YES	09-15
France	17	Saint Margaret Mary, Apostle of the Sacred Heart	Vintrou, Francoise	Along the Paths of the Gospel	2000	YES	07-10
France	17	Saints for Girls (St. Margaret Mary Alacoque)	Muus, Solveig and Bart Tesoriero	Aquinas Kids	2012	NO	05-09
France	17	Saints of the Americas (St. Isaac Jogues)	Winkler, Rev. Jude	St. Joseph Picture	2006	NO	05 and up

Country	Century	Title	Author	Publisher	Year	In Print	Age
France	17	Story of St. Isaac Jogues, A	Ernest, Brother	Footsteps of the Saints	1958, 2011	NO	06-09
France	17	Story of St. Louise de Marillac	Ernest, Brother	Footsteps of the Saints	1960, 2010	NO	06-09
France	17	Woman Who Loved (A), Louise de Marillac	Dollen, Charles	Encounter Books	1987	YES	09 and up
France	17 & 18	Army in Battle Array, An (St. Louis de Montfort)	Dorcy, Sister Mary Jean	Dorcy Biography	1955	YES	10 and up
France	17 & 18	Book of Saints, Part 1 (St. John Baptist de La Salle)	Lovasik, Fr. Lawrence	St. Joseph Picture	1981	NO	05 and up
France	17 & 18	Book of Saints, Part 9 (St. Louis de Montfort)	Lovasik, Fr. Lawrence	St. Joseph Picture	1996	NO	05 and up
France	17 & 18	Lives of the Saints: Modern Saints (St. John Baptist de La Salle)	Tesoriero, Bart	Aquinas Kids	2012	NO	05-09
France	17 & 18	St. Louis de Montfort, The Story of Our Lady's Slave	Windeatt, Mary Fabyan	Windeatt Saint Series	1991	NO	12 and up
France	18	Book of Saints, Part 6 (St. Benedict Labre)	Lovasik, Fr. Lawrence	St. Joseph Picture	1985	NO	05 and up
France	18	Boy of Philadelphia: A Story about the Continental Congress	Morriss, Frank	Catholic Treasury	1955	YES	10 and up
France	18	Daughter of the Seine (A), A Life of Madame Roland	Eaton, Jeannette	Newbery	1929	YES	10 and up
France	18	Figs from Thistles: St. John Baptist de la Salle	Robbins, Brother Gerald	Holy Cross Press	1964	YES	09 and up
France	18	Frontier Bishop: Simon Gabriel Bruté	Hughes, Riley	Catholic Treasury	1959, 2012	NO	10 and up
France	18	Red Bonnet, The	Garnett, Henry	Clarion Books	1964, 1974	YES	09 and up
France	18	Stepping Stones to Heaven, A Story of St. Gaspar del Bufalo	Flavius, Brother	In the Footsteps of the Saints	1964, 2010	NO	09-12
France	18	Under Three Flags: The Story of Gabriel Richard	Abodaher, David J.	Hawthorn Junior Biography	1965	YES	11 and up
France	18 & 19	Book of Saints, Part 4 (St. John Vianney)	Lovasik, Fr. Lawrence	St. Joseph Picture	1982	NO	05 and up
France	18 & 19	Book of Saints, Part 6 (St. Madeleine Sophie Barat)	Lovasik, Father Lawrence	St. Joseph Picture Books	1985	NO	05 and up
France	18 & 19	Book of Saints, Part 10 (St. Eugene de Mazenod)	Lovasik, Fr. Lawrence	St. Joseph Picture	1997	NO	05 and up
France	18 & 19	Book of Saints, Part 11 (St. Madeleine Sophie Barat)	Lovasik, Father Lawrence	St. Joseph Picture Books	1997	NO	05 and up

France	18 & 19	Candle Burns for France, A (Cure d'Ars)	Thompson, Blanche Jennings	Favorite Catholic Books	1946	YES	07 and up
France	18 & 19	Country Road Home, The Story of St. John Vianney, Cure of Ars	Daughters of St. Paul	Encounter Books	1966, 1987	YES	09 and up
France	18 & 19	Cure of Ars, The Priest Who Outtalked the Devil	Lomask, Milton	Vision Books	1958, 1998	NO	09-15
France	18 & 19	Cure of Ars (The), The Story of St. John Vianney, Patron Saint of Parish Priests	Windeatt, Mary Fabyan	Windeatt Saint Series	1991	NO	10 and up
France	18 & 19	Dear Philippine: The Mission of Mother Duchesne	Hubbard, Margaret Ann	Vision Books	1964	YES	09-15
France	18 & 19	Father of the American Navy, Captain John Barry	Anderson, Floyd	Banner Books	1959, 2011	NO	09-15
France	18 & 19	Lives of the Saints: Modern Saints (St. John Vianney)	Tesoriero, Bart	Aquinas Kids	2012	NO	05-09
France	18 & 19	Man Who Could Read Stones: Champollion and the Rosetta Stone	Honour, Alan	Hawthorn Junior Biography	1966	YES	11 and up
France	18 & 19	Mother Barat's Vineyard	Hubbard, Margaret	Vision Books	1962	YES	09-15
France	18 & 19	Rochambeau and Our French Allies	Lomask, Milton	American Background	1965	YES	10-15
France	18 & 19	Saint John Vianney: Priest for All People	DeDomenico, Elizabeth Marie	Encounter the Saints	2008	NO	09 and up
France	18 & 19	Saint Julie Billiart: The Smiling Saint	Glavich, Mary	Encounter the Saints	2002	YES	09 and up
France	18 & 19	Simon Bruté and the Western Adventure	Bartelme, Elizabeth	American Background	1959, 2012	NO	10-15
France	18 & 19	Story of St. John Vianney, A	Ryan, Brother Ernest	Dujarie Press Reprint	1959, 2008	NO	06-09
France	19	Bernadette and the Lady	Pauli, Hertha	Vision Books	1956, 1999	NO	09-15
France	19	Book of Saints, Part 2 (St. Bernadette)	Lovasik, Fr. Lawrence	St. Joseph Picture	1981	NO	05 and up
France	19	Book of Saints, Part 2 (St. Therese of the Child Jesus)	Lovasik, Fr. Lawrence	St. Joseph Picture Books	1981	NO	05 and up
France	19	Book of Saints, Part 3 (St. Catherine Laboure)	Lovasik, Fr. Lawrence	St. Joseph Picture	1982	NO	05 and up
France	19	Book of Saints, Part 6 (St. Anthony Mary Claret)	Lovasik, Fr. Lawrence	St. Joseph Picture	1985	NO	05 and up
France	19	Book of Saints, Part 9 (St. Peter Julian Eymard)	Lovasik, Fr. Lawrence	St. Joseph Picture	1996	NO	05 and up

France	19	Candle Burns for France, A (Blessed Catherine Laboure)	Thompson, Blanche Jennings	Favorite Catholic Books	1946	YES	07 and up
France	19	Candle Burns for France, A (St. Bernadette)	Thompson, Blanche Jennings	Favorite Catholic Books	1946	YES	07 and up
France	19	Candle Burns for France, A (St. Therese)	Thompson, Blanche Jennings	Favorite Catholic Books	1946	YES	07 and up
France	19	Children of La Salette, The	Windeatt, Mary Fabyan	Windeatt Saint Series	1951	YES	14 and up
France	19	Flowery Kingdom, The (St. John Gabriel)	Daughters of Charity	Catholic Stories, Volume IV	1995	NO	07-10
France	19	Great Gift of Our Lady, The (St. Catherine Laboure)	Daughters of Charity	Catholic Stories, Volume I	1987	NO	07-10
France	19	Journey into Light: The Story of Louis Braille	Webster, Gary	Hawthorn Junior Bio.	1964	YES	11 and up
France	19	Light in the Grotto, Life of St. Bernadette	Daughters of St. Paul	Encounter Books	1967, 1978	YES	09 and up
France	19	Little Dove of Our Lady, The (St. Catherine Laboure)	Daughters of Charity	Catholic Stories, Volume I	1987	NO	07-10
France	19	Little Flower (The), The Story of Saint Therese of the Child Jesus	Windeatt, Mary Fabyan	Windeatt Saint Series	1991	NO	09 and up
France	19	Lives of the Saints: Modern Saints (St. Bernadette Soubirous)	Tesoriero, Bart	Aquinas Kids	2012	NO	05-09
France	19	Lives of the Saints: Modern Saints (St. Therese of Lisieux)	Tesoriero, Bart	Aquinas Kids	2012	NO	05-09
France	19	Master Mariner: The Adventurous Life of Joseph Conrad	Smaridge, Norah	Hawthorn Junior Biography	1966	YES	11 and up
France	19	Miraculous Medal (The), The Story of Our Lady's Appearances to St. Catherine Laboure	Windeatt, Mary Fabyan	Windeatt Saint Series	1991	NO	09 and up
France	19	More Saints of the Eucharist: Little Queen in Her Little Way (St. Therese of the Child Jesus)	Francis, Father	Father Francis Coloring Books	1959	NO	06 and up
France	19	Music Master, The Story of Herman Cohen	Rodino, Amedeo	Encounter Books	1968	YES	09 and up
France	19	Our Lady Came to Pontmain	Ernest, Brother	Footsteps of the Saints	1954, 2010	NO	09-12

Country	Century	Title	Author	Series	Year	In Print	Age
France	19	Our Lady Comes to Paris, A Story of St. Catherine Laboure	Ernest, Brother	In the Footsteps of the Saints	1953, 2009	NO	09-12
France	19	Our Lady of La Salette	Windeatt, Mary Fabyan	Windeatt Coloring	1954	NO	04 and up
France	19	Our Lady of Lourdes	Windeatt, Mary Fabyan	Windeatt Coloring	1954	YES	04 and up
France	19	Our Lady of Lourdes	Lovasik, Fr. Lawrence	St. Joseph Picture	1985	NO	05 and up
France	19	Our Lady of Pellevoisin	Windeatt, Mary Fabyan	Windeatt Coloring	1954	NO	04 and up
France	19	Our Lady of Pontmain	Windeatt, Mary Fabyan	Windeatt Coloring	1954	NO	04 and up
France	19	Our Lady of the Miraculous Medal	Windeatt, Mary Fabyan	Windeatt Coloring	1954	NO	04 and up
France	19	Pauline Jaricot, Foundress of the Living Rosary and the Society for the Propagation of the Faith	Windeatt, Mary Fabyan	Windeatt Saint Series	1993	NO	12 and up
France	19	Saint Bernadette Soubirous: Light in the Grotto	Heffernan, Anne Eileen	Encounter the Saints	1999	NO	09 and up
France	19	Saint Catherine Laboure: And Our Lady of the Miraculous Medal	Trouvé, Marianne Lorraine	Encounter the Saints	2012	NO	09 and up
France	19	Saint Catherine Laboure and the Miraculous Medal	Power-Waters, Alma	Vision Books	1962, 2000	NO	09-15
France	19	Saint Catherine Laboure: Mary's Messenger	Roux, Marie-Genevieve and Sister Elisabeth Charpy	Along the Paths of the Gospel	2000	YES	07-10
France	19	Saint Therese and the Roses	Homan, Helen Walker	Vision Books	1955, 1995	NO	09-15
France	19	Saint Therese of Lisieux: And the "Little Way" of Love	Baudouin-Croix, Marie	Along the Paths of the Gospel	1999	YES	07-10
France	19	Saint Therese of Lisieux: The Way of Love	Glavich, Mary Kathleen SND	Encounter the Saints	2003	NO	09 and up
France	19	Saint Therese of the Child Jesus	Winkler, Father Jude	St. Joseph Picture	2000	NO	05 and up
France	19	Saints for Girls (St. Bernadette Soubirous)	Muus, Solveig and Bart Tesoriero	Aquinas Kids	2012	NO	05-09
France	19	Saints for Girls (St. Therese of Lisieux)	Muus, Solveig and Bart Tesoriero	Aquinas Kids	2012	NO	05-09

Country	Century	Title	Author	Series	Year	In Print	Ages
France	19	Show Us Your Face, A Story of Venerable Leo Papin Dupont	Hagemann, Brother Gerard	In the Footsteps of the Saints	1962, 2011	NO	09-12
France	19	Story of a Soul, The	Therese of Lisieux, Saint	Favorite Catholic Books	1898, etc.	NO	12 and up
France	19	Story of Louis Braille, A	Ernest, Brother	Footsteps of the Saints	1962, 2010	NO	06-09
France	19	Story of Millet, A	Ernest, Brother	Footsteps of the Saints	1961, 2010	NO	06-09
France	19	Story of St. Bernadette, A	Ernest, Brother	Footsteps of the Saints	1958, 2009	NO	06-09
France	19	Story of St. Therese, A	Ernest, Brother	Footsteps of the Saints	1957, 2009	NO	06-09
France	19	They Became Saints (St. Bernadette: And Our Lady of Lourdes)	Francis, Father	Father Francis Coloring Books	1951	NO	07 and up
France	19	They Became Saints (St. Therese of the Child Jesus: And Her Little Way)	Francis, Father	Fr. Francis Coloring Books	1951	NO	07 and up
France	19 & 20	Charles de Foucauld, Adventurer of the Desert	Garnett, Emmeline	Vision Books	1962	YES	09-15
France	20	Fighting Father Duffy	Bishop, Jim & Virginia Lee	Vision Books	1956	YES	09-15
France	20	I Lay Down My Life, Biography of Joyce Kilmer	Cargas, Harry	Similar to Encounter Books	1964	YES	09 and up
France	20	Pancakes-Paris	Bishop, Claire Huchet	Newbery	1947	YES	08 and up
France	20	Pen and Bayonet: The Story of Joyce Kilmer	Smaridge, Norah	Hawthorn Junior Bio.	1962	YES	11 and up
France	20	You're Never Alone: The Story of Thomas Merton	Collins, David R.	Weaver Books	1996	YES	09-12
Germany	08	Bring Me an Ax, A Story of St. Boniface of Germany	Roberto, Brother	In the Footsteps of the Saints	1964, 2008	NO	09-12
Germany	08	Book of Saints, Part 4 (St. Boniface)	Lovasik, Fr. Lawrence	St. Joseph Picture	1982	NO	05 and up
Germany	09	Saint Meinrad	Windeatt, Mary Fabyan	Windeatt Coloring	1954	NO	04 and up
Germany	11 & 12	Book of Saints, Part 11 (Bl. Jutta of Diessenberg)	Lovasik, Fr. Lawrence	St. Joseph Picture	1997	NO	05 and up
Germany	12	Book of Saints, Part 9 (St. Hildegard of Bingen)	Lovasik, Fr. Lawrence	St. Joseph Picture	1996	NO	05 and up
Germany	12	Book of Saints, Part 9 (St. Hildegund)	Lovasik, Fr. Lawrence	St. Joseph Picture	1996	NO	05 and up
Germany	13	Master Albert, The Story of Saint Albert the Great	Dorcy, Sister Mary Jean	Dorcy Biography	1955	YES	12 and up

Germany	13	Truth Was Their Star (St. Albert the Great)	Dorcy, Sister Mary Jean	Dorcy Biography	1947, 1999	NO	10 and up
Germany	14	Book of Saints, Part 5 (St. Vincent Ferrer)	Lovasik, Fr. Lawrence	St. Joseph Picture	1985	NO	05 and up
Germany	16	Book of Saints, Part 5 (St. Peter Canisius)	Lovasik, Fr. Lawrence	St. Joseph Picture	1985	NO	05 and up
Germany	17	Book of Saints, Part 7 (St. Lawrence of Brindisi)	Lovasik, Fr. Lawrence	St. Joseph Picture	1993	NO	05 and up
Germany	18	Story of Beethoven, A	Ryan, Brother Ernest	Dujarie Press Reprint	1960, 2005	NO	06-09
Germany	19	Music Master, The Story of Herman Cohen	Rodino, Amedeo	Encounter Books	1968	YES	09 and up
Germany	19	Story of Blessed Pauline von Mallinckrodt, A	Ernest, Brother	Footsteps of the Saints	1961, 2010	NO	06-09
Germany	19 & 20	Blessed by the Cross: St. Edith Stein	Hill, Mary Lea FSP	Encounter the Saints	1999	NO	09 and up
Germany	19 & 20	Book of Saints, Part 9 (Bl. Teresa - Edith Stein)	Lovasik, Father Lawrence	St. Joseph Picture Books	1996	NO	05 and up
Germany	20	Joseph from Germany	Mohan, Claire Jordan	Mohan Biographies	2007	YES	09 and up
Germany	20	Story of Pope Benedict XVI for Children, The	Mohan, Claire Jordan	Mohan Biographies	2007	NO	09 and up
Greece	01	Eagle of God: A Life of St. John the Evangelist	Premont, Br. Jeremy	Holy Cross Press	1964	YES	09 and up
Greece	01	Lives of the Saints: The Early Church (St. Luke)	Tesoriero, Bart	Aquinas Kids	2010	NO	05-09
Greece	01	Saints for Boys and Girls (St. Dennis or Dionysius)	Beebe, Catherine	Beebe Biography	1959	YES	09-14
Greece	08 & 09	Book of Saints, Part 10 (St. George the Younger)	Lovasik, Fr. Lawrence	St. Joseph Picture	1997	NO	05 and up
Greece	09	Book of Saints, Part 4 (Sts. Cyril and Methodius)	Lovasik, Fr. Lawrence	St. Joseph Picture	1982	NO	05 and up
Greece	16	Blood Red Crescent	Garnett, Henry	Clarion Books	1960, 2004, 2007	NO	09 and up
Guate-mala	16	Friar Among Savages, Father Luis Cancer	Kurt, Br. and Br. Antoninus	Banner Books	1958, 2011	NO	09-15
Guate-mala	20	Fire of Freedom: The Story of Colonel Carlos Castillo Armas	Steffan, Jack	Hawthorn Junior Biography	1963	YES	11 and up
Haiti	18 & 19	Pierre Toussaint, Pioneer in Brotherhood	Sheehan, Arthur and Elizabeth	American Background	1963	YES	10-15
Hawaii	19	Father Damien and the Bells	Sheehan, Arthur and Elizabeth	Junior Vision	1962	YES	09-11

Hawaii	19	Father Damien and the Bells	Sheehan, Arthur and Elizabeth	Vision Books	1957, 2004	NO	09-15
Hawaii	19	No Greater Love, The Life of Father Damien of Molokai	Daughters of St. Paul	Encounter Books	1979	YES	09 and up
Hawaii	19	Saint Damien of Molokai: Hero of Hawaii	Richards, Virginia	Encounter the Saints	2009	NO	09 and up
Holland	14	Book of Saints, Part 5 (St. Vincent Ferrer)	Lovasik, Fr. Lawrence	St. Joseph Picture	1985	NO	05 and up
Holland	16	Army in Battle Array, An (St. John of Gorkum or Cologne)	Dorcy, Sister Mary Jean	Dorcy Biography	1955	YES	10 and up
Holland	16	Book of Saints, Part 5 (St. Peter Canisius)	Lovasik, Fr. Lawrence	St. Joseph Picture	1985	NO	05 and up
Holland	20	Light Within: The Story of Maria Montessori	Smaridge, Norah	Hawthorn Junior Bio.	1965	YES	11 and up
Holland	20	Winged Watchman, The	Van Stockum, Hilda	Favorite Catholic Books	1962, 1997	NO	10 and up
Holy Land	B.C.	David, King of Israel	Schmid, Brother Evan	Footsteps of the Saints	1966, 2011	NO	09-12
Holy Land	B.C.	David and Goliath	de Paola, Tomie	de Paola Biography	1984	YES	04-08
Holy Land	B.C.	David of Jerusalem	de Wohl, Louis	de Wohl Biography	1963	YES	15 and up
Holy Land	B.C.	David, the Shepherd King	Beebe, Catherine	Beebe Biography	1966	YES	10 and up
Holy Land	B.C.	David, The Shepherd King	Beebe, Catherine	Holy Cross Press	1966	YES	09 and up
Holy Land	B.C.	King David and His Songs, A Story of the Psalms	Windeatt, Mary Fabyan	Windeatt Saint Series	1993	NO	09 and up
Holy Land	01	Eagle of God: A Life of St. John the Evangelist	Premont, Brother Jeremy	Holy Cross Press	1964	YES	09 and up
Holy Land	04	Helena	Harris, Mary	Patron Saint Books	1964	YES	08 and up
Holy Land	04	Living Wood (The), A Novel of St. Helena	de Wohl, Louis	de Wohl Biography	1947	YES	15 and up
Holy Land	04	Saint Helena and the True Cross	de Wohl, Louis	Vision Books	1958, 2012	NO	09-15
Holy Land	04 & 05	Book of Saints, Part 6 (St. Jerome)	Lovasik, Fr. Lawrence	St. Joseph Picture	1985	NO	05 and up
Holy Land	04 & 05	Saint Jerome and the Bible	Sanderlin, George	Vision Books	1961	YES	09-15
Holy Land	12	Crusader: The Story of Richard the Lion-Heart (Richard I)	Power-Waters, Alma	Hawthorn Junior Biography	1964	YES	11 and up

Holy Land	13	Brown Scapular, The (St. Simon Stock)	Windeatt, Mary Fabyan	Windeatt Coloring	1956	YES	04 and up
Holy Land	13	Simon o' The Stock	Heagney, Anne	Catholic Treasury	1955	YES	10 and up
Holy Land	13	Story of St. Simon of Stock, A	Ernest, Brother	Footsteps of the Saints	1959, 2008	NO	06-09
Holy Land	16	Saint Ignatius and the Company of Jesus	Derleth, August	Vision Books	1956, 1999	NO	09-15
Hong Kong	20	Hong Kong Altar Boy	Hanson, Joseph E.	Similar to Catholic Treasury	1965	YES	10 and up
Hungary	04	Book of Saints, Part 6 (St. Martin of Tours)	Lovasik, Fr. Lawrence	St. Joseph Picture	1985	NO	05 and up
Hungary	11	Book of Saints, Part 10 (St. Gerard Sagredo)	Lovasik, Fr. Lawrence	St. Joseph Picture	1997	NO	05 and up
Hungary	13	Book of Saints, Part 3 (St. Elizabeth)	Lovasik, Fr. Lawrence	St. Joseph Picture	1982	NO	05 and up
Hungary	13	Elizabeth	Harris, Mary	Patron Saint Books	1961	YES	08 and up
Hungary	13	Hunters of Souls (St. Margaret of Hungary)	Dorcy, Sister Mary Jean	Dorcy Biography	1949, 1999	YES	10 and up
Hungary	13	Queen of the Poor, A Story of Elizabeth of Hungary	Daly, Brother Marco	In the Footsteps of the Saints	1961, 2009	NO	09-12
Hungary	13	Saint Elizabeth's Three Crowns	Thompson, Blanche Jennings	Junior Vision	1962	YES	09-11
Hungary	13	Saint Elizabeth's Three Crowns	Thompson, Blanche	Vision Books	1958, 1996	NO	09-15
Hungary	13	Story of St. Elizabeth of Hungary, A	Ernest, Brother	Footsteps of the Saints	1960, 2009	NO	06-09
Hungary	15	Torch in the Darkness (A), A Story of St. John Capistrano	Roberto, Brother	In the Footsteps of the Saints	1956, 2010	NO	09-12
Hungary	19	Christmas Anna Angel, The	Sawyer, Ruth	Caldecott	1944	YES	04 and up
Iceland	06	Fingal's Quest	Polland, Madeleine	Clarion Books	1961, 2003	NO	09 and up
Iceland	06	Irish Saints (St. Brendan)	Reilly, Robert T.	Vision Books	1964, 1981, 2002	YES	09-15
Iceland	06	Story of Rolf and the Viking Bow, The	French, Allen	Favorite Catholic Books	1924, 1995	NO	10 and up
Iceland	11	King's Men, A Story of St. Olaf of Norway	Boucher, Alan	Clarion Books	1962	YES	09 and up
Iceland	11	Sword of Clontarf	Brady, Charles A.	Clarion Books	1960, 2006	NO	09 and up

India	01	Book of Saints, Part 8 (St. Bartholomew or Nathaniel)	Lovasik, Father Lawrence	St. Joseph Picture Books	1993	NO	05 and up
India	16	Lives of the Saints: The Middle Ages (St. Francis Xavier)	Tesoriero, Bart	Aquinas Kids	2010	NO	05-09
India	16	Saints for Boys (St. Francis Xavier)	Muus, Solveig and Bart Tesoriero	Aquinas Kids	2012	NO	05-09
India	20	Bld. Teresa of Calcutta: Missionary of Charity	Glavich, Mary Kathleen SND	Encounter the Saints	2003	NO	09 and up
India	20	Light Within: The Story of Maria Montessori	Smaridge, Norah	Hawthorn Junior Biography	1965	YES	11 and up
India	20	Mother Teresa	Winkler, Father Jude	St. Joseph Picture	2002	NO	05 and up
Ireland	04	Book of Saints, Part 11 (St. Grimonia)	Lovasik, Father Lawrence	St. Joseph Picture Books	1997	NO	05 and up
Ireland	04 & 05	Lives of the Saints: The Monastic Era (St. Patrick)	Tesoriero, Bart	Aquinas Kids	2010	NO	05-09
Ireland	04 & 05	Saints for Boys (St. Patrick)	Muus, Solveig and Bart Tesoriero	Aquinas Kids	2012	NO	05-09
Ireland	05	Book of Saints, Part 1 (St. Patrick)	Lovasik, Fr. Lawrence	St. Joseph Picture	1981	NO	05 and up
Ireland	05	Flame over Tara	Polland, Madeleine	Clarion Books	1964, 2004	NO	09 and up
Ireland	05	Irish Saints (St. Patrick)	Reilly, Robert T.	Vision Books	1964, 1981, 2002	YES	09-15
Ireland	05	Land of Erin, The (St. Patrick)	Daughters of Charity	Catholic Stories, Volume IV	1995	NO	07-10
Ireland	05	Patrick	Hunt, Marigold	Patron Saint Books	1964	YES	08 and up
Ireland	05	Patrick, Patron Saint of Ireland	de Paola, Tomie	de Paola Biography	1994	NO	04-08
Ireland	05	Saint Brigid and the Cows	Betz, Eva K.	Saints and Friendly Beasts	1964, 2004	NO	08 and up
Ireland	05	Saint Patrick	Lovasik, Fr. Lawrence	St. Joseph Picture	1984	NO	05 and up
Ireland	05	Saint Patrick, Apostle of Ireland	Beebe, Catherine	Beebe Biography	1968	YES	08-14
Ireland	05	Story of St. Briget, A	Ernest, Brother	Footsteps of the Saints	1959, 2008	NO	06-09
Ireland	05	Story of St. Patrick, A	Ernest, Brother	Footsteps of the Saints	1958, 2011	NO	06-09

Ireland	05	When Saints Were Young (St. Patrick)	Thompson, Blanche	Vision Books	1960	YES	09-15
Ireland	05 & 06	Irish Saints (St. Brendan)	Reilly, Robert T.	Vision Books	1964, 1981, 2002	YES	09-15
Ireland	05 & 06	Irish Saints (St. Brigid)	Reilly, Robert T.	Vision Books	1964, 2002	YES	09-15
Ireland	06	Irish Saints (St. Columcille)	Reilly, Robert T.	Vision Books	1964, 1981, 2002	YES	09-15
Ireland	06	Saint Colum and the Crane	Betz, Eva K.	Saints and Friendly Beasts	1961, 2003	NO	08 and up
Ireland	06 & 07	Irish Saints (St. Columban)	Reilly, Robert T.	Vision Books	1964, 1981, 2002	YES	09-15
Ireland	06 & 07	Little Patron of Gardeners: Good St. Fiacre	Beebe, Catherine	Beebe Biography	1948, 2012	NO	08 and up
Ireland	06 & 07	Saints for Boys and Girls (St. Kevin)	Beebe, Catherine	Beebe Biography	1959	YES	09-14
Ireland	07	Begga's Bracelet	Daughters of Charity	Catholic Stories, Volume III	1995	NO	07-10
Ireland	07	Book of Saints, Part 2 (St. Dymphna)	Lovasik, Fr. Lawrence	St. Joseph Picture	1981	NO	05 and up
Ireland	07	Book of Saints, Part 9 (St. Cuthbert)	Lovasik, Fr. Lawrence	St. Joseph Picture	1996	NO	05 and up
Ireland	07	Lives of the Saints: The Monastic Era (St. Dymphna)	Tesoriero, Bart	Aquinas Kids	2010	NO	05-09
Ireland	11	Saints for Boys and Girls (Blessed Brian Lacey)	Beebe, Catherine	Beebe Biography	1959	YES	09-14
Ireland	11	Sword of Clontarf	Brady, Charles A.	Clarion Books	1960, 2006	NO	09 and up
Ireland	11 & 12	Irish Saints (St. Malachy)	Reilly, Robert T.	Vision Books	1964, 1981, 2002	YES	09-15
Ireland	12	Irish Saints (St. Laurence O'Toole)	Reilly, Robert T.	Vision Books	1964, 1981	YES	09-15
Ireland	14	Book of Saints, Part 5 (St. Vincent Ferrer)	Lovasik, Fr. Lawrence	St. Joseph Picture	1985	NO	05 and up
Ireland	16	Red Hugh, Prince of Donegal	Reilly, Robert T.	Catholic Treasury	1957, 1997	NO	10 and up
Ireland	17	Irish Saints (Blessed Oliver Plunkett)	Reilly, Robert T.	Vision Books	1964, 1981, 2002	YES	09-15
Ireland	18	Story of Captain John Barry, A	Flavius, Brother	Footsteps of the Saints	1965, 2012	NO	06-09

Ireland	18 & 19	Courageous Catherine: Mother Mary Catherine McAuley, The First Sister of Mercy	Marie, Sister Raymond	Catholic Treasury	1958	YES	10 and up
Ireland	18 & 19	Father of the American Navy, Captain John Barry	Anderson, Floyd	Banner Books	1959, 2011	NO	09-15
Ireland	18 & 19	Irish Saints (Bishop Edward J. Galvin)	Reilly, Robert T.	Vision Books	1964, 1981, 2002	YES	09-15
Ireland	18 & 19	Irish Saints (Father Theobald Mathew)	Reilly, Robert T.	Vision Books	1964, 2002	YES	09-15
Ireland	18 & 19	Irish Saints (Matt Talbot)	Reilly, Robert T.	Vision Books	1964, 1981, 2002	YES	09-15
Ireland	18 & 19	Irish Saints (Mother Catherine McAuley)	Reilly, Robert T.	Vision Books	1964, 1981, 2002	YES	09-15
Ireland	18 & 19	Mathew Carey, Pamphleter for Freedom	Hindman, Jane F.	American Background	1960	YES	10-15
Ireland	18 & 19	Story of Venerable Mother Catherine McAuley	Ernest, Brother	In the Footsteps of the Saints	1959, 2011	NO	06-09
Ireland	19	Frances Warde and the First Sisters of Mercy	Christopher, Sister Marie	Vision Books	1960	YES	09-15
Ireland	19	King of Song: The Story of John McCormack	Hume, Ruth and Paul	Hawthorn Junior Biography	1964	YES	11 and up
Ireland	19	Our Lady of Knock	Windeatt, Mary Fabyan	Windeatt Coloring	1954	YES	04 and up
Ireland	19	Thunder Maker: General Thomas Meagher	Lamers, William M.	Catholic Treasury	1959	YES	10 and up
Ireland	20	Edel Quinn: Beneath the Southern Cross	Brown, Evelyn M.	Vision Books	1967	YES	09-15
Ireland	20	Father Flanagan, Builder of Boys	Stevens, Clifford J.	American Background	1967	YES	10-15
Ireland	20	Operation Escape: The Adventure of Father O'Flaherty	Madden, Daniel	Hawthorn Junior Biography	1962	YES	11 and up
Ireland	various	Big Tree of Bunlahy, Stories of My Own Countryside	Colum, Padraic	Newbery	1933	YES	09 and up
Island of Rhodes	16	Knights Besieged	Faulkner, Nancy	Clarion Books	1964	YES	09 and up
Israel	B.C.	Anne (grandmother of Jesus)	Richardson, M.K.	Patron Saint Books	1960	YES	08 and up
Israel	B.C.	Book of Saints, Part 1 (St. Anne)	Lovasik, Fr. Lawrence	St. Joseph Picture	1981	NO	05 and up
Israel	B.C.	Book of Saints, Part 4 (St. Joachim)	Lovasik, Fr. Lawrence	St. Joseph Picture	1982	NO	05 and up

Saint Series Books by Geographical Setting

Israel	B.C.	Lives of the Saints: The Early Church (Blessed Virgin Mary)	Tesoriero, Bart	Aquinas Kids	2010	NO	05-09
Israel	B.C.	Lives of the Saints: The Early Church (St. Anne)	Tesoriero, Bart	Aquinas Kids	2010	NO	05-09
Israel	B.C.	Lives of the Saints: The Early Church (St. Joseph)	Tesoriero, Bart	Aquinas Kids	2010	NO	05-09
Israel	B.C.	Saints for Boys (St. Joseph)	Muus, Solveig & Bart Tesoriero	Aquinas Kids	2012	NO	05-09
Israel	B.C.	Saints for Boys and Girls (St. Anne)	Beebe, Catherine	Beebe Biography	1959	YES	09-14
Israel	B.C.	Saints for Boys and Girls (St. Joseph)	Beebe, Catherine	Beebe Biography	1959	YES	09-14
Israel	B.C.	Saints for Girls (St. Anne)	Muus, Solveig and Bart Tesoriero	Aquinas Kids	2012	NO	05-09
Israel	01	Ageless Story	Ford, Lauren	Caldecott	1939	YES	04 and up
Israel	01	Apostles of the Lord, The	Beebe, Catherine	Beebe Biography	1958	YES	08-14
Israel	01	Baboushka and the Three Kings	Robbins, Ruth	Caldecott	1960	NO	04 and up
Israel	01	Book of Saints, Part 1 (St. Stephen)	Lovasik, Fr. Lawrence	St. Joseph Picture	1981	NO	05 and up
Israel	01	Book of Saints, Part 3 (Our Lady, Queen)	Lovasik, Fr. Lawrence	St. Joseph Picture	1982	NO	05 and up
Israel	01	Book of Saints, Part 3 (St. John the Baptist)	Lovasik, Fr. Lawrence	St. Joseph Picture	1982	NO	05 and up
Israel	01	Book of Saints, Part 8 (St. Bartholomew or Nathaniel)	Lovasik, Father Lawrence	St. Joseph Picture Books	1993	NO	05 and up
Israel	01	Book of Saints, Part 8 (St. James the Greater)	Lovasik, Fr. Lawrence	St. Joseph Picture	1993	NO	05 and up
Israel	01	Book of Saints, Part 8 (St. Joseph)	Lovasik, Fr. Lawrence	St. Joseph Picture	1993	NO	05 and up
Israel	01	Book of Saints, Part 8 (St. Jude Thaddeus)	Lovasik, Fr. Lawrence	St. Joseph Picture	1993	NO	05 and up
Israel	01	Book of Saints, Part 8 (St. Matthew)	Lovasik, Fr. Lawrence	St. Joseph Picture	1993	NO	05 and up
Israel	01	Book of Saints, Part 8 (St. Matthias)	Lovasik, Fr. Lawrence	St. Joseph Picture	1993	NO	05 and up
Israel	01	Book of Saints, Part 8 (St. Peter)	Lovasik, Fr. Lawrence	St. Joseph Picture	1993	NO	05 and up
Israel	01	Book of Saints, Part 8 (St. Thomas)	Lovasik, Fr. Lawrence	St. Joseph Picture	1993	NO	05 and up
Israel	01	Came the Dawn: Mary of Nazareth, God's Mother and Ours	Daughters of St. Paul	Encounter Books	1982	YES	09 and up

Israel	01	Fisher Prince (The): The Life of St. Peter, Apostle	Daughters of St. Paul	Encounter Books	1966, 1984	YES	09 and up
Israel	01	Good Saint Joseph	Lovasik, Fr. Lawrence	St. Joseph Picture	1978	NO	05 and up
Israel	01	Great Hero (The), St. Paul the Apostle	Daughters of St. Paul	Encounter Books	1963	YES	09 and up
Israel	01	Great Men of the Bible: New Testament (Joseph, John the Baptist, Jesus, Peter, John, James the Greater, James the Lesser, Matthew, Jude, Judas, Stephen, Paul, Philip, Mark, and Luke)	Winkler, Father Jude	St. Joseph Picture Books	1987	NO	05 and up
Israel	01	Great Women of the Bible (Mary, Martha and Mary, and Mary Magdalene)	Winkler, Father Jude	St. Joseph Picture Books	1986, 1990	NO	05 and up
Israel	01	Holy Family, The	Winkler, Father Jude	St. Joseph Picture	2005	NO	05 and up
Israel	01	Jesus Our Savior: The Life of Jesus for the Very Young (Book 1, His Early Life)	Francis, Father	Father Francis Coloring Books	1954	NO	06 and up
Israel	01	Jesus Our Savior: The Life of Jesus for the Very Young (Book 2, His Public Life)	Francis, Father	Father Francis Coloring Books	1954	NO	06-09
Israel	01	Joseph (St. Joseph)	Daughters of Charity	Catholic Stories, Volume III	1995	NO	07-10
Israel	01	Joseph (St. Joseph)	Sheed, Wilfrid	Patron Saint Books	1958	YES	08 and up
Israel	01	Last Apostle, The (St. Paul)	Eleanor, Mother Mary	Catholic Treasury	1956	YES	10 and up
Israel	01	Lives of the Saints: The Early Church (St. John the Apostle)	Tesoriero, Bart	Aquinas Kids	2010	NO	05-09
Israel	01	Lives of the Saints: The Early Church (St. Martha)	Tesoriero, Bart	Aquinas Kids	2010	NO	05-09
Israel	01	Lives of the Saints: The Early Church (St. Matthew)	Tesoriero, Bart	Aquinas Kids	2010	NO	05-09
Israel	01	Lives of the Saints: The Early Church (St. Peter)	Tesoriero, Bart	Aquinas Kids	2010	NO	05-09
Israel	01	Lives of the Saints: The Early Church (St. Veronica)	Tesoriero, Bart	Aquinas Kids	2010	NO	05-09
Israel	01	Mary (mother of Jesus)	Dorcy, Sister Mary Jean	Patron Saint Books	1958	YES	08 and up
Israel	01	Mary, Full of Grace	Francis, Father	Fr. Francis Coloring	1954, 1997	NO	04 and up

Israel	01	Mary, Mother of Jesus	de Paola, Tomie	de Paola Biography	1995	YES	04-08
Israel	01	Mary, My Mother	Lovasik, Fr. Lawrence	St. Joseph Picture	1978	NO	05 and up
Israel	01	Mary, My Mother: A Mary-book for Little Boys and Girls	Dorcy, Sister Mary Jean	Dorcy Biography	1944	YES	05 and up
Israel	01	Miracles of Jesus	de Paola, Tomie	de Paola Biography	1987, 2008	NO	04-08
Israel	01	Our Mother Mary	Francis, Father	Father Francis Coloring	1959	NO	04 and up
Israel	01	Parables of Jesus	de Paola, Tomie	de Paola Biography	1987, 1995	YES	04-08
Israel	01	Saint Peter the Apostle	Lovasik, Fr. Lawrence	St. Joseph Picture Books	1980, 1987	NO	05 and up
Israel	01	Saints for Boys and Girls (Mary the Virgin Mother of Our Lord)	Beebe, Catherine	Beebe Biography	1959	YES	09-14
Israel	01	Saints for Boys (St. John the Baptist)	Muus, Solveig and Bart Tesoriero	Aquinas Kids	2012	NO	05-09
Israel	01	Saints for Boys (St. Jude Thaddeus)	Muus, Solveig and Bart Tesoriero	Aquinas Kids	2012	NO	05-09
Israel	01	Saints for Boys (St. Peter)	Muus, Solveig and Bart Tesoriero	Aquinas Kids	2012	NO	05-09
Israel	01	Saints for Boys and Girls (St. Jude)	Beebe, Catherine	Beebe Biography	1959	YES	09-14
Israel	01	Saints for Girls (Blessed Virgin Mary)	Muus, Solveig and Bart Tesoriero	Aquinas Kids	2012	NO	05-09
Israel	01	Spear (The), A Novel of the Crucifixion	de Wohl, Louis	de Wohl Biography	1955, 1998	NO	15 and up
Israel	01	St. Paul: The Thirteenth Apostle	Wallace, Susan Helen	Encounter the Saints	2007	NO	09 and up
Israel	01	Story of Jesus for Boys and Girls, The	Beebe, Catherine	Beebe Biography	1945	YES	09-14
Israel	01	Story of Jesus, The	Lovasik, Father Lawrence	St. Joseph Picture Books	1999	NO	05 and up
Israel	01	Story of Mary, The Mother of Jesus	Beebe, Catherine	Beebe Biography	1950	YES	09-14
Israel	01	Story of St. Joseph, A	Ernest, Brother	Footsteps of the Saints	1957, 2011	NO	06-09
Israel	01	Story of St. Peter, A	Ernest, Brother	Footsteps of the Saints	1961, 2011	NO	06-09

Israel	01	Story of St. Stephen, A	Ernest, Brother	Footsteps of the Saints	1962, 2008	NO	06-09
Israel	01	Story of the Birth of Jesus, The	Winkler, Rev. Jude	St. Joseph Bible Story	1989	NO	05-09
Israel	01	Story of the Three Wise Kings, The	de Paola, Tomie	de Paola Biography	1983	YES	04-08
Israel	03	Saints for Boys and Girls (St. George)	Beebe, Catherine	Beebe Biography	1959	YES	09-14
Israel	03	They Became Saints (St. Christopher: And His Mighty Monarch)	Francis, Father	Father Francis Coloring	1951	NO	07 and up
Israel	03 & 04	Saints of the Byzantine World (St. Hilarion)	Thompson, Blanche Jennings	Vision Books	1961	YES	09-15
Israel	04	Book of Saints, Part 4 (St. Helen)	Lovasik, Fr. Lawrence	St. Joseph Picture Books	1982	NO	05 and up
Israel	04	Book of Saints, Part 5 (St. Basil the Great)	Lovasik, Fr. Lawrence	St. Joseph Picture	1985	NO	05 and up
Israel	04	Noble Lady, The Life of St. Helen	Daughters of St. Paul	Encounter Books	1966	YES	09 and up
Israel	04	Saints for Boys and Girls (Saint Helen)	Beebe, Catherine	Beebe Biography	1959	YES	09-14
Israel	04	Saints of the Byzantine World (Saint Basil the Great)	Thompson, Blanche Jennings	Vision Books	1961	YES	09-15
Israel	04	Saints of the Byzantine World (St. Cyril of Jerusalem)	Thompson, Blanche Jennings	Vision Books	1961	YES	09-15
Israel	06	Book of Saints, Part 5 (St. Christopher)	Lovasik, Fr. Lawrence	St. Joseph Picture	1985	NO	05 and up
Israel	06	Christopher, The Holy Giant	de Paola, Tomie	de Paola Biography	1994	YES	04-08
Israel	06	Lives of the Saints: The Early Church (St. Christopher)	Tesoriero, Bart	Aquinas Kids	2010	NO	05-09
Israel	06	Saint Christopher for Boys and Girls	Beebe, Catherine	Beebe Biography	1955, 2012	NO	09-14
Israel	06	Saints for Boys (St. Christopher)	Muus, Solveig and Bart Tesoriero	Aquinas Kids	2012	NO	05-09
Israel	11	Blue Gonfalon (First Crusade)	Hubbard, Margaret	Clarion Books	1960, 2004	NO	09 and up
Israel	13	Where Valor Lies (Seventh Crusade)	de Leeau, Adele & Cateau	Clarion Books	1959, 2007	NO	09 and up
Israel	19 & 20	Monuments to Glory: The Story of Antonio Barluzzi, Architect of the Holy Land	Madden, Daniel M.	Hawthorn Junior Biography	1964	YES	11 and up

Country	#	Title	Author	Publisher	Year	Illustrated	Age
Israel	20	Desert Fighter: The Story of General Yigael Yadin and the Dead Sea Scrolls	Miller, Shane	Hawthorn Junior Biography	1967	YES	11 and up
Italy	01	Lives of the Saints: The Early Church (St. Paul)	Tesoriero, Bart	Aquinas Kids	2010	NO	05-09
Italy	01	Saint Peter the Apostle	Lovasik, Fr. Lawrence	St. Joseph Picture	1980, 1987	NO	05 and up
Italy	03	Book of Saints, Part 1 (St. Lawrence)	Lovasik, Fr. Lawrence	St. Joseph Picture	1981	NO	05 and up
Italy	03	Lives of the Saints: The Monastic Era (St. Adrian of Nicomedia))	Tesoriero, Bart	Aquinas Kids	2010	NO	05-09
Italy	03	Lives of the Saints: The Monastic Era (St. Florian)	Tesoriero, Bart	Aquinas Kids	2010	NO	05-09
Italy	03	Lives of the Saints: The Early Church (St. Lucy)	Tesoriero, Bart	Aquinas Kids	2010	NO	05-09
Italy	03	Saints for Boys and Girls (St. Dennis)	Beebe, Catherine	Beebe Biography	1959	YES	09-14
Italy	03	Saints for Girls (St. Lucy)	Muus, Solveig and Bart Tesoriero	Aquinas Kids	2012	NO	05-09
Italy	03	Story of St. Agatha, A	Ernest, Brother	Footsteps of the Saints	1960, 2009	NO	06-09
Italy	03	Story of St. Lawrence, A	Emge, Brother Lawrence	In the Footsteps of the Saints	1961, 2012	NO	06-09
Italy	03	Story of St. Lawrence, A	Emge, Brother Lawrence	Dujarie Press Reprint	1961, 2009	NO	06-09
Italy	03	Story of St. Lucy, A	Ernest, Brother	Footsteps of the Saints	1957, 2012	NO	06-09
Italy	04	Book of Saints, Part 6 (St. Ambrose)	Lovasik, Fr. Lawrence	St. Joseph Picture	1985	NO	05 and up
Italy	04	Book of Saints, Part 6 (St. Jerome)	Lovasik, Fr. Lawrence	St. Joseph Picture	1985	NO	05 and up
Italy	04	Book of Saints, Part 6 (St. Martin of Tours)	Lovasik, Fr. Lawrence	St. Joseph Picture	1985	NO	05 and up
Italy	04	Lives of the Saints: The Monastic Era (St. Adrian of Nicomedia)	Tesoriero, Bart	Aquinas Kids	2010	NO	05-09
Italy	04	Lives of the Saints: The Monastic Era (St. Florian)	Tesoriero, Bart	Aquinas Kids	2010	NO	05-09
Italy	04	Saint Jerome and the Bible	Sanderlin, George	Vision Books	1961	YES	09-15
Italy	05	Book of Saints, Part 5 (St. Leo the Great)	Lovasik, Fr. Lawrence	St. Joseph Picture	1985	NO	05 and up
Italy	05	Mountain of God (The): A Life of St. Benedict	Willet, Brother Franciscus (Orrin Primm)	Holy Cross Press	1965	YES	09 and up

Italy	05 & 06	Book of Saints, Part 3 (St. Benedict)	Lovasik, Fr. Lawrence	St. Joseph Picture	1982	NO	05 and up
Italy	05 & 06	Book of Saints, Part 12 (St. Anthony of Lerins)	Lovasik, Fr. Lawrence	St. Joseph Picture Books	1999	NO	05 and up
Italy	05 & 06	Holy Twins, The (Sts. Benedict and Scholastica)	de Paola, Tomie	de Paola Biography	2001	NO	04-08
Italy	05 & 06	Lives of the Saints: The Monastic Era (St. Benedict)	Tesoriero, Bart	Aquinas Kids	2010	NO	05-09
Italy	05 & 06	St. Benedict	Forbes, F.A.	Forbes Biography	1921	YES	12 and up
Italy	05 & 06	Saint Benedict, Hero of the Hills	Windeatt, Mary Fabyan	Vision Books	1958, 2001	NO	09-15
Italy	05 & 06	Saint Benedict, The Story of the Father of the Western Monks	Windeatt, Mary Fabyan	Windeatt Saint Series	1993	NO	09 and up
Italy	05 & 06	Saints for Boys (St. Benedict)	Muus, Solveig and Bart Tesoriero	Aquinas Kids	2012	NO	05-09
Italy	05 & 06	Story of St. Benedict, A	Ernest, Brother	Footsteps of the Saints	1958, 2012	NO	06-09
Italy	06	Citadel of God, A Novel of St. Benedict	de Wohl, Louis	de Wohl Biography	1959, 1994	NO	15 and up
Italy	06	Mountain of God (The): A Life of St. Benedict	Willet, Brother Franciscus	Holy Cross Press	1965	YES	09 and up
Italy	06 & 07	Augustine Came to Kent	Willard, Barbara	Clarion	1963, 1996	NO	09 and up
Italy	06 & 07	Book of Saints, Part 5 (St. Gregory the Great)	Lovasik, Fr. Lawrence	St. Joseph Picture	1985	NO	05 and up
Italy	06 & 07	Saint Gregory the Great, Consul of God	Sanderlin, George	Vision Books	1964	YES	09-15
Italy	07	Irish Saints (Saint Columban)	Reilly, Robert T.	Vision Books	1964, 1981, 2002	YES	09-15
Italy	10 & 11	Bernard (of Menthon)	Smaridge, Norah	Patron Saint Books	1960	YES	08 and up
Italy	11	Book of Saints, Part 10 (St. Gerard Sagredo)	Lovasik, Fr. Lawrence	St. Joseph Picture	1997	NO	05 and up
Italy	12 & 13	Book of Saints, Part 6 (St. Francis of Assisi)	Lovasik, Fr. Lawrence	St. Joseph Picture	1985	NO	05 and up
Italy	12 & 13	Children's Saint Francis, The (St. Francis of Assisi)	Beebe, Catherine	Beebe Biography	1941, 1946	YES	08-14
Italy	12 & 13	Francis and Clare, Saints of Assisi	Homan, Helen Walker	Junior Vision	1962	YES	09-11
Italy	12 & 13	Francis and Clare, Saints of Assisi	Homan, Helen Walker	Vision Books	1956, 1994	NO	09-15
Italy	12 & 13	Francis, The Poor Man of Assisi (includes St. Clare)	de Paola, Tomie	de Paola Biography	1982, 1990	YES	04-08

Italy	12 & 13	Gentle Revolutionary Life of St. Francis of Assisi	Daughters of St. Paul	Encounter Books	1978	YES	09 and up
Italy	12 & 13	Joyful Beggar, A Novel of St. Francis of Assisi	de Wohl, Louis	de Wohl Biography	1958, 2001	NO	15 and up
Italy	12 & 13	Lives of the Saints: The Monastic Era (St. Francis of Assisi)	Tesoriero, Bart	Aquinas Kids	2010	NO	05-09
Italy	12 & 13	Saint Clare of Assisi: A Light for the World	Trouvé, Marianne	Encounter the Saints	2009	NO	09 and up
Italy	12 & 13	Saint Francis	Francis, Mary	Patron Saint Books	1959	YES	08 and up
Italy	12 & 13	Saint Francis of Assisi	Windeatt, Mary Fabyan	Windeatt Coloring	1956	NO	04 and up
Italy	12 & 13	Saint Francis of Assisi	Lovasik, Fr. Lawrence	St. Joseph Picture	1980	NO	05 and up
Italy	12 & 13	Saint Francis of Assisi: Gentle Revolutionary	Alves, Mary Emmanuel	Encounter the Saints	1999	NO	09 and up
Italy	12 & 13	Saint Francis of Assisi: God's Gentle Knight	Vintrou, Francoise	Paths of the Gospel	1998	YES	07-10
Italy	12 & 13	Saints for Boys (St. Francis of Asssi)	Muus, Solveig and Bart Tesoriero	Aquinas Kids	2012	NO	05-09
Italy	12 & 13	Song of Francis	de Paola, Tomie	de Paola Biography	2009	NO	02-08
Italy	12 & 13	Story of St. Clare, A	Ernest, Brother	Footsteps of the Saints	1957, 2010	NO	06-09
Italy	12 & 13	They Became Saints (St. Francis and the Wolf of Gubbio)	Francis, Father	Father Francis Coloring	1951	NO	07 and up
Italy	13	Book of Saints, Part 1 (St. Anthony of Padua)	Lovasik, Fr. Lawrence	St. Joseph Picture	1981	NO	05 and up
Italy	13	Book of Saints, Part 3 (St. Clare)	Lovasik, Fr. Lawrence	St. Joseph Picture	1982	NO	05 and up
Italy	13	Book of Saints, Part 3 (St. Thomas Aquinas)	Lovasik, Fr. Lawrence	St. Joseph Picture	1982	NO	05 and up
Italy	13	Book of Saints, Part 6 (St. Bonaventure)	Lovasik, Fr. Lawrence	St. Joseph Picture	1985	NO	05 and up
Italy	13	Book of Saints, Part 7 (St. Margaret of Cortona)	Lovasik, Fr. Lawrence	St. Joseph Picture	1993	NO	05 and up
Italy	13	Book of Saints, Part 7 (St. Zita)	Lovasik, Fr. Lawrence	St. Joseph Picture	1993	NO	05 and up
Italy	13	Book of Saints, Part 9 (St. Agnes of Assisi)	Lovasik, Fr. Lawrence	St. Joseph Picture	1996	NO	05 and up
Italy	13	Book of Saints, Part 11 (St. Margaret of Cortona)	Lovasik, Fr. Lawrence	St. Joseph Picture	1997	NO	05 and up
Italy	13	Book of Saints, Part 12 (St. Philip Benizi)	Lovasik, Fr. Lawrence	St. Joseph Picture	1999	NO	05 and up

Country	Century	Title	Author	Publisher	Year	In Print	Age
Italy	13	Children's Saint Anthony, The (St. Anthony of Padua)	Beebe, Catherine	Beebe Biography	1939, 1943	YES	08-14
Italy	13	Hunters of Souls (Blessed Albert of Bergamo)	Dorcy, Sister Mary Jean	Dorcy Biography	1949, 1999	YES	10 and up
Italy	13	Hunters of Souls (Blessed James or Jacopo of Voragine)	Dorcy, Sister Mary Jean	Dorcy Biography	1949, 1999	YES	10 and up
Italy	13	Hunters of Souls (Blessed Sadoc and Martyrs of Sandomir)	Dorcy, Sister Mary Jean	Dorcy Biography	1949, 1999	YES	10 and up
Italy	13	Hunters of Souls (St. Peter, Martyr of Verona)	Dorcy, Sister Mary Jean	Dorcy Biography	1949, 1999	YES	10 and up
Italy	13	Lives of the Saints: The Middle Ages (St. Anthony)	Tesoriero, Bart	Aquinas Kids	2010	NO	05-09
Italy	13	Lives of the Saints: The Middle Ages (St. Thomas Aquinas)	Tesoriero, Bart	Aquinas Kids	2010	NO	05-09
Italy	13	Master Albert, The Story of St. Albert the Great	Dorcy, Sister Mary Jean	Dorcy Biography	1955	YES	12 and up
Italy	13	Ox Was an Angel (The), A Story of St. Thomas Aquinas	Overstreet, Brother Edward	In the Footsteps of the Saints	1961, 2013	NO	12-15
Italy	13	Pillar in the Twilight, The Life of St. Thomas Aquinas	Daughters of St. Paul	Encounter Books	1967, 1978	YES	09 and up
Italy	13	Quiet Light (The), A Novel of St. Thomas Aquinas	de Wohl, Louis	de Wohl Biography	1950, 1996	NO	15 and up
Italy	13	Saint Anthony and the Christ Child	Homan, Helen Walker	Junior Vision	1963	YES	09-11
Italy	13	Saint Anthony and the Christ Child	Homan, Helen Walker	Vision Books	1958, 1997	NO	09-15
Italy	13	Saint Anthony of Padua	Windeatt, Mary Fabyan	Windeatt Coloring	1955	NO	04 and up
Italy	13	Saint Anthony of Padua	Lovasik, Fr. Lawrence	St. Joseph Picture	1984	NO	05 and up
Italy	13	Saint Anthony of Padua: Fire and Light	Kerry, Margaret and Mary Tebo	Encounter the Saints	1999	NO	09 and up
Italy	13	Saint Anthony of Padua: Proclaimer of the Good News	Baudouin-Croix, Marie	Along the Paths of the Gospel	1999	YES	07-10
Italy	13	Saint Clare of Assisi: A Light for the World	Trouvé, Marianne Lorraine	Encounter the Saints	2009	NO	09 and up

Italy	13	Saint Thomas Aquinas and the Preaching Beggars	Larnen, Brendan and Milton Lomask	Vision Books	1957, 2005	NO	09-15
Italy	13	Saints for Boys (St. Anthony of Padua)	Muus, Solveig and Bart Tesoriero	Aquinas Kids	2012	NO	05-09
Italy	13	Saints for Boys (St. Thomas Aquinas)	Muus, Solveig and Bart Tesoriero	Aquinas Kids	2012	NO	05-09
Italy	13	Saints for Boys and Girls (St. Anthony of Padua)	Beebe, Catherine	Beebe Biography	1959	YES	09-14
Italy	13	Saints for Girls (St. Clare)	Muus, Solveig and Bart Tesoriero	Aquinas Kids	2012	NO	05-09
Italy	13	St. Thomas Aquinas, The Story of "The Dumb Ox"	Windeatt, Mary Fabyan	Windeatt Saint Series	1993	NO	08 and up
Italy	13	Story of St. Anthony, A	Ernest, Brother	Footsteps of the Saints	1960, 2009	NO	06-09
Italy	13	Truth Was Their Star (St. Albert the Great)	Dorcy, Sister Mary Jean	Dorcy Biography	1947, 1999	NO	10 and up
Italy	13	Truth Was Their Star (St. Thomas Aquinas)	Dorcy, Sister Mary Jean	Dorcy Biography	1947, 1999	NO	10 and up
Italy	13 & 14	Army in Battle Array, An (Bld. Margaret of Castello)	Dorcy, Sister Mary Jean	Dorcy Biography	1955	YES	10 and up
Italy	13 & 14	Book of Saints, Part 7 (St. Peregrine)	Lovasik, Fr. Lawrence	St. Joseph Picture	1993	NO	05 and up
Italy	13 & 14	Book of Saints, Part 9 (St. Juliana Falconieri)	Lovasik, Fr. Lawrence	St. Joseph Picture	1996	NO	05 and up
Italy	13 & 14	Dante and His Journey	Schmid, Brother Evan	Footsteps of the Saints	1961, 2013	NO	12-15
Italy	13 & 14	Lives of the Saints: The Middle Ages (St. Peregrime)	Tesoriero, Bart	Aquinas Kids	2010	NO	05-09
Italy	13 & 14	Mary's Pilgrim, The Life of St. Peregrine	Daughters of St. Paul	Encounter Books	1972	YES	09 and up
Italy	13 & 14	Story of St. Peregrine, A	Ernest, Brother	Footsteps of the Saints	1958, 2008	NO	06-09
Italy	13 & 14	Truth Was Their Star (St. Agnes of Montepulciano)	Dorcy, Sister Mary Jean	Dorcy Biography	1947, 1999	NO	10 and up
Italy	14	Book of Saints, Part 5 (St. Vincent Ferrer)	Lovasik, Fr. Lawrence	St. Joseph Picture	1985	NO	05 and up
Italy	14	Book of Saints, Part 6 (St. Catherine of Siena)	Lovasik, Fr. Lawrence	St. Joseph Picture	1985	NO	05 and up
Italy	14	Catherine of Siena	Sorgia, Fr. Raimondo	Encounter Books	1975	YES	09 and up
Italy	14	Her Dream Came True, The Life of Blessed Imelda Lambertini	Daughters of St. Paul	Encounter Books	1967	YES	09 and up

Country	Age	Title	Author	Publisher	Year	Series?	Ages
Italy	14	Lay Siege to Heaven, A Novel of St. Catherine of Siena	de Wohl, Louis	de Wohl Biography	1960, 1991	NO	15 and up
Italy	14	Lives of the Saints: The Middle Ages (St. Catherine of Siena)	Tesoriero, Bart	Aquinas Kids	2010	NO	05-09
Italy	14	Patron Saint of First Communicants, The Story of Bld. Imelda Lambertini	Windeatt, Mary Fabyan	Windeatt Saint Series	1991	NO	09 and up
Italy	14	Saint Catherine of Siena	Forbes, F.A.	Forbes Biography	1913, 1998	NO	12 and up
Italy	14	Saints for Boys and Girls (Blessed Imelda)	Beebe, Catherine	Beebe Biography	1959	YES	09-14
Italy	14	Saints for Girls (St. Catherine of Siena)	Muus, Solveig and Bart Tesoriero	Aquinas Kids	2012	NO	05-09
Italy	14	Saints of the Eucharist: God's Little White Saint (Blessed Imelda)	Francis, Father	Father Francis Coloring	1958	NO	06 and up
Italy	14	St. Catherine of Siena, The Story of the Girl Who Saw Saints in the Sky	Windeatt, Mary Fabyan	Windeatt Saint Series	1993	NO	09 and up
Italy	14	They Became Saints (Bld. Imelda: And Her First Holy Communion)	Francis, Father	Father Francis Coloring	1951	NO	07 and up
Italy	14	Truth Was Their Star (Blessed Imelda)	Dorcy, Sister Mary Jean	Dorcy Biography	1947, 1999	NO	10 and up
Italy	14	Truth Was Their Star (St. Catherine of Siena)	Dorcy, Sister Mary Jean	Dorcy Biography	1947, 1999	NO	10 and up
Italy	14	When Saints Were Young (St. Catherine of Siena)	Thompson, Blanche Jennings	Vision Books	1960	YES	09-15
Italy	14 & 15	Army in Battle Array, An (Blessed Peter Geremia)	Dorcy, Sister Mary Jean	Dorcy Biography	1955	YES	10 and up
Italy	14 & 15	Book of Saints, Part 4 (St. Rita)	Lovasik, Fr. Lawrence	St. Joseph Picture	1982	NO	05 and up
Italy	14 & 15	Lives of the Saints: The Middle Ages (St. Bernadine of Siena)	Tesoriero, Bart	Aquinas Kids	2010	NO	05-09
Italy	14 & 15	Lives of the Saints: The Middle Ages (St. Rita)	Tesoriero, Bart	Aquinas Kids	2010	NO	05-09
Italy	14 & 15	Saints for Girls (St. Joan of Arc)	Muus, Solveig and Bart Tesoriero	Aquinas Kids	2012	NO	05-09
Italy	14 & 15	Story of St. Rita, A	Ernest, Brother	Footsteps of the Saints	1959, 2008	NO	06-09
Italy	14 & 15	Truth Was Their Star (St. Antoninus of Florence)	Dorcy, Sister Mary Jean	Dorcy Biography	1947, 1999	YES	10 and up

Italy	15	Torch in the Darkness (A), A Story of St. John Capistrano	Roberto, Brother	In the Footsteps of the Saints	1956, 2010	NO	09-12
Italy	15	Apprentice of Florence	Kyle, Ann	Newbery	1933	YES	11 and up
Italy	15	Army in Battle Array, An (Blessed James of Ulm	Dorcy, Sister Mary Jean	Dorcy Biography	1955	YES	10 and up
Italy	15	Book of Saints, Part 10 (Bl. Helen of Udine)	Lovasik, Fr. Lawrence	St. Joseph Picture Books	1997	NO	05 and up
Italy	15	Book of Saints, Part 10 (St. Catherine of Genoa)	Lovasik, Fr. Lawrence	St. Joseph Picture	1997	NO	05 and up
Italy	15	Book of Saints, Part 11 (Bl. Osanna of Mantua)	Lovasik, Fr. Lawrence	St. Joseph Picture	1997	NO	05 and up
Italy	15	King of Colors (The), A Story of Fra Angelico	Roberto, Brother	Footsteps of the Saints	1962, 2010	NO	09-12
Italy	15	Saint Angela Merici: Leading People to God	Keefe, Sister Maryellen	Along the Paths of the Gospel	2000	YES	07-10
Italy	15	Saint Francis of Paola (Paula)	Winkler, Father Jude	St. Joseph Picture	2006	NO	05 and up
Italy	15	Story of Michaelangelo, A	Ernest, Brother	Footsteps of the Saints	1961, 2012	NO	06-09
Italy	15 & 16	Book of Saints, Part 4 (St. Angela Merici)	Lovasik, Fr. Lawrence	St. Joseph Picture	1982	NO	05 and up
Italy	15 & 16	Hunters of Souls (Bld. Catherine of Racconigi)	Dorcy, Sister Mary Jean	Dorcy Biography	1949, 1999	YES	10 and up
Italy	15 & 16	Promise to Angela (The): A Life of St. Angela Merici	McKern, Pat	Holy Cross Press	1966	YES	09 and up
Italy	15 & 16	Story of St. Angeli Merici, A	Ernest, Brother	Footsteps of the Saints	1960, 2011	NO	06-09
Italy	15 & 16	When Saints Were Young (St. Angela Merici)	Thompson, Blanche	Vision Books	1960	YES	09-15
Italy	15 & 16	Wings of an Eagle: The Story of Michelangelo	Peck, Anne Merriman	Hawthorn Junior Biography	1963	YES	11 and up
Italy	16	Army in Battle Array, An (Pope St. Pius V)	Dorcy, Sister Mary Jean	Dorcy Biography	1955	YES	10 and up
Italy	16	Army in Battle Array, An (St. Catherine de Ricci	Dorcy, Sister Mary Jean	Dorcy Biography	1955	YES	10 and up
Italy	16	Army in Battle Array, An (St. John of Gorkum or Cologne)	Dorcy, Sister Mary Jean	Dorcy Biography	1955	YES	10 and up
Italy	16	Blood Red Crescent	Garnett, Henry	Clarion Books	1960, 2004, 2007	NO	09 and up
Italy	16	Book of Saints, Part 2 (St. Aloysius Gonzaga)	Lovasik, Fr. Lawrence	St. Joseph Picture	1981	NO	05 and up

Italy	16	Book of Saints, Part 3 (St. Charles Borromeo)	Lovasik, Fr. Lawrence	St. Joseph Picture	1982	NO	05 and up
Italy	16	Book of Saints, Part 5 (St. Philip Neri)	Lovasik, Fr. Lawrence	St. Joseph Picture	1985	NO	05 and up
Italy	16	Book of Saints, Part 6 (St. Pius V)	Lovasik, Fr. Lawrence	St. Joseph Picture	1985	NO	05 and up
Italy	16	Book of Saints, Part 9 (St. Benedict the Black)	Lovasik, Fr. Lawrence	St. Joseph Picture	1996	NO	05 and up
Italy	16	Book of Saints, Part 12 (St. Andrew Avellino)	Lovasik, Fr. Lawrence	St. Joseph Picture	1999	NO	05 and up
Italy	16	Don't Turn Back, A Story of St. Ignatius Loyola	Roberto, Brother	Footsteps of the Saints	1958, 2013	NO	12-15
Italy	16	Footsteps of A Giant, Life of St. Charles Borromeo	Daughters of St. Paul	Encounter Books	1970	YES	09 and up
Italy	16	Golden Thread (The), A Novel of St. Ignatius Loyola	de Wohl, Louis	de Wohl Biography	1952, 2002	NO	15 and up
Italy	16	Lives of the Saints: The Middle Ages (St. Charles Borromeo)	Tesoriero, Bart	Aquinas Kids	2010	NO	05-09
Italy	16	No Place for Defeat, Life of St. Pius V	Daughters of St. Paul	Encounter Books	1970, 1987	YES	09 and up
Italy	16	Robert	Richardson, M.K.	Patron Saint Books	1961	YES	08 and up
Italy	16	Saint Angela Merici: Leading People to God	Keefe, Sister Maryellen	Along the Paths of the Gospel	2000	YES	07-10
Italy	16	Saint Ignatius and the Company of Jesus	Derleth, August	Vision Books	1956, 1999	NO	09-15
Italy	16	Saint Ignatius Loyola, Founder of the Jesuits	Forbes, F.A.	Forbes Biography	1913, 1998	NO	12 and up
Italy	16	Saint Ignatius of Loyola: For the Greater Glory of God	Giaimo, Donna and Patricia Jablonski	Encounter the Saints	2000	NO	09 and up
Italy	16	Saint Philip of the Joyous Heart	Connolly, Francis X.	Vision Books	1957, 1993	NO	09-15
Italy	16	Story of St. Charles, A	Ernest, Brother	Footsteps of the Saints	1962, 2009	NO	06-09
Italy	16	Story of St. Stanislaus Kostka, A	Ernest, Brother	Footsteps of the Saints	1958, 2009	NO	06-09
Italy	16	They Became Saints (St. Aloysius: Prince and Jesuit Scholastic)	Francis, Father	Father Francis Coloring	1951	NO	07 and up
Italy	16	When Saints Were Young (St. Aloysius Gonzaga)	Thompson, Blanche Jennings	Vision Books	1960	YES	09-15
Italy	16	When Saints Were Young (St. Charles Borromeo)	Thompson, Blanche	Vision Books	1960	YES	09-15

Italy	16	When Saints Were Young (St. Stanislaus Kostka)	Thompson, Blanche Jennings	Vision Books	1960	YES	09-15
Italy	16 & 17	Book of Saints, Part 5 (St. Camillus of Lellis)	Lovasik, Fr. Lawrence	St. Joseph Picture Books	1985	NO	05 and up
Italy	16 & 17	Book of Saints, Part 5 (St. Robert Bellarmine)	Lovasik, Fr. Lawrence	St. Joseph Picture	1985	NO	05 and up
Italy	16 & 17	Gamble for God (A), St. Camillus de Lellis	Daughters of St. Paul	Encounter Books	1983	YES	09 and up
Italy	16 & 17	Story of St. Camillus, A	Ernest, Brother	Footsteps of the Saints	1954, 2012	NO	06-09
Italy	17	Book of Saints, Part 2 (St. John Berchmans)	Lovasik, Fr. Lawrence	St. Joseph Picture	1981	NO	05 and up
Italy	17	Book of Saints, Part 7 (St. Lawrence of Brindisi)	Lovasik, Fr. Lawrence	St. Joseph Picture	1993	NO	05 and up
Italy	17	Desert Padre: Eusebio Francisco Kino	Thayer, Jack	Catholic Treasury	1959	YES	10 and up
Italy	17	Father Kino, Priest to the Pimas	Clark, Ann Nolan	Vision Books	1963	YES	09-15
Italy	17	Little Friar Who Flew, The (St. Joseph of Copertino)	Gauch, Patricia	Favorite Catholic Books	1980	YES	10 and up
Italy	17	Robert	Richardson, M.K.	Patron Saint Books	1961	YES	08 and up
Italy	17	Saints for Boys and Girls (St. John Berchmans)	Beebe, Catherine	Beebe Biography	1959	YES	09-14
Italy	17	Two Trumpeters of Vienna, The	Pauli, Hertha	Clarion Books	1961	YES	09 and up
Italy	17 & 18	Book of Saints, Part 12 (Bl. Mary Fontanella or Mary of the Angels)	Lovasik, Fr. Lawrence	St. Joseph Picture Books	1999	NO	05 and up
Italy	17 & 18	Book of Saints, Part 12 (St. Lucy Filippini)	Lovasik, Fr. Lawrence	St. Joseph Picture	1999	NO	05 and up
Italy	18	Book of Saints, Part 2 (St. Gerard Majella)	Lovasik, Fr. Lawrence	St. Joseph Picture	1981	NO	05 and up
Italy	18	Book of Saints, Part 4 (St. Alphonsus Liguori)	Lovasik, Fr. Lawrence	St. Joseph Picture	1982	NO	05 and up
Italy	18	Book of Saints, Part 5 (St. Paul of the Cross)	Lovasik, Fr. Lawrence	St. Joseph Picture	1985	NO	05 and up
Italy	18	Book of Saints, Part 6 (St. Benedict Labre)	Lovasik, Fr. Lawrence	St. Joseph Picture	1985	NO	05 and up
Italy	18	Book of Saints, Part 12 (St. Teresa Margaret Redi)	Lovasik, Fr. Lawrence	St. Joseph Picture Books	1999	NO	05 and up
Italy	18	Lives of the Saints: Modern Saints (St. Gerard)	Tesoriero, Bart	Aquinas Kids	2012	NO	05-09

Country	Century	Title	Author	Publisher/Series	Year	Illustrated	Age
Italy	18	Miracle Man of Muro (The), A Story of St. Gerard Majella	Ernest, Brother	In the Footsteps of the Saints	1950, 2011	NO	09-12
Italy	18	More Saints of the Eucharist: A Playmate of Jesus (St. Gerard Majella)	Francis, Father	Father Francis Coloring Books	1959	NO	06 and up
Italy	18	Saints for Boys and Girls (St. Gerard Majella)	Beebe, Catherine	Beebe Biography	1959	YES	09-14
Italy	18 & 19	Anina (daughter of St. Elizabeth Seton)	Daughters of Charity	Catholic Stories, Volume II	1992	NO	07-10
Italy	18 & 19	Book of Saints, Part 11 (St. Clement Mary Hofbauer)	Lovasik, Fr. Lawrence	St. Joseph Picture	1997	NO	05 and up
Italy	18 & 19	Champion of the Apostolate: The Life of St. Vincent Pallotti	Greene, Brother Ellis	Holy Cross Press	1967	YES	09 and up
Italy	19	Ahead of the Crowd, The Story of St. Dominic Savio	Daughters of St. Paul	Encounter Books	1970	YES	09 and up
Italy	19	Anvil Chorus: The Story of Giuseppe Verdi	Kaufman, Helen L.	Hawthorn Junior Bio.	1964	YES	11 and up
Italy	19	Book of Saints, Part 1 (St. John Bosco)	Lovasik, Fr. Lawrence	St. Joseph Picture	1981	NO	05 and up
Italy	19	Book of Saints, Part 2 (St. Dominic Savio)	Lovasik, Fr. Lawrence	St. Joseph Picture	1981	NO	05 and up
Italy	19	Book of Saints, Part 3 (St. Frances Cabrini)	Lovasik, Fr. Lawrence	St. Joseph Picture	1982	NO	05 and up
Italy	19	Book of Saints, Part 10 (St. Justin de Jacobis)	Lovasik, Fr. Lawrence	St. Joseph Picture	1997	NO	05 and up
Italy	19	Book of Saints, Part 12 (St. Mary Mazzarello)	Lovasik, Fr. Lawrence	St. Joseph Picture	1999	NO	05 and up
Italy	19	Man Who Found Out Why: The Story of Gregor Mendel	Webster, Gary	Hawthorn Junior Biography	1963	YES	11 and up
Italy	19	Maria Domenica Mazzarello	Fino, Catherine	Along the Paths of the Gospel	2002	YES	07-10
Italy	19	Mother Cabrini, Missionary to the World	Keyes, Frances Parkinson	Vision Books	1959, 1997	NO	09-15
Italy	19	Saint Dominic Savio	Windeatt, Mary Fabyan	Windeatt Coloring Books	1955	NO	04 and up
Italy	19	Saint Frances Cabrini	Windeatt, Mary Fabyan	Windeatt Coloring	1956	NO	04 and up
Italy	19	Saint Frances Xavier Cabrini: Cecchina's Dream	Dority, Victoria and Mary Andes	Encounter the Saints	2005	YES	09 and up

Italy	19	Saint John Bosco and the Children's Saint, Dominic Savio	Beebe, Catherine	Vision Books	1955, 1992	NO	09-15
Italy	19	Saint John Bosco: The Friend of Children and Young People	Monmarche, Carole and the Salesians of Don Bosco	Along the Paths of the Gospel	1997	YES	07-10
Italy	19	Saint John Bosco, The Friend of Youth	Forbes, F.A.	Forbes Biography	1935, 2000	NO	12 and up
Italy	19	Saints for Boys and Girls (St. Frances Xavier Cabrini)	Beebe, Catherine	Beebe Biography	1959	YES	09-14
Italy	19	Saints for Girls (St. Frances Cabrini)	Muus, Solveig and Bart Tesoriero	Aquinas Kids	2012	NO	05-09
Italy	19	Saints of the Americas (St. Frances Cabrini)	Winkler, Rev. Jude	St. Joseph Picture	2006	NO	05 and up
Italy	19	Saints of the Eucharist: A Lily in God's Garden (St. Maria Goretti)	Francis, Father	Father Francis Coloring	1958	NO	06 and up
Italy	19	Story of John Bosco, A	Ryan, Brother Ernest	Dujarie Press Reprint	1958, 2005	NO	06-09
Italy	19	Story of St. Dominic Savio, A	Ernest, Brother	Footsteps of the Saints	1957, 2011	NO	06-09
Italy	19	Story of St. John Bosco, A	Ernest, Brother	Footsteps of the Saints	1958, 2011	NO	06-09
Italy	19	They Became Saints (St. Dominic Savio: The Classroom Friend)	Francis, Father	Father Francis Coloring	1951	NO	07 and up
Italy	19	To the Ends of the Earth, A Story of St. Frances Xavier Cabrini	Greene, Brother Genard	In the Footsteps of the Saints	1955, 2009	NO	09-12
Italy	19 & 20	Apostle of Peace, The Story of Pope Pius XII	Hatch, Alden	Hawthorn Junior Bio.	1965	YES	11 and up
Italy	19 & 20	Book of Saints, Part 1 (St. Pius X)	Lovasik, Fr. Lawrence	St. Joseph Picture	1981	NO	05 and up
Italy	19 & 20	Book of Saints, Part 5 (St. Gemma Galgani)	Lovasik, Fr. Lawrence	St. Joseph Picture	1985	NO	05 and up
Italy	19 & 20	Good Pope John (Pope John XXIII)	Sheehan, Elizabeth Odell	Vision Books	1966	YES	09-15
Italy	19 & 20	Light Within: The Story of Maria Montessori	Smaridge, Norah	Hawthorn Junior Bio.	1965	YES	11 and up
Italy	19 & 20	Lives of the Saints: Modern Saints (St. Pio of Pietrelcina)	Tesoriero, Bart	Aquinas Kids	2012	NO	05-09
Italy	19 & 20	More Saints of the Eucharist: A Gem of the Eucharist (St. Gemma)	Francis, Father	Father Francis Coloring	1959	NO	06 and up

Country	Century	Title	Author	Publisher	Year	In Print	Ages
Italy	19 & 20	Padre Pio	Winkler, Father Jude	St. Joseph Picture Books	1999	NO	05 and up
Italy	19 & 20	Pope Pius XII, The World's Shepherd	de Wohl, Louis	Vision Books	1961	YES	09-15
Italy	19 & 20	Pope St. Pius X	Forbes, F.A.	Forbes Biography	1918, 1987	NO	12 and up
Italy	19 & 20	Rich in Love: The Story of Padre Pio of Pietrelcina	Bertanzetti, Eileen Dunn	Weaver Books	1999	YES	09-12
Italy	19 & 20	Saint Pius X	Windeatt, Mary Fabyan	Windeatt Coloring	1955	NO	04 and up
Italy	19 & 20	Saint Pius X, The Farm Boy Who Became Pope	Diethelm, Walter	Junior Vision	1963	YES	09-11
Italy	19 & 20	Saint Pius X, The Farm Boy Who Became Pope	Diethelm, Walter	Vision Books	1956, 1994	NO	09-15
Italy	19 & 20	Saints of the Eucharist: The Pope of Little Children (St. Pius X)	Francis, Father	Father Francis Coloring	1958	NO	06 and up
Italy	19 & 20	Story of St. Gemma, A	Ernest, Brother	Footsteps of the Saints	1957, 2010	NO	06-09
Italy	19 & 20	They Became Saints (St. Mary Goretti: "The Lily of the Marshes")	Francis, Father	Father Francis Coloring	1951	NO	07 and up
Italy	19 & 20	Way of the Cross (The), A Story of Padre Pio	Mohan, Claire Jordan	Mohan Biographies	2002	NO	09-12
Italy	20	Assignment to the Council	Lomask, Milton	Clarion Books	1966	YES	09 and up
Italy	20	Blessed Pier Giorgio Frassati: Journey to the Summit	Vazquez, Ana Maria and Jennings Dean	Encounter the Saints	2004	NO	09 and up
Italy	20	Book of Saints, Part 2 (St. Maria Goretti)	Lovasik, Fr. Lawrence	St. Joseph Picture	1981	NO	05 and up
Italy	20	Boy Who Was, The	Hallock, Grace	Newbery	1928	YES	10/ up
Italy	20	Father Flanagan, Builder of Boys	Stevens, Clifford J.	American Background	1967	YES	10-15
Italy	20	Lucrezia Bori of the Metropolitan Opera	Marion, John Francis	American Background	1962	YES	10-15
Italy	20	Nino	Angelo, Valenti	Newbery	1938	YES	09 and up
Italy	20	Operation Escape: The Adventure of Father O'Flaherty	Madden, Daniel	Hawthorn Junior Biography	1962	YES	11 and up
Italy	20	Saint Gianna Beretta Molla: The Gift of Life	Wallace, Susan Helen	Encounter the Saints	2012	NO	09 and up
Italy	20	Saint Maria Goretti	Windeatt, Mary Fabyan	Windeatt Coloring	1955	NO	04 and up
Italy	20	Saint Pio of Pietrelcina: Rich in Love	Bertanzetti, Eileen Dunn	Encounter the Saints	2002	NO	09 and up

Italy	20	Saints of the Eucharist: A Lily in God's Garden (St. Maria Goretti)	Francis, Father	Father Francis Coloring	1958	NO	06 and up
Italy	20	Yes Is Forever! Mother Thecla Merlo, The First Daughter of St. Paul	Daughters of St. Paul	Encounter Books	1981	YES	09 and up
Italy	20 & 21	Blessed John Paul II: Be Not Afraid	Wallace, Susan Helen	Encounter the Saints	2011	NO	09 and up
Italy	20 & 21	Pope John Paul II	Winkler, Jude Rev.	St. Joseph Picture	2005	NO	05 and up
Italy	20 & 21	Story of Pope Benedict XVI for Children, The	Mohan, Claire Jordan	Mohan Biographies	2007	NO	09 and up
Japan	16	Lives of the Saints: The Middle Ages (St. Francis Xavier)	Tesoriero, Bart	Aquinas Kids	2010	NO	05-09
Japan	16	Saints for Boys (St. Francis Xavier)	Muus, Solveig and Bart Tesoriero	Aquinas Kids	2012	NO	05-09
Japan	17	Army in Battle Array, An (Blessed Alphonsus Navarrette and Companions)	Dorcy, Sister Mary Jean	Dorcy Biography	1955	YES	10 and up
Japan	20	Dawn From the West: The Story of Genevieve Caulfield	Rau, Margaret	Hawthorn Junior Biography	1964	YES	11 and up
Laos	20	Doctor America: The Story of Tom Dooley	Morris, Terry	Hawthorn Junior Biography	1963	YES	11 and up
Laos	20	I Charge Each of You: The Story of Dr. Tom Dooley	O'Brien, Sr. Mary Celine	Holy Cross Press	1966	YES	09 and up
Lithuania	19 & 20	Kaze's True Home, The Young Life of a Modern Day Saint, Mother Maria Kaupas	Mohan, Claire Jordan	Mohan Biographies	1992	YES	09-12
Luxembourg	19 & 20	Mother Alfred and the Doctors Mayo	Richardson, James P.	Banner Books	1959	YES	09-15
Mexico	16	Blessed Sebastian and the Oxen	Betz, Eva K.	Saints and Friendly Beasts	1961, 2003	NO	08 and up
Mexico	16	Cross in the West, The	Boesch, Mark	Vision Books	1956	YES	09-15
Mexico	16	Friar and the Knight, (The), Padre Olmedo and Cortez	Strousse, Flora	American Background	1957	YES	10-15
Mexico	16	Miracle in Mexico: The Story of Juan Diego	Tinkle, Lon	Hawthorn Junior Bio.	1965	YES	11 and up
Mexico	16	Our Lady of Guadalupe	Windeatt, Mary Fabyan	Windeatt Coloring Books	1954	YES	04 and up

Mexico	16	Our Lady of Guadalupe	de Paola, Tomie	de Paola Biography	1980	YES	04-08
Mexico	16	Our Lady of Guadalupe	Lovasik, Fr. Lawrence	St. Joseph Picture	1985, 1990	NO	05 and up
Mexico	16	Saint Juan Diego: and Our Lady of Guadalupe	Nobisso, Josephine	Encounter the Saints	2002	NO	09 and up
Mexico	16	Saints of the Americas (St. Juan Diego)	Winkler, Rev. Jude	St. Joseph Picture	2006	NO	05 and up
Mexico	16	Story of Our Lady of Guadalupe, A	Ernest, Brother	Footsteps of the Saints	1957, 2012	NO	06-09
Mexico	17	Desert Padre: Eusebio Francisco Kino	Thayer, Jack	Catholic Treasury	1959	YES	10 and up
Mexico	17 & 18	Don Diego de Vargas	Buchanan, Rosemary	American Background	1963	YES	10-15
Mexico	17 & 18	Father Kino, Priest to the Pimas	Clark, Ann Nolan	Vision Books	1963	YES	09-15
Mexico	17 & 18	Padre Kino and the Trail to the Pacific	Steffan, Jack	American Background	1960	YES	10-15
Mexico	18	Desert Padre: Eusebio Francisco Kino	Thayer, Jack	Catholic Treasury	1959	YES	10 and up
Mexico	18	First Californian: The Story of Fray Junipero Serra	Demarest, Donald	Hawthorn Junior Biography	1963	YES	11 and up
Mexico	18	Saints of the Americas (Bld. Junipero Serra)	Winkler, Rev. Jude	St. Joseph Picture	2006	NO	05 and up
Mexico	19 & 20	Dawn Brings Glory, A Story of Blessed Miguel Pro	Roberto, Brother	In the Footsteps of the Saints	1956, 2013	NO	12-15
Mexico	19 & 20	God's Secret Agent, The Life of Father Michael Augustine Pro, S.J.	Daughters of St. Paul	Encounter Books	1967	YES	09 and up
Mexico	19 & 20	Jose Finds the King, A Blessed Miguel Pro Story	Ball, Ann	Glory of America	2002	NO	7-12
Mexico	19 & 20	Saints of the Americas (Bld. Miguel Agustin Pro)	Winkler, Rev. Jude	St. Joseph Picture	2006	NO	05 and up
Mexico	20	Nine Days to Christmas, A Story of Mexico	Ets, Marie and Aurora Labastida	Caldecott	1959	YES	04 and up
Mexico	20	Padre Pro, Mexican Hero	Royer, Fanchon	American Background	1963	YES	10-15
Middle East	B.C.	Abraham and Isaac	Arnsteen, Katy Keck	Kid Scripts	1997	NO	04-08
Middle East	B.C.	Deborah	Arnsteen, Katy Keck	Kid Scripts	1997	NO	04-08
Middle East	B.C.	Great Men of the Bible: Old Testament (Adam, Cain and Abel, Noah, Abraham, Joseph, Moses, Samuel, David,	Winkler, Father Jude	St. Joseph Picture	1987	NO	05 and up

Setting	Era	Title	Author	Publisher	Year	Illus.	Ages
		Solomon, Elijah, Isaiah, Jeremiah, Job, Jonah, Judas Maccabee)					
Middle East	B.C.	Great Women of the Bible (Eve, Sarah, Rebekah, Rachel and Leah, Rahab, Deborah, Ruth, Hannah, Michal, Abigail, Bathsheba, Jezebel, Judith, and Esther)	Winkler, Father Jude	St. Joseph Picture	1986, 1990	NO	05 and up
Middle East	B.C.	Joseph and the Dreams	Arnsteen, Katy Keck	Kid Scripts	1997	NO	04-08
Middle East	B.C.	Joshua, God's General	Arnsteen, Katy Keck	Kid Scripts	1997	NO	04-08
Middle East	B.C.	Naomi and Ruth	Arnsteen, Katy Keck	Kid Scripts	1997	NO	04-08
Middle East	B.C.	Noah and the Ark	de Paola, Tomie	de Paola Biography	1983	YES	04-08
Middle East	B.C.	Noah's Ark	Pinkney, Jerry	Caldecott	2002	NO	04 and up
Middle East	B.C.	Noah's Ark	Spier, Peter	Caldecott	1977	NO	04 and up
Middle East	B.C.	Story of Abraham, The	Winkler, Rev. Jude	St. Joseph Bible Story	1988, 1994	YES	05-09
Middle East	B.C.	Story of Isaac and Jacob, The	Winkler, Rev. Jude	St. Joseph Bible Story	1988, 1994	YES	05-09
Middle East	B.C.	Story of Joseph and His Brothers, The	Winkler, Rev. Jude	St. Joseph Bible Story	1988, 1994	YES	05-09
Middle East	B.C.	Story of Joshua, The	Winkler, Rev. Jude	St. Joseph Bible Story Books	1988, 1994	NO	05-09
Middle East	B.C.	Story of Noah and the Flood, The	Winkler, Rev. Jude	St. Joseph Bible Story Books	1989, 2004	NO	05-09
Middle East	B.C.	Story of Ruth, The	Winkler, Rev. Jude	St. Joseph Bible Story	1988	YES	05-09
Middle East	B.C.- 01 A.D.	Bible Story (The), The Promised Lord and His Coming	Beebe, Catherine	Vision Books	1957	YES	09-15
Middle East	01	Book of Saints, Part 8 (St. Andrew)	Lovasik, Fr. Lawrence	St. Joseph Picture	1993	NO	05 and up
Middle East	01	Book of Saints, Part 8 (St. John)	Lovasik, Fr. Lawrence	St. Joseph Picture	1993	NO	05 and up
Middle East	01	Book of Saints, Part 8 (St. Luke)	Lovasik, Fr. Lawrence	St. Joseph Picture	1993	NO	05 and up
Middle East	01	Book of Saints, Part 8 (St. Mark)	Lovasik, Fr. Lawrence	St. Joseph Picture	1993	NO	05 and up
Middle East	01	Book of Saints, Part 8 (St. Paul)	Lovasik, Fr. Lawrence	St. Joseph Picture	1993	NO	05 and up

Middle East	01	Book of Saints, Part 8 (St. Simon)	Lovasik, Fr. Lawrence	St. Joseph Picture	1993	NO	05 and up
Middle East	01	Book of Saints, Part 8 (Sts. Philip and James)	Lovasik, Fr. Lawrence	St. Joseph Picture	1993	NO	05 and up
Middle East	01	Glorious Folly, A Novel of the Time of St. Paul	de Wohl, Louis	de Wohl Biography	1957	YES	15 and up
Middle East	01	Great Hero (The), St. Paul the Apostle	Daughters of St. Paul	Encounter Books	1963	YES	09 and up
Middle East	01	Great Men of the Bible: New Testament (Peter, John, James the Greater, James the Lesser, Matthew, Jude, Judas, Stephen, Paul, Philip, Mark, and Luke)	Winkler, Father Jude	St. Joseph Picture Books	1987	NO	05 and up
Middle East	01	Last Apostle, The (St. Paul)	Eleanor, Mother Mary	Catholic Treasury	1956	YES	10 and up
Middle East	01	Lives of the Saints: The Early Church (St. John the Apostle)	Tesoriero, Bart	Aquinas Kids	2010	NO	05-09
Middle East	01	Lives of the Saints: The Early Church (St. Luke)	Tesoriero, Bart	Aquinas Kids	2010	NO	05-09
Middle East	01	Lives of the Saints: The Early Church (St. Paul)	Tesoriero, Bart	Aquinas Kids	2010	NO	05-09
Middle East	01	Peter and Paul: The Rock and the Sword	Thompson, Blanche	Vision Books	1964	YES	09-15
Middle East	01	Saint Paul the Apostle	Lovasik, Fr. Lawrence	St. Joseph Picture	1980, 1990	NO	05 and up
Middle East	01	Saint Paul the Apostle, The Story of the Apostle to the Gentiles	Windeatt, Mary Fabyan	Windeatt Saint Series	1993	NO	12 and up
Middle East	01	Saints for Boys (St. Paul)	Muus, Solveig and Bart Tesoriero	Aquinas Kids	2012	NO	05-09
Middle East	01	St. Paul: The Thirteenth Apostle	Wallace, Susan Helen	Encounter the Saints	2007	NO	09 and up
Middle East	01	Story of St. Andrew, A	Danielski, S.E.	Footsteps of the Saints	1966, 2010	NO	06-09
Middle East	03	Book of Saints, Part 7 (Sts. Cosmas and Damian)	Lovasik, Fr. Lawrence	St. Joseph Picture	1993	NO	05 and up
Middle East	04	Book of Saints, Part 11 (St. Epiphanius of Salamis)	Lovasik, Fr. Lawrence	St. Joseph Picture	1997	NO	05 and up
Middle East	04	Book of Saints, Part 11 (St. Macrina the Younger)	Lovasik, Fr. Lawrence	St. Joseph Picture	1997	NO	05 and up
Middle East	04	Lives of the Saints: The Monastic Era (St. Nicholas)	Tesoriero, Bart	Aquinas Kids	2010	NO	05-09

Location	#	Title	Author	Publisher	Year	In Series?	Ages
Middle East	04	Saints of the Byzantine World (St. Gregory Nazianzen)	Thompson, Blanche Jennings	Vision Books	1961	YES	09-15
Middle East	04	Saints of the Byzantine World (St. Gregory of Nyssa	Thompson, Blanche Jennings	Vision Books	1961	YES	09-15
Middle East	04	Saints of the Byzantine World (St. Nicholas of Myra)	Thompson, Blanche Jennings	Vision Books	1961	YES	09-15
Middle East	04 & 05	Book of Saints, Part 7 (St. John Chrysostom)	Lovasik, Fr. Lawrence	St. Joseph Picture	1993	NO	05 and up
Middle East	04 & 05	Saints of the Byzantine World (St. John Chrysostom)	Thompson, Blanche Jennings	Vision Books	1961	YES	09-15
Middle East	07 & 08	Saints of the Byzantine World (St. John Damascene)	Thompson, Blanche Jennings	Vision Books	1961	YES	09-15
Morocco	13	Saints for Boys and Girls (St. Daniel)	Beebe, Catherine	Beebe Biography	1959	YES	09-14
Morocco	20	Charles de Foucauld, Adventurer of the Desert	Garnett, Emmeline	Vision Books	1962	YES	09-15
Netherlands	19 & 20	Book of Saints, Part 9 (Bl. Teresa - Edith Stein)	Lovasik, Fr. Lawrence	St. Joseph Picture	1996	NO	05 and up
Netherlands	19 & 20	Book of Saints, Part 9 (Bl. Titus Brandsma)	Lovasik, Fr. Lawrence	St. Joseph Picture	1996	NO	05 and up
North Africa	04 & 05	Book of Saints, Part 3 (St. Augustine)	Lovasik, Fr. Lawrence	St. Joseph Picture	1982	NO	05 and up
North Africa	04 & 05	Restless Flame (The), A Novel of St. Augustine	de Wohl, Louis	de Wohl Biography	1950, 1997	NO	15 and up
North Africa	04 & 05	Saint Augustine and His Search for Faith	Lomask, Milton	Vision Books	1957	YES	09-15
northern Europe	09	Book of Saints, Part 4 (Sts. Cyril and Methodius)	Lovasik, Fr. Lawrence	St. Joseph Picture	1982	NO	05 and up
northern Europe	12	Saint Hyacinth of Poland, The Story of the Apostle of the North	Windeatt, Mary Fabyan	Windeatt Saint Series	1993	NO	11 and up
northern Europe	12 & 13	Hunters of Souls (St. Hyacinth of Poland)	Dorcy, Sister Mary Jean	Dorcy Biography	1949, 1999	YES	10 and up
northern Europe	13	Saint Hyacinth of Poland, The Story of the Apostle of the North	Windeatt, Mary Fabyan	Windeatt Saint Series	1993	NO	11 and up
northern Europe	13	Story of St. Hyacinth, A	Ernest, Brother	Footsteps of the Saints	1960, 2008	NO	06-09
Norway	11	King's Men, A Story of St. Olaf of Norway	Boucher, Alan	Clarion Books	1962	YES	09 and up
Norway	19 & 20	Knute Rockne, Football Wizard of Notre Dame	Daley, Arthur	American Background	1960	YES	10-15
Paraguay	17	Chuiraquimba and the Black Robes	Polland, Madeleine	Clarion Books	1962, 2010	NO	09 and up

Persia	B.C.	Queen Esther	Arnsteen, Katy Keck	Kid Scripts	1997	NO	04-08
Persia	B.C.	Queen Esther	de Paola, Tomie	de Paola Biography	1986	YES	04-08
Persia	01	Book of Saints, Part 8 (St. Jude Thaddeus)	Lovasik, Fr. Lawrence	St. Joseph Picture	1993	NO	05 and up
Persia (Parthia)	01	Book of Saints, Part 8 (St. Thomas)	Lovasik, Fr. Lawrence	St. Joseph Picture	1993	NO	05 and up
Peru	16	St. Rose of Lima, The Story of the First Canonized Saint of the Americas	Windeatt, Mary Fabyan	Windeatt Saint Series	1993	NO	09 and up
Peru	16 & 17	Army in Battle Array, An (Bld. Martin de Porres)	Dorcy, Sister Mary Jean	Dorcy Biography	1955	YES	10 and up
Peru	16 & 17	Army in Battle Array, An (St. Rose of Lima)	Dorcy, Sister Mary Jean	Dorcy Biography	1955	YES	10 and up
Peru	16 & 17	Book of Saints, Part 2 (St. Rose of Lima)	Lovasik, Fr. Lawrence	St. Joseph Picture Books	1981	NO	05 and up
Peru	16 & 17	Book of Saints, Part 7 (St. Martin de Porres)	Lovasik, Fr. Lawrence	St. Joseph Picture Books	1993	NO	05 and up
Peru	16 & 17	Girl Who Laughed at Satan (The), A Story of St. Rose of Lima	Roberto, Brother	In the Footsteps of the Saints	1956, 2008	NO	09-12
Peru	16 & 17	Linda (St. Rose of Lima)	Richardson, M.K.	Patron Saint Books	1960	YES	08 and up
Peru	16 & 17	Lives of the Saints: Modern Saints (St. Martin de Porres)	Tesoriero, Bart	Aquinas Kids	2012	NO	05-09
Peru	16 & 17	Lives of the Saints: Modern Saints (St. Rose of Lima)	Tesoriero, Bart	Aquinas Kids	2012	NO	05-09
Peru	16 & 17	Martin de Porres, Saint of the New World	Tarry, Ellen	Vision Books	1963	YES	09-15
Peru	16 & 17	Saint Martin de Porres	Lovasik, Fr. Lawrence	St. Joseph Picture	1983	NO	05 and up
Peru	16 & 17	Saint Martin de Porres and the Mice	Betz, Eva K.	Saints and Friendly Beasts	1963, 2003	NO	08 and up
Peru	16 & 17	Saint Martin de Porres, The Story of the Little Doctor of Lima, Peru	Windeatt, Mary Fabyan	Windeatt Saint Series	1993	NO	09 and up
Peru	16 & 17	Saint Martin de Porres: Humble Healer	DeDomenico, Elizabeth	Encounter the Saints	2005	NO	09 and up
Peru	16 & 17	Saints for Boys and Girls (St. Rose of Lima)	Beebe, Catherine	Beebe Biography	1959	YES	09-14
Peru	16 & 17	Saints for Boys (St. Martin de Porres)	Muus, Solveig and Bart Tesoriero	Aquinas Kids	2012	NO	05-09

Saint Series Books by Geographical Setting

Peru	16 & 17	Saints for Girls (St. Rose of Lima)	Muus, Solveig and Bart Tesoriero	Aquinas Kids	2012	NO	05-09
Peru	16 & 17	Saints of the Americas (Sts. Rose of Lima and Martin de Porres)	Winkler, Rev. Jude	St. Joseph Picture Books	2006	NO	05 and up
Peru	16 & 17	They Became Saints (St. Martin de Porres: The Holy Negro of Lima)	Francis, Father	Father Francis Coloring	1951	NO	07 and up
Peru	16 & 17	They Became Saints (St. Rose of Lima: The First American Saint)	Francis, Father	Father Francis Coloring Books	1951	NO	07 and up
Peru	17	Saint John Masias, Marvelous Dominican Gatekeeper of Lima, Peru	Windeatt, Mary Fabyan	Windeatt Saint Series	1993	NO	10 and up
Peru	17	Saint Martin de Porres, The Story of the Little Doctor of Lima, Peru	Windeatt, Mary Fabyan	Windeatt Saint Series	1993	NO	09 and up
Peru	17	Saint Rose of Lima, The Story of the First Canonized Saint of the Americas	Windeatt, Mary Fabyan	Windeatt Saint Series	1993	NO	09 and up
Peru	17	Truth Was Their Star (Blessed John Masias)	Dorcy, Sister Mary Jean	Dorcy Biography	1947, 1999	NO	10 and up
Peru	20	Trailblazer for the Sacred Heart, Fr. Mateo Crawley-Boevey (Globe-Trotter for the Sacred Heart)	Balskus, Pat	Encounter Books	1976	YES	09 and up
Philippines	20	Island Hero: The Story of Ramon Magsaysay	Gray, Marvin M.	Hawthorn Junior Biography	1965	YES	11 and up
Poland	01	Book of Saints, Part 8 (St. Andrew)	Lovasik, Fr. Lawrence	St. Joseph Picture	1993	NO	05 and up
Poland	12	Saint Hyacinth of Poland, The Story of the Apostle of the North	Windeatt, Mary Fabyan	Windeatt Saint Series	1993	NO	11 and up
Poland	13	Hunters of Souls (Blessed Sadoc and Martyrs of Sandomir)	Dorcy, Sister Mary Jean	Dorcy Biography	1949, 1999	YES	10 and up
Poland	13	Master Albert, The Story of St. Albert the Great	Dorcy, Sister Mary Jean	Dorcy Biography	1955	YES	12 and up
Poland	13	Saint Hyacinth of Poland, The Story of the Apostle of the North	Windeatt, Mary Fabyan	Windeatt Saint Series	1993	NO	11 and up
Poland	13	Truth Was Their Star (St. Albert the Great)	Dorcy, Sister Mary Jean	Dorcy Biography	1947, 1999	NO	10 and up
Poland	16	Book of Saints, Part 2 (St. Stanislaus Kostka)	Lovasik, Fr. Lawrence	St. Joseph Picture	1981	NO	05 and up

Poland	16	Story of St. Stanislaus Kostka, A	Ernest, Brother	Footsteps of the Saints	1958, 2009	NO	06-09
Poland	16	When Saints Were Young (St. Stanislaus Kostka)	Thompson, Blanche Jennings	Vision Books	1960	YES	09-15
Poland	18	Cavalry Hero, Casimir Pulaski	Adams, Dorothy	American Background	1957	YES	10-15
Poland	19	Master Mariner: The Adventurous Life of Joseph Conrad	Smaridge, Norah	Hawthorn Junior Biography	1966	YES	11 and up
Poland	19	Red Rose for Frania (A): A Story of the Young Life of Francis Siedliska	Mohan, Claire Jordan	Mohan Biographies	1989	YES	09-12
Poland	19 & 20	Blessed by the Cross: St. Edith Stein	Hill, Mary Lea FSP	Encounter the Saints	1999	NO	09 and up
Poland	19 & 20	Book of Saints, Part 6 (St. Maximilian Kolbe)	Lovasik, Fr. Lawrence	St. Joseph Picture	1985	NO	05 and up
Poland	19 & 20	Book of Saints, Part 9 (Bl. Teresa - Edith Stein)	Lovasik, Fr. Lawrence	St. Joseph Picture	1996	NO	05 and up
Poland	19 & 20	Lion of Poland: The Story of Paderewski	Hume, Ruth and Paul	Hawthorn Junior Bio.	1962, 2012	NO	11 and up
Poland	19 & 20	Lives of the Saints: Modern Saints (St. Maximilian Kolbe)	Tesoriero, Bart	Aquinas Kids	2012	NO	05-09
Poland	19 & 20	Music from the Hunger Pit, A Story of St. Maximillian Kolbe	Roberto, Brother	In the Footsteps of the Saints	1954, 2008	NO	09-12
Poland	20	Blessed John Paul II: Be Not Afraid	Wallace, Susan Helen	Encounter the Saints	2011	NO	09 and up
Poland	20	More Than a Knight, The True Story of St. Maximilian Kolbe	Daughters of St. Paul	Encounter Books	1982	YES	09 and up
Poland	20	Pope John Paul II	Winkler, Jude Rev.	St. Joseph Picture	2005	NO	05 and up
Poland	20	St. Faustina Kowalska: Messenger of Mercy,	Wallace, Susan Helen	Encounter the Saints	2007	NO	09 and up
Poland	20	Saint Maximilian Kolbe: Mary's Knight	Jablonski, Patricia	Encounter the Saints	2001	NO	09 and up
Poland	20	St. Maximiliam Kolbe, The Story of the Two Crowns	Mohan, Claire Jordan	Mohan Biographies	1999	YES	09-12
Poland	20	Young Life of Pope John Paul II, The	Mohan, Claire Jordan	Mohan Biographies	1995, 2005	NO	09-12
Poland	20	Young Life of Saint Maria Faustina, The	Mohan, Claire Jordan	Mohan Biographies	2000	NO	09-12
Poland	20	Young Life of Sister Faustina, The	Mohan, Claire Jordan	Mohan Biographies	2000	YES	09-12
Portugal	07	Book of Saints, Part 10 (St. Fructuosus of Braga)	Lovasik, Fr. Lawrence	St. Joseph Picture	1997	NO	05 and up

Saint Series Books by Geographical Setting

Portugal	13	Children's Saint Anthony, The (Anthony of Padua)	Beebe, Catherine	Beebe Biography	1939, 1943	YES	08-14
Portugal	13	Saint Anthony and the Christ Child	Homan, Helen Walker	Junior Vision	1963	YES	09-11
Portugal	13	Saint Anthony and the Christ Child	Homan, Helen Walker	Vision Books	1958, 1997	NO	09-15
Portugal	13	Saint Anthony of Padua	Windeatt, Mary Fabyan	Windeatt Coloring Books	1955	NO	04 and up
Portugal	13	Saint Anthony of Padua	Lovasik, Fr. Lawrence	St. Joseph Picture	1984	NO	05 and up
Portugal	13	Saint Anthony of Padua: Fire and Light	Kerry, Margaret and Mary Tebo	Encounter the Saints	1999	NO	09 and up
Portugal	13	Saint Anthony of Padua: Proclaimer of the Good News	Baudouin-Croix, Marie	Along the Paths of the Gospel	1999	YES	07-10
Portugal	13	Saints for Boys and Girls (St. Anthony of Padua)	Beebe, Catherine	Beebe Biography	1959	YES	09-14
Portugal	13	Story of St. Anthony, A	Ernest, Brother	In the Footsteps of the Saints	1960, 2009	NO	06-09
Portugal	15	Book of Saints, Part 10 (St. Beatrice Da Silva Meneses)	Lovasik, Fr. Lawrence	St. Joseph Picture	1997	NO	05 and up
Portugal	15	Crown for Joanna, A	Dorcy, Sister Mary Jean	Dorcy Biography	1946	YES	10 and up
Portugal	15	Truth Was Their Star (Blessed Joanna of Portugal)	Dorcy, Sister Mary Jean	Dorcy Biography	1947, 1999	NO	10 and up
Portugal	15 & 16	Book of Saints, Part 4 (St. John of God)	Lovasik, Fr. Lawrence	St. Joseph Picture	1982	NO	05 and up
Portugal	15 & 16	Lives of the Saints: The Middle Ages (St. John of God)	Tesoriero, Bart	Aquinas Kids	2010	NO	05-09
Portugal	17	Book of Saints, Part 7 (St. Lawrence of Brindisi)	Lovasik, Fr. Lawrence	St. Joseph Picture	1993	NO	05 and up
Portugal	20	Blessed Jacinta and Francisco Marto: Shepherds of Fatima	Heffernan, Anne and Patricia Jablonski	Encounter the Saints	2000	NO	09 and up
Portugal	20	Boy with a Mission, The Life of Francis Marto of Fatima	Daughters of St. Paul	Encounter Books	1967, 1981	YES	09 and up
Portugal	20	Children of Fatima and Our Lady's Message to the World, The	Windeatt, Mary Fabyan	Windeatt Saint Series	1991	NO	09 and up
Portugal	20	Our Lady Came to Fatima	Hume, Ruth Fox	Vision Books	1957, 2005	NO	09-15

Portugal	20	Our Lady of Fatima	Richomme, Agnes	Catholic Children's Library	1965, 2012	NO	10 and up
Portugal	20	Our Lady of Fatima	Windeatt, Mary Fabyan	Windeatt Coloring	1954	NO	04 and up
Portugal	20	Our Lady of Fatima	Lovasik, Fr. Lawrence	St. Joseph Picture	1984, 1991	NO	05 and up
Portugal	20	Story of Our Lady of Fatima, A	Ernest, Brother	Footsteps of the Saints	1957, 2010	NO	06-09
Rome	01	Book of Saints, Part 8 (St. Paul)	Lovasik, Fr. Lawrence	St. Joseph Picture	1993	NO	05 and up
Rome	01	Book of Saints, Part 8 (St. Peter)	Lovasik, Fr. Lawrence	St. Joseph Picture	1993	NO	05 and up
Rome	01	City of the Golden House	Polland, Madeleine	Clarion Books	1963, 2005	NO	09 and up
Rome	01	Great Hero (The), St. Paul the Apostle	Daughters of St. Paul	Encounter Books	1963	YES	09 and up
Rome	01	Last Apostle, The (St. Paul)	Eleanor, Mother Mary	Catholic Treasury	1956	YES	10 and up
Rome	01	Saint Philomena	Windeatt, Mary Fabyan	Windeatt Coloring	1955	YES	04 and up
Rome	01	Saints for Boys (St. Paul)	Muus, Solveig and Bart Tesoriero	Aquinas Kids	2012	NO	05-09
Rome	01	Saints for Boys (St. Peter)	Muus, Solveig and Bart Tesoriero	Aquinas Kids	2012	NO	05-09
Rome	01	Story of St. Peter, A	Ernest, Brother	Footsteps of the Saints	1961, 2011	NO	06-09
Rome	02	Book of Saints, Part 6 (St. Ignatius of Antioch)	Lovasik, Fr. Lawrence	St. Joseph Picture	1985	NO	05 and up
Rome	02	Lives of the Saints: The Early Church (St. Cecilia)	Tesoriero, Bart	Aquinas Kids	2010	NO	05-09
Rome	02	No Tears for the Bride, A Story of St. Perpetua	Roberto, Brother	Footsteps of the Saints	1958, 2008	NO	09-12
Rome	03	Book of Saints, Part 3 (St. Cecilia)	Lovasik, Fr. Lawrence	St. Joseph Picture	1982	NO	05 and up
Rome	03	Book of Saints, Part 7 (St. Valentine)	Lovasik, Fr. Lawrence	St. Joseph Picture	1993	NO	05 and up
Rome	03	Fabiola	Wiseman, Nicholas Cardinal Patrick	Favorite Catholic Books	1854, etc.	NO	12 and up
Rome	03	Lives of the Saints: The Monastic Era (St. Sebastian)	Tesoriero, Bart	Aquinas Kids	2010	NO	05-09
Rome	03	Lion Tamer, The (martyr Martina)	Daughters of Charity	Catholic Stories, Volume IV	1995	NO	07-10

Rome	03	No Tears for the Bride, A Story of St. Perpetua	Roberto, Brother	Footsteps of the Saints	1958, 2008	NO	09-12
Rome	03	Story of St. Cecilia, A	Ernest, Brother	Footsteps of the Saints	1959, 2009	NO	06-09
Rome	03 & 04	Marc's Choice: A Story of the Time of Diocletian	Cornelius, Sister Mary	Catholic Treasury	1957	YES	10 and up
Rome	04	Book of Saints, Part 2 (St. Agnes)	Lovasik, Fr. Lawrence	St. Joseph Picture	1981	NO	05 and up
Rome	04	Book of Saints, Part 2 (St. Tarcisius)	Lovasik, Fr. Lawrence	St. Joseph Picture	1981	NO	05 and up
Rome	04	Book of Saints, Part 4 (St. Helen)	Lovasik, Fr. Lawrence	St. Joseph Picture	1982	NO	05 and up
Rome	04	Book of Saints, Part 4 (St. Sebastian)	Lovasik, Fr. Lawrence	St. Joseph Picture	1982	NO	05 and up
Rome	04	Book of Saints, Part 7 (St. George)	Lovasik, Fr. Lawrence	St. Joseph Picture	1993	NO	05 and up
Rome	04	Helena	Harris, Mary	Patron Saint Books	1964	YES	08 and up
Rome	04	Living Wood (The), A Novel of St. Helena	de Wohl, Louis	de Wohl Biography	1947	YES	15 and up
Rome	04	Saints for Boys and Girls (St. Agnes)	Beebe, Catherine	Beebe Biography	1959	YES	09-14
Rome	04	Saints of the Eucharist: A Boy who Carried Jesus (St. Tarcisius)	Francis, Father	Father Francis Coloring	1958	NO	06 and up
Rome	04	St. Tarcisius	Bernadi, Mary R.	Similar to Encounter	1983	YES	09 and up
Rome	04	Story of St. Sebastian, A	Ernest, Brother	Footsteps of the Saints	1959, 2010	NO	06-09
Rome	04	They Became Saints (St. Agnes: The Fearless Virgin)	Francis, Father	Father Francis Coloring	1951	NO	07 and up
Rome	04	They Became Saints (St. Tarcisius: Boy Martyr of the Holy Eucharist)	Francis, Father	Father Francis Coloring	1951	NO	07 and up
Rome	04 & 05	Restless Flame (The), A Novel of St. Augustine	de Wohl, Louis	de Wohl Biography	1950, 1997	NO	15 and up
Rome	04 & 05	Saint Augustine and His Search for Faith	Lomask, Milton	Vision Books	1957	YES	09-15
Rome	05 & 06	Book of Saints, Part 9 (St. Galla)	Lovasik, Fr. Lawrence	St. Joseph Picture	1996	NO	05 and up
Rome	09	Book of Saints, Part 4 (Sts. Cyril and Methodius)	Lovasik, Fr. Lawrence	St. Joseph Picture	1982	NO	05 and up
Rome	14	Book of Saints, Part 7 (St. Bridget)	Lovasik, Fr. Lawrence	St. Joseph Picture	1993	NO	05 and up
Russia	01	Book of Saints, Part 8 (St. Andrew)	Lovasik, Fr. Lawrence	St. Joseph Picture	1993	NO	05 and up

Russia	04	Book of Saints, Part 4 (St. Nicholas)	Lovasik, Fr. Lawrence	St. Joseph Picture	1982	NO	05 and up
Russia	09 & 10	Book of Saints, Part 9 (St. Olga)	Lovasik, Fr. Lawrence	St. Joseph Picture	1996	NO	05 and up
Russia	20	Lion of Poland: The Story of Paderewski	Hume, Ruth and Paul	Hawthorn Junior Bio.	1962, 2012	NO	11 and up
San Salvador	15	Columbus and the New World	Derleth, August	Vision Books	1957	YES	09-15
San Salvador	15	Golden Caravel, The (Christopher Columbus)	Bemister, Margaret	Catholic Treasury	1962	YES	10 and up
San Salvador	15	Pedro of the Water Jars (Christopher Columbus)	Daughters of Charity	Catholic Stories, Volume I	1987	NO	07-10
Saxony (Germany)	13 & 14	Book of Saints, Part 7 (St. Gertrude)	Lovasik, Fr. Lawrence	St. Joseph Picture	1993	NO	05 and up
Scotland	06	Irish Saints (St. Columcille)	Reilly, Robert T.	Vision Books	1964, 1981, 2002	YES	09-15
Scotland	10	Black Fox of Lorne, The	de Angeli, Marguerite	Newbery	1956	YES	09 and up
Scotland	11	Margaret (St. Margaret of Scotland)	Sister M. Juliana of Maryknoll	Patron Saint Books	1959	NO	08 and up
Scotland	12	Outlaws of Ravenhurst	Wallace, Sr. M. Imelda	Favorite Catholic Books	1950, 1996	NO	10 and up
Scotland	14	Book of Saints, Part 5 (St. Vincent Ferrer)	Lovasik, Fr. Lawrence	St. Joseph Picture Books	1985	NO	05 and up
Scotland	16 & 17	Book of Saints, Part 10 (St. John Ogilvie)	Lovasik, Fr. Lawrence	St. Joseph Picture	1997	NO	05 and up
Sicily	04	Book of Saints, Part 2 (St. Lucy)	Lovasik, Fr. Lawrence	St. Joseph Picture	1981	NO	05 and up
Sicily	06 & 07	Book of Saints, Part 10 (St. Zozimus)	Lovasik, Fr. Lawrence	St. Joseph Picture	1997	NO	05 and up
Sinai	B.C.	Moses	Arnsteen, Katy Keck	Kid Scripts	1997	NO	04-08
Sinai	B.C.	Story of Moses, The	Winkler, Rev. Jude	St. Joseph Bible Story	1988, 1994	YES	05-09
South America	16 & 17	Saint Francis Solano, Wonderworker of the New World and Apostle of Argentina and Peru	Windeatt, Mary Fabyan	Windeatt Saint Series	1994	NO	11 and up
South America	17	Book of Saints, Part 1 (St. Peter Claver)	Lovasik, Fr. Lawrence	St. Joseph Picture	1981	NO	05 and up
South America	17	Peter Claver, Saint Among Slaves	Roos, Ann	Vision Books	1965	YES	09-15
South America	17	Saints of the Americas (St. Peter Claver)	Winkler, Rev. Jude	St. Joseph Picture	2006	NO	05 and up

Spain	01	Book of Saints, Part 8 (St. James the Greater)	Lovasik, Fr. Lawrence	St. Joseph Picture	1993	NO	05 and up
Spain	03	Book of Saints, Part 11 (St. Eulalia of Merida)	Lovasik, Fr. Lawrence	St. Joseph Picture	1997	NO	05 and up
Spain	06	Book of Saints, Part 11 (St. Hermenegild)	Lovasik, Fr. Lawrence	St. Joseph Picture	1997	NO	05 and up
Spain	06 & 07	Book of Saints, Part 5 (St. Isidore of Seville)	Lovasik, Fr. Lawrence	St. Joseph Picture	1985	NO	05 and up
Spain	06 & 07	Lives of the Saints: The Monastic Era (St. Isidore of Seville)	Tesoriero, Bart	Aquinas Kids	2010	NO	05-09
Spain	07	Book of Saints, Part 10 (St. Fructuosus of Braga)	Lovasik, Fr. Lawrence	St. Joseph Picture	1997	NO	05 and up
Spain	11 & 12	Lives of the Saints: The Monastic Era (St. Isidore the Farmer)	Tesoriero, Bart	Aquinas Kids	2010	NO	05-09
Spain	12	Book of Saints, Part 3 (St. Isidore)	Lovasik, Fr. Lawrence	St. Joseph Picture	1982	NO	05 and up
Spain	12	Saint Dominic and the Rosary	Beebe, Catherine	Vision Books	1956, 1996	NO	09-15
Spain	12 & 13	Book of Saints, Part 4 (St. Dominic)	Lovasik, Fr. Lawrence	St. Joseph Picture	1982	NO	05 and up
Spain	12 & 13	Hunters of Souls (St. Dominic)	Dorcy, Sister Mary Jean	Dorcy Biography	1949, 1999	YES	10 and up
Spain	12 & 13	Hunters of Souls (St. Raymond of Pennafort)	Dorcy, Sister Mary Jean	Dorcy Biography	1949, 1999	YES	10 and up
Spain	12 & 13	Saint Dominic	Dorcy, Sister Mary Jean	Dorcy Biography	1959, 1982, 2009	NO	14 and up
Spain	12 & 13	Saint Dominic de Guzman	Ordonez, Emilio	Along the Paths of the Gospel	2000	YES	07-10
Spain	12 & 13	St. Dominic, Preacher of the Rosary and Founder of the Dominican Order	Windeatt, Mary Fabyan	Windeatt Saint Series	1993	NO	09 and up
Spain	12 & 13	Story of St. Dominic, A	Ernest, Brother	Footsteps of the Saints	1959, 2008	NO	06-09
Spain	12 & 13	When All Ships Failed, A Story of St. Raymond of Pennafort	Ernest, Brother	In the Footsteps of the Saints	1953, 2010	NO	09-12
Spain	13	Book of Saints, Part 1 (St. Anthony of Padua)	Lovasik, Fr. Lawrence	St. Joseph Picture	1981	NO	05 and up
Spain	14	Truth Was Their Star (St. Vincent Ferrer)	Dorcy, Sister Mary Jean	Dorcy Biography	1947, 1999	NO	10 and up
Spain	14 & 15	Book of Saints, Part 5 (St. Vincent Ferrer)	Lovasik, Fr. Lawrence	St. Joseph Picture	1985	NO	05 and up
Spain	14 & 15	Lives of the Saints: The Middle Ages (St. Vincent Ferrer)	Tesoriero, Bart	Aquinas Kids	2010	NO	05-09

Spain	15	Book of Saints, Part 10 (St. Beatrice Da Silva Meneses)	Lovasik, Fr. Lawrence	St. Joseph Picture	1997	NO	05 and up
Spain	15	Book of Saints, Part 11 (St. John of Sahagun)	Lovasik, Fr. Lawrence	St. Joseph Picture	1997	NO	05 and up
Spain	15	Columbus and the New World	Derleth, August	Vision Books	1957	YES	09-15
Spain	15	Golden Caravel, The (Christopher Columbus)	Bemister, Margaret	Catholic Treasury	1962	YES	10 and up
Spain	15	Pedro of the Water Jars (Christopher Columbus)	Daughters of Charity	Catholic Stories, Volume I	1987	NO	07-10
Spain	15 & 16	Book of Saints, Part 5 (St. Ignatius Loyola)	Lovasik, Fr. Lawrence	St. Joseph Picture	1985	NO	05 and up
Spain	15 & 16	Don't Turn Back, A Story of St. Ignatius Loyola	Roberto, Brother	Footsteps of the Saints	1958, 2013	NO	12-15
Spain	15 & 16	Lives of the Saints: The Middle Ages (St. Ignatius of Loyola)	Tesoriero, Bart	Aquinas Kids	2010	NO	05-09
Spain	15 & 16	Saints for Boys (St. Ignatius Loyola)	Muus, Solveig and Bart Tesoriero	Aquinas Kids	2012	NO	05-09
Spain	16	Blessed Sebastian and the Oxen	Betz, Eva K.	Saints and Friendly Beasts	1961, 2003	NO	08 and up
Spain	16	Blood Red Crescent	Garnett, Henry	Clarion Books	1960, 2004, 2007	NO	09 and up
Spain	16	Book of Saints, Part 1 (St. Teresa of Avila)	Lovasik, Fr. Lawrence	St. Joseph Picture Books	1981	NO	05 and up
Spain	16	Book of Saints, Part 2 (St. Aloysius Gonzaga)	Lovasik, Fr. Lawrence	St. Joseph Picture	1981	NO	05 and up
Spain	16	Book of Saints, Part 3 (St. Francis Xavier)	Lovasik, Fr. Lawrence	St. Joseph Picture	1982	NO	05 and up
Spain	16	Book of Saints, Part 3 (St. John of the Cross)	Lovasik, Fr. Lawrence	St. Joseph Picture	1982	NO	05 and up
Spain	16	Book of Saints, Part 12 (St. Peter of Alcantara)	Lovasik, Fr. Lawrence	St. Joseph Picture Books	1999	NO	05 and up
Spain	16	Flame in the Night, The Life of St. Francis Xavier	Daughters of St. Paul	Encounter Books	1967, 1981	YES	09 and up
Spain	16	Golden Thread, A Novel of St. Ignatius Loyola	de Wohl, Louis	de Wohl Biography	1952, 2002	NO	15 and up
Spain	16	I Serve the King, A Story of St. Francis Borgia	Roberto, Brother	Footsteps of the Saints	1954, 2010	NO	09-12
Spain	16	Leaving Matters to God, The Life of St. Teresa of Avila	Cantoni, Louise Bellucci	Encounter Books	1982, 1984	YES	09 and up

Saint Series Books by Geographical Setting

Spain	16	Lives of the Saints: The Middle Ages (St. Francis Xavier)	Tesoriero, Bart	Aquinas Kids	2010	NO	05-09
Spain	16	Lives of the Saints: The Middle Ages (St. Teresa of Avila)	Tesoriero, Bart	Aquinas Kids	2010	NO	05-09
Spain	16	More Saints of the Eucharist: The Patron of the Eucharist (St. Paschal)	Francis, Father	Father Francis Coloring	1959	NO	06 and up
Spain	16	Pascual and the Kitchen Angels (St. Pascal Baylon)	de Paola, Tomie	de Paola Biography	2006	NO	04-08
Spain	16	Pedro Menendez de Aviles and the Founding of St. Augustine	Stone, Elaine Murray	American Background	1969	YES	10-15
Spain	16	Saint Francis of the Seven Seas	Nevins, Albert J.	Junior Vision	1963	YES	09-11
Spain	16	Saint Francis of the Seven Seas	Nevins, Albert J.	Vision Books	1955, 1995	NO	09-15
Spain	16	Saint Francis Solano, Wonderworker of the New World and Apostle of Argentina and Peru	Windeatt, Mary Fabyan	Windeatt Saint Series	1994	NO	11 and up
Spain	16	Saint Francis Xavier	Marchand, Fr. Norbert	Catholic Children's	1965, 2012	NO	10 and up
Spain	16	Saint Ignatius and the Company of Jesus	Derleth, August	Vision Books	1956, 1999	NO	09-15
Spain	16	Saint Ignatius Loyola, Founder of the Jesuits	Forbes, F.A.	Forbes Biography	1913, 1998	NO	12 and up
Spain	16	Saint Ignatius of Loyola: For the Greater Glory of God	Giaimo, Donna and Patricia Jablonski	Encounter the Saints	2000	NO	09 and up
Spain	16	Saint Teresa of Avila	Windeatt, Mary Fabyan	Windeatt Coloring	1955	NO	04 and up
Spain	16	Saint Teresa of Avila: Joyful in the Lord	Wallace, Susan Helen	Encounter the Saints	2008	NO	09 and up
Spain	16	Saint Teresa of Avila, Reformer of Carmel	Forbes, F.A.	Forbes Biography	1917, 1998	NO	12 and up
Spain	16	Saints for Boys (St. Francis Xavier)	Muus, Solveig and Bart Tesoriero	Aquinas Kids	2012	NO	05-09
Spain	16	Sea Tiger: The Story of Pedro Menendez	Kolars, Frank	Hawthorn Junior Bio.	1963	YES	11 and up
Spain	16	Set All Afire, A Novel of St. Francis Xavier	de Wohl, Louis	de Wohl Biography	1951, 1991	NO	15 and up
Spain	16	Story of Paschal Baylon, A	Ernest, Brother	Footsteps of the Saints	1960, 2011	NO	06-09
Spain	16	They Became Saints (St. Aloysius: Prince and Jesuit Scholastic)	Francis, Father	Father Francis Coloring	1951	NO	07 and up

Country	Century	Title	Author	Publisher	Year	Illustrated	Age
Spain	16	Truth Was Their Star (St. Louis Bertrand)	Dorcy, Sister Mary Jean	Dorcy Biography	1947, 1999	NO	10 and up
Spain	16	When Saints Were Young (St. Aloysius Gonzaga)	Thompson, Blanche Jennings	Vision Books	1960	YES	09-15
Spain	16	When Saints Were Young (St. Teresa of Avila)	Thompson, Blanche Jennings	Vision Books	1960	YES	09-15
Spain	16 & 17	Army in Battle Array, An (Blessed Alphonsus Navarrette and Companions)	Dorcy, Sister Mary Jean	Dorcy Biography	1955	YES	10 and up
Spain	16 & 17	Book of Saints, Part 1 (St. Peter Claver)	Lovasik, Fr. Lawrence	St. Joseph Picture	1981	NO	05 and up
Spain	16 & 17	Peter Claver, Saint Among Slaves	Roos, Ann	Vision Books	1965	YES	09-15
Spain	16 & 17	Saint John Masias, Marvelous Dominican Gatekeeper of Lima, Peru	Windeatt, Mary Fabyan	Windeatt Saint Series	1993	NO	10 and up
Spain	16 & 17	Saints of the Americas (St. Peter Claver)	Winkler, Rev. Jude	St. Joseph Picture	2006	NO	05 and up
Spain	16 & 17	Truth Was Their Star (Blessed John Masias)	Dorcy, Sister Mary Jean	Dorcy Biography	1947, 1999	NO	10 and up
Spain	17 & 18	Don Diego de Vargas	Buchanan, Rosemary	American Background	1963	YES	10-15
Spain	18	First Californian: The Story of Fray Junipero Serra	Demarest, Donald	Hawthorn Junior Biography	1963	YES	11 and up
Spain	18	Saints of the Americas (Bld. Junipero Serra)	Winkler, Rev. Jude	St. Joseph Picture	2006	NO	05 and up
Spain	19	Book of Saints, Part 6 (St. Anthony Mary Claret)	Lovasik, Fr. Lawrence	St. Joseph Picture	1985	NO	05 and up
Spain	19	Book of Saints, Part 10 (St. Mary Soledad)	Lovasik, Fr. Lawrence	St. Joseph Picture	1997	NO	05 and up
Spain	19	Book of Saints, Part 12 (St. Mary Soledad)	Lovasik, Fr. Lawrence	St. Joseph Picture	1999	NO	05 and up
Spain	19 & 20	Book of Saints, Part 11 (Bl. Angela of the Cross Guerrero)	Lovasik, Fr. Lawrence	St. Joseph Picture Books	1997	NO	05 and up
Spain	20	Book of Saints, Part 9 (St. Miguel Cordero)	Lovasik, Fr. Lawrence	St. Joseph Picture	1996	NO	05 and up
Spain	20	Lucrezia Bori of the Metropolitan Opera	Marion, John Francis	American Background	1962	YES	10-15
Spain	20	Saints of the Americas (St. Miguel Cordero)	Winkler, Rev. Jude	St. Joseph Picture	2006	NO	05 and up
Sweden	07	King's Thane (Edwin and Beorn)	Brady, Charles A.	Clarion Books	1961, 2009	NO	09 and up
Sweden	14	Book of Saints, Part 7 (St. Bridget)	Lovasik, Fr. Lawrence	St. Joseph Picture	1993	NO	05 and up

Country	#	Title	Author	Publisher	Year	In Print	Ages
Sweden	14	Face in the Flames (The), A Story of St. Bridget of Sweden	Flavius, Brother	In the Footsteps of the Saints	1959, 2011	NO	09-12
Switzerland	09	Book of Saints, Part 11 (St. Wiborada)	Lovasik, Fr. Lawrence	St. Joseph Picture	1997	NO	05 and up
Switzerland	09	Saint Meinrad	Windeatt, Mary Fabyan	Windeatt Coloring	1954	NO	04 and up
Switzerland	13	Apple and the Arrow, The	Buff, Mary and Conrad	Newbery	1959	NO	09 and up
Switzerland	14	Mountains Are Free	Adams, Julie Davis	Newbery	1930	YES	09 and up
Switzerland	16	Book of Saints, Part 5 (St. Peter Canisius)	Lovasik, Fr. Lawrence	St. Joseph Picture	1985	NO	05 and up
Syria	01	Lives of the Saints: The Early Church (St. Luke)	Tesoriero, Bart	Aquinas Kids	2010	NO	05-09
Syria	01 & 02	Book of Saints, Part 6 (St. Ignatius of Antioch)	Lovasik, Fr. Lawrence	St. Joseph Picture	1985	NO	05 and up
Syria	04 & 05	Saints of the Byzantine World (Simeon Stylites)	Thompson, Blanche	Vision Books	1961	YES	09-15
Syria	06	Book of Saints, Part 12 (St. Simeon Stylites the Younger)	Lovasik, Fr. Lawrence	St. Joseph Picture	1999	NO	05 and up
Tasmania	19	Thunder Maker: General Thomas Meagher	Lamers, William M.	Catholic Treasury	1959	YES	10 and up
Thailand	20	Dawn From the West: The Story of Genevieve Caulfield	Rau, Margaret	Hawthorn Junior Biography	1964	YES	11 and up
Tunisia	06	Book of Saints, Part 9 (St. Fulgentius of Ruspe)	Lovasik, Fr. Lawrence	St. Joseph Picture Books	1996	NO	05 and up
Turkey	01	Love as Strong as Death, The Story of St. Thecla	Panunzi, Rev. Paul	Encounter Books	1966	YES	09 and up
Turkey	04	Helena	Harris, Mary	Patron Saint Books	1964	YES	08 and up
Turkey	05	Saints for Boys and Girls (St. Daniel)	Beebe, Catherine	Beebe Biography	1959	YES	09-14
Turkey	16	Knights Besieged	Faulkner, Nancy	Clarion Books	1964	YES	09 and up
Turkey	19	Florence Nightingale's Nuns	Garnett, Emmeline	Vision Books	1961, 2009	NO	09-15
Uganda	19	African Triumph, The Life of Charles Lwanga	Dollen, Charles	Encounter Books	1967, 1978	YES	09 and up
Uganda	19	Uganda Martyrs	Bouin, Fr. Paul	Catholic Children's Library	1964, 2012	NO	10 and up
United States	06	Irish Saints (St. Brendan)	Reilly, Robert T.	Vision Books	1964, 1981, 2002	YES	09-15

Country	Ch.	Title	Author	Publisher	Year	In Print	Ages
United States	16	Cross in the West, The	Boesch, Mark	Vision Books	1956	YES	09-15
United States	16	Friar Among Savages, Father Luis Cancer	Kurt, Br. and Br. Atoninus	Banner Books	1958, 2011	NO	09-15
United States	16	Pedro Menendez de Aviles and the Founding of St. Augustine	Stone, Elaine Murray	American Background	1969	YES	10-15
United States	16	Sea Tiger: The Story of Pedro Menendez	Kolars, Frank	Hawthorn Junior Bio.	1963	YES	11 and up
United States	16 & 17	Wilderness Explorer: The Story of Samuel de Champlain	Wilson, Charles Morrow	Hawthorn Junior Biography	1963	YES	11 and up
United States	17	Adventurous Lady, Margaret Brent of Maryland	Grant, Dorothy Fremont	American Background	1957	YES	10-15
United States	17	Black Robe (St. Isaac Jogues)	Daughters of Charity	Catholic Stories, Volume I	1987	NO	07-10
United States	17	Blessed Kateri Tekakwitha	Windeatt, Mary Fabyan	Windeatt Coloring Books	1955	YES	04 and up
United States	17	Blessed Kateri Tekakwitha, The Lily of the Mohawks	Lovasik, Fr. Lawrence	St. Joseph Picture Books	1981, 1996	YES	05 and up
United States	17	Book of Saints, Part 1 (St. Isaac Jogues)	Lovasik, Fr. Lawrence	St. Joseph Picture Books	1981	NO	05 and up
United States	17	Book of Saints, Part 2 (Bld. Kateri Tekakwitha)	Lovasik, Fr. Lawrence	St. Joseph Picture	1981	NO	05 and up
United States	17	Cheerful Warrior, The Life of St. Charles Garnier	Dollen, Charles	Encounter Books	1967	YES	09 and up
United States	17	Colonial Governor, Thomas Dongan of New York	Hopkins, J.G.E.	American Background	1957	YES	10-15
United States	17	Cross Among the Tomahawks	Lomask, Milton	Clarion Books	1961, 2011	NO	09 and up
United States	17	Crusaders of the Great River, Marquette and Joliet	Doty, Rev. William	Banner Books	1958	YES	09-15
United States	17	Desert Padre: Eusebio Francisco Kino	Thayer, Jack	Catholic Treasury	1959	YES	10 and up
United States	17	Father Marquette and the Great Rivers	Derleth, August	Junior Vision	1962	YES	09-11
United States	17	Father Marquette and the Great Rivers	Derleth, August	Vision Books	1955, 1998	NO	09-15
United States	17	Forty-Ninth Star (The), Alaska	Savage, Alma	Banner Books	1959, 2011	NO	09-15
United States	17	Joseph the Huron	Bosco, Antoinette	American Background	1961	YES	10-15

Country	Century	Title	Author	Publisher	Year	Chapter Book	Age
United States	17	Kateri Tekakwitha, Mohawk Maid	Brown, Evelyn M.	Vision Books	1958, 1991	NO	09-15
United States	17	Kateri Tekakwitha, The Little Iroquois Girl	Richomme, Agnes	Catholic Children's Library	1965, 2012	NO	10 and up
United States	17	Lives of the Saints: Modern Saints (St. Kateri Tekakwitha)	Tesoriero, Bart	Aquinas Kids	2012	NO	05-09
United States	17	Lydia Longley, The First American Nun	McCarthy, Helen A.	Vision Books	1958	YES	09-15
United States	17	Marylanders: A Story of the Puritan Revolt in Lord Baltimore's Colony	Heagney, Anne	Catholic Treasury	1957	YES	10 and up
United States	17	Ottawanta (Our Lady of the Fields)	Daughters of Charity	Catholic Stories, Volume II	1992	NO	07-10
United States	17	Saint Isaac and the Indians	Lomask, Milton	Vision Books	1956, 1991	NO	09-15
United States	17	Saint Isaac Jogues: With Burning Heart	Orfeo, Christine & Mary E. Tebo	Encounter the Saints	2002	NO	09 and up
United States	17	Saint Kateri Tekakwitha: Courgeous Faith	Fisher, Lillian	Encounter the Saints	2012	NO	09 and up
United States	17	Saint Kateri Tekakwitha, The Lily of the Mohawks	Lovasik, Fr. Lawrence	St. Joseph Picture Books	2012	NO	05 and up
United States	17	Saints for Girls (Blessed Kateri Tekakwitha)	Muus, Solveig and Bart Tesoriero	Aquinas Kids	2012	NO	05-09
United States	17	Saints of the Americas (Kateri Tekakwitha)	Winkler, Rev. Jude	St. Joseph Picture	2006	NO	05 and up
United States	17	Saints of the Americas (St. Isaac Jogues)	Winkler, Rev. Jude	St. Joseph Picture	2006	NO	05 and up
United States	17	Star of the Mohawk, Kateri Tekakwitha	MacDonald, Francis	Banner Books	1958, 2011	NO	09-15
United States	17	Story of St. Isaac Jogues, A	Ernest, Brother	Footsteps of the Saints	1958, 2011	NO	06-09
United States	17	They Became Saints (Kateri Tekakwitha: "The Lily of the Mohawks")	Francis, Father	Father Francis Coloring	1951	NO	07 and up
United States	17 & 18	Daniel Duluth, Explorer of the Northlands	Abodaher, Daniel	American Background	1966	YES	10-15
United States	17 & 18	De Tonti of the Iron Hand and the Exploration of the Mississippi	Heagney, Anne	American Background	1959	YES	10-15
United States	17 & 18	Don Diego de Vargas	Buchanan, Rosemary	American Background	1963	YES	10-15
United States	17 & 18	Father Kino, Priest to the Pimas	Clark, Ann Nolan	Vision Books	1963	YES	09-15

United States	17 & 18	Padre Kino and the Trail to the Pacific	Steffan, Jack	American Background	1960	YES	10-15
United States	18	Bishop's Boy (John Carroll)	Anderson, Floyd	Catholic Treasury	1957	YES	10 and up
United States	18	Boy of Philadelphia: A Story about the Continental Congress	Morriss, Frank	Catholic Treasury	1955	YES	10 and up
United States	18	Cavalry Hero, Casimir Pulaski	Adams, Dorothy	American Background	1957	YES	10-15
United States	18	Desert Padre: Eusebio Francisco Kino	Thayer, Jack	Catholic Treasury	1959	YES	10 and up
United States	18	First Californian: The Story of Fray Junipero Serra	Demarest, Donald	Hawthorn Junior Biography	1963	YES	11 and up
United States	18	Forty-Ninth Star (The), Alaska	Savage, Alma	Banner Books	1959, 2011	NO	09-15
United States	18	John Carroll: Bishop and Patriot	Lomask, Milton	Vision Books	1956	YES	09-15
United States	18	Road to the King's Mountain, The (Junipero Serra)	Hubbard, Margaret Ann	Clarion Books	1963	YES	09 and up
United States	18	Saints of the Americas (Bld. Junipero Serra)	Winkler, Rev. Jude	St. Joseph Picture	2006	NO	05 and up
United States	18	Story of Captain John Barry, A	Flavius, Brother	Footsteps of the Saints	1965, 2012	NO	06-09
United States	18 & 19	Anina (daughter of St. Elizabeth Seton)	Daughters of Charity	Catholic Stories, Volume II	1992	NO	07-10
United States	18 & 19	Book of Saints, Part 1 (St. Elizabeth Ann Seton)	Lovasik, Fr. Lawrence	St. Joseph Picture	1981	NO	05 and up
United States	18 & 19	Charles Carroll and the American Revolution	Lomask, Milton	American Background	1959	YES	10-15
United States	18 & 19	Elizabeth Bayley Seton	Daughters of Charity	Catholic Stories, Volume II	1992	NO	07-10
United States	18 & 19	Fanny Allen, Green Mountain Rebel	Betz, Eva K.	American Background	1962	YES	10-15
United States	18 & 19	Father of the American Navy, Captain John Barry	Anderson, Floyd	Banner Books	1959, 2011	NO	09-15
United States	18 & 19	Frontier Priest and Congressman, Father Gabriel Richard	Alois, Brother	Banner Books	1958	YES	09-15
United States	18 & 19	God and the General's Daughter	Heagney, Anne	Similar to Catholic Treasury	1953	YES	10 and up
United States	18 & 19	Lives of the Saints: Modern Saints (St. Elizabeth Ann Seton)	Tesoriero, Bart	Aquinas Kids	2012	NO	05-09

Saint Series Books by Geographical Setting

United States	18 & 19	Mathew Carey, Pamphleter for Freedom	Hindman, Jane F.	American Background	1960	YES	10-15
United States	18 & 19	Mother Seton and the Sisters of Charity	Power-Waters, Alma	Junior Vision	1963	YES	09-11
United States	18 & 19	Mother Seton and the Sisters of Charity	Power-Waters, Alma	Vision Books	1957, 2000	NO	09-15
United States	18 & 19	Mother Seton: Wife, Mother, Educator, Foundress, Saint	Daughters of St. Paul	Similar to Encounter Books	1975	YES	09 and up
United States	18 & 19	Pierre Toussaint, Pioneer in Brotherhood	Sheehan, Arthur and Elizabeth	American Background	1963	YES	10-15
United States	18 & 19	Priest, Patriot and Leader, The Story of Archbishop Carroll	Betz, Eva K.	Banner Books	1960, 2011	NO	09-15
United States	18 & 19	Rochambeau and Our French Allies	Lomask, Milton	American Background	1965	YES	10-15
United States	18 & 19	Saint Elizabeth Ann Seton	Lovasik, Fr. Lawrence	St. Joseph Picture	1981, 1990	NO	05 and up
United States	18 & 19	Saint Elizabeth Ann Seton: Daughter of America	Grunwell, Jeanne Marie and Mari Goering	Encounter the Saints	1999	NO	09 and up
United States	18 & 19	Saints for Girls (St. Elizabeth Ann Seton)	Muus, Solveig and Bart Tesoriero	Aquinas Kids	2012	NO	05-09
United States	18 & 19	Saints of the Americas (St. Elizabeth Ann Seton)	Winkler, Rev. Jude	St. Joseph Picture Books	2006	NO	05 and up
United States	18 & 19	Simon Bruté and the Western Adventure	Bartelme, Elizabeth	American Background	1959, 2012	NO	10-15
United States	18 & 19	Story of Mother Elizabeth Seton, A	Ryan, Brother Ernest	Dujarie Press Reprint	1960, 2008	NO	06-09
United States	18 & 19	Under Three Flags: The Story of Gabriel Richard	Abodaher, David J.	Hawthorn Junior Bio.	1965	YES	11 and up
United States	18 & 19	Virgil Barber, New England Pied Piper	Betz, Eva K.	American Background	1963	YES	10-15
United States	18 & 19	William Gaston, Fighter for Justice	Betz, Eva K.	American Background	1964	YES	10-15
United States	18-20	Ursulines, Nuns of Adventure: The Story of the New Orleans Community	Kane, Harnett T.	Vision Books	1959	YES	09-15
United States	19	Adventures of Broken Hand	Morriss, Frank	Catholic Treasury	1957	YES	10 and up
United States	19	Apostle of Ice and Snow: A Life of Bishop Charles Seghers	Betz, Eva	Holy Cross Press	1964	YES	09 and up

Country	Century	Title	Author	Publisher	Year	In Print	Ages
United States	19	Armorer of the Confederacy, Secretary Mallory	Durkin, Rev. Joseph T.	Banner Books	1960	YES	09-15
United States	19	Black Robe Peacemaker, Pierre de Smet	Hopkins, J.G.E.	American Background	1958	YES	10-15
United States	19	Book of Saints, Part 6 (St. John Neumann)	Lovasik, Fr. Lawrence	St. Joseph Picture Books	1985	NO	05 and up
United States	19	Chaplain in Gray, Abram Ryan	Heagney, H.J.	American Background	1958	YES	10-15
United States	19	Charity Goes to War (Civil War and the Sisters of Charity)	Heagney, Anne	Catholic Treasury	1961	YES	10 and up
United States	19	Charles John Seghers, Pioneer in Alaska	Bosco, Antoinette	American Background	1960	YES	10-15
United States	19	Courageous Catherine: Mother Mary Catherine McAuley, The First Sister of Mercy	Marie, Sister Raymond	Catholic Treasury	1958	YES	10 and up
United States	19	Dawn From the West: The Story of Genevieve Caulfield	Rau, Margaret	Hawthorn Junior Biography	1964	YES	11 and up
United States	19	Dear Philippine: The Mission of Mother Duchesne	Hubbard, Margaret Ann	Vision Books	1964	YES	09-15
United States	19	First Sioux Nun, Sister Marie-Josephine Nebraska (1859-1894)	Hilger, Sister Mary Ione	Similar to Catholic Treasury	1963	YES	10 and up
United States	19	Fold It Gently, A Story of Fr. Abram Ryan	Donahoe, Br. Bernard	Footsteps of the Saints	1960, 2010	NO	09-12
United States	19	Forked Lightning: The Story of Philip H. Sheridan	Orbaan, Albert	Hawthorn Junior Biography	1964	YES	11 and up
United States	19	Forty-Ninth Star (The), Alaska	Savage, Alma	Banner Books	1959, 2011	NO	09-15
United States	19	Frances Warde and the First Sisters of Mercy	Christopher, Sister Marie	Vision Books	1960	YES	09-15
United States	19	Frontier Bishop: Simon Gabriel Bruté	Hughes, Riley	Catholic Treasury	1959, 2012	NO	10 and up
United States	19	General Phil Sheridan and the Union Cavalry	Lomask, Milton	American Background	1959	YES	10-15
United States	19	Giant of the Western Trail, Father Peter de Smet	McHugh, Rev. Michael	Banner Books	1958, 2003, 2011	NO	09-15
United States	19	Gold Rush Bishop (Patrick Manogue)	Anderson, Floyd	Catholic Treasury	1962, 2012	NO	10 and up
United States	19	Great Black Robe, The (Father Peter de Smet)	Pitrone, Jean Maddern	Similar to Encounter Books	1964, 1965, 1981	YES	09 and up

United States	19	Hand Raised at Gettysburg (Irish Brigade)	Johnson, Grace and Harold	Catholic Treasury	1955, 2012	NO	10 and up
United States	19	Hands of Mercy, The Story of Sister-Nurses in the Civil War	Smaridge, Norah	Banner Books	1960, 2011	NO	09-15
United States	19	I Lay Down My Life, Biography of Joyce Kilmer	Cargas, Harry	Similar to Encounter Books	1964	YES	09 and up
United States	19	Irish Saints (Bishop Edward J. Galvin)	Reilly, Robert T.	Vision Books	1964, 1981, 2002	YES	09-15
United States	19	Irish Saints (Father Theobald Mathew)	Reilly, Robert T.	Vision Books	1964, 2002	YES	09-15
United States	19	John Hughes, Eagle of the Church	Hurley, Doran	American Background	1961	YES	10-15
United States	19	John Neumann, The Children's Bishop	Sheehan, Elizabeth	Vision Books	1965	YES	09-15
United States	19	Kat Finds a Friend, A St. Elizabeth Ann Seton Story	Stromberg, Joan	Glory of America series	1999	NO	07-12
United States	19	Kit Carson of the Old West	Boesch, Mark	Vision Books	1959	YES	09-15
United States	19	Lady and the Pirate, The (Battle of New Orleans in 1814)	Riordan, Robert	Similar to Catholic Treasury	1957	YES	10 and up
United States	19	Light in the Early West, Berenice Chouteau	Schlafy, Rev. James	Banner Books	1959, 2011	NO	09-15
United States	19	Lives of the Saints: Modern Saints (St. John Neumann)	Tesoriero, Bart	Aquinas Kids	2012	NO	05-09
United States	19	Margaret Haughery, Bread Woman of New Orleans	Strousse, Flora	American Background	1961	YES	10-15
United States	19	Massacre At Ash Hollow	Reilly, Robert T.	Catholic Treasury	1960	YES	10 and up
United States	19	Medicine for Wildcat: A Life Story about Samuel Charles Mazzuchelli	Riordan, Robert	Catholic Treasury	1956	YES	10 and up
United States	19	Orphans Find a Home (The), A St. Frances Xavier Cabrini Story	Stromberg, Joan	Glory of America series	1998	NO	07-12
United States	19	Prairie Venture (Colorado homesteading)	Jacks, Leo Vincent	Similar to Catholic Treasury	1959	YES	10 and up
United States	19	Quiet Flame: Mother Marianne of Molokai	Betz, Eva K.	Catholic Treasury	1963	YES	10 and up
United States	19	Raphael Semmes, Confederate Admiral	Daly, Robert W.	American Background	1965	YES	10-15

Country	Century	Title	Author	Publisher	Year	Illustrated	Ages
United States	19	Rebels in the Shadows	Reilly, Robert T.	similiar to Catholic Treasury	1962, 1979	NO	10 and up
United States	19	Rose Greenhow, Confederate Secret Agent	Grant, Dorothy Fremont	American Background	1961	YES	10-15
United States	19	Saints of the Americas (St. John Neumann)	Winkler, Rev. Jude	St. Joseph Picture	2006	NO	05 and up
United States	19	Sarah Peter: The Dream and the Harvest	Power-Waters, Alma	Vision Books	1965	YES	09-15
United States	19	Servant to the Slaves: The Story of Henriette Delille	Collins, David R.	Weaver Books	2000	YES	09-12
United States	19	Spaldings of Old Kentucky, The	Heagney, Anne	Similar to Catholic Treasury	1964	YES	10 and up
United States	19	Story of Venerable Mother Catherine McAuley	Ernest, Brother	In the Footsteps of the Saints	1959, 2011	NO	06-09
United States	19	Stout Hearts and Gentle Hands: The Life of Mother Angela of the Sisters of the Holy Cross	Betz, Eva	Holy Cross Press	1964	YES	09 and up
United States	19	Thomas Finds a Treasure, A St. John Neumann Story	Stromberg, Joan	Glory of America series	2001	NO	07-12
United States	19	Thunder Maker: General Thomas Meagher	Lamers, William M.	Catholic Treasury	1959	YES	10 and up
United States	19	Turquoise Rosary	Jacks, Leo Vincent	Catholic Treasury	1960	YES	10 and up
United States	19	Web Begun, The (Civil War)	Betz, Eva K.	Similar to Catholic Treasury	1961	YES	10 and up
United States	19	Willy Finds Victory, A Blessed Francis Seelos Story	Stromberg, Joan	Glory of America series	2004	NO	07-12
United States	19	Wires West (telegraph)	Jacks, Leo Vincent	Catholic Treasury	1957	YES	10 and up
United States	19 & 20	Amazing John Tabb (Civil War)	Betz, Eva K.	Catholic Treasury	1958	YES	10 and up
United States	19 & 20	Book of Saints, Part 3 (St. Frances Cabrini)	Lovasik, Fr. Lawrence	St. Joseph Picture	1982	NO	05 and up
United States	19 & 20	Brother Dutton of Molokai	Crouch, Howard E.	Catholic Treasury	1958	YES	10 and up
United States	19 & 20	Catholic Campuses, Stories of American Catholic Colleges	Staudacher, Rosemarian	Vision Books	1958	YES	09-15
United States	19 & 20	Door of Hope: The Story of Katharine Drexel	Burton, Katherine	Hawthorn Junior Biography	1963	YES	11 and up

Saint Series Books by Geographical Setting

United States	19 & 20	Fighting Father Duffy	Bishop, Jim and Virginia	Vision Books	1956	YES	09-15
United States	19 & 20	Fighting Irishman: The Story of "Wild Bill" Donovan"	Wilhelm, Maria	Hawthorn Junior Biography	1964	YES	11 and up
United States	19 & 20	Governor Al Smith	Farley, James and James Conniff	Vision Books	1959	YES	09-15
United States	19 & 20	John LaFarge, Gentle Jesuit	Strousse, Flora	American Background	1968	YES	10-15
United States	19 & 20	Katharine Drexel, Friend of the Neglected	Tarry, Ellen	Vision Books	1958, 2000	NO	09-15
United States	19 & 20	Katie, The Young Life of Mother Katharine Drexel	Mohan, Claire Jordan	Mohan Biographies	2000	NO	09-12
United States	19 & 20	Kaze's True Home, The Young Life of a Modern Day Saint, Mother Maria Kaupas	Mohan, Claire Jordan	Mohan Biographies	1992	YES	09-12
United States	19 & 20	Knute Rockne, Football Wizard of Notre Dame	Daley, Arthur	American Background	1960	YES	10-15
United States	19 & 20	Long Trail (The), The Story of Buffalo Bill	Kolars, Frank	Banner Books	1960, 2011	NO	09-15
United States	19 & 20	Magnificent Failure: The Story of Fr. Solanus Casey	Collins, David R.	Weaver Books	1999	YES	09-12
United States	19 & 20	Mother Alfred and the Doctors Mayo	Richardson, James P.	Banner Books	1959	YES	09-15
United States	19 & 20	Mother Cabrini, Missionary to the World	Keyes, Frances	Vision Books	1959, 1997	NO	09-15
United States	19 & 20	Pen and Bayonet: The Story of Joyce Kilmer	Smaridge, Norah	Hawthorn Junior Bio.	1962	YES	11 and up
United States	19 & 20	Rose Hawthorne: The Pilgrimage of Nathaniel's Daughter	Sheehan, Arthur & Elizabeth	Vision Books	1959	YES	09-15
United States	19 & 20	Saint Frances Cabrini	Windeatt, Mary Fabyan	Windeatt Coloring	1956	NO	04 and up
United States	19 & 20	Saint Frances Xavier Cabrini: Cecchina's Dream	Dority, Victoria and Mary Andes	Encounter the Saints	2005	YES	09 and up
United States	19 & 20	Saint Katharine Drexel: The Total Gift	Wallace, Susan Helen	Encounter the Saints	2003	NO	09 and up
United States	19 & 20	Saints for Boys and Girls (St. Frances Xavier Cabrini)	Beebe, Catherine	Beebe Biography	1959	YES	09-14
United States	19 & 20	Saints for Girls (St. Frances Cabrini)	Muus, Solveig and Bart Tesoriero	Aquinas Kids	2012	NO	05-09
United States	19 & 20	Saints of the Americas (St. Frances Cabrini)	Winkler, Rev. Jude	St. Joseph Picture	2006	NO	05 and up
United States	19 & 20	Saints of the Americas (St. Katharine Drexel)	Winkler, Rev. Jude	St. Joseph Picture	2006	NO	05 and up

United States	19 & 20	Sidewalk Statesman, Alfred E. Smith	Schofield, William G.	American Background	1958	YES	10-15
United States	19 & 20	Search for a Shepherd (A), A Story of Fr. Paul of Graymoor	Roberto, Brother	In the Footsteps of the Saints	1959, 2011	NO	09-12
United States	19 & 20	Submarine Pioneer: John Philip Holland	Morriss, Frank	Catholic Treasury	1961, 2012	NO	10 and up
United States	19 & 20	To the Ends of the Earth, A Story of St. Frances Xavier Cabrini	Greene, Brother Genard	In the Footsteps of the Saints	1955, 2009	NO	09-12
United States	20	Beyond the Clouds: The Story of Christa McAuliffe	Collins, David R.	Weaver Books	1996	YES	09-12
United States	20	Champions in Sports and Spirit (Gil Hodges, Rocky Marciano, Maureen Connolly, Maurice Richard, Bob Cousy, Terry Brennan, and Yogi Berra)	Fitzgerald, Ed	Vision Books	1956	YES	09-15
United States	20	Doctor America: The Story of Tom Dooley	Morris, Terry	Hawthorn Junior Bio.	1963	YES	11 and up
United States	20	Father Flanagan, Builder of Boys	Stevens, Clifford J.	American Background Books	1967	YES	10-15
United States	20	Forty-Ninth Star (The), Alaska	Savage, Alma	Banner Books	1959, 2011	NO	09-15
United States	20	Got a Penny? The Story of Dorothy Day	Collins, David R.	Weaver Books	1996	YES	09-12
United States	20	I Charge Each of You: The Story of Dr. Tom Dooley	O'Brien, Sr. Mary Celine	Holy Cross Press	1966	YES	09 and up
United States	20	I Lay Down My Life, Biography of Joyce Kilmer	Cargas, Harry	Similar to Encounter Books	1964	YES	09 and up
United States	20	In American Vineyards: Religious Orders in the United States	Staudacher, Rosemarian	Vision Books	1966	YES	09-15
United States	20	John Fitzgerald Kennedy, Man of Courage	Strousse, Flora	American Background Books	1964	YES	10-15
United States	20	Juanita	Politi, Leo	Caldecott	1948	NO	04 and up
United States	20	Lion of Poland: The Story of Paderewski	Hume, Ruth and Paul	Hawthorn Junior Bio.	1962, 2012	NO	11 and up
United States	20	Lucrezia Bori of the Metropolitan Opera	Marion, John Francis	American Background	1962	YES	10-15
United States	20	More Champions in Sports and Spirit (Stan Musial, Carmen Basilio, Alex Olmedo, Juan Manuel Fangio, Ron	Fitzgerald, Ed	Vision Books	1959	YES	09-15

		Delany, Eddie Arcaro, Jean Beliveau, and Herb Score)					
United States	20	My Eskimos: A Priest in the Arctic	Buliard, Roger P.	Vision Books	1956	YES	09-15
United States	20	Pedro, The Angel of Olvera Street	Politi, Leo	Caldecott	1946	NO	04 and up
United States	20	Prisoner of Lost Island (Catholic fiction)	Kolars, Frank	Similar to Catholic Treasury	1961	YES	10 and up
United States	20	Song of the Swallows	Politi, Leo	Caldecott	1949	NO	04 and up
United States	20	Tall American: The Story of Gary Cooper	Gehman, Richard	Hawthorn Junior Bio.	1963	YES	11 and up
United States	20	To Far Places: The Story of Francis X. Ford	Betz, Eva K.	Hawthorn Junior Bio.	1962	YES	11 and up
United States	20	You're Never Alone: The Story of Thomas Merton	Collins, David R.	Weaver Books	1996	YES	09-12
United States	20	King of Song: The Story of John McCormack	Hume, Ruth and Paul	Hawthorn Junior Bio.	1964	YES	11 and up
various	19 & 20	Journeys with Mary: Apparitions of Our Lady	de Santis, Zerlina	Encounter the Saints	2001, 2002	NO	09 and up
various	20	King of Song: The Story of John McCormack	Hume, Ruth and Paul	Hawthorn Junior Bio.	1964	YES	11 and up
Vietnam	20	Doctor America: The Story of Tom Dooley	Morris, Terry	Hawthorn Junior Bio.	1963	YES	11 and up
Vietnam	20	I Charge Each of You: The Story of Dr. Tom Dooley	O'Brien, Sr. Mary Celine	Holy Cross Press	1966	YES	09 and up
Wales	06	David	Betz, Eva K.	Patron Saint Books	1960	YES	08 and up
Wales	07	Book of Saints, Part 12 (St. Winifred)	Lovasik, Fr. Lawrence	St. Joseph Picture	1999	NO	05 and up
western Europe	14 & 15	Lives of the Saints: The Middle Ages (St. Vincent Ferrer)	Tesoriero, Bart	Aquinas Kids	2010	NO	05-09
western Europe	14 & 15	Truth Was Their Star (St. Vincent Ferrer)	Dorcy, Sister Mary Jean	Dorcy Biography	1947, 1999	NO	10 and up
world	16	Book of Saints, Part 3 (St. Francis Xavier)	Lovasik, Fr. Lawrence	St. Joseph Picture	1982	NO	05 and up
world	16	Flame in the Night, The Life of St. Francis Xavier	Daughters of St. Paul	Encounter Books	1967, 1981	YES	09 and up
world	16	Saint Francis Xavier	Marchand, Fr. Norbert	Catholic Children's Library	1965, 2012	NO	10 and up
world	16	Saint Francis of the Seven Seas	Nevins, Albert J.	Junior Vision	1963	YES	09-11
world	16	Saint Francis of the Seven Seas	Nevins, Albert J.	Vision Books	1955, 1995	NO	09-15

world	16	Set All Afire, A Novel of Saint Francis Xavier	de Wohl, Louis	de Wohl Biography	1951, 1991	NO	15 and up
world	16	Ship's Boy with Magellan	Lomask, Milton	Clarion Books	1960, 2010	NO	09 and up
world	20	Trailblazer for the Sacred Heart, Fr. Mateo Crawley-Boevey (Globe-Trotter for the Sacred Heart)	Balskus, Pat	Encounter Books	1976	YES	09 and up
Yugoslavia	20	Mother Teresa's Someday, The Young Life of Mother Teresa of Calcutta	Mohan, Claire Jordan	Mohan Biographies	1990	NO	09-12
Yugoslavia	20	Young Life of Mother Teresa of Calcutta, The	Mohan, Claire Jordan	Mohan Biographies	1997	YES	09-12

Saint Series Books in Chronological Order

The following pages list the saint series books in chronological order (by century). The "OOP" column indicates whether the book is currently out of print—as of April 2013.

Cen.	Country	Book Title	Author	Series	Year	OOP	Ages
B.C.	Assyria	Jonah, The Whale and the Vine	Arnsteen, Katy Keck	Kid Scripts	1997	NO	04-08
B.C.	Egypt	Joseph and the Dreams	Arnsteen, Katy Keck	Kid Scripts	1997	NO	04-08
B.C.	Egypt	Moses	Arnsteen, Katy Keck	Kid Scripts	1997	NO	04-08
B.C.	Egypt	Story of Joseph and His Brothers, The	Winkler, Rev. Jude	St. Joseph Bible Story Books	1988, 1994	YES	05-09
B.C.	Egypt	Story of Moses, The	Winkler, Rev. Jude	St. Joseph Bible Story	1988, 1994	YES	05-09
B.C	Holy Land	David, King of Israel	Schmid, Brother Evan	Footsteps of the Saints	1966, 2011	NO	09-12
B.C.	Holy Land	David and Goliath	de Paola, Tomie	de Paola Biography	1984	YES	04-08
B.C.	Holy Land	David of Jerusalem	de Wohl, Louis	de Wohl Biography	1963	YES	15 and up
B.C.	Holy Land	David, The Shepherd King	Beebe, Catherine	Beebe Biography	1966	YES	10 and up
B.C.	Holy Land	David, The Shepherd King	Beebe, Catherine	Holy Cross Press	1966	YES	09 and up
B.C.	Holy Land	King David and His Songs, A Story of the Psalms	Windeatt, Mary Fabyan	Windeatt Saint Series	1993	NO	09 and up
B.C.	Israel	Anne (grandmother of Jesus)	Richardson, M.K.	Patron Saint Books	1960	YES	08 and up
B.C.	Israel	Book of Saints, Part 1 (St. Anne)	Lovasik, Fr. Lawrence	St. Joseph Picture	1981	NO	05 and up
B.C.	Israel	Book of Saints, Part 4 (St. Joachim)	Lovasik, Fr. Lawrence	St. Joseph Picture	1982	YES	05 and up
B.C.	Israel	Lives of the Saints: The Early Church (Blessed Virgin Mary)	Tesoriero, Bart	Aquinas Kids	2010	NO	05-09
B.C.	Israel	Lives of the Saints: The Early Church (St. Anne)	Tesoriero, Bart	Aquinas Kids	2010	NO	05-09
B.C.	Israel	Lives of the Saints: The Early Church (St. Joseph)	Tesoriero, Bart	Aquinas Kids	2010	NO	05-09
B.C.	Israel	Mary (mother of Jesus)	Dorcy, Sister Mary Jean	Patron Saint Books	1958	YES	08 and up
B.C.	Israel	Saints for Boys (St. Joseph)	Muus, Solveig and Bart Tesoriero	Aquinas Kids	2012	NO	05-09

159

B.C.	Israel	Saints for Boys and Girls (St. Anne)	Beebe, Catherine	Beebe Biography	1959	YES	09-14
B.C.	Israel	Saints for Boys and Girls (St. Jude)	Beebe, Catherine	Beebe Biography	1959	YES	09-14
B.C.	Israel	Saints for Girls (St. Anne)	Muus, Solveig and Bart Tesoriero	Aquinas Kids	2012	NO	05-09
B.C.	Israel	Story of Mary, The Mother of Jesus	Beebe, Catherine	Beebe Biography	1950	YES	09-14
B.C.	Israel	Story of the Three Wise Kings (Epiphany)	de Paola, Tomie	de Paola Biography	1983	YES	04-08
B.C.	Middle East	Abraham and Isaac	Arnsteen, Katy Keck	Kid Scripts	1997	NO	04-08
B.C.	Middle East	Deborah	Arnsteen, Katy Keck	Kid Scripts	1997	NO	04-08
B.C.	Middle East	Great Men of the Bible: Old Testament (Adam, Cain, Abel, Noah, Abraham, Joseph, Moses, Samuel, David, Solomon, Elijah, Isaiah, Jeremiah, Job, Jonah, Judas Maccabee)	Winkler, Father Jude	St. Joseph Picture Books	1987	NO	05 and up
B.C.	Middle East	Great Women of the Bible (Eve, Rebekah, Rachel and Leah, Sarah, Rahab, Deborah, Ruth, Hannah, Michal, Abigail, Bathsheba, Jezebel, Judith, and Esther)	Winkler, Father Jude	St. Joseph Picture Books	1986, 1990	NO	05 and up
B.C.	Middle East	Joseph and the Dreams	Arnsteen, Katy Keck	Kid Scripts	1997	NO	04-08
B.C.	Middle East	Joshua, God's General	Arnsteen, Katy Keck	Kid Scripts	1997	NO	04-08
B.C.	Middle East	Naomi and Ruth	Arnsteen, Katy Keck	Kid Scripts	1997	NO	04-08
B.C.	Middle East	Noah and the Ark	de Paola, Tomie	de Paola Biography	1983	YES	04-08
B.C.	Middle East	Noah's Ark	Pinkney, Jerry	Caldecott	2002	NO	04 and up
B.C.	Middle East	Noah's Ark	Spier, Peter	Caldecott	1977	NO	04 and up
B.C.	Middle East	Story of Abraham, The	Winkler, Rev. Jude	St. Joseph Bible Story Books	1988, 1994	YES	05-09
B.C.	Middle East	Story of Isaac and Jacob, The	Winkler, Rev. Jude	St. Joseph Bible Story	1988, 1994	YES	05-09
B.C.	Middle East	Story of Joseph and His Brothers, The	Winkler, Rev. Jude	St. Joseph Bible Story	1988, 1994	YES	05-09

Saint Series Books in Chronological Order

B.C.	Middle East	Story of Joshua, The	Winkler, Rev. Jude	St. Joseph Bible Story	1988, 1994	NO	05-09
B.C.	Middle East	Story of Noah and the Flood, The	Winkler, Rev. Jude	St. Joseph Bible Story	1989, 2004	NO	05-09
B.C.	Middle East	Story of Ruth, The	Winkler, Rev. Jude	St. Joseph Bible Story	1988	YES	05-09
B.C.	Persia	Queen Esther	Arnsteen, Katy Keck	Kid Scripts	1997	NO	04-08
B.C.	Persia	Queen Esther	de Paola, Tomie	de Paola Biography	1986	YES	04-08
B.C.	Sinai	Moses	Arnsteen, Katy Keck	Kid Scripts	1997	NO	04-08
B.C.	Sinai	Story of Moses, The	Winkler, Rev. Jude	St. Joseph Bible Story	1988, 1994	YES	05-09
B.C.-01 A.D.	Middle East	Bible Story (The), The Promised Lord and His Coming	Beebe, Catherine	Vision Books	1957	YES	09-15
01	Arabia	Book of Saints, Part 11 (St. Bartholomew or Nathaniel)	Lovasik, Fr. Lawrence	St. Joseph Picture	1997	NO	05 and up
01	Armenia	Saints for Boys (St. Jude Thaddeus)	Muus, Solveig and Bart Tesoriero	Aquinas Kids	2012	NO	05-09
01	Ethiopia	Book of Saints, Part 8 (St. Matthias)	Lovasik, Fr. Lawrence	St. Joseph Picture	1993	NO	05 and up
01	Europe	Book of Saints, Part 8 (St. Simon)	Lovasik, Fr. Lawrence	St. Joseph Picture	1993	NO	05 and up
01	Greece	Eagle of God: A Life of St. John the Evangelist	Premont, Br. Jeremy	Holy Cross Press	1964	YES	09 and up
01	Greece	Lives of the Saints: The Early Church (St. Luke)	Tesoriero, Bart	Aquinas Kids	2010	NO	05-09
01	Greece	Saints for Boys and Girls (St. Dennis or Dionysius)	Beebe, Catherine	Beebe Biography	1959	YES	09-14
01	Holy Land	Eagle of God: A Life of St. John the Evangelist	Premont, Br. Jeremy	Holy Cross Press	1964	YES	09 and up
01	India	Book of Saints, Part 8 (St. Bartholomew or Nathaniel)	Lovasik, Fr. Lawrence	St. Joseph Picture	1993	NO	05 and up
01	Israel	Ageless Story	Ford, Lauren	Caldecott	1939	YES	04 and up
01	Israel	Apostles of the Lord, The	Beebe, Catherine	Beebe Biography	1958	YES	08-14
01	Israel	Baboushka and the Three Kings	Robbins, Ruth	Caldecott	1960	NO	04 and up
01	Israel	Book of Saints, Part 1 (St. Stephen)	Lovasik, Fr. Lawrence	St. Joseph Picture	1981	NO	05 and up
01	Israel	Book of Saints, Part 3 (Our Lady, Queen)	Lovasik, Fr. Lawrence	St. Joseph Picture	1982	NO	05 and up

01	Israel	Book of Saints, Part 3 (St. John the Baptist)	Lovasik, Fr. Lawrence	St. Joseph Picture	1982	NO	05 and up
01	Israel	Book of Saints, Part 8 (St. Bartholomew or Nathaniel)	Lovasik, Fr. Lawrence	St. Joseph Picture	1993	NO	05 and up
01	Israel	Book of Saints, Part 8 (St. James the Greater)	Lovasik, Fr. Lawrence	St. Joseph Picture	1993	NO	05 and up
01	Israel	Book of Saints, Part 8 (St. Joseph)	Lovasik, Fr. Lawrence	St. Joseph Picture	1993	NO	05 and up
01	Israel	Book of Saints, Part 8 (St. Jude Thaddeus)	Lovasik, Fr. Lawrence	St. Joseph Picture	1993	NO	05 and up
01	Israel	Book of Saints, Part 8 (St. Matthew)	Lovasik, Fr. Lawrence	St. Joseph Picture	1993	NO	05 and up
01	Israel	Book of Saints, Part 8 (St. Matthias)	Lovasik, Fr. Lawrence	St. Joseph Picture	1993	NO	05 and up
01	Israel	Book of Saints, Part 8 (St. Peter)	Lovasik, Fr. Lawrence	St. Joseph Picture	1993	NO	05 and up
01	Israel	Book of Saints, Part 8 (St. Thomas)	Lovasik, Fr. Lawrence	St. Joseph Picture	1993	NO	05 and up
01	Israel	Came the Dawn, Mary of Nazareth, God's Mother and Ours	Daughters of St. Paul	Encounter Books	1982	YES	09 and up
01	Israel	Fisher Prince: The Life of St. Peter, Apostle	Daughters of St. Paul	Encounter Books	1966, 1984	YES	09 and up
01	Israel	Good Saint Joseph	Lovasik, Fr. Lawrence	St. Joseph Picture	1978	NO	05 and up
01	Israel	Great Hero (The), St. Paul the Apostle	Daughters of St. Paul	Encounter Books	1963	YES	09 and up
01	Israel	Great Men of the Bible: New Testament (Joseph, John the Baptist, Jesus, Peter, John, James the Greater, James the Lesser, Matthew, Jude, Judas, Stephen, Paul, Philip, Mark, and Luke)	Winkler, Father Jude	St. Joseph Picture	1987	NO	05 and up
01	Israel	Great Women of the Bible (Mary, Martha and Mary, and Mary Magdalene)	Winkler, Father Jude	St. Joseph Picture Books	1986, 1990	NO	05 and up
01	Israel	Holy Family, The	Winkler, Father Jude	St. Joseph Picture	2005	NO	05 and up
01	Israel	Jesus Our Savior: The Life of Jesus for the Very Young (Book 1, His Early Life)	Francis, Father	Father Francis Coloring Books	1954	NO	06 and up
01	Israel	Jesus Our Savior: The Life of Jesus for the Very Young (Book 2, His Public Life)	Francis, Father	Father Francis Coloring Books	1954	NO	06 and up

01	Israel	Joseph	Sheed, Wilfrid	Patron Saint Books	1958	YES	08 and up
01	Israel	Joseph (St. Joseph)	Daughters of Charity	Catholic Stories, Volume III	1995	NO	07-10
01	Israel	Last Apostle, The (St. Paul)	Eleanor, Mother Mary	Catholic Treasury	1956	YES	10 and up
01	Israel	Lives of the Saints: The Early Church (St. John the Apostle)	Tesoriero, Bart	Aquinas Kids	2010	NO	05-09
01	Israel	Lives of the Saints: The Early Church (St. Martha)	Tesoriero, Bart	Aquinas Kids	2010	NO	05-09
01	Israel	Lives of the Saints: The Early Church (St. Matthew)	Tesoriero, Bart	Aquinas Kids	2010	NO	05-09
01	Israel	Lives of the Saints: The Early Church (St. Peter)	Tesoriero, Bart	Aquinas Kids	2010	NO	05-09
01	Israel	Lives of the Saints: The Early Church (St. Veronica)	Tesoriero, Bart	Aquinas Kids	2010	NO	05-09
01	Israel	Mary, Full of Grace	Francis, Father	Fr. Francis Coloring	1954, 1997	NO	06 and up
01	Israel	Mary, Mother of Jesus	de Paola, Tomie	de Paola Biography	1995	YES	04-08
01	Israel	Mary, My Mother	Lovasik, Fr. Lawrence	St. Joseph Picture	1978	NO	05 and up
01	Israel	Mary, My Mother: A Mary-book for Little Boys and Girls	Dorcy, Sister Mary Jean	Dorcy Biography	1944	YES	05-09
01	Israel	Miracles of Jesus	de Paola, Tomie	de Paola Biography	1987, 1996, 2008	NO	04-08
01	Israel	Our Mother Mary	Francis, Father	Fr. Francis Coloring	1959	NO	04 and up
01	Israel	Parables of Jesus	de Paola, Tomie	de Paola Biography	1987, 1995	YES	04-08
01	Israel	St. Paul: The Thirteenth Apostle	Wallace, Susan Helen	Encounter the Saints	2007	NO	09 and up
01	Israel	Saint Peter the Apostle	Lovasik, Fr. Lawrence	St. Joseph Picture	1980, 1987	NO	05 and up
01	Israel	Saints for Boys (St. John the Baptist)	Muus, Solveig and Bart Tesoriero	Aquinas Kids	2012	NO	05-09
01	Israel	Saints for Boys (St. Jude Thaddeua)	Muus, Solveig and Bart Tesoriero	Aquinas Kids	2012	NO	05-09
01	Israel	Saints for Boys (St. Peter)	Muus, Solveig and Bart Tesoriero	Aquinas Kids	2012	NO	05-09

01	Israel	Saints for Boys and Girls (Mary the Virgin Mother of Our Lord)	Beebe, Catherine	Beebe Biography	1959	YES	09-14
01	Israel	Saints for Boys and Girls (St. Joseph)	Beebe, Catherine	Beebe Biography	1959	YES	09-14
01	Israel	Saints for Girls (Blessed Virgin Mary)	Muus, Solveig and Bart Tesoriero	Aquinas Kids	2012	NO	05-09
01	Israel	Spear (The), A Novel of the Crucifixion	de Wohl, Louis	de Wohl Biography	1955, 1998	NO	15 and up
01	Israel	Story of Jesus for Boys and Girls, The	Beebe, Catherine	Beebe Biography	1945	YES	09-14
01	Israel	Story of Jesus, The	Lovasik, Fr. Lawrence	St. Joseph Picture Books	1999	NO	05 and up
01	Israel	Story of Mary, The Mother of Jesus	Beebe, Catherine	Beebe Biography	1950	YES	09-14
01	Israel	Story of St. Joseph, A	Ernest, Brother	Footsteps of the Saints	1957, 2011	NO	06-09
01	Israel	Story of St. Peter, A	Ernest, Brother	Footsteps of the Saints	1961, 2011	NO	06-09
01	Israel	Story of St. Stephen, A	Ernest, Brother	Footsteps of the Saints	1962, 2008	NO	06-09
01	Israel	Story of the Birth of Jesus, The	Winkler, Rev. Jude	St. Joseph Bible Story	1989	NO	05-09
01	Italy	Lives of the Saints: The Early Church (St. Peter)	Tesoriero, Bart	Aquinas Kids	2010	NO	05-09
01	Italy	Saint Peter the Apostle	Lovasik, Fr. Lawrence	St. Joseph Picture Books	1980, 1987	NO	05 and up
01	Middle East	Book of Saints, Part 8 (St. Andrew)	Lovasik, Fr. Lawrence	St. Joseph Picture	1993	NO	05 and up
01	Middle East	Book of Saints, Part 8 (St. John)	Lovasik, Fr. Lawrence	St. Joseph Picture	1993	NO	05 and up
01	Middle East	Book of Saints, Part 8 (St. Luke)	Lovasik, Fr. Lawrence	St. Joseph Picture	1993	NO	05 and up
01	Middle East	Book of Saints, Part 8 (St. Mark)	Lovasik, Fr. Lawrence	St. Joseph Picture	1993	NO	05 and up
01	Middle East	Book of Saints, Part 8 (St. Paul)	Lovasik, Fr. Lawrence	St. Joseph Picture	1993	NO	05 and up
01	Middle East	Book of Saints, Part 8 (St. Simon)	Lovasik, Fr. Lawrence	St. Joseph Picture	1993	NO	05 and up
01	Middle East	Book of Saints, Part 8 (Sts. Philip and James)	Lovasik, Fr. Lawrence	St. Joseph Picture	1993	NO	05 and up
01	Middle East	Glorious Folly, A Novel of the Time of Saint Paul	de Wohl, Louis	de Wohl Biography	1957	YES	15 and up
01	Middle East	Great Hero (The), St. Paul the Apostle	Daughters of St. Paul	Encounter Books	1963	YES	09 and up

01	Middle East	Great Men of the Bible: New Testament (Peter, John, James the Greater, James the Lesser, Matthew, Jude, Judas, Stephen, Paul, Philip, Mark, and Luke)	Winkler, Father Jude	St. Joseph Picture Books	1987	NO	05 and up
01	Middle East	Last Apostle, The (St. Paul)	Eleanor, Mother Mary	Catholic Treasury	1956	YES	10 and up
01	Middle East	Lives of the Saints: The Early Church (St. John the Apostle)	Tesoriero, Bart	Aquinas Kids	2010	NO	05-09
01	Middle East	Lives of the Saints: The Early Church (St. Luke)	Tesoriero, Bart	Aquinas Kids	2010	NO	05-09
01	Middle East	Lives of the Saints: The Early Church (St. Paul)	Tesoriero, Bart	Aquinas Kids	2010	NO	05-09
01	Middle East	Peter and Paul: The Rock and the Sword	Thompson, Blanche Jennings	Vision Books	1964	YES	09-15
01	Middle East	Saint Paul the Apostle	Lovasik, Fr. Lawrence	St. Joseph Picture	1980, 1990	NO	05 and up
01	Middle East	Saint Paul the Apostle, The Story of the Apostle to the Gentiles	Windeatt, Mary Fabyan	Windeatt Saint Series	1993	NO	12 and up
01	Middle East	St. Paul: The Thirteenth Apostle	Wallace, Susan Helen	Encounter the Saints	2007	NO	09 and up
01	Middle East	Saints for Boys (St. Paul)	Muus, Solveig and Bart Tesoriero	Aquinas Kids	2012	NO	05-09
01	Middle East	Story of St. Andrew, A	Danielski, S.E.	Footsteps of the Saints	1966, 2010	NO	06-09
01	Persia	Book of Saints, Part 8 (St. Jude Thaddeus)	Lovasik, Fr. Lawrence	St. Joseph Picture	1993	NO	05 and up
01	Persia (Parthia)	Book of Saints, Part 8 (St. Thomas)	Lovasik, Fr. Lawrence	St. Joseph Picture	1993	NO	05 and up
01	Poland	Book of Saints, Part 8 (St. Andrew)	Lovasik, Fr. Lawrence	St. Joseph Picture	1993	NO	05 and up
01	Rome	Book of Saints, Part 8 (St. Paul)	Lovasik, Fr. Lawrence	St. Joseph Picture	1993	NO	05 and up
01	Rome	Book of Saints, Part 8 (St. Peter)	Lovasik, Fr. Lawrence	St. Joseph Picture	1993	NO	05 and up
01	Rome	City of the Golden House	Polland, Madeleine	Clarion Books	1963, 2005	NO	09 and up
01	Rome	Great Hero (The), St. Paul the Apostle	Daughters of St. Paul	Encounter Books	1963	YES	09 and up
01	Rome	Last Apostle, The (St. Paul)	Eleanor, Mother Mary	Catholic Treasury	1956	YES	10 and up
01	Rome	Saint Philomena	Windeatt, Mary Fabyan	Windeatt Coloring	1955	YES	04 and up

01	Rome	Saints for Boys (St. Paul)	Muus, Solveig and Bart Tesoriero	Aquinas Kids	2012	NO	05-09
01	Rome	Saints for Boys (St. Peter)	Muus, Solveig and Bart Tesoriero	Aquinas Kids	2012	NO	05-09
10	Rome	Story of St. Peter, A	Ernest, Brother	Footsteps of the Saints	1961, 2011	NO	06-09
01	Russia	Book of Saints, Part 8 (St. Andrew)	Lovasik, Fr. Lawrence	St. Joseph Picture	1993	NO	05 and up
01	Spain	Book of Saints, Part 8 (St. James the Greater)	Lovasik, Fr. Lawrence	St. Joseph Picture	1993	NO	05 and up
01	Syria	Book of Saints, Part 6 (St. Ignatius of Antioch)	Lovasik, Fr. Lawrence	St. Joseph Picture	1985	YES	05 and up
01	Israel	Lives of the Saints: The Early Church (St. Luke)	Tesoriero, Bart	Aquinas Kids	2010	NO	05-09
01	Turkey	Love as Strong as Death, The Story of St. Thecla	Panunzi, Rev. Paul	Encounter Books	1966	YES	09 and up
01	various	Apostles of Jesus, The	Lovasik, Fr. Lawrence	St. Joseph Picture	1980, 1990	NO	05 and up
01	various	Twelve Apostles, The	Lovasik, Fr. Lawrence	St. Joseph Picture	2002	NO	05 and up
01-15	various	Christmas and the Saints	Pauli, Hertha	Vision Books	1956	YES	09-15
02	Egypt	Lives of the Saints: The Monastic Era (St. Catherine of Alexandria)	Tesoriero, Bart	Aquinas Kids	2010	NO	05-09
02	Rome	Book of Saints, Part 6 (St. Ignatius of Antioch)	Lovasik, Fr. Lawrence	St. Joseph Picture	1985	YES	05 and up
02	Rome	Lives of the Saints: The Early Church (St. Cecilia)	Tesoriero, Bart	Aquinas Kids	2010	NO	05-09
02	Rome	No Tears for the Bride, A Story of St. Perpetua	Roberto, Brother	Footsteps of the Saints	1958, 2008	NO	09-12
02	Syria	Book of Saints, Part 6 (St. Ignatius of Antioch)	Lovasik, Fr. Lawrence	St. Joseph Picture	1985	YES	05 and up
03	Africa	Saint Christopher	Windeatt, Mary Fabyan	Windeatt Coloring	1955	YES	04 and up
03	Africa	Story of St. Cyprian, A	Ernest, Brother	Footsteps of the Saints	1960, 2012	NO	06-09
03	Egypt	Barbara	Richardson, M.K.	Patron Saint Books	1959	YES	08 and up
03	Egypt	Book of Saints, Part 4 (St. Barbara)	Lovasik, Fr. Lawrence	St. Joseph Picture	1982	YES	05 and up
03	Egypt	Book of Saints, Part 5 (St. Anthony the Abbot)	Lovasik, Fr. Lawrence	St. Joseph Picture	1985	YES	05 and up
03	Egypt	Book of Saints, Part 7 (St. Catherine of Alexandria)	Lovasik, Fr. Lawrence	St. Joseph Picture Books	1993	NO	05 and up

03	Egypt	Lives of the Saints: The Monastic Era (St. Apollonia)	Tesoriero, Bart	Aquinas Kids	2010	NO	05-09
03	Egypt	Lives of the Saints: The Monastic Era (St. Barbara)	Tesoriero, Bart	Aquinas Kids	2010	NO	05-09
03	Egypt	Lives of the Saints: The Monastic Era (St. Catherine of Alexandria)	Tesoriero, Bart	Aquinas Kids	2010	NO	05-09
03	Egypt	Saints for Boys and Girls (St. Barbara)	Beebe, Catherine	Beebe Biography	1959	YES	09-14
03	Egypt	Saints for Boys and Girls (St. Catherine Alexandria)	Beebe, Catherine	Beebe Biography	1959	YES	09-14
03	Egypt	Saints for Girls (St. Barbara)	Muus, Solveig and Bart Tesoriero	Aquinas Kids	2012	NO	05-09
03	Egypt	Saints of the Byzantine World (St. Anthony of Egypt and St. Paul the Hermit)	Thompson, Blanche Jennings	Vision Books	1961	YES	09-15
03	Egypt	Story of St. Catherine of Alexandria, A	Flavius, Brother	Dujarie Press Reprint	1965, 2005	NO	06-09
03	Egypt	Story of St. Catherine of Alexandria, A	Flavius, Brother	Footsteps of the Saints	1965, 2012	NO	06-09
03	England	Book of Saints, Part 4 (St. Helen)	Lovasik, Fr. Lawrence	St. Joseph Picture	1982	YES	05 and up
03	England	Living Wood (The), A Novel of Saint Helena	de Wohl, Louis	de Wohl Biography	1947	YES	15 and up
03	England	Saint Helena and the True Cross	de Wohl, Louis	Vision Books	1958, 2012	NO	09-15
03	England	Saints for Boys and Girls (St. Helen)	Beebe, Catherine	Beebe Biography	1959	YES	09-14
03	France	Saints for Boys and Girls (St. Dennis)	Beebe, Catherine	Beebe Biography	1959	YES	09-14
03	Israel	Saints for Boys and Girls (St. George)	Beebe, Catherine	Beebe Biography	1959	YES	09-14
03	Israel	Saints of the Byzantine World (St. Hilarion)	Thompson, Blanche	Vision Books	1961	YES	09-15
03	Israel	They Became Saints (St. Christopher: And His Mighty Monarch)	Francis, Father	Father Francis Coloring	1951	NO	07 and up
03	Italy	Book of Saints, Part 1 (St. Lawrence)	Lovasik, Fr. Lawrence	St. Joseph Picture	1981	NO	05 and up
03	Italy	Lives of the Saints: The Monastic Era (St. Adrian of Nicomedia)	Tesoriero, Bart	Aquinas Kids	2010	NO	05-09
03	Italy	Lives of the Saints: The Monastic Era (St. Florian)	Tesoriero, Bart	Aquinas Kids	2010	NO	05-09

03	Italy	Lives of the Saints: The Early Church (St. Lucy)	Tesoriero, Bart	Aquinas Kids	2010	NO	05-09
03	Italy	Saints for Boys and Girls (St. Dennis)	Beebe, Catherine	Beebe Biography	1959	YES	09-14
03	Italy	Saints for Girls (St. Lucy)	Muus, Solveig and Bart Tesoriero	Aquinas Kids	2012	NO	05-09
03	Italy	Story of St. Agatha, A	Ernest, Brother	Footsteps of the Saints	1960, 2009	NO	06-09
03	Italy	Story of St. Lawrence, A	Emge, Br. Lawrence	Footsteps of the Saints	1961, 2012	NO	06-09
03	Italy	Story of St. Lawrence, A	Emge, Brother Lawrence	Dujarie Press Reprint	1961, 2009	NO	06-09
03	Italy	Story of St. Lucy, A	Ernest, Brother	Footsteps of the Saints	1957, 2012	NO	06-09
03	Middle East	Book of Saints, Part 7 (Sts. Cosmas and Damian)	Lovasik, Fr. Lawrence	St. Joseph Picture	1993	NO	05 and up
03	Rome	Book of Saints, Part 3 (St. Cecilia)	Lovasik, Fr. Lawrence	St. Joseph Picture	1982	NO	05 and up
03	Rome	Book of Saints, Part 7 (St. Valentine)	Lovasik, Fr. Lawrence	St. Joseph Picture	1993	NO	05 and up
03	Rome	Fabiola	Wiseman, Nicholas Cardinal	Favorite Catholic Books	1854, etc.	NO	12 and up
03	Rome	Lives of the Saints: The Monastic Era (St. Sebastian)	Tesoriero, Bart	Aquinas Kids	2010	NO	05-09
03	Rome	Lion Tamer, The (martyr Martina)	Daughters of Charity	Catholic Stories, Volume IV	1995	NO	07-10
03	Rome	Marc's Choice: A Story of the Time of Diocletian	Cornelius, Sister Mary	Catholic Treasury	1957	YES	10 and up
03	Rome	No Tears for the Bride, A Story of St. Perpetua	Roberto, Brother	Footsteps of the Saints	1958, 2008	NO	09-12
03	Spain	Book of Saints, Part 11 (St. Eulalia of Merida)	Lovasik, Fr. Lawrence	St. Joseph Picture	1997	NO	05 and up
04	Africa	Monica, Model for Christian Mothers	Forbes, F.A.	Forbes Biography	1915, 1998	NO	12 and up
04	Africa	Saints for Boys (St. Augustine of Hippo)	Muus, Solveig and Bart Tesoriero	Aquinas Kids	2012	NO	05-09
04	Armenia	Book of Saints, Part 7 (St. Blase)	Lovasik, Fr. Lawrence	St. Joseph Picture	1993	NO	05 and up
04	Armenia	Lives of the Saints: The Monastic Era (St. Blaise)	Tesoriero, Bart	Aquinas Kids	2010	NO	05-09
04	Armenia	Story of St. Blaise, A	Cullen, Br. Franlkin	Footsteps of the Saints	1958, 2010	NO	06-09

04	Egypt	Book of Saints, Part 5 (St. Anthony the Abbot)	Lovasik, Fr. Lawrence	St. Joseph Picture	1985	YES	05 and up
04	Egypt	Book of Saints, Part 10 (St. Moses the Black)	Lovasik, Fr. Lawrence	St. Joseph Picture	1997	NO	05 and up
04	Egypt	Saint Athanasius, The Father of Orthodoxy	Forbes, F.A.	Forbes Biography	1919, 1998	NO	12 and up
04	Egypt	Saints of the Byzantine World (St. Athanasius)	Thompson, Blanche	Vision Books	1961	YES	09-15
04	Egypt	Saints of the Byzantine World (St. Anthony of Egypt)	Thompson, Blanche Jennings	Vision Books	1961	YES	09-15
04	Egypt	Saints of the Byzantine World (St. Cyril of Alexandria)	Thompson, Blanche Jennings	Vision Books	1961	YES	09-15
04	Egypt	Saints of the Byzantine World (St. Hilarion)	Thompson, Blanche	Vision Books	1961	YES	09-15
04	Egypt	Saints of the Byzantine World (St. Pachomius)	Thompson, Blanche	Vision Books	1961	YES	09-15
04	Egypt	Saints of the Byzantine World (St. Paul the Hermit)	Thompson, Blanche Jennings	Vision Books	1961	YES	09-15
04	England	Noble Lady, The Life of St. Helen	Daughters of St. Paul	Encounter Books	1966	YES	09 and up
04	England	Saint George and the Dragon, A Golden Legend	Hodges, Margaret (adaptor)	Caldecott	1984	NO	04 and up
04	England	Saint Helena and the True Cross	de Wohl, Louis	Vision Books	1958, 2012	NO	09-15
04	England	Saints for Boys and Girls (St. Helen)	Beebe, Catherine	Beebe Biography	1959	YES	09-14
04	Ethiopia	Book of Saints, Part 10 (St. Moses the Black)	Lovasik, Fr. Lawrence	St. Joseph Picture	1997	NO	05 and up
04	France	Book of Saints, Part 6 (St. Ambrose)	Lovasik, Fr. Lawrence	St. Joseph Picture	1985	YES	05 and up
04	France	Book of Saints, Part 6 (St. Martin of Tours)	Lovasik, Fr. Lawrence	St. Joseph Picture	1985	YES	05 and up
04	France	Book of Saints, Part 11 (St. Grimonia)	Lovasik, Fr. Lawrence	St. Joseph Picture	1997	NO	05 and up
04	Holy Land	Book of Saints, Part 4 (St. Helen)	Lovasik, Fr. Lawrence	St. Joseph Picture	1982	YES	05 and up
04	Holy Land	Book of Saints, Part 6 (St. Jerome)	Lovasik, Fr. Lawrence	St. Joseph Picture	1985	YES	05 and up
04	Holy Land	Helena	Harris, Mary	Patron Saint Books	1964	YES	08 and up
04	Holy Land	Living Wood (The), A Novel of Saint Helena	de Wohl, Louis	de Wohl Biography	1947	YES	15 and up
04	Holy Land	Noble Lady, The Life of St. Helen	Daughters of St. Paul	Encounter Books	1966	YES	09 and up

04	Holy Land	Saint Helena and the True Cross	de Wohl, Louis	Vision Books	1958, 2012	NO	09-15
04	Holy Land	Saint Jerome and the Bible	Sanderlin, George	Vision Books	1961	YES	09-15
04	Holy Land	Saints for Boys and Girls (St. Helen)	Beebe, Catherine	Beebe Biography	1959	YES	09-14
04	Hungary	Book of Saints, Part 6 (St. Martin of Tours)	Lovasik, Fr. Lawrence	St. Joseph Picture	1985	YES	05 and up
04	Ireland	Book of Saints, Part 11 (St. Grimonia)	Lovasik, Fr. Lawrence	St. Joseph Picture	1997	NO	05 and up
04	Ireland	Lives of the Saints: The Monastic Era (St. Patrick)	Tesoriero, Bart	Aquinas Kids	2010	NO	05-09
04	Ireland	Saints for Boys (St. Patrick)	Muus, Solveig and Bart Tesoriero	Aquinas Kids	2012	NO	05-09
04	Israel	Book of Saints, Part 5 (St. Basil the Great)	Lovasik, Fr. Lawrence	St. Joseph Picture Books	1985	YES	05 and up
04	Israel	Saints of the Byzantine World (St. Basil the Great)	Thompson, Blanche	Vision Books	1961	YES	09-15
04	Israel	Saints of the Byzantine World (St. Cyril of Jerusalem)	Thompson, Blanche Jennings	Vision Books	1961	YES	09-15
04	Israel	Saints of the Byzantine World (St. Hilarion)	Thompson, Blanche	Vision Books	1961	YES	09-15
04	Italy	Book of Saints, Part 6 (St. Ambrose)	Lovasik, Fr. Lawrence	St. Joseph Picture	1985	YES	05 and up
04	Italy	Book of Saints, Part 6 (St. Jerome)	Lovasik, Fr. Lawrence	St. Joseph Picture	1985	YES	05 and up
04	Italy	Book of Saints, Part 6 (St. Martin of Tours)	Lovasik, Fr. Lawrence	St. Joseph Picture	1985	YES	05 and up
04	Italy	Lives of the Saints: The Monastic Era (St. Adrian of Nicomedia)	Tesoriero, Bart	Aquinas Kids	2010	NO	05-09
04	Italy	Lives of the Saints: The Monastic Era (St. Florian)	Tesoriero, Bart	Aquinas Kids	2010	NO	05-09
04	Italy	Saint Jerome and the Bible	Sanderlin, George	Vision Books	1961	YES	09-15
04	Middle East	Book of Saints, Part 7 (St. John Chrysostom)	Lovasik, Fr. Lawrence	St. Joseph Picture	1993	NO	05 and up
04	Middle East	Book of Saints, Part 11 (St. Epiphanius of Salamis)	Lovasik, Fr. Lawrence	St. Joseph Picture	1997	NO	05 and up
04	Middle East	Book of Saints, Part 11 (St. Macrina the Younger)	Lovasik, Fr. Lawrence	St. Joseph Picture	1997	NO	05 and up
04	Middle East	Lives of the Saints: The Monastic Era (St. Nicholas)	Tesoriero, Bart	Aquinas Kids	2010	NO	05-09

04	Middle East	Saints of the Byzantine World (St. Gregory Nazianzen)	Thompson, Blanche Jennings	Vision Books	1961	YES	09-15
04	Middle East	Saints of the Byzantine World (St. Gregory of Nyssa	Thompson, Blanche Jennings	Vision Books	1961	YES	09-15
04	Middle East	Saints of the Byzantine World (St. John Chrysostom)	Thompson, Blanche Jennings	Vision Books	1961	YES	09-15
04	Middle East	Saints of the Byzantine World (St. Nicholas of Myra)	Thompson, Blanche Jennings	Vision Books	1961	YES	09-15
04	North Africa	Book of Saints, Part 3 (St. Augustine)	Lovasik, Fr. Lawrence	St. Joseph Picture Books	1982	NO	05 and up
04	North Africa	Lives of the Saints: The Monastic Era (St. Augustine)	Tesoriero, Bart	Aquinas Kids	2010	NO	05-09
04	North Africa	Restless Flame, A Novel of Saint Augustine	de Wohl, Louis	de Wohl Biography	1950, 1997	NO	15 and up
04	North Africa	Saint Augustine and His Search for Faith	Lomask, Milton	Vision Books	1957	YES	09-15
04	Rome	Book of Saints, Part 2 (St. Agnes)	Lovasik, Fr. Lawrence	St. Joseph Picture	1981	NO	05 and up
04	Rome	Book of Saints, Part 2 (St. Tarcisius)	Lovasik, Fr. Lawrence	St. Joseph Picture	1981	NO	05 and up
04	Rome	Book of Saints, Part 4 (St. Helen)	Lovasik, Fr. Lawrence	St. Joseph Picture	1982	YES	05 and up
04	Rome	Book of Saints, Part 4 (St. Sebastian)	Lovasik, Fr. Lawrence	St. Joseph Picture	1982	YES	05 and up
04	Rome	Book of Saints, Part 7 (St. George)	Lovasik, Fr. Lawrence	St. Joseph Picture	1993	NO	05 and up
04	Rome	Helena	Harris, Mary	Patron Saint Books	1964	YES	08 and up
04	Rome	Living Wood (The), A Novel of St. Helena	de Wohl, Louis	de Wohl Biography	1947	YES	15 and up
04	Rome	Marc's Choice: A Story of the Time of Diocletian	Cornelius, Sister Mary	Catholic Treasury	1957	YES	10 and up
04	Rome	Restless Flame, A Novel of St. Augustine	de Wohl, Louis	de Wohl Biography	1950, 1997	NO	15 and up
04	Rome	Saints for Boys and Girls (Saint Agnes)	Beebe, Catherine	Beebe Biography	1959	YES	09-14
04	Rome	Saints of the Eucharist: A Boy who Carried Jesus (St. Tarcisius)	Francis, Father	Father Francis Coloring	1958	NO	06 and up
04	Rome	St. Tarcisius	Bernadi, Mary R.	Similar to Encounter	1983	YES	09 and up
04	Rome	Story of St. Sebastian, A	Ernest, Brother	Footsteps of the Saints	1959, 2010	NO	06-09

04	Rome	They Became Saints (St. Agnes: The Fearless Virgin)	Francis, Father	Father Francis Coloring	1951	NO	07 and up
04	Rome	They Became Saints (St. Tarcisius: Boy Martyr of the Holy Eucharist)	Francis, Father	Father Francis Coloring	1951	NO	07 and up
04	Russia	Book of Saints, Part 4 (St. Nicholas)	Lovasik, Fr. Lawrence	St. Joseph Picture	1982	YES	05 and up
04	Sicily	Book of Saints, Part 2 (St. Lucy)	Lovasik, Fr. Lawrence	St. Joseph Picture	1981	NO	05 and up
04	Syria	Saints of the Byzantine World (Simeon Stylites)	Thompson, Blanche	Vision Books	1961	YES	09-15
04	Turkey	Helena	Harris, Mary	Patron Saint Books	1964	YES	08 and up
05	Africa	Saints for Boys (St. Augustine of Hippo)	Muus, Solveig and Bart Tesoriero	Aquinas Kids	2012	NO	05-09
05	Egypt	Saints of the Byzantine World (St. Cyril of Alexandria)	Thompson, Blanche Jennings	Vision Books	1961	YES	09-15
05	France	Book of Saints, Part 12 (St. Anthony of Lerins)	Lovasik, Fr. Lawrence	St. Joseph Picture Books	1999	NO	05 and up
05	France	Candle Burns for France, A (St. Genevieve)	Thompson, Blanche Jennings	Favorite Catholic Books	1946	YES	07 and up
05	France	Land of Erin, The (St. Patrick)	Daughters of Charity	Catholic Stories, Volume IV	1995	NO	07-10
05	France	Story of St. Patrick, A	Ernest, Brother	Footsteps of the Saints	1958, 2011	NO	06-09
05	France	When Saints Were Young (St. Genevieve of Nanterre)	Thompson, Blanche Jennings	Vision Books	1960	YES	09-15
05	Holy Land	Book of Saints, Part 6 (St. Jerome)	Lovasik, Fr. Lawrence	St. Joseph Picture	1985	YES	05 and up
05	Holy Land	Saint Jerome and the Bible	Sanderlin, George	Vision Books	1961	YES	09-15
05	Ireland	Book of Saints, Part 1 (St. Patrick)	Lovasik, Fr. Lawrence	St. Joseph Picture	1981	NO	05 and up
05	Ireland	Flame over Tara	Polland, Madeleine	Clarion Books	1964, 2004	NO	09 and up
05	Ireland	Irish Saints (St. Brendan)	Reilly, Robert T.	Vision Books	1964, 1981, 2002	YES	09-15
05	Ireland	Irish Saints (St. Brigid)	Reilly, Robert T.	Vision Books	1964, 1981, 2002	YES	09-15

05	Ireland	Irish Saints (St. Patrick)	Reilly, Robert T.	Vision Books	1964, 1981, 2002	YES	09-15
05	Ireland	Land of Erin, The (St. Patrick)	Daughters of Charity	Catholic Stories, Volume IV	1995	NO	07-10
05	Ireland	Lives of the Saints: The Monastic Era (St. Patrick)	Tesoriero, Bart	Aquinas Kids	2010	NO	05-09
05	Ireland	Patrick	Hunt, Marigold	Patron Saint Books	1964	YES	08 and up
05	Ireland	Patrick, Patron Saint of Ireland	de Paola, Tomie	de Paola Biography	1994	NO	04-08
05	Ireland	Saint Brigid and the Cows	Betz, Eva K.	Saints and Friendly Beasts	1964, 2004	NO	08 and up
05	Ireland	Saint Patrick	Lovasik, Fr. Lawrence	St. Joseph Picture	1984	NO	05 and up
05	Ireland	Saint Patrick, Apostle of Ireland	Beebe, Catherine	Beebe Biography	1968	YES	08 and up
05	Ireland	Saints for Boys (St. Patrick)	Muus, Solveig and Bart Tesoriero	Aquinas Kids	2012	NO	05-09
05	Ireland	Story of St. Briget, A	Ernest, Brother	Footsteps of the Saints	1959, 2008	NO	06-09
05	Ireland	Story of St. Patrick, A	Ernest, Brother	Footsteps of the Saints	1958, 2011	NO	06-09
05	Ireland	When Saints Were Young (St. Patrick)	Thompson, Blanche	Vision Books	1960	YES	09-15
05	Italy	Book of Saints, Part 3 (St. Benedict)	Lovasik, Fr. Lawrence	St. Joseph Picture	1982	NO	05 and up
05	Italy	Book of Saints, Part 5 (St. Leo the Great)	Lovasik, Fr. Lawrence	St. Joseph Picture	1985	YES	05 and up
05	Italy	Book of Saints, Part 12 (St. Anthony of Lerins)	Lovasik, Fr. Lawrence	St. Joseph Picture	1999	NO	05 and up
05	Italy	Holy Twins, The (Sts. Benedict and Scholastica)	de Paola, Tomie	de Paola Biography	2001	NO	04-08
05	Italy	Lives of the Saints: The Monastic Era (St. Benedict)	Tesoriero, Bart	Aquinas Kids	2010	NO	05-09
05	Italy	Mountain of God (The): A Life of St. Benedict	Willet, Br. Franciscus	Holy Cross Press	1965	YES	09 and up
05	Italy	Saint Benedict, Hero of the Hills	Windeatt, Mary Fabyan	Vision Books	1958, 2001	NO	09-15
05	Italy	Saint Benedict, The Story of the Father of the Western Monks	Windeatt, Mary Fabyan	Windeatt Saint Series	1993	NO	09 and up
05	Italy	St. Benedict	Forbes, F.A.	Forbes Biography	1921	YES	12 and up

05	Italy	Saints for Boys (St. Benedict)	Muus, Solveig and Bart Tesoriero	Aquinas Kids	2012	NO	05-09
05	Italy	Story of St. Benedict, A	Ernest, Brother	Footsteps of the Saints	1958, 2012	NO	06-09
05	Middle East	Book of Saints, Part 7 (St. John Chrysostom)	Lovasik, Fr. Lawrence	St. Joseph Picture	1993	NO	05 and up
05	Middle East	Saints of the Byzantine World (St. John Chrysostom)	Thompson, Blanche Jennings	Vision Books	1961	YES	09-15
05	North Africa	Book of Saints, Part 3 (St. Augustine)	Lovasik, Fr. Lawrence	St. Joseph Picture	1982	NO	05 and up
05	North Africa	Lives of the Saints: The Monastic Era (St. Augustine)	Tesoriero, Bart	Aquinas Kids	2010	NO	05-09
05	North Africa	Restless Flame (The), A Novel of St. Augustine	de Wohl, Louis	de Wohl Biography	1950, 1997	NO	15 and up
05	North Africa	Saint Augustine and His Search for Faith	Lomask, Milton	Vision Books	1957	YES	09-15
05	Rome	Book of Saints, Part 9 (St. Galla)	Lovasik, Fr. Lawrence	St. Joseph Picture	1996	NO	05 and up
05	Rome	Restless Flame (The), A Novel of St. Augustine	de Wohl, Louis	de Wohl Biography	1950, 1997	NO	15 and up
05	Syria	Saints of the Byzantine World (Simeon Stylites)	Thompson, Blanche	Vision Books	1961	YES	09-15
05	Turkey	Saints for Boys and Girls (Saint Daniel)	Beebe, Catherine	Beebe Biography	1959	YES	09-14
06	Denmark	Locked Crowns, The	Garthwaite, Marion	Clarion Books	1963	YES	09 and up
06	England	Augustine Came to Kent	Willard, Barbara	Clarion	1963, 1996	NO	09 and up
06	England	Locked Crowns, The	Garthwaite, Marion	Clarion Books	1963	YES	09 and up
06	France	Book of Saints, Part 10 (St. Monegundis)	Lovasik, Fr. Lawrence	St. Joseph Picture	1997	NO	05 and up
06	France	Book of Saints, Part 12 (St. Anthony of Lerins)	Lovasik, Fr. Lawrence	St. Joseph Picture	1999	NO	05 and up
06	France	Book of Saints, Part 12 (St. Bertrand of Le Mans)	Lovasik, Fr. Lawrence	St. Joseph Picture	1999	NO	05 and up
06	France	Fingal's Quest	Polland, Madeleine	Clarion Books	1961, 2003	NO	09 and up
06	France	Irish Saints (St. Columban)	Reilly, Robert T.	Vision Books	1964, 1981, 2002	YES	09-15
06	France	When Saints Were Young (St. Genevieve of Nanterre)	Thompson, Blanche	Vision Books	1960	YES	09-15
06	Iceland	Fingal's Quest	Polland, Madeleine	Clarion Books	1961, 2003	NO	09 and up

06	Iceland	Irish Saints (St. Brendan)	Reilly, Robert T.	Vision Books	1964, 1981, 2002	YES	09-15
06	Iceland	Irish Saints (St. Columcille)	Reilly, Robert T.	Vision Books	1964, 1981, 2002	YES	09-15
06	Iceland	Story of Rolf and the Viking Bow, The	French, Allen	Favorite Catholic Books	1924, 1995	NO	10 & up
06	Ireland	Irish Saints (St. Brendan)	Reilly, Robert T.	Vision Books	1964, 1981, 2002	YES	09-15
06	Ireland	Irish Saints (St. Brigid)	Reilly, Robert T.	Vision Books	1964, 1981, 2002	YES	09-15
06	Ireland	Irish Saints (St. Columban)	Reilly, Robert T.	Vision Books	1964, 1981, 2002	YES	09-15
06	Ireland	Little Patron of Gardeners: Good St. Fiacre	Beebe, Catherine	Beebe Biography	1948, 2012	NO	08 and up
06	Ireland	Saint Colum and the Crane	Betz, Eva K.	Saints and Friendly Beasts	1961, 2003	NO	08 and up
06	Ireland	Saints for Boys and Girls (St. Kevin)	Beebe, Catherine	Beebe Biography	1959	YES	09-14
06	Israel	Book of Saints, Part 5 (St. Christopher)	Lovasik, Fr. Lawrence	St. Joseph Picture Books	1985	YES	05 and up
06	Israel	Christopher, The Holy Giant	de Paola, Tomie	de Paola Biography	1994	YES	04-08
06	Israel	Lives of the Saints: The Early Church (St. Christopher)	Tesoriero, Bart	Aquinas Kids	2010	NO	05-09
06	Israel	Saint Christopher for Boys and Girls	Beebe, Catherine	Beebe Biography	1955, 2012	NO	09-14
06	Israel	Saints for Boys (St. Christopher)	Muus, Solveig and Bart Tesoriero	Aquinas Kids	2012	NO	05-09
06	Italy	Augustine Came to Kent	Willard, Barbara	Clarion	1963, 1996	NO	09 and up
06	Italy	Book of Saints, Part 3 (St. Benedict)	Lovasik, Fr. Lawrence	St. Joseph Picture	1982	NO	05 and up
06	Italy	Book of Saints, Part 5 (St. Gregory the Great)	Lovasik, Fr. Lawrence	St. Joseph Picture	1985	YES	05 and up
06	Italy	Book of Saints, Part 12 (St. Anthony of Lerins)	Lovasik, Fr. Lawrence	St. Joseph Picture	1999	NO	05 and up
06	Italy	Citadel of God, A Novel of St. Benedict	de Wohl, Louis	de Wohl Biography	1959, 1994	NO	15 and up

06	Italy	Holy Twins, The (Sts. Benedict and Scholastica)	de Paola, Tomie	de Paola Biography	2001	NO	04-08
06	Italy	Lives of the Saints: The Monastic Era (St. Benedict)	Tesoriero, Bart	Aquinas Kids	2010	NO	05-09
06	Italy	Mountain of God (The): A Life of St. Benedict	Willet, Br. Franciscus	Holy Cross Press	1965	YES	09 and up
06	Italy	Saint Benedict, Hero of the Hills	Windeatt, Mary Fabyan	Vision Books	1958, 2001	NO	09-15
06	Italy	Saint Benedict, The Story of the Father of the Western Monks	Windeatt, Mary Fabyan	Windeatt Saint Series	1993	NO	09 and up
06	Italy	Saint Gregory the Great, Consul of God	Sanderlin, George	Vision Books	1964	YES	09-15
06	Italy	Saints for Boys (St. Benedict)	Muus, Solveig and Bart Tesoriero	Aquinas Kids	2012	NO	05-09
06	Italy	St. Benedict	Forbes, F.A.	Forbes Biography	1921	YES	12 and up
06	Italy	Story of St. Benedict, A	Ernest, Brother	Footsteps of the Saints	1958, 2012	NO	06-09
06	Rome	Book of Saints, Part 9 (St. Galla)	Lovasik, Fr. Lawrence	St. Joseph Picture	1996	NO	05 and up
06	Scotland	Irish Saints (St. Columcille)	Reilly, Robert T.	Vision Books	1964, 1981, 2002	YES	09-15
06	Sicliy	Book of Saints, Part 10 (St. Zozimus)	Lovasik, Fr. Lawrence	St. Joseph Picture	1997	NO	05 and up
06	Spain	Book of Saints, Part 5 (St. Isidore of Seville)	Lovasik, Fr. Lawrence	St. Joseph Picture	1985	YES	05 and up
06	Spain	Book of Saints, Part 8 (St. Hermenegild)	Lovasik, Fr. Lawrence	St. Joseph Picture	1993	NO	05 and up
06	Spain	Lives of the Saints: The Monastic Era (St. Isidore of Seville)	Tesoriero, Bart	Aquinas Kids	2010	NO	05-09
06	Syria	Book of Saints, Part 12 (St. Simeon Stylites the Younger)	Lovasik, Fr. Lawrence	St. Joseph Picture	1999	NO	05 and up
06	Tunisia	Book of Saints, Part 9 (St. Fulgentius of Ruspe)	Lovasik, Fr. Lawrence	St. Joseph Picture	1996	NO	05 and up
06	United States	Irish Saints (St. Brendan)	Reilly, Robert T.	Vision Books	1964, 2002	YES	09-15
06	Wales	David	Betz, Eva K.	Patron Saint Books	1960	YES	08 and up
07	Belgium	Book of Saints, Part 2 (St. Dymphna)	Lovasik, Fr. Lawrence	St. Joseph Picture	1981	NO	05 and up
07	England	Augustine Came to Kent	Willard, Barbara	Clarion	1963, 1996	NO	09 and up

07	England	Book of Saints, Part 4 (St. Boniface)	Lovasik, Fr. Lawrence	St. Joseph Picture	1982	YES	05 and up
07	England	Book of Saints, Part 10 (St. Ermengild)	Lovasik, Fr. Lawrence	St. Joseph Picture	1997	NO	05 and up
07	England	Book of Saints, Part 10 (St. Mildred)	Lovasik, Fr. Lawrence	St. Joseph Picture	1997	NO	05 and up
07	England	Bring Me an Ax, A Story of St. Boniface of Germany	Roberto, Brother	In the Footsteps of the Saints	1964, 2008	NO	09-12
07	England	King's Thane (Edwin and Beorn)	Brady, Charles A.	Clarion Books	1961, 2009	NO	09 and up
07	France	Archer Saint (The), A Story of St. Hubert	Ernest, Brother	Footsteps of the Saints	1950, 2009	NO	09-12
07	France	Book of Saints, Part 12 (St. Bertrand of Le Mans)	Lovasik, Fr. Lawrence	St. Joseph Picture Books	1999	NO	05 and up
07	France	Irish Saints (St. Columban)	Reilly, Robert T.	Vision Books	1964, 1981, 2002	YES	09-15
07	France	Little Patron of Gardeners: Good Saint Fiacre	Beebe, Catherine	Beebe Biography	1948, 2012	NO	08 and up
07	Ireland	Begga's Bracelet	Daughters of Charity	Catholic Stories, Volume III	1995	NO	07-10
07	Ireland	Book of Saints, Part 2 (St. Dymphna)	Lovasik, Fr. Lawrence	St. Joseph Picture	1981	NO	05 and up
07	Ireland	Book of Saints, Part 9 (St. Cuthbert)	Lovasik, Fr. Lawrence	St. Joseph Picture	1996	NO	05 and up
07	Ireland	Irish Saints (St. Columban)	Reilly, Robert T.	Vision Books	1964, 1981, 2002	YES	09-15
07	Ireland	Little Patron of Gardeners: Good Saint Fiacre	Beebe, Catherine	Beebe Biography	1948, 2012	NO	08 and up
07	Ireland	Lives of the Saints: The Monastic Era (St. Dymphna)	Tesoriero, Bart	Aquinas Kids	2010	NO	05-09
07	Ireland	Saints for Boys and Girls (St. Kevin)	Beebe, Catherine	Beebe Biography	1959	YES	09-14
07	Italy	Augustine Came to Kent	Willard, Barbara	Clarion	1963, 1996	NO	09 and up
07	Italy	Book of Saints, Part 5 (St. Gregory the Great)	Lovasik, Fr. Lawrence	St. Joseph Picture	1985	YES	05 and up
07	Italy	Irish Saints (St. Columban)	Reilly, Robert T.	Vision Books	1964, 1981, 2002	YES	09-15
07	Italy	Saint Gregory the Great, Consul of God	Sanderlin, George	Vision Books	1964	YES	09-15

07	Middle East	Saints of the Byzantine World (St. John Damascene)	Thompson, Blanche Jennings	Vision Books	1961	YES	09-15
07	Portugal	Book of Saints, Part 10 (St. Fructuosus of Braga)	Lovasik, Fr. Lawrence	St. Joseph Picture	1997	NO	05 and up
07	Sicily	Book of Saints, Part 10 (St. Zozimus)	Lovasik, Fr. Lawrence	St. Joseph Picture	1997	NO	05 and up
07	Spain	Book of Saints, Part 10 (St. Fructuosus of Braga)	Lovasik, Fr. Lawrence	St. Joseph Picture	1997	NO	05 and up
07	Spain	Book of Saints, Part 5 (St. Isidore of Seville)	Lovasik, Fr. Lawrence	St. Joseph Picture	1985	YES	05 and up
07	Spain	Lives of the Saints: The Monastic Era (St. Isidore of Seville)	Tesoriero, Bart	Aquinas Kids	2010	NO	05-09
07	Sweden	King's Thane (Edwin and Beorn)	Brady, Charles A.	Clarion Books	1961, 2009	NO	09 and up
07	Wales	Book of Saints, Part 12 (St. Winifred)	Lovasik, Fr. Lawrence	St. Joseph Picture	1999	NO	05 and up
08	Europe	Son of Charlemagne	Willard, Barbara	Clarion	1959, 1998	NO	09 and up
08	France	Archer Saint (The), A Story of St. Hubert	Ernest, Brother	Footsteps of the Saints	1950, 2009	NO	09-12
08	France	Hammer of Gaul: The Story of Charles Martel	Miller, Shane	Hawthorn Junior Bio.	1964	YES	11 and up
08	France	Son of Charlemagne	Willard, Barbara	Clarion	1959, 1998	NO	09 and up
08	Germany	Book of Saints, Part 4 (St. Boniface)	Lovasik, Fr. Lawrence	St. Joseph Picture	1982	YES	05 and up
08	Germany	Bring Me an Ax, A Story of St. Boniface of Germany	Roberto, Brother	In the Footsteps of the Saints	1964, 2008	NO	09-12
08	Greece	Book of Saints, Part 10 (St. George the Younger)	Lovasik, Fr. Lawrence	St. Joseph Picture Books	1997	NO	05 and up
08	Middle East	Saints of the Byzantine World (St. John Damascene)	Thompson, Blanche Jennings	Vision Books	1961	YES	09-15
09	England	Alfred of Wessex: The King Who Saved His Country	Morriss, Frank	Catholic Treasury	1959	YES	10 and up
09	Europe	Son of Charlemagne	Willard, Barbara	Clarion	1959, 1998	NO	09 and up
09	Germany	Saint Meinrad	Windeatt, Mary Fabyan	Windeatt Coloring	1954	NO	04 and up
09	Greece	Book of Saints, Part 10 (St. George the Younger)	Lovasik, Fr. Lawrence	St. Joseph Picture Books	1997	NO	05 and up
09	Greece	Book of Saints, Part 4 (Sts. Cyril and Methodius)	Lovasik, Fr. Lawrence	St. Joseph Picture	1982	YES	05 and up

Saint Series Books in Chronological Order

09	northern Europe	Book of Saints, Part 4 (Sts. Cyril & Methodius)	Lovasik, Fr. Lawrence	St. Joseph Picture	1982	YES	05 and up
09	Rome	Book of Saints, Part 4 (Sts. Cyril & Methodius)	Lovasik, Fr. Lawrence	St. Joseph Picture	1982	YES	05 and up
09	Russia	Book of Saints, Part 9 (St. Olga)	Lovasik, Fr. Lawrence	St. Joseph Picture	1996	NO	05 and up
09	Switzerland	Book of Saints, Part 11 (St. Wiborada)	Lovasik, Fr. Lawrence	St. Joseph Picture	1997	NO	05 and up
09	Switzerland	Saint Meinrad	Windeatt, Mary Fabyan	Windeatt Coloring Books	1954	NO	04 and up
10	Bohemia	Story of St. Wenceslaus, A	Ernest, Brother	In the Footsteps of the Saints	1961, 2008	NO	06-09
10	France	Bernard (of Menthon)	Smaridge, Norah	Patron Saint Books	1960	YES	08 and up
10	Italy	Bernard (of Menthon)	Smaridge, Norah	Patron Saint Books	1960	YES	08 and up
10	Russia	Book of Saints, Part 9 (St. Olga)	Lovasik, Fr. Lawrence	St. Joseph Picture	1996	NO	05 and up
10	Scotland	Black Fox of Lorne, The	de Angeli, Marguerite	Newbery	1956	YES	09 and up
11	England	Book of Saints, Part 6 (St. Edward)	Lovasik, Fr. Lawrence	St. Joseph Picture	1985	YES	05 and up
11	England	Margaret (St. Margaret of Scotland)	Sr. M. Juliana of Maryknoll	Patron Saint Books	1959	NO	08 and up
11	England	Saints for Boys and Girls (St. Edward the Confessor)	Beebe, Catherine	Beebe Biography	1959	YES	09-14
11	England	Saints for Boys and Girls (St. Robert)	Beebe, Catherine	Beebe Biography	1959	YES	09-14
11	England	Silver King: Edward the Confessor, The Last Great Anglo-Saxon Ruler	Stanley-Wrench, Margaret	Hawthorn Junior Biography	1966	YES	11 and up
11	England	Story of St. Margaret of Scotland, A	Ernest, Brother	Footsteps of the Saints	1957, 2009	NO	06-09
11	Europe	Blue Gonfalon (First Crusade)	Hubbard, Margaret	Clarion Books	1960, 2004	NO	09 and up
11	France	Bells of Conquest, Life of St. Bernard of Clairvaux	Daughters of St. Paul	Encounter Books	1968, 1987	YES	09 and up
11	France	Bernard (of Menthon)	Smaridge, Norah	Patron Saint Books	1960	YES	08 and up
11	France	Book of Saints, Part 11 (St. Alberic)	Lovasik, Fr. Lawrence	St. Joseph Picture	1997	NO	05 and up
11	France	Book of Saints, Part 12 (St. Bertrand of Comminges)	Lovasik, Fr. Lawrence	St. Joseph Picture	1999	NO	05 and up
11	France	Hide the Children, A Story of St. Bernard of Clairvaux	Roberto, Brother	In the Footsteps of the Saints	1962, 2010	NO	09-12

11	France	Saints for Boys and Girls (St. Edward the Confessor)	Beebe, Catherine	Beebe Biography	1959	YES	09-14
11	France	Silver King: Edward the Confessor, The Last Great Anglo-Saxon Ruler	Stanley-Wrench, Margaret	Hawthorn Junior Biography	1966	YES	11 and up
11	France	Thunder of Silence, Life of St. Bernard of Clairvaux	Willett, Br. Franciscus	Holy Cross Press	1964	YES	09 and up
11	Germany	Book of Saints, Part 11 (Bl. Jutta of Diessenberg)	Lovasik, Fr. Lawrence	St. Joseph Picture	1997	NO	05 and up
11	Hungary	Book of Saints, Part 10 (St. Gerard Sagredo)	Lovasik, Fr. Lawrence	St. Joseph Picture	1997	NO	05 and up
11	Iceland	King's Men, A Story of St. Olaf of Norway	Boucher, Alan	Clarion Books	1962	YES	09 and up
11	Iceland	Sword of Clontarf	Brady, Charles A.	Clarion Books	1960, 2006	NO	09 and up
11	Ireland	Irish Saints (St. Malachy)	Reilly, Robert T.	Vision Books	1964, 1981, 2002	YES	09-15
11	Ireland	Saints for Boys and Girls (Bld. Brian Lacey)	Beebe, Catherine	Beebe Biography	1959	YES	09-14
11	Ireland	Sword of Clontarf	Brady, Charles A.	Clarion Books	1960, 2006	NO	09 and up
11	Israel	Blue Gonfalon (First Crusade)	Hubbard, Margaret	Clarion Books	1960, 2004	NO	09 and up
11	Italy	Bernard (of Menthon)	Smaridge, Norah	Patron Saint Books	1960	YES	08 and up
11	Italy	Book of Saints, Part 10 (St. Gerard Sagredo)	Lovasik, Fr. Lawrence	St. Joseph Picture	1997	NO	05 and up
11	Norway	King's Men, A Story of St. Olaf of Norway	Boucher, Alan	Clarion Books	1962	YES	09 and up
11	Scotland	Margaret (St. Margaret of Scotland)	Sr. M. Juliana of Maryknoll	Patron Saint Books	1959	NO	08 and up
11	Spain	Lives of the Saints: The Monastic Era (St. Isidore the Farmer)	Tesoriero, Bart	Aquinas Kids	2010	NO	05-09
12	Cyprus	Crusader: The Story of Richard the Lion-Heart (Richard I)	Power-Waters, Alma	Hawthorn Junior Biography	1964	YES	11 and up
12	England	Book of Saints, Part 12 (St. William of York)	Lovasik, Fr. Lawrence	St. Joseph Picture	1999	NO	05 and up
12	England	Brown Scapular, The (St. Simon Stock)	Windeatt, Mary Fabyan	Windeatt Coloring	1956	YES	04 and up
12	England	Crusader: The Story of Richard the Lion-Heart (Richard I)	Power-Waters, Alma	Hawthorn Junior Biography	1964	YES	11 and up
12	England	Hidden Treasure of Glaston, The	Jewett, Eleanore M.	Newbery	1946, 1966, 2000	NO	10 and up

12	England	If All the Swords in England (Thomas Becket and Henry II)	Willard, Barbara	Clarion	1961, 2000	NO	09 and up
12	England	Richard	Richardson, M.K.	Patron Saint Books	1959	YES	08 and up
12	England	Saints for Boys and Girls (St. Robert)	Beebe, Catherine	Beebe Biography	1959	YES	09-14
12	England	Saints for Boys and Girls (St. William of Rochester)	Beebe, Catherine	Beebe Biography	1959	YES	09-14
12	England	Simon o' The Stock	Heagney, Anne	Catholic Treasury	1955	YES	10 and up
12	England	Story of St. Simon of Stock, A	Ernest, Brother	Footsteps of the Saints	1959, 2008	NO	06-09
12	England	When Saints Were Young (St. Thomas of Canterbury or St. Thomas Becket)	Thompson, Blanche Jennings	Vision Books	1960	YES	09-15
12	France	Bells of Conquest, The Life of St. Bernard of Clairvaux	Daughters of St. Paul	Encounter Books	1968, 1987	YES	09 and up
12	France	Book of Saints, Part 3 (St. Bernard)	Lovasik, Fr. Lawrence	St. Joseph Picture	1982	NO	05 and up
12	France	Book of Saints, Part 11 (St. Alberic)	Lovasik, Fr. Lawrence	St. Joseph Picture	1997	NO	05 and up
12	France	Book of Saints, Part 12 (St. Bertrand of Comminges)	Lovasik, Fr. Lawrence	St. Joseph Picture	1999	NO	05 and up
12	France	Crusader: The Story of Richard the Lion-Heart (Richard I)	Power-Waters, Alma	Hawthorn Junior Biography	1964	YES	11 and up
12	France	Hide the Children, A Story of St. Bernard of Clairvaux	Roberto, Brother	In the Footsteps of the Saints	1962, 2010	NO	09-12
12	France	Hunters of Souls (St. Dominic)	Dorcy, Sister Mary Jean	Dorcy Biography	1949, 1999	YES	10 and up
12	France	If All the Swords in England (Thomas Becket and Henry II)	Willard, Barbara	Clarion	1961, 2000	NO	09 and up
12	France	Irish Saints (St .Laurence O'Toole)	Reilly, Robert T.	Vision Books	1964, 1981, 2002	YES	09-15
12	France	Saint Dominic	Dorcy, Sister Mary Jean	Dorcy Biography	1959, 1982, 2009	NO	14 and up
12	France	Saint Dominic and the Rosary	Beebe, Catherine	Vision Books	1956, 1996	NO	09-15
12	France	Saint Dominic de Guzman	Ordonez, Emilio	Along the Paths of the Gospel	2000	YES	07-10
12	France	Thunder of Silence, Life of St. Bernard of Clairvaux	Willett, Br. Franciscus	Holy Cross Press	1964	YES	09 and up

12	France	Truce of the Wolf and Other Tales of Old Italy	Davis, Mary Gould	Newbery	1931	YES	10 and up
12	Germany	Book of Saints, Part 9 (St. Hildegard of Bingen)	Lovasik, Fr. Lawrence	St. Joseph Picture	1996	NO	05 and up
12	Germany	Book of Saints, Part 9 (St. Hildegund)	Lovasik, Fr. Lawrence	St. Joseph Picture	1996	NO	05 and up
12	Germany	Book of Saints, Part 11 (Bl. Jutta of Diessenberg)	Lovasik, Fr. Lawrence	St. Joseph Picture	1997	NO	05 and up
12	Holy Land	Crusader: The Story of Richard the Lion-Heart (Richard I)	Power-Waters, Alma	Hawthorn Junior Biography	1964	YES	11 and up
12	Ireland	Irish Saints (St. Laurence O'Toole)	Reilly, Robert T.	Vision Books	1964, 1981, 2002	YES	09-15
12	Ireland	Irish Saints (St. Malachy)	Reilly, Robert T.	Vision Books	1964, 1981, 2002	YES	09-15
12	Italy	Book of Saints, Part 6 (St. Francis of Assisi)	Lovasik, Fr. Lawrence	St. Joseph Picture	1985	YES	05 and up
12	Italy	Children's Saint Francis, The (St. Francis of Assisi)	Beebe, Catherine	Beebe Biography	1941, 1946	YES	08-14
12	Italy	Francis and Clare, Saints of Assisi	Homan, Helen	Vision Books	1956, 1994	NO	09-11
12	Italy	Francis and Clare, Saints of Assisi	Homan, Helen	Junior Vision	1962	YES	09-11
12	Italy	Francis, The Poor Man of Assisi (includes St. Clare)	de Paola, Tomie	de Paola Biography	1982, 1990	YES	04-08
12	Italy	Gentle Revolutionary, Life of St. Francis of Assisi	Daughters of St. Paul	Encounter Books	1978	YES	09 and up
12	Italy	Joyful Beggar, A Novel of St. Francis of Assisi	de Wohl, Louis	de Wohl Biography	1958, 2001	NO	15 and up
12	Italy	Lives of the Saints: The Monastic Era (St. Francis of Assisi)	Tesoriero, Bart	Aquinas Kids	2010	NO	05-09
12	Italy	Saint Clare of Assisi: A Light for the World	Trouvé, Marianne Lorraine	Encounter the Saints	2009	NO	09 and up
12	Italy	St. Francis	Francis, Mary	Patron Saint Books	1959	YES	08 and up
12	Italy	Saint Francis of Assisi	Windeatt, Mary Fabyan	Windeatt Coloring	1956	NO	04 and up
12	Italy	Saint Francis of Assisi	Lovasik, Fr. Lawrence	St. Joseph Picture	1980	NO	05 and up
12	Italy	Saint Francis of Assisi: Gentle Revolutionary	Alves, Mary Emmanuel	Encounter the Saints	1999	NO	09 and up
12	Italy	Saint Francis of Assisi: God's Gentle Knight	Vintrou, Francoise	Along the Paths of the Gospel	1998	YES	07-10

12	Italy	Saints for Boys (St. Francis of Asssi)	Muus, Solveig and Bart Tesoriero	Aquinas Kids	2012	NO	05-09
12	Italy	Song of Francis	de Paola, Tomie	de Paola Biography	2009	NO	02-08
12	Italy	Story of St. Clare, A	Ernest, Brother	Footsteps of the Saints	1957, 2010	NO	06-09
12	Italy	They Became Saints (St. Francis and the Wolf of Gubbio)	Francis, Father	Father Francis Coloring	1951	NO	07 and up
12	northern Europe	Hunters of Souls (St. Hyacinth of Poland)	Dorcy, Sister Mary Jean	Dorcy Biography	1949, 1999	YES	10 and up
12	northern Europe	St. Hyacinth of Poland, The Story of the Apostle of the North	Windeatt, Mary Fabyan	Windeatt Saint Series	1993	NO	11 and up
12	northern Eurpoe	Story of St. Hyacinth, A	Ernest, Brother	Footsteps of the Saints	1960, 2008	NO	06-09
12	Portugal	Saints for Boys (St. Anthony of Padua)	Muus, Solveig and Bart Tesoriero	Aquinas Kids	2012	NO	05-09
12	Scotland	Outlaws of Ravenhurst	Wallace, Sister M. Imelda S. L.	Favorite Catholic Books	1950, 1996	NO	10 and up
12	Spain	Book of Saints, Part 3 (St. Isidore)	Lovasik, Fr. Lawrence	St. Joseph Picture	1982	NO	05 and up
12	Spain	Book of Saints, Part 4 (St. Dominic)	Lovasik, Fr. Lawrence	St. Joseph Picture	1982	YES	05 and up
12	Spain	Hunters of Souls (St. Dominic)	Dorcy, Sister Mary Jean	Dorcy Biography	1949, 1999	YES	10 and up
12	Spain	Hunters of Souls (St. Raymond of Pennafort)	Dorcy, Sister Mary Jean	Dorcy Biography	1949, 1999	YES	10 and up
12	Spain	Lives of the Saints: The Monastic Era (St. Isidore the Farmer)	Tesoriero, Bart	Aquinas Kids	2010	NO	05-09
12	Spain	Saint Dominic	Dorcy, Sister Mary Jean	Dorcy Biography	1959, 1982, 2009	NO	14 and up
12	Spain	Saint Dominic and the Rosary	Beebe, Catherine	Vision Books	1956, 1996	NO	09-15
12	Spain	Saint Dominic de Guzman	Ordonez, Emilio	Paths of the Gospel	2000	YES	07-10
12	Spain	St. Dominic, Preacher of the Rosary and Founder of the Dominican Order	Windeatt, Mary Fabyan	Windeatt Saint Series	1993	NO	09 and up
12	Spain	Story of St. Dominic, A	Ernest, Brother	Footsteps of the Saints	1959, 2008	NO	06-09
12	Spain	When All Ships Failed, A Story of St. Raymond of Pennafort	Ernest, Brother	In the Footsteps of the Saints	1953, 2010	NO	09-12

13	Bohemia	Hunters of Souls (Bld. Zedislava of Bohemia)	Dorcy, Sister Mary Jean	Dorcy Biography	1949, 1999	YES	10 and up
13	Cyprus	Where Valor Lies (Seventh Crusade)	de Leeau, Adele & Cateau	Clarion Books	1959, 2007	NO	09 and up
13	Czech Republic	Hunters of Souls (Bld. Zedislava of Bohemia)	Dorcy, Sister Mary Jean	Dorcy Biography	1949, 1999	YES	10 and up
13	Egypt	Where Valor Lies (Seventh Crusade)	de Leeau, Adele & Cateau	Clarion Books	1959, 2007	NO	09 and up
13	England	Brown Scapular, The (St. Simon Stock)	Windeatt, Mary Fabyan	Windeatt Coloring	1956	YES	04 and up
13	England	Cedric the Forester	Marshall, Bernard	Newbery	1921, 2012	NO	10 and up
13	England	Richard	Richardson, M.K.	Patron Saint Books	1959	YES	08 and up
13	England	Saints for Boys and Girls (St. William of Rochester)	Beebe, Catherine	Beebe Biography	1959	YES	09-14
13	England	Simon o' The Stock	Heagney, Anne	Catholic Treasury	1955	YES	10 and up
13	France	Book of Saints, Part 4 (St. Dominic)	Lovasik, Fr. Lawrence	St. Joseph Picture	1982	YES	05 and up
13	France	Saint Dominic de Guzman	Ordonez, Emilio	Along the Paths of the Gospel	2000	YES	07-10
13	France	St. Dominic, Preacher of the Rosary and Founder of the Dominican Order	Windeatt, Mary Fabyan	Windeatt Saint Series	1993	NO	09 and up
13	France	Story of St. Dominic, A	Ernest, Brother	Footsteps of the Saints	1959, 2008	NO	06-09
13	France	Saint Louis and the Last Crusade	Hubbard, Margaret	Vision Books	1958, 2013	NO	09-15
13	France	Saint on Horseback (The): A Story of St. Louis, King of France	Gazagne, Brother Louis	In the Footsteps of the Saints	1953, 2009	NO	09-12
13	France	Story of St. Simon of Stock, A	Ernest, Brother	Footsteps of the Saints	1959, 2008	NO	06-09
13	France	They Became Saints (St. Louis: King of France)	Francis, Father	Father Francis Coloring	1951	NO	07 and up
13	France	Truce of the Wolf and Other Tales of Old Italy	Davis, Mary Gould	Newbery	1931	YES	10 and up
13	France	Where Valor Lies (Seventh Crusade)	de Leeau, Adele & Cateau	Clarion Books	1959, 2007	NO	09 and up
13	Germany	Master Albert, The Story of St. Albert the Great	Dorcy, Sister Mary Jean	Dorcy Biography	1955	YES	12 and up
13	Germany	Truth Was Their Star (St. Albert the Great)	Dorcy, Sister Mary Jean	Dorcy Biography	1947, 1999	NO	10 and up
13	Holy Land	Brown Scapular, The (St. Simon Stock)	Windeatt, Mary Fabyan	Windeatt Coloring	1956	YES	04 and up

13	Holy Land	Simon o' The Stock	Heagney, Anne	Catholic Treasury	1955	YES	10 and up
13	Holy Land	Story of St. Simon of Stock, A	Ernest, Brother	Footsteps of the Saints	1959, 2008	NO	06-09
13	Hungary	Book of Saints, Part 3 (St. Elizabeth)	Lovasik, Fr. Lawrence	St. Joseph Picture Books	1982	NO	05 and up
13	Hungary	Elizabeth	Harris, Mary	Patron Saint Books	1961	YES	08 and up
13	Hungary	Hunters of Souls (St. Margaret of Hungary)	Dorcy, Sister Mary Jean	Dorcy Biography	1949, 1999	YES	10 and up
13	Hungary	Queen of the Poor, A Story of Elizabeth of Hungary	Daly, Brother Marco	In the Footsteps of the Saints	1961, 2009	NO	09-12
13	Hungary	Saint Elizabeth's Three Crowns	Thompson, Blanche	Junior Vision	1962	YES	09-11
13	Hungary	Saint Elizabeth's Three Crowns	Thompson, Blanche	Vision Books	1958, 1996	NO	09-15
13	Hungary	Story of St. Elizabeth of Hungary, A	Ernest, Brother	Footsteps of the Saints	1960, 2009	NO	06-09
13	Israel	Where Valor Lies (Seventh Crusade)	de Leeau, Adele &Cateau	Clarion Books	1959, 2007	NO	09 and up
13	Italy	Army in Battle Array, An (Bld. Margaret of Castello)	Dorcy, Sister Mary Jean	Dorcy Biography	1955	YES	10 and up
13	Italy	Book of Saints, Part 1 (St. Anthony of Padua)	Lovasik, Fr. Lawrence	St. Joseph Picture	1981	NO	05 and up
13	Italy	Book of Saints, Part 3 (St. Clare)	Lovasik, Fr. Lawrence	St. Joseph Picture	1982	NO	05 and up
13	Italy	Book of Saints, Part 3 (St. Thomas Aquinas)	Lovasik, Fr. Lawrence	St. Joseph Picture	1982	NO	05 and up
13	Italy	Book of Saints, Part 6 (St. Bonaventure)	Lovasik, Fr. Lawrence	St. Joseph Picture	1985	YES	05 and up
13	Italy	Book of Saints, Part 6 (St. Francis of Assisi)	Lovasik, Fr. Lawrence	St. Joseph Picture	1985	YES	05 and up
13	Italy	Book of Saints, Part 7 (St. Margaret of Cortona)	Lovasik, Fr. Lawrence	St. Joseph Picture	1993	NO	05 and up
13	Italy	Book of Saints, Part 7 (St. Peregrine)	Lovasik, Fr. Lawrence	St. Joseph Picture	1993	NO	05 and up
13	Italy	Book of Saints, Part 7 (St. Zita)	Lovasik, Fr. Lawrence	St. Joseph Picture	1993	NO	05 and up
13	Italy	Book of Saints, Part 9 (St. Agnes of Assisi)	Lovasik, Fr. Lawrence	St. Joseph Picture	1996	NO	05 and up
13	Italy	Book of Saints, Part 9 (St. Juliana Falconieri)	Lovasik, Fr. Lawrence	St. Joseph Picture	1996	NO	05 and up
13	Italy	Book of Saints, Part 11 (St. Margaret of Cortona)	Lovasik, Fr. Lawrence	St. Joseph Picture	1997	NO	05 and up
13	Italy	Book of Saints, Part 12 (St. Philip Benizi)	Lovasik, Fr. Lawrence	St. Joseph Picture	1999	NO	05 and up

13	Italy	Children's Saint Anthony, The (Anthony of Padua)	Beebe, Catherine	Beebe Biography	1939, 1943	YES	08-14
13	Italy	Children's Saint Francis, The (St. Francis of Assisi)	Beebe, Catherine	Beebe Biography	1941, 1946	YES	08-14
13	Italy	Dante and His Journey	Schmid, Brother Evan	Footsteps of the Saints	1961, 2013	NO	12-15
13	Italy	Francis and Clare, Saints of Assisi	Homan, Helen	Junior Vision	1962	YES	09-11
13	Italy	Francis and Clare, Saints of Assisi	Homan, Helen	Vision Books	1956, 1994	NO	09-15
13	Italy	Francis, Poor Man of Assisi (includes St. Clare)	de Paola, Tomie	de Paola Biography	1982, 1990	YES	04-08
13	Italy	Hunters of Souls (Bld. Albert of Bergamo)	Dorcy, Sister Mary Jean	Dorcy Biography	1949, 1999	YES	10 and up
13	Italy	Hunters of Souls (Bld. James/Jacopo of Voragine)	Dorcy, Sister Mary Jean	Dorcy Biography	1949, 1999	YES	10 and up
13	Italy	Hunters of Souls (Bld. Sadoc and Martyrs of Sandomir)	Dorcy, Sister Mary Jean	Dorcy Biography	1949, 1999	YES	10 and up
13	Italy	Hunters of Souls (St. Peter, Martyr of Verona)	Dorcy, Sister Mary Jean	Dorcy Biography	1949, 1999	YES	10 and up
13	Italy	Joyful Beggar, A Novel of St. Francis of Assisi	de Wohl, Louis	de Wohl Biography	1958, 2001	NO	15 and up
13	Italy	Lives of the Saints: The Middle Ages (St. Anthony)	Tesoriero, Bart	Aquinas Kids	2010	NO	05-09
13	Italy	Lives of the Saints: The Monastic Era (St. Francis of Assisi)	Tesoriero, Bart	Aquinas Kids	2010	NO	05-09
13	Italy	Lives of the Saints: The Middle Ages (St. Peregrime)	Tesoriero, Bart	Aquinas Kids	2010	NO	05-09
13	Italy	Lives of the Saints: The Middle Ages (St. Thomas Aquinas)	Tesoriero, Bart	Aquinas Kids	2010	NO	05-09
13	Italy	Mary's Pilgrim, The Life of St. Peregrine	Daughters of St. Paul	Encounter Books	1972	YES	09 and up
13	Italy	Master Albert, The Story of St. Albert the Great	Dorcy, Sister Mary Jean	Dorcy Biography	1955	YES	12 and up
13	Italy	Ox Was an Angel (The), A Story of St. Thomas Aquinas	Overstreet, Brother Edward	In the Footsteps of the Saints	1961, 2013	NO	12-15
13	Italy	Pillar in the Twilight, Life of St. Thomas Aquinas	Daughters of St. Paul	Encounter Books	1967, 1978	YES	09 and up
13	Italy	Quiet Light, A Novel of St. Thomas Aquinas	de Wohl, Louis	de Wohl Biography	1950, 1996	NO	15 and up
13	Italy	Saint Anthony and the Christ Child	Homan, Helen	Junior Vision	1963	YES	09-11

13	Italy	Saint Anthony and the Christ Child	Homan, Helen	Vision Books	1958, 1997	NO	09-15
13	Italy	Saint Anthony of Padua	Windeatt, Mary Fabyan	Windeatt Coloring	1955	NO	04 and up
13	Italy	Saint Anthony of Padua	Lovasik, Fr. Lawrence	St. Joseph Picture	1984	NO	05 and up
13	Italy	Saint Anthony of Padua: Fire and Light	Kerry, Margaret and Mary Tebo	Encounter the Saints	1999	NO	09 and up
13	Italy	Saint Anthony of Padua: Proclaimer of the Good News	Baudouin-Croix, Marie	Along the Paths of the Gospel	1999	YES	07-10
13	Italy	Saint Clare of Assisi: A Light for the World	Trouvé, Marianne	Encounter the Saints	2009	NO	09 and up
13	Italy	Saint Francis of Assisi	Windeatt, Mary Fabyan	Windeatt Coloring	1956	NO	04 and up
13	Italy	Saint Francis of Assisi	Lovasik, Fr. Lawrence	St. Joseph Picture	1980	NO	05 and up
13	Italy	Saint Francis of Assisi: God's Gentle Knight	Vintrou, Francoise	Along the Paths of the Gospel	1998	YES	07-10
13	Italy	Saint Thomas Aquinas and the Preaching Beggars	Larnen, Brendan and Milton Lomask	Vision Books	1957, 2005	NO	09-15
13	Italy	Saints for Boys (St. Anthony of Padua)	Muus, Solveig and Bart Tesoriero	Aquinas Kids	2012	NO	05-09
13	Italy	Saints for Boys (St. Francis of Asssi)	Muus, Solveig and Bart Tesoriero	Aquinas Kids	2012	NO	05-09
13	Italy	Saints for Boys (St. Thomas Aquinas)	Muus, Solveig and Bart Tesoriero	Aquinas Kids	2012	NO	05-09
13	Italy	Saints for Boys and Girls (St. Anthony of Padua)	Beebe, Catherine	Beebe Biography	1959	YES	09-14
13	Italy	Saints for Girls (St. Clare)	Muus, Solveig and Bart Tesoriero	Aquinas Kids	2012	NO	05-09
13	Italy	Song of Francis	de Paola, Tomie	de Paola Biography	2009	NO	02-08
13	Italy	St. Francis	Francis, Mary	Patron Saint Books	1959	YES	08 and up
13	Italy	St. Thomas Aquinas, The Story of "The Dumb Ox"	Windeatt, Mary Fabyan	Windeatt Saint Series	1993	NO	08 and up
13	Italy	Story of St. Anthony, A	Ernest, Brother	Footsteps of the Saints	1960, 2009	NO	06-09
13	Italy	Story of St. Peregrine, A	Ernest, Brother	Footsteps of the Saints	1958, 2008	NO	06-09

13	Italy	Story of St. Clare, A	Ernest, Brother	Footsteps of the Saints	1957, 2010	NO	06-09
13	Italy	They Became Saints (Saint Francis and the Wolf of Gubbio)	Francis, Father	Father Francis Coloring	1951	NO	07 and up
13	Italy	Truth Was Their Star (St. Agnes of Montepulciano)	Dorcy, Sister Mary Jean	Dorcy Biography	1947, 1999	NO	10 and up
13	Italy	Truth Was Their Star (St. Albert the Great)	Dorcy, Sister Mary Jean	Dorcy Biography	1947, 1999	NO	10 and up
13	Italy	Truth Was Their Star (St. Thomas Aquinas)	Dorcy, Sister Mary Jean	Dorcy Biography	1947, 1999	NO	10 and up
13	Morocco	Saints for Boys and Girls (St. Daniel)	Beebe, Catherine	Beebe Biography	1959	YES	09-14
13	northern Europe	Hunters of Souls (St. Hyacinth of Poland)	Dorcy, Sister Mary Jean	Dorcy Biography	1949, 1999	YES	10 and up
13	northern Europe	St. Hyacinth of Poland, The Story of the Apostle of the North	Windeatt, Mary Fabyan	Windeatt Saint Series	1993	NO	11 and up
13	Poland	Hunters of Souls (Blessed Sadoc and Martyrs of Sandomir)	Dorcy, Sister Mary Jean	Dorcy Biography	1949, 1999	YES	10 and up
13	Poland	Master Albert, The Story of St. Albert the Great	Dorcy, Sister Mary Jean	Dorcy Biography	1955	YES	12 and up
13	Poland	Truth Was Their Star (St. Albert the Great)	Dorcy, Sister Mary Jean	Dorcy Biography	1947, 1999	NO	10 and up
13	Portugal	Children's Saint Anthony, (St. Anthony of Padua)	Beebe, Catherine	Beebe Biography	1939, 1943	YES	08-14
13	Portugal	Saint Anthony and the Christ Child	Homan, Helen	Junior Vision	1963	YES	09-11
13	Portugal	Saint Anthony and the Christ Child	Homan, Helen	Vision Books	1958, 1997	NO	09-15
13	Portugal	Saint Anthony of Padua	Windeatt, Mary Fabyan	Windeatt Coloring	1955	NO	04 and up
13	Portugal	Saint Anthony of Padua: Fire and Light	Kerry, Margaret and Mary Tebo	Encounter the Saints	1999	NO	09 and up
13	Portugal	Saint Anthony of Padua: Proclaimer of the Good News	Baudouin-Croix, Marie	Along the Paths of the Gospel	1999	YES	07-10
13	Portugal	Saints for Boys and Girls (St. Anthony of Padua)	Beebe, Catherine	Beebe Biography	1959	YES	09-14
13	Portugal	Story of St. Anthony, A	Ernest, Brother	Footsteps of the Saints	1960, 2009	NO	06-09
13	Saxony (Germany)	Book of Saints, Part 7 (St. Gertrude)	Lovasik, Fr. Lawrence	St. Joseph Picture	1993	NO	05 and up
13	Spain	Book of Saints, Part 1 (St. Anthony of Padua)	Lovasik, Fr. Lawrence	St. Joseph Picture	1981	NO	05 and up
13	Spain	Book of Saints, Part 4 (St. Dominic)	Lovasik, Fr. Lawrence	St. Joseph Picture	1982	YES	05 and up

13	Spain	Hunters of Souls (St. Dominic)	Dorcy, Sister Mary Jean	Dorcy Biography	1949, 1999	YES	10 and up
13	Spain	Hunters of Souls (St. Raymond of Pennafort)	Dorcy, Sister Mary Jean	Dorcy Biography	1949, 1999	YES	10 and up
13	Spain	Saint Dominic	Dorcy, Sister Mary Jean	Dorcy Biography	1959, 1982, 2009	NO	14 and up
13	Spain	Saint Dominic de Guzman	Ordonez, Emilio	Along the Paths of the Gospel	2000	YES	07-10
13	Spain	St. Dominic, Preacher of the Rosary and Founder of the Dominican Order	Windeatt, Mary Fabyan	Windeatt Saint Series	1993	NO	09 and up
13	Spain	Story of St. Dominic, A	Ernest, Brother	Footsteps of the Saints	1959, 2008	NO	06-09
13	Spain	When All Ships Failed, A Story of St. Raymond of Pennafort	Ernest, Brother	In the Footsteps of the Saints	1953, 2010	NO	09-12
13	Switzerland	Apple and the Arrow, The	Buff, Mary and Conrad	Newbery	1959	NO	09 and up
14	Czechoslovakia	Book of Saints, Part 4 (St. John Nepomucene)	Lovasik, Fr. Lawrence	St. Joseph Picture	1982	YES	05 and up
14	England	Door in the Wall, The	de Angeli, Marguerite	Newbery	1949	NO	09 and up
14	England	Teller of Tales: The Story of Geoffrey Chaucer	Stanley-Wrench, Margaret	Hawthorn Junior Biography	1965	YES	11 and up
14	France	Book of Saints, Part 12 (St. Rosalina)	Lovasik, Fr. Lawrence	St. Joseph Picture	1999	NO	05 and up
14	France	Lives of the Saints: The Middle Ages (St. Roch)	Tesoriero, Bart	Aquinas Kids	2010	NO	05-09
14	France	Saint Colette: In the Footsteps of St. Francis and St. Clare	Poor Clares of Poligny & Sr. Elisabeth	Along the Paths of the Gospel	1998	YES	07-10
14	Italy	Army in Battle Array, An (Bld. Margaret of Castello)	Dorcy, Sister Mary Jean	Dorcy Biography	1955	YES	10 and up
14	Italy	Army in Battle Array, An (Bld. Peter Geremia)	Dorcy, Sister Mary Jean	Dorcy Biography	1955	YES	10 and up
14	Italy	Book of Saints, Part 4 (St. Rita)	Lovasik, Fr. Lawrence	St. Joseph Picture	1982	YES	05 and up
14	Italy	Book of Saints, Part 6 (St. Catherine of Siena)	Lovasik, Fr. Lawrence	St. Joseph Picture	1985	YES	05 and up
14	Italy	Book of Saints, Part 7 (St. Peregrine)	Lovasik, Fr. Lawrence	St. Joseph Picture	1993	NO	05 and up
14	Italy	Book of Saints, Part 9 (St. Juliana Falconieri)	Lovasik, Fr. Lawrence	St. Joseph Picture	1996	NO	05 and up
14	Italy	Catherine of Siena	Sorgia, Fr. Raimondo	Encounter Books	1975	YES	09 and up

14	Italy	Dante and His Journey	Schmid, Brother Evan	Footsteps of the Saints	1961, 2013	NO	12-15
14	Italy	Her Dream Came True, Life of Bld. Imelda Lambertini	Daughters of St. Paul	Encounter Books	1967	YES	09 and up
14	Italy	Lay Siege to Heaven, A Novel of St. Catherine of Siena	de Wohl, Louis	de Wohl Biography	1960, 1991	NO	15 and up
14	Italy	Lives of the Saints: The Middle Ages (St. Bernadine of Siena)	Tesoriero, Bart	Aquinas Kids	2010	NO	05-09
14	Italy	Lives of the Saints: The Middle Ages (St. Catherine of Siena)	Tesoriero, Bart	Aquinas Kids	2010	NO	05-09
14	Italy	Lives of the Saints: The Middle Ages (St. Peregrine)	Tesoriero, Bart	Aquinas Kids	2010	NO	05-09
14	Italy	Mary's Pilgrim, The Life of St. Peregrine	Daughters of St. Paul	Encounter Books	1972	YES	09 and up
14	Italy	Patron Saint of First Communicants, The Story of Blessed Imelda Lambertini	Windeatt, Mary Fabyan	Windeatt Saint Series	1991	NO	09 and up
14	Italy	Saint Catherine of Siena	Forbes, F.A.	Forbes Biography	1913, 1998	NO	12 and up
14	Italy	Saints for Boys and Girls (Blessed Imelda)	Beebe, Catherine	Beebe Biography	1959	YES	09-14
14	Italy	Saints for Girls (St. Catherine of Siena)	Muus, Solveig and Bart Tesoriero	Aquinas Kids	2012	NO	05-09
14	Italy	Saints of the Eucharist: God's Little White Saint (Blessed Imelda)	Francis, Father	Father Francis Coloring	1958	NO	06 and up
14	Italy	St. Catherine of Siena, Story of the Girl Who Saw Saints in the Sky	Windeatt, Mary Fabyan	Windeatt Saint Series	1993	NO	09 and up
14	Italy	Story of St. Peregrine, A	Ernest, Brother	Footsteps of the Saints	1958, 2008	NO	06-09
14	Italy	They Became Saints (Bld. Imelda: And Her First Holy Communion)	Francis, Father	Father Francis Coloring Books	1951	NO	07 and up
14	Italy	Torch in the Darkness (A), A Story of St. John Capistrano	Roberto, Brother	In the Footsteps of the Saints	1956, 2010	NO	09-12
14	Italy	Truth Was Their Star (Blessed Imelda)	Dorcy, Sister Mary Jean	Dorcy Biography	1947, 1999	NO	10 and up
14	Italy	Truth Was Their Star (St. Agnes of Montepulciano)	Dorcy, Sister Mary Jean	Dorcy Biography	1947, 1999	NO	10 and up

Saint Series Books in Chronological Order

14	Italy	Truth Was Their Star (St. Antoninus of Florence)	Dorcy, Sister Mary Jean	Dorcy Biography	1947, 1999	YES	10 and up
14	Italy	Truth Was Their Star (St. Catherine of Siena)	Dorcy, Sister Mary Jean	Dorcy Biography	1947, 1999	NO	10 and up
14	Italy	When Saints Were Young (St. Catherine of Siena)	Thompson, Blanche	Vision Books	1960	YES	09-15
14	Rome	Book of Saints, Part 7 (St. Bridget)	Lovasik, Fr. Lawrence	St. Joseph Picture	1993	NO	05 and up
14	Saxony (Germany)	Book of Saints, Part 7 (St. Gertrude)	Lovasik, Fr. Lawrence	St. Joseph Picture	1993	NO	05 and up
14	Spain	Book of Saints, Part 5 (St. Vincent Ferrer)	Lovasik, Fr. Lawrence	St. Joseph Picture	1985	YES	05 and up
14	Spain	Truth Was Their Star (St. Vincent Ferrer)	Dorcy, Sister Mary Jean	Dorcy Biography	1947, 1999	NO	10 and up
14	Spain	Lives of the Saints: The Middle Ages (St. Vincent Ferrer)	Tesoriero, Bart	Aquinas Kids	2010	NO	05-09
14	Sweden	Book of Saints, Part 7 (St. Bridget)	Lovasik, Fr. Lawrence	St. Joseph Picture	1993	NO	05 and up
14	Sweden	Face in the Flames (The), A Story of St. Bridget of Sweden	Flavius, Brother	In the Footsteps of the Saints	1959, 2011	NO	09-12
14	Switzerland	Mountains Are Free	Adams, Julie Davis	Newbery	1930	YES	09 and up
14	western Europe	Book of Saints, Part 5 (St. Vincent Ferrer)	Lovasik, Fr. Lawrence	St. Joseph Picture	1985	YES	05 and up
14	western Europe	Lives of the Saints: The Middle Ages (St. Vincent Ferrer)	Tesoriero, Bart	Aquinas Kids	2010	NO	05-09
14	western Europe	Truth Was Their Star (St. Vincent Ferrer)	Dorcy, Sister Mary Jean	Dorcy Biography	1947, 1999	NO	10 and up
14 & 15	Italy	Lives of the Saints: The Middle Ages (St. Rita)	Tesoriero, Bart	Aquinas Kids	2010	NO	05-09
14 & 15	Italy	Saints for Girls (St. Rita)	Muus, Solveig and Bart Tesoriero	Aquinas Kids	2012	NO	05-09
14 & 15	Italy	Story of St. Rita, A	Ernest, Brother	Footsteps of the Saints	1959, 2008	NO	06-09
15	England	Book of Saints, Part 1 (St. Thomas More)	Lovasik, Fr. Lawrence	St. Joseph Picture	1981	NO	05 and up
15	England	Cardinal Said No! The Story of St. John Fisher	Premont, Br. Jeremy	Holy Cross Press	1964	YES	09 and up
15	England	Conscience of a King (The), The Story of Thomas More	Stanley-Wrench, Margaret	Hawthorn Junior Biography	1962	YES	11 and up
15	England	Lives of the Saints: The Middle Ages (St. Thomas More)	Tesoriero, Bart	Aquinas Kids	2010	NO	05-09

15	England	Saint Thomas More of London	Ince, Elizabeth M.	Vision Books	1957, 2003	NO	09-15
15	France	Book of Saints, Part 2 (St. Joan of Arc)	Lovasik, Fr. Lawrence	St. Joseph Picture	1981	NO	05 and up
15	France	Book of Saints, Part 10 (Blessed Helen of Udine)	Lovasik, Fr. Lawrence	St. Joseph Picture Books	1997	NO	05 and up
15	France	Candle Burns for France, A (St. Jeanne d'Arc)	Thompson, Blanche Jennings	Favorite Catholic Books	1946	YES	07 and up
15	France	Joan of Arc	Richomme, Agnes	Catholic Children's Library	1950, 2012	NO	10 and up
15	France	Lives of the Saints: The Middle Ages (St. Joan of Arc)	Tesoriero, Bart	Aquinas Kids	2010	NO	05-09
15	France	Saint Colette: In the Footsteps of St. Francis and St. Clare	Poor Clares of Poligny & Sr. Elisabeth	Along the Paths of the Gospel	1998	YES	07-10
15	France	Saint Francis of Paola (Paula)	Winkler, Father Jude	St. Joseph Picture	2006	NO	05 and up
15	France	Saint Joan of Arc	Windeatt, Mary Fabyan	Windeatt Coloring	1955	YES	04 and up
15	France	Saint Joan of Arc: God's Soldier	Wallace, Susan Helen	Encounter the Saints	2002	NO	09 and up
15	France	Saint Joan, The Girl Soldier	de Wohl, Louis	Junior Vision	1962	YES	09-11
15	France	Saint Joan, The Girl Soldier	de Wohl, Louis	Vision Books	1957, 2001	NO	09-15
15	France	Saints for Girls (St. Joan of Arc)	Muus, Solveig and Bart Tesoriero	Aquinas Kids	2012	NO	05-09
15	France	Story of St. Joan of Arc, A	Ernest, Brother	Footsteps of the Saints	1958, 2009	NO	06-09
15	France	They Became Saints (St. Joan of Arc)	Francis, Father	Fr. Francis Coloring	1951	NO	07 and up
15	France	Wind and Shadows, The Story of Joan of Arc	Daughters of St. Paul	Encounter Books	1968	YES	09 and up
15	Hungary	Torch in the Darkness (A), A Story of St. John Capistrano	Roberto, Brother	In the Footsteps of the Saints	1956, 2010	NO	09-12
15	Italy	Apprentice of Florence	Kyle, Ann	Newbery	1933	YES	11 & up
15	Italy	Army in Battle Array, An (Bld. James of Ulm)	Dorcy, Sister Mary Jean	Dorcy Biography	1955	YES	10 and up
15	Italy	Army in Battle Array, An (Bld. Peter Geremia)	Dorcy, Sister Mary Jean	Dorcy Biography	1955	YES	10 and up
15	Italy	Book of Saints, Part 4 (St. Angela Merici)	Lovasik, Fr. Lawrence	St. Joseph Picture	1982	YES	05 and up

15	Italy	Book of Saints, Part 4 (St. Rita)	Lovasik, Fr. Lawrence	St. Joseph Picture	1982	YES	05 and up
15	Italy	Book of Saints, Part 10 (St. Catherine of Genoa)	Lovasik, Fr. Lawrence	St. Joseph Picture Books	1997	NO	05 and up
15	Italy	Book of Saints, Part 11 (Bl. Osanna of Mantua)	Lovasik, Fr. Lawrence	St. Joseph Picture	1997	NO	05 and up
15	Italy	Hunters of Souls (Bld. Catherine of Racconigi)	Dorcy, Sister Mary Jean	Dorcy Biography	1949, 1999	YES	10 and up
15	Italy	King of Colors (The), A Story of Fra Angelico	Roberto, Brother	Footsteps of the Saints	1962, 2010	NO	09-12
15	Italy	Lives of the Saints: The Middle Ages (St. Bernadine of Siena)	Tesoriero, Bart	Aquinas Kids	2010	NO	05-09
15	Italy	Promise to Angela (The): Life of St. Angela Merici	McKern, Pat	Holy Cross Press	1966	YES	09 and up
15	Italy	Saint Angela Merici: Leading People to God	Keefe, Sister Maryellen	Along the Paths of the Gospel	2000	YES	07-10
15	Italy	Saint Francis of Paola (Paula)	Winkler, Father Jude	St. Joseph Picture	2006	NO	05 and up
15	Italy	Story of Michaelangelo, A	Ernest, Brother	Footsteps of the Saints	1961, 2012	NO	06-09
15	Italy	Story of St. Angeli Merici, A	Ernest, Brother	Footsteps of the Saints	1960, 2011	NO	06-09
15	Italy	Torch in the Darkness (A), A Story of St. John Capistrano	Roberto, Brother	In the Footsteps of the Saints	1956, 2010	NO	09-12
15	Italy	Truth Was Their Star (St. Antoninus of Florence)	Dorcy, Sister Mary Jean	Dorcy Biography	1947, 1999	NO	10 and up
15	Italy	When Saints Were Young (St. Angela Merici)	Thompson, Blanche	Vision Books	1960	YES	09-15
15	Italy	Wings of an Eagle: The Story of Michelangelo	Peck, Anne Merriman	Hawthorn Junior Bio.	1963	YES	11 and up
15	Portugal	Book of Saints, Part 4 (St. John of God)	Lovasik, Fr. Lawrence	St. Joseph Picture	1982	YES	05 and up
15	Portugal	Book of Saints, Part 10 (St. Beatrice Da Silva Meneses)	Lovasik, Fr. Lawrence	St. Joseph Picture	1997	NO	05 and up
15	Portugal	Crown for Joanna, A	Dorcy, Sister Mary Jean	Dorcy Biography	1946	YES	10 and up
15	Portugal	Lives of the Saints: The Middle Ages (St. John of God)	Tesoriero, Bart	Aquinas Kids	2010	NO	05-09
15	Portugal	Truth Was Their Star (Bld. Joanna of Portugal)	Dorcy, Sister Mary Jean	Dorcy Biography	1947, 1999	NO	10 and up
15	San Salvador	Columbus and the New World	Derleth, August	Vision Books	1957	YES	09-15

15	San Salvador	Golden Caravel (Christopher Columbus)	Bemister, Margaret	Catholic Treasury	1962	YES	10 and up
15	San Salvador	Pedro of the Water Jars (Christopher Columbus)	Daughters of Charity	Catholic Stories, Volume I	1987	NO	07-10
15	Spain	Book of Saints, Part 5 (St. Ignatius Loyola)	Lovasik, Fr. Lawrence	St. Joseph Picture	1985	YES	05 and up
15	Spain	Book of Saints, Part 10 (St. Beatrice Da Silva Meneses)	Lovasik, Fr. Lawrence	St. Joseph Picture	1997	NO	05 and up
15	Spain	Book of Saints, Part 11 (St. John of Sahagun)	Lovasik, Fr. Lawrence	St. Joseph Picture	1997	NO	05 and up
15	Spain	Columbus and the New World	Derleth, August	Vision Books	1957	YES	09-15
15	Spain	Don't Turn Back, A Story of St. Ignatius Loyola	Roberto, Brother	Footsteps of the Saints	1958, 2013	NO	12-15
15	Spain	Golden Caravel (Christopher Columbus)	Bemister, Margaret	Catholic Treasury	1962	YES	10 and up
15	Spain	Pedro of the Water Jars (Christopher Columbus)	Daughters of Charity	Catholic Stories, Volume I	1987	NO	07-10
15	Spain	Saints for Boys (St. Ignatius Loyola)	Muus, Solveig and Bart Tesoriero	Aquinas Kids	2012	NO	05-09
15	western Europe	Book of Saints, Part 5 (St. Vincent Ferrer)	Lovasik, Fr. Lawrence	St. Joseph Picture	1985	YES	05 and up
15	western Europe	Lives of the Saints: The Middle Ages (St. Vincent Ferrer)	Tesoriero, Bart	Aquinas Kids	2010	NO	05-09
15	western Europe	Truth Was Their Star (St. Vincent Ferrer)	Dorcy, Sister Mary Jean	Dorcy Biography	1947, 1999	NO	10 and up
16	Belgium	Robert	Richardson, M.K.	Patron Saint Books	1961	YES	08 and up
16	Belgium	Saints for Boys and Girls (St. John Berchmans)	Beebe, Catherine	Beebe Biography	1959	YES	09-14
16	Canada	Wilderness Explorer: The Story of Samuel de Champlain	Wilson, Charles Morrow	Hawthorn Junior Biography	1963	YES	11 and up
16	Central America	Friar and the Knight: Padre Olmedo and Cortez	Strousse, Flora	American Background	1957	YES	10-15
16	China	Lives of the Saints: The Middle Ages (St. Francis Xavier)	Tesoriero, Bart	Aquinas Kids	2010	NO	05-09
16	China	Saints for Boys (St. Francis Xavier)	Muus, Solveig and Bart Tesoriero	Aquinas Kids	2012	NO	05-09
16	China	Mission to Cathay	Polland, Madeleine	Clarion Books	1965, 1997	NO	09 and up

16	Cuba	Friar and the Knight: Padre Olmedo and Cortez	Strousse, Flora	American Background	1957	YES	10-15
16	England	Blood Red Crescent	Garnett, Henry	Clarion Books	1960, 2004, 2007	NO	09 and up
16	England	Book of Saints, Part 1 (St. Thomas More)	Lovasik, Fr. Lawrence	St. Joseph Picture	1981	NO	05 and up
16	England	Candle for Our Lady (Cromwell and Shrine of Walsingham)	Hunt, Regina Victoria	Catholic Treasury	1955	YES	10 and up
16	England	Cardinal Said No! (The), Story of St. John Fisher	Premont, Br. Jeremy	Holy Cross Press	1964	YES	09 and up
16	England	Conscience Game, The Story of St. Thomas More	Daughters of St. Paul	Encounter Books	1967, 1981	YES	09 and up
16	England	Conscience of a King (The), The Story of Thomas More	Stanley-Wrench, Margaret	Hawthorn Junior Biography	1962	YES	11 and up
16	England	Edmund Campion, Hero of God's Underground	Gardiner, Harold C.	Vision Books	1957, 1992	NO	09-15
16	England	In the Tower of London (St. Edmund Campion)	Daughters of Charity	Catholic Stories, Volume III	1995	NO	07-10
16	England	Lives of the Saints: The Middle Ages (St. Thomas More)	Tesoriero, Bart	Aquinas Kids	2010	NO	05-09
16	England	Red Hugh, Prince of Donegal	Reilly, Robert T.	Catholic Treasury	1957, 1997	NO	10 and up
16	England	Saint Thomas More of London	Ince, Elizabeth M.	Vision Books	1957, 2003	NO	09-15
16	England	Trumpet Sounds, A	Garnett, Henry	Clarion Books	1962	YES	09 and up
16	France	Book of Saints, Part 1 (St. Vincent de Paul)	Lovasik, Fr. Lawrence	St. Joseph Picture	1981	NO	05 and up
16	France	Book of Saints, Part 3 (St. Francis de Sales)	Lovasik, Fr. Lawrence	St. Joseph Picture	1982	NO	05 and up
16	France	Candle Burns for France, A (St. Germaine)	Thompson, Blanche	Favorite Catholic	1946	YES	07 and up
16	France	Don't Turn Back, A Story of St. Ignatius Loyola	Roberto, Brother	Footsteps of the Saints	1958, 2013	NO	12-15
16	France	Fire Is His Name: A Life of St. Vincent de Paul	Lomupo, Br. Robert	Holy Cross Press	1964	YES	09 and up
16	France	Girl in the Stable (The), The Life of St. Germaine	Cantoni, Louise	Encounter Books	1967	YES	09 and up
16	France	Golden Thread, A Novel of Saint Ignatius Loyola	de Wohl, Louis	de Wohl Biography	1952, 2002	NO	15 and up
16	France	Lives of the Saints: Modern Saints (St. Francis de Sales)	Tesoriero, Bart	Aquinas Kids	2012	NO	05-09

16	France	Lives of the Saints: The Middle Ages (St. Francis Xavier)	Tesoriero, Bart	Aquinas Kids	2010	NO	05-09
16	France	Lives of the Saints: Modern Saints (St. Vincent de Paul)	Tesoriero, Bart	Aquinas Kids	2012	NO	05-09
16	France	Robert	Richardson, M.K.	Patron Saint Books	1961	YES	08 and up
16	France	Saint Francis de Sales	Thompson, Blanche	Vision Books	1965	YES	09-15
16	France	Saint Francis of Paola (Paula)	Winkler, Father Jude	St. Joseph Pictur Books	2006	NO	05 and up
16	France	Saint Germaine (Cousin) and Her Guardian Angel	Cantoni, Louise Bellucci	Similar to Encounter Books	1964	YES	09 and up
16	France	Saint Germaine and the Sheep	Betz, Eva K.	Saints and Friendly Beasts	1961, 2004	NO	08 and up
16	France	Saint Ignatius and the Company of Jesus	Derleth, August	Vision Books	1956, 1999	NO	09-15
16	France	Saint Ignatius Loyola, Founder of the Jesuits	Forbes, F.A.	Forbes Biography	1913, 1998	NO	12 and up
16	France	Saint Ignatius of Loyola: For the Greater Glory of God	Giaimo, Donna & Patricia Jablonski	Encounter the Saints	2000	NO	09 and up
16	France	Saint Vincent de Paul	Forbes, F.A.	Forbes Biography	1919, 1998	NO	12 and up
16	France	Saint Vincent de Paul: Servant of Charity	Ethievant, Sister Catherine	Along the Paths of the Gospel	1999	YES	07-10
16	France	Saints for Boys (St. Francis Xavier)	Muus, Solveig and Bart Tesoriero	Aquinas Kids	2012	NO	05-09
16	France	Shepherd and His Sheep, A (St. Vincent de Paul)	Daughters of Charity	Catholic Stories, Volume IV	1995	NO	07-10
16	France	Stairway to the Stars, A Story of St. Germaine Cousin	Roberto, Brother	In the Footsteps of the Saints	1958, 2008	NO	09-12
16	France	Story of St. Germaine, A	Ernest, Brother	Footsteps of the Saints	1956, 2009	NO	06-09
16	France	Vincent de Paul, Saint of Charity	Hubbard, Margaret Ann	Vision Books	1960, 2002	NO	09-15
16	France	Wilderness Explorer: The Story of Samuel de Champlain	Wilson, Charles Morrow	Hawthorn Junior Biography	1963	YES	11 and up
16	Germany	Book of Saints, Part 5 (St. Peter Canisius)	Lovasik, Fr. Lawrence	St. Joseph Picture	1985	YES	05 and up

16	Greece	Blood Red Crescent	Garnett, Henry	Clarion Books	1960, 2007	NO	09 and up
16	Guatemala	Friar Among Savages, Father Luis Cancer	Kurt, Br. and Br. Antoninus	Banner Books	1958, 2011	NO	09-15
16	Holland	Army in Battle Array, An (St. John of Gorkum or Cologne)	Dorcy, Sister Mary Jean	Dorcy Biography	1955	YES	10 and up
16	Holland	Book of Saints, Part 5 (St. Peter Canisius)	Lovasik, Fr. Lawrence	St. Joseph Picture	1985	YES	05 and up
16	Holy Land	Saint Ignatius and the Company of Jesus	Derleth, August	Vision Books	1956, 1999	NO	09-15
16	India	Lives of the Saints: The Middle Ages (St. Francis Xavier)	Tesoriero, Bart	Aquinas Kids	2010	NO	05-09
16	India	Saints for Boys (St. Francis Xavier)	Muus, Solveig and Bart Tesoriero	Aquinas Kids	2012	NO	05-09
16	Ireland	Red Hugh, Prince of Donegal	Reilly, Robert T.	Catholic Treasury	1957, 1997	NO	10 and up
16	Island of Rhodes	Knights Besieged	Faulkner, Nancy	Clarion Books	1964	YES	09 and up
16	Italy	Army in Battle Array, An (Pope Saint Pius V)	Dorcy, Sister Mary Jean	Dorcy Biography	1955	YES	10 and up
16	Italy	Army in Battle Array, An (St. Catherine de Ricci)	Dorcy, Sister Mary Jean	Dorcy Biography	1955	YES	10 and up
16	Italy	Army in Battle Array, An (St. John of Gorkum)	Dorcy, Sister Mary Jean	Dorcy Biography	1955	YES	10 and up
16	Italy	Blood Red Crescent	Garnett, Henry	Clarion Books	1960, 2004, 2007	NO	09 and up
16	Italy	Book of Saints, Part 2 (St. Aloysius Gonzaga)	Lovasik, Fr. Lawrence	St. Joseph Picture	1981	NO	05 and up
16	Italy	Book of Saints, Part 3 (St. Charles Borromeo)	Lovasik, Fr. Lawrence	St. Joseph Picture	1982	NO	05 and up
16	Italy	Book of Saints, Part 4 (St. Angela Merici)	Lovasik, Fr. Lawrence	St. Joseph Picture	1982	YES	05 and up
16	Italy	Book of Saints, Part 5 (St. Camillus of Lellis)	Lovasik, Fr. Lawrence	St. Joseph Picture	1985	YES	05 and up
16	Italy	Book of Saints, Part 5 (St. Philip Neri)	Lovasik, Fr. Lawrence	St. Joseph Picture	1985	YES	05 and up
16	Italy	Book of Saints, Part 5 (St. Robert Bellarrmine)	Lovasik, Fr. Lawrence	St. Joseph Picture	1985	YES	05 and up
16	Italy	Book of Saints, Part 6 (St. Pius V)	Lovasik, Fr. Lawrence	St. Joseph Picture	1985	YES	05 and up
16	Italy	Book of Saints, Part 9 (St. Benedict the Black)	Lovasik, Fr. Lawrence	St. Joseph Picture	1996	NO	05 and up
16	Italy	Book of Saints, Part 12 (St. Andrew Avellino)	Lovasik, Fr. Lawrence	St. Joseph Picture	1999	NO	05 and up

16	Italy	Don't Turn Back, A Story of St. Ignatius Loyola	Roberto, Brother	Footsteps of the Saints	1958, 2013	NO	12-15
16	Italy	Footsteps of A Giant, Life of St. Charles Borromeo	Daughters of St. Paul	Encounter Books	1970	YES	09 and up
16	Italy	Gamble for God (A), St. Camillus de Lellis	Daughters of St. Paul	Encounter Books	1983	YES	09 and up
16	Italy	Golden Thread, A Novel of St. Ignatius Loyola	de Wohl, Louis	de Wohl Biography	1952, 2002	NO	15 and up
16	Italy	Hunter of Souls (Bld. Catherine of Racconigi)	Dorcy, Sister Mary Jean	Dorcy Biography	1949, 1999	YES	10 and up
16	Italy	Lives of the Saints: The Middle Ages (St. Charles Borromeo)	Tesoriero, Bart	Aquinas Kids	2010	NO	05-09
16	Italy	No Place for Defeat, Life of St. Pius V	Daughters of St. Paul	Encounter Books	1970, 1987	YES	09 and up
16	Italy	Promise to Angela: A Life of St. Angela Merici	McKern, Pat	Holy Cross Press	1966	YES	09 and up
16	Italy	Robert	Richardson, M.K.	Patron Saint Books	1961	YES	08 and up
16	Italy	Saint Angela Merici: Leading People to God	Keefe, Sister Maryellen	Along the Paths of the Gospel	2000	YES	07-10
16	Italy	Saint Ignatius and the Company of Jesus	Derleth, August	Vision Books	1956, 1999	NO	09-15
16	Italy	Saint Ignatius Loyola, Founder of the Jesuits	Forbes, F.A.	Forbes Biography	1913, 1998	NO	12 and up
16	Italy	Saint Ignatius of Loyola: For the Greater Glory of God	Giaimo, Donna & Patricia Jablonski	Encounter the Saints	2000	NO	09 and up
16	Italy	Saint Philip of the Joyous Heart	Connolly, Francis X.	Vision Books	1957, 1993	NO	09-15
16	Italy	Story of St. Angeli Merici, A	Ernest, Brother	Footsteps of the Saints	1960, 2011	NO	06-09
16	Italy	Story of St. Camillus, A	Ernest, Brother	Footsteps of the Saints	1954, 2012	NO	06-09
16	Italy	Story of St. Charles, A	Ernest, Brother	Footsteps of the Saints	1962, 2009	NO	06-09
16	Italy	Story of St. Stanislaus Kostka, A	Ernest, Brother	Footsteps of the Saints	1958, 2009	NO	06-09
16	Italy	They Became Saints (St. Aloysius: Prince and Jesuit Scholastic)	Francis, Father	Father Francis Coloring	1951	NO	07 and up
16	Italy	When Saints Were Young (St. Aloysius Gonzaga)	Thompson, Blanche Jennings	Vision Books	1960	YES	09-15
16	Italy	When Saints Were Young (St. Angela Merici)	Thompson, Blanche Jennings	Vision Books	1960	YES	09-15

16	Italy	When Saints Were Young (St. Charles Borromeo)	Thompson, Blanche Jennings	Vision Books	1960	YES	09-15
16	Italy	When Saints Were Young (St. Stanislaus Kostka)	Thompson, Blanche Jennings	Vision Books	1960	YES	09-15
16	Italy	Wings of an Eagle: The Story of Michelangelo	Peck, Anne Merriman	Hawthorn Junior Bio.	1963	YES	11 and up
16	Japan	Lives of the Saints: The Middle Ages (St. Francis Xavier)	Tesoriero, Bart	Aquinas Kids	2010	NO	05-09
16	Japan	Saints for Boys (St. Francis Xavier)	Muus, Solveig and Bart Tesoriero	Aquinas Kids	2012	NO	05-09
16	Mexico	Blessed Sebastian and the Oxen	Betz, Eva K.	Saints and Friendly Beasts	1961, 2003	NO	08 and up
16	Mexico	Cross in the West, The	Boesch, Mark	Vision Books	1956	YES	09-15
16	Mexico	Friar and the Knight: Padre Olmedo and Cortez	Strousse, Flora	American Background	1957	YES	10-15
16	Mexico	Miracle in Mexico: The Story of Juan Diego	Tinkle, Lon	Hawthorn Junior Biography	1965	YES	11 and up
16	Mexico	Our Lady of Guadalupe	Windeatt, Mary Fabyan	Windeatt Coloring	1954	YES	04 and up
16	Mexico	Our Lady of Guadalupe	de Paola, Tomie	de Paola Biography	1980, 1988	YES	04-08
16	Mexico	Our Lady of Guadalupe	Lovasik, Fr. Lawrence	St. Joseph Picture	1985, 1990	NO	05 and up
16	Mexico	Saint Juan Diego: and Our Lady of Guadalupe	Nobisso, Josephine	Encounter the Saints	2002	NO	09 and up
16	Mexico	Saints of the Americas (St. Juan Diego)	Winkler, Rev. Jude	St. Joseph Picture	2006	NO	05 and up
16	Mexico	Story of Our Lady of Guadalupe, A	Ernest, Brother	Footsteps of the Saints	1957, 2012	NO	06-09
16	Peru	Army in Battle Array, An (Bld. Martin de Porres)	Dorcy, Sister Mary Jean	Dorcy Biography	1955	YES	10 and up
16	Peru	Army in Battle Array, An (Saint Rose of Lima)	Dorcy, Sister Mary Jean	Dorcy Biography	1955	YES	10 and up
16	Peru	Book of Saints, Part 2 (St. Rose of Lima)	Lovasik, Fr. Lawrence	St. Joseph Picture	1981	NO	05 and up
16	Peru	Book of Saints, Part 7 (St. Martin de Porres)	Lovasik, Fr. Lawrence	St. Joseph Picture	1993	NO	05 and up
16	Peru	Girl Who Laughed at Satan (The), A Story of St. Rose of Lima	Roberto, Brother	In the Footsteps of the Saints	1956, 2008	NO	09-12
16	Peru	Linda (St. Rose of Lima)	Richardson, M.K.	Patron Saint Books	1960	YES	08 and up

16	Peru	Lives of the Saints: Modern Saints (St. Martin de Porres)	Tesoriero, Bart	Aquinas Kids	2012	NO	05-09
16	Peru	Lives of the Saints: Modern Saints (St. Rose of Lima)	Tesoriero, Bart	Aquinas Kids	2012	NO	05-09
16	Peru	Martin de Porres, Saint of the New World	Tarry, Ellen	Vision Books	1963	YES	09-15
16	Peru	Saint Martin de Porres	Lovasik, Fr. Lawrence	St. Joseph Picture	1983	NO	05 and up
16	Peru	Saint Martin de Porres and the Mice	Betz, Eva K.	Saints and Friendly Beasts	1963, 2003	NO	08 and up
16	Peru	Saint Martin de Porres: Humble Healer	DeDomenico, Elizabeth Marie	Encounter the Saints	2005	NO	09 and up
16	Peru	Saint Martin de Porres, The Story of the Little Doctor of Lima, Peru	Windeatt, Mary Fabyan	Windeatt Saint Series	1993	NO	09 and up
16	Peru	Saints for Boys (St. Martin de Porres)	Muus, Solveig and Bart Tesoriero	Aquinas Kids	2012	NO	05-09
16	Peru	Saints for Boys and Girls (St. Rose of Lima)	Beebe, Catherine	Beebe Biography	1959	YES	09-14
16	Peru	Saints for Girls (St. Rose of Lima)	Muus, Solveig and Bart Tesoriero	Aquinas Kids	2012	NO	05-09
16	Peru	Saints of the Americas (Sts. Rose of Lima and Martin de Porres)	Winkler, Rev. Jude	St. Joseph Picture	2006	NO	05 and up
16	Peru	St. Rose of Lima, The Story of the First Canonized Saint of the Americas	Windeatt, Mary Fabyan	Windeatt Saint Series	1993	NO	09 and up
16	Peru	They Became Saints (St. Martin de Porres: The Holy Negro of Lima)	Francis, Father	Father Francis Coloring	1951	NO	07 and up
16	Peru	They Became Saints (St. Rose of Lima: The First American Saint)	Francis, Father	Father Francis Coloring	1951	NO	07 and up
16	Poland	Book of Saints, Part 2 (St. Stanislaus Kostka)	Lovasik, Fr. Lawrence	St. Joseph Picture	1981	NO	05 and up
16	Poland	When Saints Were Young (St. Stanislaus Kostka)	Thompson, Blanche	Vision Books	1960	YES	09-15
16	Portugal	Book of Saints, Part 4 (St. John of God)	Lovasik, Fr. Lawrence	St. Joseph Picture	1982	YES	05 and up
16	Portugal	Lives of the Saints: The Middle Ages (St. John of God)	Tesoriero, Bart	Aquinas Kids	2010	NO	05-09

16	Scotland	Book of Saints, Part 10 (St. John Ogilvie)	Lovasik, Fr. Lawrence	St. Joseph Picture	1997	NO	05 and up
16	South America	Saint Francis Solano, Wonderworker of the New World and Apostle of Argentina and Peru	Windeatt, Mary Fabyan	Windeatt Saint Series	1994	NO	11 and up
16	Spain	Army in Battle Array, An (Blessed Alphonsus Navarrette & Companions)	Dorcy, Sister Mary Jean	Dorcy Biography	1955	YES	10 and up
16	Spain	Blessed Sebastian and the Oxen	Betz, Eva K.	Saints and Friendly Beasts	1961, 2003	NO	08 and up
16	Spain	Blood Red Crescent	Garnett, Henry	Clarion Books	1960, 2004, 2007	NO	09 and up
16	Spain	Book of Saints, Part 1 (St. Peter Claver)	Lovasik, Fr. Lawrence	St. Joseph Picture Books	1981	NO	05 and up
16	Spain	Book of Saints, Part 1 (St. Teresa of Avila)	Lovasik, Fr. Lawrence	St. Joseph Picture	1981	NO	05 and up
16	Spain	Book of Saints, Part 2 (St. Aloysius Gonzaga)	Lovasik, Fr. Lawrence	St. Joseph Picture	1981	NO	05 and up
16	Spain	Book of Saints, Part 3 (St. Francis Xavier)	Lovasik, Fr. Lawrence	St. Joseph Picture	1982	NO	05 and up
16	Spain	Book of Saints, Part 3 (St. John of the Cross)	Lovasik, Fr. Lawrence	St. Joseph Picture	1982	NO	05 and up
16	Spain	Book of Saints, Part 5 (St. Ignatius Loyola)	Lovasik, Fr. Lawrence	St. Joseph Picture	1985	YES	05 and up
16	Spain	Book of Saints, Part 12 (St. Peter of Alcantara)	Lovasik, Fr. Lawrence	St. Joseph Picture	1999	NO	05 and up
16	Spain	Flame in the Night, The Life of St. Francis Xavier	Daughters of St. Paul	Encounter Books	1967, 1981	YES	09 and up
16	Spain	Golden Thread, A Novel of Saint Ignatius Loyola	de Wohl, Louis	de Wohl Biography	1952, 2002	NO	15 and up
16	Spain	I Serve the King, A Story of St. Francis Borgia	Roberto, Brother	In the Footsteps of the Saints	1954, 2010	NO	09-12
16	Spain	Leaving Matters to God, The Life of St. Teresa of Avila	Cantoni, Louise Bellucci	Encounter Books	1982, 1984	YES	09 and up
16	Spain	Lives of the Saints: The Middle Ages (St. Francis Xavier)	Tesoriero, Bart	Aquinas Kids	2010	NO	05-09
16	Spain	Lives of the Saints: The Middle Ages (St. Ignatius of Loyola)	Tesoriero, Bart	Aquinas Kids	2010	NO	05-09
16	Spain	Lives of the Saints: The Middle Ages (St. Teresa of Avila)	Tesoriero, Bart	Aquinas Kids	2010	NO	05-09

16	Spain	More Saints of the Eucharist: Patron of the Eucharist (St. Paschal)	Francis, Father	Father Francis Coloring	1959	NO	06 and up
16	Spain	Pascual and the Kitchen Angels (St. Pascal Baylon)	de Paola, Tomie	de Paola Biography	2006	NO	04-08
16	Spain	Pedro Menendez de Aviles and the Founding of St. Augustine	Stone, Elaine Murray	American Background	1969	YES	10-15
16	Spain	Peter Claver, Saint Among Slaves	Roos, Ann	Vision Books	1965	YES	09-15
16	Spain	Saint Francis of the Seven Seas	Nevins, Albert J.	Junior Vision	1963	YES	09-11
16	Spain	Saint Francis of the Seven Seas	Nevins, Albert J.	Vision Books	1955, 1995	NO	09-15
16	Spain	Saint Francis Solano, Wonderworker of the New World and Apostle of Argentina and Peru	Windeatt, Mary Fabyan	Windeatt Saint Series	1994	NO	11 and up
16	Spain	Saint Francis Xavier	Marchand, Fr. Norbert	Catholic Children's Library	1965, 2012	NO	10 and up
16	Spain	Saint Ignatius and the Company of Jesus	Derleth, August	Vision Books	1956, 1999	NO	09-15
16	Spain	Saint Ignatius Loyola, Founder of the Jesuits	Forbes, F.A.	Forbes Biography	1913, 1998	NO	12 and up
16	Spain	Saint Ignatius of Loyola: For the Greater Glory of God	Giaimo, Donna & Patricia Jablonski	Encounter the Saints	2000	NO	09 and up
16	Spain	Saint John Masias, Marvelous Dominican Gatekeeper of Lima, Peru	Windeatt, Mary Fabyan	Windeatt Saint Series	1993	NO	10 and up
16	Spain	Saint Teresa of Avila	Windeatt, Mary Fabyan	Windeatt Coloring	1955	NO	04 and up
16	Spain	Saint Teresa of Avila: Joyful in the Lord	Wallace, Susan Helen	Encounter the Saints	2008	NO	09 and up
16	Spain	Saint Teresa of Avila, Reformer of Carmel	Forbes, F.A.	Forbes Biography	1917, 1998	NO	12 and up
16	Spain	Saints for Boys (St. Francis Xavier)	Muus, Solveig and Bart Tesoriero	Aquinas Kids	2012	NO	05-09
16	Spain	Saints for Boys (St. Ignatius Loyola)	Muus, Solveig and Bart Tesoriero	Aquinas Kids	2012	NO	05-09
16	Spain	Saints of the Americas (St. Peter Claver)	Winkler, Rev. Jude	St. Joseph Picture	2006	NO	05 and up
16	Spain	Sea Tiger: The Story of Pedro Menendez	Kolars, Frank	Hawthorn Junior Bio.	1963	YES	11 and up
16	Spain	Set All Afire, A Novel of Saint Francis Xavier	de Wohl, Louis	de Wohl Biography	1951, 1991	NO	15 and up

16	Spain	Story of Paschal Baylon, A	Ernest, Brother	Footsteps of the Saints	1960, 2011	NO	06-09
16	Spain	They Became Saints (St. Aloysius: Prince and Jesuit Scholastic)	Francis, Father	Father Francis Coloring	1951	NO	07 and up
16	Spain	Truth Was Their Star (Blessed John Masias)	Dorcy, Sister Mary Jean	Dorcy Biography	1947, 1999	NO	10 and up
16	Spain	Truth Was Their Star (St. Louis Bertrand)	Dorcy, Sister Mary Jean	Dorcy Biography	1947, 1999	NO	10 and up
16	Spain	When Saints Were Young (St. Aloysius Gonzaga)	Thompson, Blanche	Vision Books	1960	YES	09-15
16	Spain	When Saints Were Young (St. Teresa of Avila)	Thompson, Blanche	Vision Books	1960	YES	09-15
16	Switzerland	Book of Saints, Part 5 (St. Peter Canisius)	Lovasik, Fr. Lawrence	St. Joseph Picture	1985	YES	05 and up
16	Turkey	Knights Besieged	Faulkner, Nancy	Clarion Books	1964	YES	09 and up
16	United States	Cross in the West, The	Boesch, Mark	Vision Books	1956	YES	09-15
16	United States	Friar Among Savages, Father Luis Cancer	Kurt, Br. and Br. Antoninus	Banner Books	1958, 2011	NO	09-15
16	United States	Pedro Menendez de Aviles and the Founding of St. Augustine	Stone, Elaine Murray	American Background	1969	YES	10-15
16	United States	Sea Tiger: The Story of Pedro Menendez	Kolars, Frank	Hawthorn Junior Bio.	1963	YES	11 and up
16	United States	Wilderness Explorer: The Story of Samuel de Champlain	Wilson, Charles Morrow	Hawthorn Junior Biography	1963	YES	11 and up
16	world	Book of Saints, Part 3 (St. Francis Xavier)	Lovasik, Fr. Lawrence	St. Joseph Picture	1982	NO	05 and up
16	world	Flame in the Night, Life of St. Francis Xavier	Daughters of St. Paul	Encounter Books	1967, 1981	YES	09 and up
16	world	Saint Francis of the Seven Seas	Nevins, Albert J.	Junior Vision	1963	YES	09-11
16	world	Saint Francis of the Seven Seas	Nevins, Albert J.	Vision Books	1955, 1995	NO	09-15
16	world	Saint Francis Xavier	Marchand, Fr. Norbert	Catholic Children's Library	1965, 2012	NO	10 and up
16	world	Set All Afire, A Novel of Saint Francis Xavier	de Wohl, Louis	de Wohl Biography	1951, 1991	NO	15 and up
16	world	Ship's Boy with Magellan	Lomask, Milton	Clarion Books	1960, 2010	NO	09 and up
16 & 17	Bohemia	Story of the Infant Jesus of Prague, A	Ernest, Brother	Footsteps of the Saints	1956, 2009	NO	06-09
16 & 17	Czech Republic	Story of the Infant Jesus of Prague, A	Ernest, Brother	Footsteps of the Saints	1956, 2009	NO	06-09

17	Austria	Book of Saints, Part 7 (St. Lawrence of Brindisi)	Lovasik, Fr. Lawrence	St. Joseph Picture	1993	NO	05 and up
17	Belgium	Book of Saints, Part 2 (St. John Berchmans)	Lovasik, Fr. Lawrence	St. Joseph Picture	1981	NO	05 and up
17	Belgium	Robert	Richardson, M.K.	Patron Saint Books	1961	YES	08 and up
17	Belgium	Saints for Boys and Girls (St. John Berchmans)	Beebe, Catherine	Beebe Biography	1959	YES	09-14
17	Canada	Anne (shrine at Beaupre)	Richardson, M.K.	Patron Saint Books	1960	YES	08 and up
17	Canada	Black Robe (St. Isaac Jogues)	Daughters of Charity	Catholic Stories, Volume I	1987	NO	07-10
17	Canada	Blessed Kateri Tekakwitha	Windeatt, Mary Fabyan	Windeatt Coloring	1955	YES	04 and up
17	Canada	Blessed Kateri Tekakwitha, The Lily of the Mohawks	Lovasik, Fr. Lawrence	St. Joseph Picture	1981, 1996	YES	05 and up
17	Canada	Blessed Marie of New France, The Story of the First Missionary Sisters in Canada	Windeatt, Mary Fabyan	Windeatt Saint Series	1994	NO	10 and up
17	Canada	Book of Saints, Part 1 (St. Isaac Jogues)	Lovasik, Fr. Lawrence	St. Joseph Picture	1981	NO	05 and up
17	Canada	Book of Saints, Part 2 (Blessed Kateri Tekakwitha)	Lovasik, Fr. Lawrence	St. Joseph Picture	1981	NO	05 and up
17	Canada	Commandant Paul and the Founding of Montreal	Wilson, Charles Morrow	American Background	1966	YES	10-15
17	Canada	Cross Among the Tomahawks	Lomask, Milton	Clarion Books	1961, 2011	NO	09 and up
17	Canada	Crusaders of the Great River, Marquette & Joliet	Doty, Rev. William	Banner Books	1958, 2011	NO	09-15
17	Canada	Daniel Duluth, Explorer of the Northlands	Abodaher, Daniel	American Background	1966	YES	10-15
17	Canada	Father Marquette and the Great Rivers	Derleth, August	Junior Vision	1962	YES	09-11
17	Canada	Father Marquette and the Great Rivers	Derleth, August	Vision Books	1955, 1998	NO	09-15
17	Canada	Joseph the Huron	Bosco, Antoinette	American Background	1961	YES	10-15
17	Canada	Kateri Tekakwitha, Mohawk Maid	Brown, Evelyn M.	Vision Books	1958, 1991	NO	09-15
17	Canada	Kateri Tekakwitha, The Little Iroquois Girl	Richomme, Agnes	Catholic Children's	1965, 2012	NO	10 and up
17	Canada	Lives of the Saints: Modern Saints (St. Kateri Tekakwitha)	Tesoriero, Bart	Aquinas Kids	2012	NO	05-09

17	Canada	Lydia Longley, The First American Nun	McCarthy, Helen A.	Vision Books	1958	YES	09-15
17	Canada	Marguerite Bourgeoys, Pioneer Teacher	Genevieve, Sr. St. Mary	Vision Books	1963	YES	09-15
17	Canada	Mère Marie of New France	Windeatt, Mary Fabyan	American Background	1958	YES	10-15
17	Canada	Saint Isaac and the Indians	Lomask, Milton	Vision Books	1956, 1991	NO	09-15
17	Canada	Saint Isaac Jogues: With Burning Heart	Orfeo, Christine and Mary E. Tebo	Encounter the Saints	2002	NO	09 and up
17	Canada	Saint Kateri Tekakwitha: Courgeous Faith	Fisher, Lillian	Encounter the Saints	2012	NO	09 and up
17	Canada	Saint Kateri Tekakwitha, The Lily of the Mohawks	Lovasik, Fr. Lawrence	St. Joseph Picture	2012	NO	05 and up
17	Canada	Saints for Girls (Blessed Kateri Tekakwitha)	Muus, Solveig and Bart Tesoriero	Aquinas Kids	2012	NO	05-09
17	Canada	Saints of the Americas (Kateri Tekakwitha)	Winkler, Rev. Jude	St. Joseph Picture	2006	NO	05 and up
17	Canada	Saints of the Americas (St. Isaac Jogues)	Winkler, Rev. Jude	St. Joseph Picture	2006	NO	05 and up
17	Canada	Star of the Mohawk, Kateri Tekakwitha	MacDonald, Francis	Banner Books	1958, 2011	NO	09-15
17	Canada	Story of St. Isaac Jogues, A	Ernest, Brother	Footsteps of the Saints	1958, 2011	NO	06-09
17	Canada	They Became Saints (Kateri Tekakwitha: "The Lily of the Mohawks")	Francis, Father	Father Francis Coloring	1951	NO	07 and up
17	Canada	Wilderness Explorer: The Story of Samuel de Champlain	Wilson, Charles Morrow	Hawthorn Junior Biography	1963	YES	11 and up
17	Ecuador	Book of Saints, Part 9 (St. Mariana of Quito)	Lovasik, Fr. Lawrence	St. Joseph Picture	1996	NO	05 and up
17	Ecuador	Saints of the Americas (St. Mariana of Quito)	Winkler, Rev. Jude	St. Joseph Picture	2006	NO	05 and up
17	England	Adventurous Lady: Margaret Brent of Maryland	Grant, Dorothy Fremont	American Background	1957	YES	10-15
17	England	Bright Banners (St. Claude de la Colombiere)	Hunt, Regina Victoria	Catholic Treasury	1956	YES	10 and up
17	England	Saints for Boys and Girls (Bld. Richard Herst)	Beebe, Catherine	Beebe Biography	1959	YES	09-14
17	France	Anne (shrine at Auray)	Richardson, M.K.	Patron Saint Books	1960	YES	08 and up
17	France	Army in Battle Array, An (St. Louis de Montfort)	Dorcy, Sister Mary Jean	Dorcy Biography	1955	YES	10 and up

17	France	Black Robe (St. Isaac Jogues)	Daughters of Charity	Catholic Stories, Volume I	1987	NO	07-10
17	France	Blessed Marie of New France, The Story of the First Missionary Sisters in Canada	Windeatt, Mary Fabyan	Windeatt Saint Series	1994	NO	10 and up
17	France	Book of Saints, Part 1 (St. Isaac Jogues)	Lovasik, Fr. Lawrence	St. Joseph Picture	1981	NO	05 and up
17	France	Book of Saints, Part 1 (St. John Baptist de La Salle)	Lovasik, Fr. Lawrence	St. Joseph Picture	1981	NO	05 and up
17	France	Book of Saints, Part 1 (St. Margaret Mary Alacoque)	Lovasik, Fr. Lawrence	St. Joseph Picture	1981	NO	05 and up
17	France	Book of Saints, Part 1 (St. Vincent de Paul)	Lovasik, Fr. Lawrence	St. Joseph Picture	1981	NO	05 and up
17	France	Book of Saints, Part 3 (St. Francis de Sales)	Lovasik, Fr. Lawrence	St. Joseph Picture	1982	NO	05 and up
17	France	Book of Saints, Part 4 (St. Louise de Marillac)	Lovasik, Fr. Lawrence	St. Joseph Picture	1982	YES	05 and up
17	France	Book of Saints, Part 5 (St. John Eudes)	Lovasik, Fr. Lawrence	St. Joseph Picture	1985	YES	05 and up
17	France	Book of Saints, Part 7 (St. Jane Frances de Chantel)	Lovasik, Fr. Lawrence	St. Joseph Picture	1993	NO	05 and up
17	France	Book of Saints, Part 9 (St. Louis de Montfort)	Lovasik, Fr. Lawrence	St. Joseph Picture	1996	NO	05 and up
17	France	Cheerful Warrior, Life of St. Charles Garnier	Dollen, Charles	Encounter Books	1967	YES	09 and up
17	France	Commandant Paul and the Founding of Montreal	Wilson, Charles Morrow	American Background	1966	YES	10-15
17	France	Crusaders of the Great River, Marquette & Joliet	Doty, Rev. William	Banner Books	1958, 2011	NO	09-15
17	France	Father Marquette and the Great Rivers	Derleth, August	Junior Vision	1962	YES	09-11
17	France	Father Marquette and the Great Rivers	Derleth, August	Vision Books	1955, 1998	NO	09-15
17	France	Figs from Thistles: St. John Baptist de la Salle	Robbins, Br. Gerald	Holy Cross Press	1964	YES	09 and up
17	France	Fire Is His Name: A Life of St. Vincent de Paul	Lomupo, Br. Robert	Holy Cross Press	1964	YES	09 and up
17	France	Lives of the Saints: Modern Saints (St. Francis de Sales)	Tesoriero, Bart	Aquinas Kids	2012	NO	05-09
17	France	Lives of the Saints: Modern Saints (St. John Baptist de La Salle)	Tesoriero, Bart	Aquinas Kids	2012	NO	05-09
17	France	Lives of the Saints: Modern Saints (St. Louise de Marillac)	Tesoriero, Bart	Aquinas Kids	2012	NO	05-09

17	France	Lives of the Saints: Modern Saints (St. Vincent de Paul)	Tesoriero, Bart	Aquinas Kids	2012	NO	05-09
17	France	Louise (St. Louise de Marillac)	Daughters of Charity	Catholic Stories, Volume III	1995	NO	07-10
17	France	Mademoiselle Louise, Life of Louise de Marillac	Dollen, Charles	Encounter Books	1967	YES	09 and up
17	France	Marguerite Bourgeoys, Pioneer Teacher	Genevieve, Sr. St. Mary	Vision Books	1963	YES	09-15
17	France	Mère Marie of New France	Windeatt, Mary Fabyan	American Background	1958	YES	10-15
17	France	Robert	Richardson, M.K.	Patron Saint Books	1961	YES	08 and up
17	France	Saint Francis de Sales	Thompson, Blanche	Vision Books	1965	YES	09-15
17	France	Saint Isaac and the Indians	Lomask, Milton	Vision Books	1956, 1991	NO	09-15
17	France	Saint Isaac Jogues: With Burning Heart	Orfeo, Christine	Encounter the Saints	2002	NO	09 and up
17	France	Saints of the Americas (St. Isaac Jogues)	Winkler, Rev. Jude	St. Joseph Picture	2006	NO	05 and up
17	France	St. Louis de Montfort, The Story of Our Lady's Slave	Windeatt, Mary Fabyan	Windeatt Saint Series	1991	NO	12 and up
17	France	Saint Louise de Marillac	Roux, Marie-Genevieve and Elisabeth Charpy	Along the Paths of the Gospel	2001	YES	07-10
17	France	Saint Margaret Mary and the Promises of the Sacred Heart of Jesus	Windeatt, Mary Fabyan	Windeatt Saint Series	1994	NO	11 and up
17	France	Saint Margaret Mary, Apostle of the Sacred Heart	Vintrou, Francoise	Along the Paths of the Gospel	2000	YES	07-10
17	France	Saint Vincent de Paul	Forbes, F.A.	Forbes Biography	1919, 1998	NO	12 and up
17	France	Saint Vincent de Paul: Servant of Charity	Ethievant, Sister Catherine	Along the Paths of the Gospel	1999	YES	07-10
17	France	Saints for Girls (St. Margaret Mary Alacoque)	Muus, Solveig and Bart Tesoriero	Aquinas Kids	2012	NO	05-09
17	France	Shepherd and His Sheep, A (St. Vincent de Paul)	Daughters of Charity	Catholic Stories, Volume IV	1995	NO	07-10
17	France	St. Margaret Mary, Apostle of the Sacred Heart	Hume, Ruth Fox	Vision Books	1960	YES	09-15

17	France	Story of St. Isaac Jogues, A	Ernest, Brother	Footsteps of the Saints	1958, 2011	NO	06-09
17	France	Story of St. Louise de Marillac, A	Ernest, Brother	Footsteps of the Saints	1960, 2010	NO	06-09
17	France	Vincent de Paul, Saint of Charity	Hubbard, Margaret	Vision Books	1960, 2002	NO	09-15
17	France	Wilderness Explorer: The Story of Samuel de Champlain	Wilson, Charles Morrow	Hawthorn Junior Biography	1963	YES	11 and up
17	France	Woman Who Loved (A), Louise de Marillac	Dollen, Charles	Encounter Books	1987	YES	09 and up
17	Germany	Book of Saints, Part 7 (St. Lawrence of Brindisi)	Lovasik, Fr. Lawrence	St. Joseph Picture Books	1993	NO	05 and up
17	Ireland	Irish Saints (Blessed Oliver Plunkett)	Reilly, Robert T.	Vision Books	1964, 1981, 2002	YES	09-15
17	Italy	Book of Saints, Part 2 (St. John Berchmans)	Lovasik, Fr. Lawrence	St. Joseph Picture	1981	NO	05 and up
17	Italy	Book of Saints, Part 5 (St. Camillus of Lellis)	Lovasik, Fr. Lawrence	St. Joseph Picture	1985	YES	05 and up
17	Italy	Book of Saints, Part 5 (St. Robert Bellarrmine)	Lovasik, Fr. Lawrence	St. Joseph Picture	1985	YES	05 and up
17	Italy	Book of Saints, Part 7 (St. Lawrence of Brindisi)	Lovasik, Fr. Lawrence	St. Joseph Picture	1993	NO	05 and up
17	Italy	Book of Saints, Part 12 (Bld. Mary Fontanella or Mary of the Angels)	Lovasik, Father Lawrence	St. Joseph Picture Books	1999	NO	05 and up
17	Italy	Desert Padre: Eusebio Francisco Kino	Thayer, John	Catholic Treasury	1959	YES	10 and up
17	Italy	Father Kino, Priest to the Pimas	Clark, Ann Nolan	Vision Books	1963	YES	09-15
17	Italy	Gamble for God (A), St. Camillus de Lellis	Daughters of St. Paul	Encounter Books	1983	YES	09 and up
17	Italy	Little Friar Who Flew, (St. Joseph of Copertino)	Gauch, Patricia	Favorite Catholic Books	1980	YES	10 and up
17	Italy	Lives of the Saints: Modern Saints (St. Francis de Sales)	Tesoriero, Bart	Aquinas Kids	2012	NO	05-09
17	Italy	Robert	Richardson, M.K.	Patron Saint Books	1961	YES	08 and up
17	Italy	Saints for Boys and Girls (St. John Berchmans)	Beebe, Catherine	Beebe Biography	1959	YES	09-14
17	Italy	Story of St. Camillus, A	Ernest, Brother	Footsteps of the Saints	1954, 2012	NO	06-09
17	Italy	Two Trumpeters of Vienna, The	Pauli, Hertha	Clarion Books	1961	YES	09 and up

17	Japan	Army in Battle Array, An (Blessed Alphonsus Navarrette and Companions)	Dorcy, Sister Mary Jean	Dorcy Biography	1955	YES	10 and up
17	Mexico	Desert Padre: Eusebio Francisco Kino	Thayer, John	Catholic Treasury	1959	YES	10 and up
17	Mexico	Don Diego de Vargas	Buchanan, Rosemary	American Background	1963	YES	10-15
17	Mexico	Father Kino, Priest to the Pimas	Clark, Ann Nolan	Vision Books	1963	YES	09-15
17	Mexico	Padre Kino and the Trail to the Pacific	Steffan, Jack	American Background	1960	YES	10-15
17	Paraguay	Chuiraquimba and the Black Robes	Polland, Madeleine	Clarion Books	1962, 2010	NO	09 and up
17	Peru	Army in Battle Array, An (Bld. Martin de Porres)	Dorcy, Sister Mary Jean	Dorcy Biography	1955	YES	10 and up
17	Peru	Army in Battle Array, An (St. Rose of Lima)	Dorcy, Sister Mary Jean	Dorcy Biography	1955	YES	10 and up
17	Peru	Book of Saints, Part 2 (St. Rose of Lima)	Lovasik, Fr. Lawrence	St. Joseph Picture	1981	NO	05 and up
17	Peru	Book of Saints, Part 7 (St. Martin de Porres)	Lovasik, Fr. Lawrence	St. Joseph Picture	1993	NO	05 and up
17	Peru	Girl Who Laughed at Satan (The), A Story of St. Rose of Lima	Roberto, Brother	In the Footsteps of the Saints	1956, 2008	NO	09-12
17	Peru	Linda (St. Rose of Lima)	Richardson, M.K.	Patron Saint Books	1960	YES	08 and up
17	Peru	Lives of the Saints: Modern Saints (St. Martin de Porres)	Tesoriero, Bart	Aquinas Kids	2012	NO	05-09
17	Peru	Lives of the Saints: Modern Saints (St. Rose of Lima)	Tesoriero, Bart	Aquinas Kids	2012	NO	05-09
17	Peru	Martin de Porres, Saint of the New World	Tarry, Ellen	Vision Books	1963	YES	09-15
17	Peru	Saint John Masias, Marvelous Dominican Gatekeeper of Lima, Peru	Windeatt, Mary Fabyan	Windeatt Saint Series	1993	NO	10 and up
17	Peru	Saint Martin de Porres	Lovasik, Fr. Lawrence	St. Joseph Picture	1983	NO	05 and up
17	Peru	Saint Martin de Porres and the Mice	Betz, Eva K.	Saints and Friendly Beasts	1963, 2003	NO	08 and up
17	Peru	Saint Martin de Porres: Humble Healer	DeDomenico, Elizabeth	Encounter the Saints	2005	NO	09 and up
17	Peru	Saint Martin de Porres, The Story of the Little Doctor of Lima, Peru	Windeatt, Mary Fabyan	Windeatt Saint Series	1993	NO	09 and up

17	Peru	Saint Rose of Lima, Story of the First Canonized Saint of the Americas	Windeatt, Mary Fabyan	Windeatt Saint Series	1993	NO	09 and up
17	Peru	Saints for Boys (St. Martin de Porres)	Muus, Solveig and Bart Tesoriero	Aquinas Kids	2012	NO	05-09
17	Peru	Saints for Boys and Girls (St. Rose of Lima)	Beebe, Catherine	Beebe Biography	1959	YES	09-14
17	Peru	Saints of the Americas (Sts. Rose of Lima and Martin de Porres)	Winkler, Rev. Jude	St. Joseph Picture Books	2006	NO	05 and up
17	Peru	They Became Saints (St. Martin de Porres: The Holy Negro of Lima)	Francis, Father	Father Francis Coloring	1951	NO	07 and up
17	Peru	They Became Saints (St. Rose of Lima: The First American Saint)	Francis, Father	Father Francis Coloring	1951	NO	07 and up
17	Peru	Truth Was Their Star (Blessed John Masias)	Dorcy, Sister Mary Jean	Dorcy Biography	1947, 1999	NO	10 and up
17	Portugal	Book of Saints, Part 7 (St. Lawrence of Brindisi)	Lovasik, Fr. Lawrence	St. Joseph Picture	1993	NO	05 and up
17	Scotland	Book of Saints, Part 10 (St. John Ogilvie)	Lovasik, Fr. Lawrence	St. Joseph Picture	1997	NO	05 and up
17	South America	Book of Saints, Part 1 (St. Peter Claver)	Lovasik, Fr. Lawrence	St. Joseph Picture	1981	NO	05 and up
17	South America	Peter Claver, Saint Among Slaves	Roos, Ann	Vision Books	1965	YES	09-15
17	South America	Saint Francis Solano, Wonderworker of the New World and Apostle of Argentina and Peru	Windeatt, Mary Fabyan	Windeatt Saint Series	1994	NO	11 and up
17	South America	Saints of the Americas (St. Peter Claver)	Winkler, Rev. Jude	St. Joseph Picture	2006	NO	05 and up
17	Spain	Book of Saints, Part 1 (St. Peter Claver)	Lovasik, Fr. Lawrence	St. Joseph Picture	1981	NO	05 and up
17	Spain	Don Diego de Vargas	Buchanan, Rosemary	American Background	1963	YES	10-15
17	Spain	Peter Claver, Saint Among Slaves	Roos, Ann	Vision Books	1965	YES	09-15
17	Spain	Saint John Masias, Marvelous Dominican Gatekeeper of Lima, Peru	Windeatt, Mary Fabyan	Windeatt Saint Series	1993	NO	10 and up
17	Spain	Saints of the Americas (St. Peter Claver)	Winkler, Rev. Jude	St. Joseph Picture	2006	NO	05 and up
17	Spain	Truth Was Their Star (Blessed John Masias)	Dorcy, Sister Mary Jean	Dorcy Biography	1947, 1999	NO	10 and up
17	United States	Adventurous Lady: Margaret Brent of Maryland	Grant, Dorothy Fremont	American Background	1957	YES	10-15

17	United States	Black Robe (St. Isaac Jogues)	Daughters of Charity	Catholic Stories for Boys & Girls, Volume I	1987	NO	07-10
17	United States	Blessed Kateri Tekakwitha	Windeatt, Mary Fabyan	Windeatt Coloring	1955	YES	04 and up
17	United States	Bld. Kateri Tekakwitha, Lily of the Mohawks	Lovasik, Fr. Lawrence	St. Joseph Picture	1981, 1996	YES	05 and up
17	United States	Book of Saints, Part 1 (St. Isaac Jogues)	Lovasik, Fr. Lawrence	St. Joseph Picture	1981	NO	05 and up
17	United States	Book of Saints, Part 2 (Bld. Kateri Tekakwitha)	Lovasik, Fr. Lawrence	St. Joseph Picture	1981	NO	05 and up
17	United States	Cheerful Warrior, Life of St. Charles Garnier	Dollen, Charles	Encounter Books	1967	YES	09 and up
17	United States	Colonial Governor, Thomas Dongan of New York	Hopkins, J.G.E.	American Background	1957	YES	10-15
17	United States	Cross Among the Tomahawks	Lomask, Milton	Clarion Books	1961, 2011	NO	09 and up
17	United States	Crusaders of the Great River, Marquette and Joliet	Doty, Rev. William	Banner Books	1958, 2011	NO	09-15
17	United States	Daniel Duluth, Explorer of the Northlands	Abodaher, Daniel	American Background	1966	YES	10-15
17	United States	De Tonti of the Iron Hand and the Exploration of the Mississippi	Heagney, Anne	American Background	1959	YES	10-15
17	United States	Desert Padre: Eusebio Francisco Kino	Thayer, John	Catholic Treasury	1959	YES	10 and up
17	United States	Don Diego de Vargas	Buchanan, Rosemary	American Background	1963	YES	10-15
17	United States	Father Kino, Priest to the Pimas	Clark, Ann Nolan	Vision Books	1963	YES	09-15
17	United States	Father Marquette and the Great Rivers	Derleth, August	Junior Vision	1962	YES	09-11
17	United States	Father Marquette and the Great Rivers	Derleth, August	Vision Books	1955, 1998	NO	09-15
17	United States	Forty-Ninth Star (The), Alaska	Savage, Alma	Banner Books	1959, 2011	NO	09-15
17	United States	Joseph the Huron	Bosco, Antoinette	American Background	1961	YES	10-15
17	United States	Kateri Tekakwitha, Mohawk Maid	Brown, Evelyn M.	Vision Books	1958, 1991	NO	09-15
17	United States	Kateri Tekakwitha, The Little Iroquois Girl	Richomme, Agnes	Catholic Children's Library	1965, 2012	NO	10 and up
17	United States	Lives of the Saints: Modern Saints (St. Kateri Tekakwitha)	Tesoriero, Bart	Aquinas Kids	2012	NO	05-09

17	United States	Lydia Longley, The First American Nun	McCarthy, Helen A.	Vision Books	1958	YES	09-15
17	United States	Marylanders: A Story of the Puritan Revolt in Lord Baltimore's Colony	Heagney, Anne	Catholic Treasury	1957	YES	10 and up
17	United States	Ottawanta (Our Lady of the Fields)	Daughters of Charity	Catholic Stories, Volume II	1992	NO	07-10
17	United States	Padre Kino and the Trail to the Pacific	Steffan, Jack	American Background	1960	YES	10-15
17	United States	Saint Isaac and the Indians	Lomask, Milton	Vision Books	1956, 1991	NO	09-15
17	United States	Saint Isaac Jogues: With Burning Heart	Orfeo, Christine & Mary E. Tebo	Encounter the Saints	2002	NO	09 and up
17	United States	Saint Kateri Tekakwitha: Courgeous Faith	Fisher, Lillian	Encounter the Saints	2012	NO	09 and up
17	United States	Saint Kateri Tekakwitha, Lily of the Mohawks	Lovasik, Fr. Lawrence	St. Joseph Picture	2012	NO	05 and up
17	United States	Saints for Girls (Blessed Kateri Tekakwitha)	Muus, Solveig and Bart Tesoriero	Aquinas Kids	2012	NO	05-09
17	United States	Saints of the Americas (Kateri Tekakwitha)	Winkler, Rev. Jude	St. Joseph Picture	2006	NO	05 and up
17	United States	Saints of the Americas (St. Isaac Jogues)	Winkler, Rev. Jude	St. Joseph Picture	2006	NO	05 and up
17	United States	Star of the Mohawk, Kateri Tekakwitha	MacDonald, Francis	Banner Books	1958, 2011	NO	09-15
17	United States	Story of St. Isaac Jogues, A	Ernest, Brother	Footsteps of the Saints	1958, 2011	NO	06-09
17	United States	They Became Saints (Venerable Kateri Tekakwitha: "The Lily of the Mohawks")	Francis, Father	Father Francis Coloring Books	1951	NO	07 and up
17	United States	Wilderness Explorer: The Story of Samuel de Champlain	Wilson, Charles Morrow	Hawthorn Junior Biography	1963	YES	11 and up
18	Austria (Moravia)	Book of Saints, Part 11 (St. Clement Mary Hofbauer)	Lovasik, Fr. Lawrence	St. Joseph Picture	1997	NO	05 and up
18	Austria	Story of Franz Schubert, A	Ernest, Brother	In the Footsteps of the Saints	1961, 2011	NO	06-09
18	Belgium	Great Black Robe, The (Father Peter de Smet)	Pitrone, Jean Maddern	Similar to Encounter Books	1964, 1965, 1981	YES	09 and up
18	Canada	Daniel Duluth, Explorer of the Northlands	Abodaher, Daniel	American Background	1966	YES	10-15
18	Canada	Lydia Longley, The First American Nun	McCarthy, Helen A.	Vision Books	1958	YES	09-15

18	Egypt	Man Who Could Read Stones: Champollion and the Rosetta Stone	Honour, Alan	Hawthorn Junior Biography	1966	YES	11 and up
18	Far East	Father of the American Navy, Captain John Barry	Anderson, Floyd	Banner Books	1959, 2011	NO	09-15
18	France	Army in Battle Array, An (St. Louis de Montfort)	Dorcy, Sister Mary Jean	Dorcy Biography	1955	YES	10 and up
18	France	Book of Saints, Part 1 (St. John Baptist de La Salle)	Lovasik, Fr. Lawrence	St. Joseph Picture	1981	NO	05 and up
18	France	Book of Saints, Part 4 (St. John Vianney)	Lovasik, Fr. Lawrence	St. Joseph Picture	1982	YES	05 and up
18	France	Book of Saints, Part 6 (St. Benedict Labre)	Lovasik, Fr. Lawrence	St. Joseph Picture	1985	YES	05 and up
18	France	Book of Saints, Part 6 (St. Madeleine Sophie Barat)	Lovasik, Fr. Lawrence	St. Joseph Picture	1985	YES	05 and up
18	France	Book of Saints, Part 9 (St. Louis de Montfort)	Lovasik, Fr. Lawrence	St. Joseph Picture	1996	NO	05 and up
18	France	Book of Saints, Part 10 (St. Eugene de Mazenod)	Lovasik, Fr. Lawrence	St. Joseph Picture Books	1997	NO	05 and up
18	France	Book of Saints, Part 11 (St. Madeleine Sophie Barat)	Lovasik, Fr. Lawrence	St. Joseph Picture Books	1997	NO	05 and up
18	France	Boy of Philadelphia: A Story about the Continental Congress	Morriss, Frank	Catholic Treasury	1955	YES	10 and up
18	France	Candle Burns for France, A (Cure d'Ars)	Thompson, Blanche Jennings	Favorite Catholic Books	1946	YES	07 and up
18	France	Country Road Home, The Story of St. John Vianney, Cure of Ars	Daughters of St. Paul	Encounter Books	1966, 1987	YES	09 and up
18	France	Cure of Ars (The), The Priest Who Out-talked the Devil	Lomask, Milton	Vision Books	1958, 1998	NO	09-15
18	France	Cure of Ars, The Story of St. John Vianney, Patron Saint of Parish Priests	Windeatt, Mary Fabyan	Windeatt Saint Series	1991	NO	10 and up
18	France	Daughter of the Seine, A Life of Madame Roland	Eaton, Jeannette	Newbery	1929	YES	10 and up
18	France	Dear Philippine: Mission of Mother Duchesne	Hubbard, Margaret	Vision Books	1964	YES	09-15
18	France	Father of the American Navy, Captain John Barry	Anderson, Floyd	Banner Books	1959, 2011	NO	09-15
18	France	Figs from Thistles: St. John Baptist de la Salle	Robbins, Br. Gerald	Holy Cross Press	1964	YES	09 and up
18	France	Frontier Bishop: Simon Gabriel Bruté	Hughes, Riley	Catholic Treasury	1959, 2012	NO	10 and up

18	France	Lives of the Saints: Modern Saints (St. John Baptist de La Salle)	Tesoriero, Bart	Aquinas Kids	2012	NO	05-09
18	France	Man Who Could Read Stones: Champollion and the Rosetta Stone	Honour, Alan	Hawthorn Junior Biography	1966	YES	11 and up
18	France	Mother Barat's Vineyard	Hubbard, Margaret	Vision Books	1962	YES	09-15
18	France	Red Bonnet, The	Garnett, Henry	Clarion Books	1964, 1974	YES	09 and up
18	France	Rochambeau and Our French Allies	Lomask, Milton	American Background	1965	YES	10-15
18	France	Saint John Vianney: Priest for All People	DeDomenico, Elizabeth	Encounter the Saints	2008	NO	09 and up
18	France	Saint Julie Billiart: The Smiling Saint	Glavich, Mary Kathleen	Encounter the Saints	2002	YES	09 and up
18	France	St. Louis de Montfort, The Story of Our Lady's Slave	Windeatt, Mary Fabyan	Windeatt Saint Series	1991	NO	12 and up
18	France	Simon Bruté and the Western Adventure	Bartelme, Elizabeth	American Background	1959, 2012	NO	10-15
18	France	Stepping Stones to Heaven, A Story of St. Gaspar del Bufalo	Flavius, Brother	In the Footsteps of the Saints	1964, 2010	NO	09-12
18	France	Story of St. John Vianney, A	Ryan, Brother Ernest	Dujarie Press Reprint	1959, 2008	NO	06-09
18	France	Under Three Flags: The Story of Gabriel Richard	Abodaher, David J.	Hawthorn Junior Biography	1965	YES	11 and up
18	Germany	Story of Beethoven, A	Ryan, Brother Ernest	Dujarie Press Reprint	1960, 2005	NO	06-09
18	Haiti	Pierre Toussaint, Pioneer in Brotherhood	Sheehan, Arthur & Elizabeth	American Background	1963	YES	10-15
18	Ireland	Courageous Catherine: Mother Mary Catherine McAuley, The First Sister of Mercy	Marie, Sister Raymond	Catholic Treasury	1958	YES	10 and up
18	Ireland	Father of the American Navy, Captain John Barry	Anderson, Floyd	Banner Books	1959, 2011	NO	09-15
18	Ireland	Irish Saints (Bishop Edward J. Galvin)	Reilly, Robert T.	Vision Books	1964, 1981, 2002	YES	09-15
18	Ireland	Irish Saints (Father Theobald Mathew)	Reilly, Robert T.	Vision Books	1964, 1981, 2002	YES	09-15

18	Ireland	Irish Saints (Matt Talbot)	Reilly, Robert T.	Vision Books	1964, 1981, 2002	YES	09-15
18	Ireland	Irish Saints (Mother Catherine McAuley)	Reilly, Robert T.	Vision Books	1964, 1981, 2002	YES	09-15
18	Ireland	Mathew Carey, Pamphleter for Freedom	Hindman, Jane F.	American Background	1960	YES	10-15
18	Ireland	Story of Captain John Barry, A	Flavius, Brother	Footsteps of the Saints	1965, 2012	NO	06-09
18	Ireland	Story of Venerable Mother Catherine McAuley	Ernest, Brother	In the Footsteps of the Saints	1959, 2011	NO	06-09
18	Italy	Anina (daughter of St. Elizabeth Seton)	Daughters of Charity	Catholic Stories, Volume II	1992	NO	07-10
18	Italy	Book of Saints, Part 2 (St. Gerard Majella)	Lovasik, Fr. Lawrence	St. Joseph Picture	1981	NO	05 and up
18	Italy	Book of Saints, Part 4 (St. Alphonsus Liguori)	Lovasik, Fr. Lawrence	St. Joseph Picture	1982	YES	05 and up
18	Italy	Book of Saints, Part 5 (St. Paul of the Cross)	Lovasik, Fr. Lawrence	St. Joseph Picture	1985	YES	05 and up
18	Italy	Book of Saints, Part 6 (St. Benedict Labre)	Lovasik, Fr. Lawrence	St. Joseph Picture	1985	YES	05 and up
18	Italy	Book of Saints, Part 11 (St. Clement Mary Hofbauer)	Lovasik, Fr. Lawrence	St. Joseph Picture	1997	NO	05 and up
18	Italy	Book of Saints, Part 12 (Bld. Mary Fontanella or Mary of the Angels)	Lovaski, Fr. Lawrence	St. Joseph Picture Books	1999	NO	05 and up
18	Italy	Book of Saints, Part 12 (St. Lucy Filippini)	Lovasik, Fr. Lawrence	St. Joseph Picture	1999	NO	05 and up
18	Italy	Book of Saints, Part 12 (St. Teresa Margaret Redi)	Lovasik, Fr. Lawrence	St. Joseph Picture	1999	NO	05 and up
18	Italy	Champion of the Apostolate: The Life of St. Vincent Pallotti	Greene, Brother Ellis	Holy Cross Press	1967	YES	09 and up
18	Italy	Lives of the Saints: Modern Saints (St. Gerard)	Tesoriero, Bart	Aquinas Kids	2012	NO	05-09
18	Italy	Miracle Man of Muro (The), A Story of St. Gerard Majella	Ernest, Brother	In the Footsteps of the Saints	1950, 2011	NO	09-12
18	Italy	More Saints of the Eucharist: A Playmate of Jesus (St. Gerard Majella)	Francis, Father	Father Francis Coloring	1959	NO	06 and up
18	Italy	Saints for Boys and Girls (St. Gerard Majella)	Beebe, Catherine	Beebe Biography	1959	YES	09-14

18	Mexico	Desert Padre: Eusebio Francisco Kino	Thayer, John	Catholic Treasury	1959	YES	10 and up
18	Mexico	Don Diego de Vargas	Buchanan, Rosemary	American Background	1963	YES	10-15
18	Mexico	Father Kino, Priest to the Pimas	Clark, Ann Nolan	Vision Books	1963	YES	09-15
18	Mexico	First Californian, Story of Fray Junipero Serra	Demarest, Donald	Hawthorn Junior Bio.	1963	YES	11 and up
18	Mexico	Padre Kino and the Trail to the Pacific	Steffan, Jack	American Background	1960	YES	10-15
18	Mexico	Saints of the Americas (Bld. Junipero Serra)	Winkler, Rev. Jude	St. Joseph Picture	2006	NO	05 and up
18	Poland	Cavalry Hero: Casimir Pulaski	Adams, Dorothy	American Background	1957	YES	10-15
18	Spain	Don Diego de Vargas	Buchanan, Rosemary	American Background	1963	YES	10-15
18	Spain	First Californian, Story of Fray Junipero Serra	Demarest, Donald	Hawthorn Junior Bio.	1963	YES	11 and up
18	Spain	Saints of the Americas (Bld. Junipero Serra)	Winkler, Rev. Jude	St. Joseph Picture	2006	NO	05 and up
18	United States	Anina (daughter of St. Elizabeth Seton)	Daughters of Charity	Catholic Stories for Boys & Girls, Volume II	1992	NO	07-10
18	United States	Bishop's Boy (John Carroll)	Anderson, Floyd	Catholic Treasury	1957	YES	10 and up
18	United States	Book of Saints, Part 1 (St. Elizabeth Ann Seton)	Lovasik, Fr. Lawrence	St. Joseph Picture	1981	NO	05 and up
18	United States	Boy of Philadelphia: A Story about the Continental Congress	Morriss, Frank	Catholic Treasury	1955	YES	10 and up
18	United States	Cavalry Hero, Casimir Pulaski	Adams, Dorothy	American Background	1957	YES	10-15
18	United States	Charles Carroll and the American Revolution	Lomask, Milton	American Background	1959	YES	10-15
18	United States	Daniel Duluth, Explorer of the Northlands	Abodaher, Daniel	American Background	1966	YES	10-15
18	United States	De Tonti of the Iron Hand and the Exploration of the Mississippi	Heagney, Anne	American Background	1959	YES	10-15
18	United States	Desert Padre: Eusebio Francisco Kino	Thayer, John	Catholic Treasury	1959	YES	10 and up
18	United States	Don Diego de Vargas	Buchanan, Rosemary	American Background	1963	YES	10-15
18	United States	Elizabeth Bayley Seton	Daughters of Charity	Catholic Stories for Boys & Girls, Volume II	1992	NO	07-10

18	United States	Fanny Allen, Green Mountain Rebel	Betz, Eva K.	American Background	1962	YES	10-15
18	United States	Father Kino, Priest to the Pimas	Clark, Ann Nolan	Vision Books	1963	YES	09-15
18	United States	Father of the American Navy, Capt. John Barry	Anderson, Floyd	Banner Books	1959, 2011	NO	09-15
18	United States	First Californian, The Story of Fray Junipero Serra	Demarest, Donald	Hawthorn Junior Biography	1963	YES	11 and up
18	United States	Forty-Ninth Star (The), Alaska	Savage, Alma	Banner Books	1959, 2011	NO	09-15
18	United States	Frontier Priest and Congressman, Father Gabriel Richard	Alois, Brother	Banner Books	1958	YES	09-15
18	United States	God and the General's Daughter	Heagney, Anne	Similar to Catholic Treasury	1953	YES	10 and up
18	United States	Great Black Robe, The (Father Peter de Smet)	Pitrone, Jean Maddern	Similar to Encounter Books	1964, 1965, 1981	YES	09 and up
18	United States	John Carroll: Bishop and Patriot	Lomask, Milton	Vision Books	1956	YES	09-15
18	United States	Lives of the Saints: Modern Saints (St. Elizabeth Ann Seton)	Tesoriero, Bart	Aquinas Kids	2012	NO	05-09
18	United States	Mathew Carey, Pamphleter for Freedom	Hindman, Jane F.	American Background	1960	YES	10-15
18	United States	Mother Seton and the Sisters of Charity	Power-Waters, Alma	Junior Vision	1963	YES	09-11
18	United States	Mother Seton and the Sisters of Charity	Power-Waters, Alma	Vision Books	1957, 2000	NO	09-15
18	United States	Mother Seton: Wife, Mother, Educator, Foundress, Saint	Daughters of St. Paul	Similar to Encounter Books	1975	YES	10 and up
18	United States	Padre Kino and the Trail to the Pacific	Steffan, Jack	American Background	1960	YES	10-15
18	United States	Pierre Toussaint, Pioneer in Brotherhood	Sheehan, Arthur and Elizabeth	American Background	1963	YES	10-15
18	United States	Priest, Patriot and Leader, The Story of Archbishop Carroll	Betz, Eva K.	Banner Books	1960, 2011	NO	09-15
18	United States	Road to the King's Mountain, The (Junipero Serra)	Hubbard, Margaret Ann	Clarion Books	1963	YES	09 and up
18	United States	Rochambeau and Our French Allies	Lomask, Milton	American Background	1965	YES	10-15
18	United States	Saint Elizabeth Ann Seton	Lovasik, Fr. Lawrence	St. Joseph Picture	1981, 1990	NO	05 and up

18	United States	Saint Elizabeth Ann Seton: Daughter of America	Grunwell, Jeanne and Mari Goering	Encounter the Saints	1999	NO	09 and up
18	United States	Saints for Girls (St. Elizabeth Ann Seton)	Muus, Solveig and Bart Tesoriero	Aquinas Kids	2012	NO	05-09
18	United States	Saints of the Americas (Bld. Junipero Serra)	Winkler, Rev. Jude	St. Joseph Picture	2006	NO	05 and up
18	United States	Saints of the Americas (St. Elizabeth Ann Seton)	Winkler, Rev. Jude	St. Joseph Picture Books	2006	NO	05 and up
18	United States	Simon Bruté and the Western Adventure	Bartelme, Elizabeth	American Background	1959, 2012	NO	10-15
18	United States	Story of Mother Elizabeth Seton, A	Ryan, Brother Ernest	Dujarie Press Reprint	1960, 2008	NO	06-09
18	United States	Under Three Flags: The Story of Gabriel Richard	Abodaher, David J.	Hawthorn Junior Bio.	1965	YES	11 and up
18	United States	Ursulines, Nuns of Adventure: Story of the New Orleans Community	Kane, Harnett T.	Vision Books	1959	YES	09-15
18	United States	Virgil Barber, New England Pied Piper	Betz, Eva K.	American Background	1963	YES	10-15
18	United States	William Gaston, Fighter for Justice	Betz, Eva K.	American Background	1964	YES	10-15
19	Africa	Book of Saints, Part 10 (St. Justin de Jacobis)	Lovasik, Fr. Lawrence	St. Joseph Picture Books	1997	NO	05 and up
19	Africa (Sudan)	Saint Bakhita of Sudan: Forever Free	Wallace, Susan Helen	Encounter the Saints	2006	NO	09 and up
19	Africa (Uganda)	African Triumph, The Life of Charles Lwanga	Dollen, Charles	Encounter Books	1967, 1978	YES	09 and up
19	Algeria	Charles de Foucauld, Adventurer of the Desert	Garnett, Emmeline	Vision Books	1962	YES	09-15
19	Austria	Man Who Found Out Why: The Story of Gregor Mendel	Webster, Gary	Hawthorn Junior Biography	1963	YES	11 and up
19	Austria (Moravia)	Book of Saints, Part 11 (St. Clement Mary Hofbauer)	Lovasik, Fr. Lawrence	St. Joseph Picture	1997	NO	05 and up
19	Belgium	Apostle of Ice and Snow: A Life of Bishop Charles Seghers	Betz, Eva	Holy Cross Press	1964	YES	09 and up
19	Belgium	Black Robe Peacemaker, Pierre de Smet	Hopkins, J.G.E.	American Background	1958	YES	10-15
19	Belgium	Book of Saints, Part 11 (St. Mutien Marie Wiaux)	Lovasik, Fr. Lawrence	St. Joseph Picture	1997	NO	05 and up
19	Belgium	Charles John Seghers, Pioneer in Alaska	Bosco, Antoinette	American Background	1960	YES	10-15

19	Belgium	Father Damien and the Bells	Sheehan, Arthur and Elizabeth	Junior Vision	1962	YES	09-11
19	Belgium	Father Damien and the Bells	Sheehan, Arthur and Elizabeth	Vision Books	1957, 2004	NO	09-15
19	Belgium	No Greater Love, Life of Fr. Damien of Molokai	Daughters of St. Paul	Encounter Books	1979	YES	09 and up
19	Belgium	Saint Damien of Molokai: Hero of Hawaii	Richards, Virginia	Encounter the Saints	2009	NO	09 and up
19	Belgium	Story of Blessed Pauline von Mallinckrodt, A	Ernest, Brother	In the Footsteps of the Saints	1961, 2010	NO	06-09
19	Bohemia	Book of Saints, Part 6 (St. John Neumann)	Lovasik, Fr. Lawrence	St. Joseph Picture	1985	YES	05 and up
19	Bohemia	John Neumann, The Children's Bishop	Sheehan, Elizabeth Odell	Vision Books	1965	YES	09-15
19	Bohemia	Lives of the Saints: Modern Saints (St. John Neumann)	Tesoriero, Bart	Aquinas Kids	2012	NO	05-09
19	Bohemia	Saints of the Americas (St. John Neumann)	Winkler, Rev. Jude	St. Joseph Picture	2006	NO	05 and up
19	Bohemia	Wandering Minstrel (The), A Story of Antonin Dvorak	Nash, Brother Roy	In the Footsteps of the Saints	1955, 2010	NO	09-12
19	Brazil	Princess Isabel of Brazil and the Glittering Pen	Comfort, Mildred	American Background	1969	YES	10-15
19	Canada	Apostle of Ice and Snow: A Life of Bishop Charles Seghers	Betz, Eva	Holy Cross Press	1964	YES	09 and up
19	Canada	Brother Andre of Montreal	Clark, Ann Nolan	Vision Books	1967	YES	09-15
19	Canada	Charcoal Faces	Robinson, Mabel Otis	Catholic Treasury	1956	YES	10 and up
19	Canada	Charles John Seghers, Pioneer in Alaska	Bosco, Antoinette	American Background	1960	YES	10-15
19	Canada	Fighting Father Duffy	Bishop, Jim & Virginia Lee	Vision Books	1956	YES	09-15
19	Canada	First Sioux Nun, Sister Marie-Josephine Nebraska (1859-1894)	Hilger, Sister Mary Ione	Similar to Catholic Treasury	1963	YES	10 and up
19	Canada	God and the General's Daughter	Heagney, Anne	Similar to Catholic Treasury	1953	YES	10 and up
19	Canada	Just for Today, A Story of Blessed Marie Leonie	Roberto, Brother	Footsteps of the Saints	1955, 2010	NO	09-12
19	Canada	Medicine for Wildcat: A Life Story about Samuel Charles Mazzuchelli	Riordan, Robert	Catholic Treasury	1956	YES	10 and up

19	Canada	Mountain for St. Joseph: Life of Brother Andre, Miracle Man of Montreal	Bond, Ian	Holy Cross Press	1965	YES	09 and up
19	Canada	Saint Andre Bessett: Miracles in Montreal	Jablonski, Patricia Edward	Encounter the Saints	2010	NO	09 and up
19	Canada	Saints of the Americas (Bld. Marie Rose Durocher)	Winkler, Rev. Jude	St. Joseph Picture Books	2006	NO	05 and up
19	Canary Islands	Book of Saints, Part 6 (St. Anthony Mary Claret)	Lovasik, Fr. Lawrence	St. Joseph Picture	1985	YES	05 and up
19	China	Flowery Kingdom, The (St. John Gabriel)	Daughters of Charity	Catholic Stories for Boys & Girls, Volume IV	1995	NO	07-10
19	China	Irish Saints (Bishop Edward J. Galvin)	Reilly, Robert T.	Vision Books	1964, 1981, 2002	YES	09-15
19	Cuba	Book of Saints, Part 6 (St. Anthony Mary Claret)	Lovasik, Fr. Lawrence	St. Joseph Picture	1985	YES	05 and up
19	Czecho-slovaia	Man Who Found Out Why: The Story of Gregor Mendel	Webster, Gary	Hawthorn Junior Biography	1963	YES	11 and up
19	Czecho-slovia	Wandering Minstrel (The), A Story of Antonin Dvorak	Nash, Brother Roy	In the Footsteps of the Saints	1955, 2010	NO	09-12
19	Ecuador	Book of Saints, Part 9 (St. Miguel Cordero)	Lovasik, Fr. Lawrence	St. Joseph Picture	1996	NO	05 and up
19	Ecuador	Saints of the Americas (St. Miguel Cordero)	Winkler, Rev. Jude	St. Joseph Picture	2006	NO	05 and up
19	Egypt	Man Who Could Read Stones: Champollion and the Rosetta Stone	Honour, Alan	Hawthorn Junior Biography	1966	YES	11 and up
19	England	Florence Nightingale's Nuns	Garnett, Emmeline	Vision Books	1961, 2009	NO	09-15
19	England	Master Mariner: The Adventurous Life of Joseph Conrad	Smaridge, Norah	Hawthorn Junior Biography	1966	YES	11 and up
19	Far East	Father of the American Navy, Captain John Barry	Anderson, Floyd	Banner Books	1959, 2011	NO	09-15
19	France	Bernadette and the Lady	Pauli, Hertha	Vision Books	1956, 1999	NO	09-15
19	France	Book of Saints, Part 2 (St. Bernadette)	Lovasik, Fr. Lawrence	St. Joseph Picture	1981	NO	05 and up
19	France	Book of Saints, Part 2 (St. Therese of the Child Jesus)	Lovasik, Fr. Lawrence	St. Joseph Picture	1981	NO	05 and up
19	France	Book of Saints, Part 3 (St. Catherine Laboure)	Lovasik, Fr. Lawrence	St. Joseph Picture	1982	NO	05 and up

19	France	Book of Saints, Part 4 (St. John Vianney)	Lovasik, Fr. Lawrence	St. Joseph Picture	1982	YES	05 and up
19	France	Book of Saints, Part 6 (St. Anthony Mary Claret)	Lovasik, Fr. Lawrence	St. Joseph Picture	1985	YES	05 and up
19	France	Book of Saints, Part 6 (St. Madeleine Sophie Barat)	Lovasik, Fr. Lawrence	St. Joseph Picture	1985	YES	05 and up
19	France	Book of Saints, Part 9 (St. Peter Julian Eymard)	Lovasik, Fr. Lawrence	St. Joseph Picture	1996	NO	05 and up
19	France	Book of Saints, Part 10 (St. Eugene de Mazenod)	Lovasik, Fr. Lawrence	St. Joseph Picture Books	1997	NO	05 and up
19	France	Book of Saints, Part 11 (St. Madeleine Sophie Barat)	Lovasik, Fr. Lawrence	St. Joseph Picture Books	1997	NO	05 and up
19	France	Candle Burns for France, A (Blessed Catherine Laboure)	Thompson, Blanche Jennings	Favorite Catholic Books	1946	YES	07 and up
19	France	Candle Burns for France, A (Cure d'Ars)	Thompson, Blanche Jennings	Favorite Catholic Books	1946	YES	07 and up
19	France	Candle Burns for France, A (St. Bernadette)	Thompson, Blanche Jennings	Favorite Catholic Books	1946	YES	07 and up
19	France	Candle Burns for France, A (St. Therese)	Thompson, Blanche Jennings	Favorite Catholic Books	1946	YES	07 and up
19	France	Charles de Foucauld, Adventurer of the Desert	Garnett, Emmeline	Vision Books	1962	YES	09-15
19	France	Children of La Salette, The	Windeatt, Mary Fabyan	Windeatt Saint Series	1951	YES	14 and up
19	France	Country Road Home, The Story of St. John Vianney, Cure of Ars	Daughters of St. Paul	Encounter Books	1966, 1987	YES	09 and up
19	France	Cure of Ars, Story of St. John Vianney, Patron Saint of Parish Priests	Windeatt, Mary Fabyan	Windeatt Saint Series	1991	NO	10 and up
19	France	Cure of Ars , The Priest Who Out-talked the Devil	Lomask, Milton	Vision Books	1958, 1998	NO	09-15
19	France	Dear Philippine: The Mission of Mother Duchesne	Hubbard, Margaret Ann	Vision Books	1964	YES	09-15
19	France	Father of the American Navy, Captain John Barry	Anderson, Floyd	Banner Books	1959, 2011	NO	09-15
19	France	Flowery Kingdom, The (St. John Gabriel)	Daughters of Charity	Catholic Stories, Volume IV	1995	NO	07-10

19	France	Great Gift of Our Lady, The (St. Catherine Laboure)	Daughters of Charity	Catholic Stories, Volume I	1987	NO	07-10
19	France	Journey into Light: The Story of Louis Braille	Webster, Gary	Hawthorn Junior Biography	1964	YES	11 and up
19	France	Light in the Grotto, The Life of St. Bernadette	Daughters of St. Paul	Encounter Books	1967, 1978	YES	09 and up
19	France	Little Dove of Our Lady, The (St. Catherine Laboure)	Daughters of Charity	Catholic Stories, Volume I	1987	NO	07-10
19	France	Little Flower (The), The Story of St. Therese of the Child Jesus	Windeatt, Mary Fabyan	Windeatt Saint Series	1991	NO	09 and up
19	France	Lives of the Saints: Modern Saints (St. Bernadette Soubirous)	Tesoriero, Bart	Aquinas Kids	2012	NO	05-09
19	France	Lives of the Saints: Modern Saints (St. John Vianney)	Tesoriero, Bart	Aquinas Kids	2012	NO	05-09
19	France	Lives of the Saints: Modern Saints (St. Therese of Lisieux)	Tesoriero, Bart	Aquinas Kids	2012	NO	05-09
19	France	Man Who Could Read Stones: Champollion and the Rosetta Stone	Honour, Alan	Hawthorn Junior Biography	1966	YES	11 and up
19	France	Master Mariner: The Adventurous Life of Joseph Conrad	Smaridge, Norah	Hawthorn Junior Biography	1966	YES	11 and up
19	France	Miraculous Medal, The Story of Our Lady's Appearances to Saint Catherine Laboure	Windeatt, Mary Fabyan	Windeatt Saint Series	1991	NO	09 and up
19	France	More Saints of the Eucharist: Little Queen in Her Little Way (Therese of the Child Jesus)	Francis, Father	Father Francis Coloring Books	1959	NO	06 and up
19	France	Mother Barat's Vineyard	Hubbard, Margaret	Vision Books	1962	YES	09-15
19	France	Music Master, The Story of Herman Cohen	Rodino, Amedeo	Encounter Books	1968	YES	09 and up
19	France	Our Lady Came to Pontmain	Ernest, Brother	In the Footsteps of the Saints	1954, 2010	NO	09-12
19	France	Our Lady Comes to Paris, A Story of St. Catherine Laboure	Ernest, Brother	In the Footsteps of the Saints	1953, 2009	NO	09-12
19	France	Our Lady of La Salette	Windeatt, Mary Fabyan	Windeatt Coloring	1954	NO	04 and up

19	France	Our Lady of Lourdes	Windeatt, Mary Fabyan	Windeatt Coloring	1954	YES	04 and up
19	France	Our Lady of Lourdes	Lovasik, Fr. Lawrence	St. Joseph Picture	1985	NO	05 and up
19	France	Our Lady of Pellevoisin	Windeatt, Mary Fabyan	Windeatt Coloring	1954	NO	04 and up
19	France	Our Lady of Pontmain	Windeatt, Mary Fabyan	Windeatt Coloring	1954	NO	04 and up
19	France	Our Lady of the Miraculous Medal	Windeatt, Mary Fabyan	Windeatt Coloring	1954	NO	04 and up
19	France	Pauline Jaricot, Foundress of the Living Rosary and the Society for the Propagation of the Faith	Windeatt, Mary Fabyan	Windeatt Saint Series	1993	NO	12 and up
19	France	Rochambeau and Our French Allies	Lomask, Milton	American Background	1965	YES	10-15
19	France	St. Bernadette Soubirous: Light in the Grotto	Heffernan, Anne Eileen	Encounter the Saints	1999	NO	09 and up
19	France	Saint Catherine Labouré: And Our Lady of the Miraculous Medal	Trouvé, Marianne Lorraine	Encounter the Saints	2012	NO	09 and up
19	France	Saint Catherine Labouré and the Miraculous Medal	Power-Waters, Alma	Vision Books	1962, 2000	NO	09-15
19	France	Saint Catherine Labouré: Mary's Messenger	Roux, Marie-Genevieve & Elisabeth Charpy	Along the Paths of the Gospel	2000	YES	07-10
19	France	Saint John Vianney: Priest for All People	DeDomenico, Elizabeth Marie	Encounter the Saints	2008	NO	09 and up
19	France	Saint Julie Billiart: The Smiling Saint	Glavich, Mary Kathleen	Encounter the Saints	2002	YES	09 and up
19	France	Saint Therese and the Roses	Homan, Helen	Vision Books	1955, 1995	NO	09-15
19	France	Saints for Girls (St. Bernadette Soubirous)	Muus, Solveig and Bart Tesoriero	Aquinas Kids	2012	NO	05-09
19	France	Saints for Girls (St. Therese of Lisieux)	Muus, Solveig and Bart Tesoriero	Aquinas Kids	2012	NO	05-09
19	France	St. Therese of Lisieux: And the "Little Way" of Love	Baudouin-Croix, Marie	Along the Paths of the Gospel	1999	YES	07-10
19	France	St. Therese of Lisieux: The Way of Love	Glavich, Mary Kathleen	Encounter the Saints	2003	NO	09 and up
19	France	Saint Therese of the Child Jesus	Winkler, Father Jude	St. Joseph Picture	2000	NO	05 and up

19	France	Show Us Your Face, A Story of Venerable Leo Papin Dupont	Hagemann, Brother Gerard	In the Footsteps of the Saints	1962, 2011	NO	09-12
19	France	Simon Bruté and the Western Adventure	Bartelme, Elizabeth	American Background	1959, 2012	NO	10-15
19	France	Story of a Soul, The	Therese of Lisieux, Saint	Favorite Catholic Books	1898, etc.	NO	12 and up
19	France	Story of Louis Braille, A	Ernest, Brother	In the Footsteps of the Saints	1962, 2010	NO	06-09
19	France	Story of Millet, A	Ernest, Brother	In the Footsteps of the Saints	1961, 2010	NO	06-09
19	France	Story of St. Bernadette, A	Ernest, Brother	Footsteps of the Saints	1958, 2009	NO	06-09
19	France	Story of St. John Vianney, A	Ryan, Brother Ernest	Dujarie Press Reprint	1959, 2008	NO	06-09
19	France	Story of St. Therese, A	Ernest, Brother	Footsteps of the Saints	1957, 2009	NO	06-09
19	France	They Became Saints (St. Bernadette: And Our Lady of Lourdes)	Francis, Father	Father Francis Coloring	1951	NO	07 and up
19	France	They Became Saints (St. Therese of the Child Jesus and Her Little Way)	Francis, Father	Father Francis Coloring	1951	NO	07 and up
19	Germany	Blessed by the Cross: St. Edith Stein	Hill, Mary Lea FSP	Encounter the Saints	1999	NO	09 and up
19	Germany	Book of Saints, Part 9 (Blessed Teresa - Edith Stein)	Lovasik, Fr. Lawrence	St. Joseph Picture	1996	NO	05 and up
19	Germany	Music Master, The Story of Herman Cohen	Rodino, Amedeo	Encounter Books	1968	YES	09 and up
19	Germany	Story of Blessed Pauline von Mallinckrodt, A	Ernest, Brother	In the Footsteps of the Saints	1961, 2010	NO	06-09
19	Haiti	Pierre Toussaint, Pioneer in Brotherhood	Sheehan, Arthur and Elizabeth	American Background	1963	YES	10-15
19	Hawaii	Father Damien and the Bells	Sheehan, Arthur and Elizabeth	Junior Vision	1962	YES	09-11
19	Hawaii	Father Damien and the Bells	Sheehan, Arthur and Elizabeth	Vision Books	1957, 2004	NO	09-15
19	Hawaii	No Greater Love, The Life of Father Damien of Molokai	Daughters of St. Paul	Encounter Books	1979	YES	09 and up

19	Hawaii	Saint Damien of Molokai: Hero of Hawaii	Richards, Virginia Helen	Encounter the Saints	2009	NO	09 and up
19	Hungary	Christmas Anna Angel, The	Sawyer, Ruth	Caldecott	1944	YES	04 and up
19	Ireland	Courageous Catherine: Mother Mary Catherine McAuley, The First Sister of Mercy	Marie, Sister Raymond	Catholic Treasury	1958	YES	10 and up
19	Ireland	Father of the American Navy, Captain John Barry	Anderson, Floyd	Banner Books	1959, 2011	NO	09-15
19	Ireland	Frances Warde and the First Sisters of Mercy	Christopher, Sister Marie	Vision Books	1960	YES	09-15
19	Ireland	Irish Saints (Bishop Edward J. Galvin)	Reilly, Robert T.	Vision Books	1964, 1981, 2002	YES	09-15
19	Ireland	Irish Saints (Father Theobald Mathew)	Reilly, Robert T.	Vision Books	1964, 1981, 2002	YES	09-15
19	Ireland	Irish Saints (Matt Talbot)	Reilly, Robert T.	Vision Books	1964, 1981, 2002	YES	09-15
19	Ireland	Irish Saints (Mother Catherine McAuley)	Reilly, Robert T.	Vision Books	1964, 1981, 2002	YES	09-15
19	Ireland	King of Song: The Story of John McCormack	Hume, Ruth and Paul	Hawthorn Junior Bio.	1964	YES	11 and up
19	Ireland	Mathew Carey, Pamphleter for Freedom	Hindman, Jane F.	American Background	1960	YES	10-15
19	Ireland	Our Lady of Knock	Windeatt, Mary Fabyan	Windeatt Coloring	1954	YES	04 and up
19	Ireland	Story of Venerable Mother Catherine McAuley	Ernest, Brother	In the Footsteps of the Saints	1959, 2011	NO	06-09
19	Ireland	Thunder Maker: General Thomas Meagher	Lamers, William M.	Catholic Treasury	1959	YES	10 and up
19	Israel	Monuments to Glory: The Story of Antonio Barluzzi, Architect of the Holy Land	Madden, Daniel M.	Hawthorn Junior Biography	1964	YES	11 and up
19	Italy	Ahead of the Crowd, The Story of St. Dominic Savio	Daughters of St. Paul	Encounter Books	1970	YES	09 and up
19	Italy	Anina (daughter of St. Elizabeth Seton)	Daughters of Charity	Catholic Stories, Volume II	1992	NO	07-10
19	Italy	Anvil Chorus: The Story of Giuseppe Verdi	Kaufman, Helen L.	Hawthorn Junior Biography	1964	YES	11 and up

19	Italy	Apostle of Peace, The Story of Pope Pius XII	Hatch, Alden	Hawthorn Junior Bio.	1965	YES	11 and up
19	Italy	Book of Saints, Part 1 (St. John Bosco)	Lovasik, Fr. Lawrence	St. Joseph Picture	1981	NO	05 and up
19	Italy	Book of Saints, Part 1 (St. Pius X)	Lovasik, Fr. Lawrence	St. Joseph Picture	1981	NO	05 and up
19	Italy	Book of Saints, Part 2 (St. Dominic Savio)	Lovasik, Fr. Lawrence	St. Joseph Picture	1981	NO	05 and up
19	Italy	Book of Saints, Part 3 (St. Frances Cabrini)	Lovasik, Fr. Lawrence	St. Joseph Picture	1982	NO	05 and up
19	Italy	Book of Saints, Part 5 (St. Gemma Galgani)	Lovasik, Fr. Lawrence	St. Joseph Picture	1985	YES	05 and up
19	Italy	Book of Saints, Part 10 (St. Justin de Jacobis)	Lovasik, Fr. Lawrence	St. Joseph Picture	1997	NO	05 and up
19	Italy	Book of Saints, Part 11 (St. Clement Mary Hofbauer)	Lovasik, Fr. Lawrence	St. Joseph Picture	1997	NO	05 and up
19	Italy	Book of Saints, Part 12 (St. Lucy Filippini)	Lovasik, Fr. Lawrence	St. Joseph Picture	1999	NO	05 and up
19	Italy	Book of Saints, Part 12 (St. Mary Mazzarello)	Lovasik, Fr. Lawrence	St. Joseph Picture	1999	NO	05 and up
19	Italy	Champion of the Apostolate: The Life of St. Vincent Pallotti	Greene, Brother Ellis	Holy Cross Press	1967	YES	09 and up
19	Italy	Good Pope John (Pope John XXIII)	Sheehan, Elizabeth Odell	Vision Books	1966	YES	09-15
19	Italy	Light Within: The Story of Maria Montessori	Smaridge, Norah	Hawthorn Junior Bio.	1965	YES	11 and up
19	Italy	Man Who Found Out Why: The Story of Gregor Mendel	Webster, Gary	Hawthorn Junior Biography	1963	YES	11 and up
19	Italy	Maria Domenica Mazzarello	Fino, Catherine	Along the Paths of the Gospel	2002	YES	07-10
19	Italy	More Saints of the Eucharist: A Gem of the Eucharist (St. Gemma)	Francis, Father	Father Francis Coloring	1959	NO	06 and up
19	Italy	Mother Cabrini, Missionary to the World	Keyes, Frances Parkinson	Vision Books	1959, 1997	NO	09-15
19	Italy	Padre Pio	Winkler, Father Jude	St. Joseph Picture Books	2004	NO	05 and up
19	Italy	Pope Pius XII, The World's Shepherd	de Wohl, Louis	Vision Books	1961	YES	09-15
19	Italy	Pope St. Pius X	Forbes, F.A.	Forbes Biography	1918, 1987	NO	12 and up
19	Italy	Saint Dominic Savio	Windeatt, Mary Fabyan	Windeatt Coloring	1955	NO	04 and up

19	Italy	Saint Frances Cabrini	Windeatt, Mary Fabyan	Windeatt Coloring	1956	NO	04 and up
19	Italy	Saint Frances Xavier Cabrini: Cecchina's Dream	Dority, Victoria and Mary Andes	Encounter the Saints	2005	YES	09 and up
19	Italy	Saint John Bosco and the Children's Saint, Dominic Savio	Beebe, Catherine	Vision Books	1955, 1992	NO	09-15
19	Italy	Saint John Bosco, The Friend of Youth	Forbes, F.A.	Forbes Biography	1935, 2000	NO	12 and up
19	Italy	Saint John Bosco: The Friend of Children and Young People	Monmarche, Carole and the Salesians	Along the Paths of the Gospel	1997	YES	07-10
19	Italy	Saint Maria Goretti	Windeatt, Mary Fabyan	Windeatt Coloring	1955	NO	04 and up
19	Italy	Saint Pius X	Windeatt, Mary Fabyan	Windeatt Coloring	1955	NO	04 and up
19	Italy	Saint Pius X, The Farm Boy Who Became Pope	Diethelm, Walter	Junior Vision	1963	YES	09-11
19	Italy	Saint Pius X, The Farm Boy Who Became Pope	Diethelm, Walter	Vision Books	1956, 1994	NO	09-15
19	Italy	Saints for Boys and Girls (St. Frances Xavier Cabrini)	Beebe, Catherine	Beebe Biography	1959	YES	09-14
19	Italy	Saints for Girls (St. Frances Cabrini)	Muus, Solveig and Bart Tesoriero	Aquinas Kids	2012	NO	05-09
19	Italy	Saints of the Eucharist: A Lily in God's Garden (St. Maria Goretti)	Francis, Father	Father Francis Coloring Books	1958	NO	06 and up
19	Italy	Saints of the Eucharist: The Pope of Little Children (St. Pius X)	Francis, Father	Father Francis Coloring Books	1958	NO	06 and up
19	Italy	Story of John Bosco, A	Ryan, Br. Ernest	Dujarie Press Reprint	1958, 2005	NO	06-09
19	Italy	Story of St. Dominic Savio, A	Ernest, Brother	Footsteps of the Saints	1957, 2011	NO	06-09
19	Italy	Story of St. Gemma, A	Ernest, Brother	Footsteps of the Saints	1957, 2010	NO	06-09
19	Italy	Story of St. John Bosco, A	Ernest, Brother	Footsteps of the Saints	1958, 2011	NO	06-09
19	Italy	They Became Saints (St. Dominic Savio: The Classroom Friend)	Francis, Father	Father Francis Coloring	1951	NO	07 and up
19	Italy	They Became Saints (St. Mary Goretti: "The Lily of the Marshes")	Francis, Father	Father Francis Coloring	1951	NO	07 and up

19	Italy	To the Ends of the Earth, A Story of St. Frances Xavier Cabrini	Greene, Brother Genard	In the Footsteps of the Saints	1955, 2009	NO	09-12
19	Lithuania	Kaze's True Home, Young Life of a Modern Day Saint, Mother Maria Kaupas	Mohan, Claire Jordan	Mohan Biographies	1992	YES	09-12
19	Luxembourg	Mother Alfred and the Doctors Mayo	Richardson, James P.	Banner Books	1959	YES	09-15
19	Mexico	Dawn Brings Glory, A Story of Blessed Miguel Pro	Roberto, Brother	In the Footsteps of the Saints	1956, 2013	NO	12-15
19	Mexico	God's Secret Agent, The Life of Father Michael Augustine Pro, S.J.	Daughters of St. Paul	Encounter Books	1967	YES	09 and up
19	Mexico	Jose Finds the King, A Blessed Miguel Pro Story	Ball, Ann	Glory of America	2002	NO	7-12
19	Mexico	Saints of the Americas (Bld. Miguel Agustin Pro)	Winkler, Rev. Jude	St. Joseph Picture	2006	NO	05 and up
19	Moravia	Man Who Found Out Why: Story of Gregor Mendel	Webster, Gary	Hawthorn Junior Biography	1963	YES	11 and up
19	Netherlands	Book of Saints, Part 9 (Bl. Teresa - Edith Stein)	Lovasik, Fr. Lawrence	St. Joseph Picture	1996	NO	05 and up
19	Netherlands	Book of Saints, Part 9 (Bl. Titus Brandsma)	Lovasik, Fr. Lawrence	St. Joseph Picture	1996	NO	05 and up
19	Norway	Knute Rockne, Football Wizard of Notre Dame	Daley, Arthur	American Background	1960	YES	10-15
19	Poland	Blessed by the Cross: St. Edith Stein	Hill, Mary Lea FSP	Encounter the Saints	1999	NO	09 and up
19	Poland	Book of Saints, Part 6 (St. Maximilian Kolbe)	Lovasik, Fr. Lawrence	St. Joseph Picture	1985	YES	05 and up
19	Poland	Book of Saints, Part 9 (Bl. Teresa - Edith Stein)	Lovasik, Fr. Lawrence	St. Joseph Picture	1996	NO	05 and up
19	Poland	Lion of Poland: The Story of Paderewski	Hume, Ruth and Paul	Hawthorn Junior Bio.	1962, 2012	NO	11 and up
19	Poland	Master Mariner: The Adventurous Life of Joseph Conrad	Smaridge, Norah	Hawthorn Junior Biography	1966	YES	11 and up
19	Poland	Music from the Hunger Pit, A Story of St. Maximillian Kolbe	Roberto, Brother	In the Footsteps of the Saints	1954, 2008	NO	09-12
19	Poland	Red Rose for Frania: A Story of the Young Life of Francis Siedliska	Mohan, Claire Jordan	Mohan Biographies	1989	YES	09-12
19	Spain	Book of Saints, Part 6 (St. Anthony Mary Claret)	Lovasik, Fr. Lawrence	St. Joseph Picture	1985	YES	05 and up

19	Spain	Book of Saints, Part 10 (St. Mary Soledad)	Lovasik, Fr. Lawrence	St. Joseph Picture	1997	NO	05 and up
19	Spain	Book of Saints, Part 11 (Blessed Angela of the Cross Guerrero)	Lovasik, Fr. Lawrence	St. Joseph Picture	1997	NO	05 and up
19	Spain	Book of Saints, Part 12 (St. Mary Soledad)	Lovasik, Fr. Lawrence	St. Joseph Picture	1999	NO	05 and up
19	Tasmania	Thunder Maker: General Thomas Meagher	Lamers, William M.	Catholic Treasury	1959	YES	10 and up
19	Turkey	Florence Nightingale's Nuns	Garnett, Emmeline	Vision Books	1961, 2009	NO	09-15
19	Uganda	African Triumph, The Life of Charles Lwanga	Dollen, Charles	Encounter Books	1967, 1978	YES	09 and up
19	Uganda	Uganda Martyrs	Bouin, Fr. Paul	Catholic Children's Library	1964, 2012	NO	10 and up
19	United States	Adventures of Broken Hand	Morriss, Frank	Catholic Treasury	1957	YES	10 and up
19	United States	Amazing John Tabb (Civil War)	Betz, Eva K.	Catholic Treasury	1958	YES	10 and up
19	United States	Anina (daughter of St. Elizabeth Seton)	Daughters of Charity	Catholic Stories, Volume II	1992	NO	07-10
19	United States	Apostle of Ice and Snow: A Life of Bishop Charles Seghers	Betz, Eva	Holy Cross Press	1964	YES	09 and up
19	United States	Armorer of the Confederacy, Secretary Mallory	Durkin, Rev. Joseph T.	Banner Books	1960	YES	09-15
19	United States	Black Robe Peacemaker, Pierre de Smet	Hopkins, J.G.E.	American Background	1958	YES	10-15
19	United States	Book of Saints, Part 1 (St. Elizabeth Ann Seton)	Lovasik, Fr. Lawrence	St. Joseph Picture	1981	NO	05 and up
19	United States	Book of Saints, Part 3 (St. Frances Cabrini)	Lovasik, Fr. Lawrence	St. Joseph Picture	1982	NO	05 and up
19	United States	Book of Saints, Part 6 (St. John Neumann)	Lovasik, Fr. Lawrence	St. Joseph Picture	1985	YES	05 and up
19	United States	Brother Dutton of Molokai	Crouch, Howard E.	Catholic Treasury	1958	YES	10 and up
19	United States	Catholic Campuses, Stories of American Catholic Colleges	Staudacher, Rosemarian	Vision Books	1958	YES	09-15
19	United States	Chaplain in Gray, Abram Ryan	Heagney, H.J.	American Background	1958	YES	10-15
19	United States	Charity Goes to War (Civil War and the Sisters of Charity)	Heagney, Anne	Catholic Treasury	1961	YES	10 and up
19	United States	Charles Carroll and the American Revolution	Lomask, Milton	American Background	1959	YES	10-15

19	United States	Charles John Seghers, Pioneer in Alaska	Bosco, Antoinette	American Background	1960	YES	10-15
19	United States	Courageous Catherine: Mother Mary Catherine McAuley, The First Sister of Mercy	Marie, Sister Raymond	Catholic Treasury	1958	YES	10 and up
19	United States	Dawn From the West: The Story of Genevieve Caulfield	Rau, Margaret	Hawthorn Junior Biography	1964	YES	11 and up
19	United States	Dear Philippine: Mission of Mother Duchesne	Hubbard, Margaret	Vision Books	1964	YES	09-15
19	United States	Door of Hope: The Story of Katharine Drexel	Burton, Katherine	Hawthorn Junior Bio.	1963	YES	11 and up
19	United States	Elizabeth Bayley Seton	Daughters of Charity	Catholic Stories, Volume II	1992	NO	07-10
19	United States	Fanny Allen, Green Mountain Rebel	Betz, Eva K.	American Background	1962	YES	10-15
19	United States	Father of the American Navy, Captain John Barry	Anderson, Floyd	Banner Books	1959, 2011	NO	09-15
19	United States	Fighting Father Duffy	Bishop, Jim & Virginia Lee	Vision Books	1956	YES	09-15
19	United States	Fighting Irishman: The Story of "Wild Bill" Donovan"	Wilhelm, Maria	Hawthorn Junior Biography	1964	YES	11 and up
19	United States	First Sioux Nun, Sister Marie-Josephine Nebraska (1859-1894)	Hilger, Sister Mary Ione	Similar to Catholic Treasury	1963	YES	10 and up
19	United States	Fold It Gently, A Story of Fr. Abram Ryan	Donahoe, Brother Bernard	In the Footsteps of the Saints	1960, 2010	NO	09-12
19	United States	Forked Lightning: The Story of Philip H. Sheridan	Orbaan, Albert	Hawthorn Junior Biography	1964	YES	11 and up
19	United States	Forty-Ninth Star (The), Alaska	Savage, Alma	Banner Books	1959, 2011	NO	09-15
19	United States	Frances Warde and the First Sisters of Mercy	Christopher, Sister Marie	Vision Books	1960	YES	09-15
19	United States	Frontier Bishop: Simon Gabriel Bruté	Hughes, Riley	Catholic Treasury	1959, 2012	NO	10 and up
19	United States	Frontier Priest and Congressman, Father Gabriel Richard	Alois, Brother	Banner Books	1958	YES	09-15
19	United States	General Phil Sheridan and the Union Cavalry	Lomask, Milton	American Background	1959	YES	10-15
19	United States	Giant of the Western Trail, Fr. Peter de Smet	McHugh, Rev. Michael	Banner Books	1958, 2003, 2011	NO	09-15

19	United States	God and the General's Daughter	Heagney, Anne	Similar to Catholic Treasury	1953	YES	10 and up
19	United States	Gold Rush Bishop (Patrick Manogue)	Anderson, Floyd	Catholic Treasury	1962, 2012	NO	10 and up
19	United States	Governor Al Smith	Farley, James and James Conniff	Vision Books	1959	YES	09-15
19	United States	Hand Raised at Gettysburg (Irish Brigade)	Johnson, Grace & Harold	Catholic Treasury	1955, 2012	NO	10 and up
19	United States	Hands of Mercy, The Story of Sister-Nurses in the Civil War	Smaridge, Norah	Banner Books	1960, 2011	NO	09-15
19	United States	I Lay Down My Life, Biography of Joyce Kilmer	Cargas, Harry	Similar to Encounter Books	1964	YES	09 and up
19	United States	Irish Saints (Bishop Edward J. Galvin)	Reilly, Robert T.	Vision Books	1964, 1981, 2002	YES	09-15
19	United States	Irish Saints (Father Theobald Mathew)	Reilly, Robert T.	Vision Books	1964, 1981, 2002	YES	09-15
19	United States	John Hughes, Eagle of the Church	Hurley, Doran	American Background Books	1961	YES	10-15
19	United States	John LaFarge, Gentle Jesuit	Strousse, Flora	American Background Books	1968	YES	10-15
19	United States	John Neumann, The Children's Bishop	Sheehan, Elizabeth	Vision Books	1965	YES	09-15
19	United States	Kat Finds a Friend, A St. Elizabeth Ann Seton Story	Stromberg, Joan	Glory of America	1999	NO	07-12
19	United States	Katharine Drexel, Friend of the Neglected	Tarry, Ellen	Vision Books	1958, 2000	NO	09-15
19	United States	Katie, Young Life of Mother Katharine Drexel	Mohan, Claire Jordan	Mohan Biographies	2000	NO	09-12
19	United States	Kit Carson of the Old West	Boesch, Mark	Vision Books	1959	YES	09-15
19	United States	Knute Rockne, Football Wizard of Notre Dame	Daley, Arthur	American Background	1960	YES	10-15
19	United States	Lady and the Pirate, The (Battle of New Orleans in 1814)	Riordan, Robert	Similar to Catholic Treasury	1957	YES	10 and up
19	United States	Light in the Early West, Berenice Chouteau	Schlafy, Rev. James	Banner Books	1959, 2011	NO	09-15
19	United States	Lives of the Saints: Modern Saints (St. Elizabeth Ann Seton)	Tesoriero, Bart	Aquinas Kids	2012	NO	05-09

19	United States	Lives of the Saints: Modern Saints (St. John Neumann)	Tesoriero, Bart	Aquinas Kids	2012	NO	05-09
19	United States	Long Trail (The), The Story of Buffalo Bill	Kolars, Frank	Banner Books	1960, 2011	NO	09-15
19	United States	Lucrezia Bori of the Metropolitan Opera	Marion, John Francis	American Background	1962	YES	10-15
19	United States	Magnificent Failure: The Story of Father Solanus Casey	Collins, David R.	Weaver Books	1999	YES	09-12
19	United States	Margaret Haughery, Bread Woman of New Orleans	Strousse, Flora	American Background	1961	YES	10-15
19	United States	Massacre At Ash Hollow	Reilly, Robert T.	Catholic Treasury	1960	YES	10 and up
19	United States	Mathew Carey, Pamphleter for Freedom	Hindman, Jane F.	American Background	1960	YES	10-15
19	United States	Medicine for Wildcat: A Life Story about Samuel Charles Mazzuchelli	Riordan, Robert	Catholic Treasury	1956	YES	10 and up
19	United States	Mother Alfred and the Doctors Mayo	Richardson, James P.	Banner Books	1959	YES	09-15
19	United States	Mother Cabrini, Missionary to the World	Keyes, Frances Parkinson	Vision Books	1959, 1997	NO	09-15
19	United States	Mother Seton and the Sisters of Charity	Power-Waters, Alma	Junior Vision	1963	YES	09-11
19	United States	Mother Seton and the Sisters of Charity	Power-Waters, Alma	Vision Books	1957, 2000	NO	09-15
19	United States	Mother Seton: Wife, Mother, Educator, Foundress, Saint	Daughters of St. Paul	Similar to Encounter Books	1975	YES	10 and up
19	United States	Orphans Find a Home (The), A St. Frances Xavier Cabrini Story	Stromberg, Joan	Glory of America	1998	NO	07-12
19	United States	Pen and Bayonet: The Story of Joyce Kilmer	Smaridge, Norah	Hawthorn Junior Biography	1962	YES	11 and up
19	United States	Pierre Toussaint, Pioneer in Brotherhood	Sheehan, Arthur and Elizabeth	American Background	1963	YES	10-15
19	United States	Priest, Patriot and Leader, The Story of Archbishop Carroll	Betz, Eva K.	Banner Books	1960, 2011	NO	09-15
19	United States	Quiet Flame: Mother Marianne of Molokai	Betz, Eva K.	Catholic Treasury	1963	YES	10 and up
19	United States	Raphael Semmes, Confederate Admiral	Daly, Robert W.	American Background Books	1965	YES	10-15

19	United States	Rebels in the Shadows	Reilly, Robert T.	similiar to Catholic Treasury	1962, 2012	NO	10 and up
19	United States	Rochambeau and Our French Allies	Lomask, Milton	American Background	1965	YES	10-15
19	United States	Rose Greenhow, Confederate Secret Agent	Grant, Dorothy	American Background	1961	YES	10-15
19	United States	Rose Hawthorne: The Pilgrimage of Nathaniel's Daughter	Sheehan, Arthur and Elizabeth	Vision Books	1959	YES	09-15
19	United States	Saint Elizabeth Ann Seton	Lovasik, Fr. Lawrence	St. Joseph Picture Books	1981	NO	05 and up
19	United States	Saint Elizabeth Ann Seton: Daughter of America	Grunwell, Jeanne and Mari Goering	Encounter the Saints	1999	NO	09 and up
19	United States	Saint Frances Cabrini	Windeatt, Mary Fabyan	Windeatt Coloring	1956	NO	04 and up
19	United States	Saint Frances Xavier Cabrini: Cecchina's Dream	Dority, Victoria and Mary Lou Andes	Encounter the Saints	2005	YES	09 and up
19	United States	Saint Katharine Drexel: The Total Gift	Wallace, Susan Helen	Encounter the Saints	2003	NO	09 and up
19	United States	Saints for Boys and Girls (St. Frances Xavier Cabrini)	Beebe, Catherine	Beebe Biography	1959	YES	09-14
19	United States	Saints for Girls (St. Elizabeth Ann Seton)	Muus, Solveig and Bart Tesoriero	Aquinas Kids	2012	NO	05-09
19	United States	Saints for Girls (St. Frances Cabrini)	Muus, Solveig and Bart Tesoriero	Aquinas Kids	2012	NO	05-09
19	United States	Saints of the Americas (St. Elizabeth Ann Seton)	Winkler, Rev. Jude	St. Joseph Picture	2006	NO	05 and up
19	United States	Saints of the Americas (St. John Neumann)	Winkler, Rev. Jude	St. Joseph Picture	2006	NO	05 and up
19	United States	Saints of the Americas (St. Katharine Drexel)	Winkler, Rev. Jude	St. Joseph Picture	2006	NO	05 and up
19	United States	Sarah Peter: The Dream and the Harvest	Power-Waters, Alma	Vision Books	1965	YES	09-15
19	United States	Search for a Shepherd (A), A Story of Fr. Paul of Graymoor	Roberto, Brother	In the Footsteps of the Saints	1959, 2011	NO	09-12
19	United States	Servant to the Slaves: The Story of Henriette Delille	Collins, David R.	Weaver Books	2000	YES	09-12
19	United States	Sidewalk Statesman, Alfred E. Smith	Schofield, William G.	American Background	1958	YES	10-15

19	United States	Simon Bruté and the Western Adventure	Bartelme, Elizabeth	American Background	1959, 2012	NO	10-15
19	United States	Spaldings of Old Kentucky, The	Heagney, Anne	Similar to Catholic Treasury	1964	YES	10 and up
19	United States	Story of Mother Elizabeth Seton, A	Ryan, Brother Ernest	Dujarie Press Reprint	1960, 2008	NO	06-09
19	United States	Story of Venerable Mother Catherine McAuley	Ernest, Brother	In the Footsteps of the Saints	1959, 2011	NO	06-09
19	United States	Stout Hearts and Gentle Hands: The Life of Mother Angela of the Sisters of the Holy Cross	Betz, Eva	Holy Cross Press	1964	YES	09 and up
19	United States	Submarine Pioneer: John Philip Holland	Morriss, Frank	Catholic Treasury	1961, 2012	NO	10 and up
19	United States	Thomas Finds a Treasure, A St. John Neumann Story	Stromberg, Joan	Glory of America series	2001	NO	07-12
19	United States	Thunder Maker: General Thomas Meagher	Lamers, William M.	Catholic Treasury	1959	YES	10 and up
19	United States	To the Ends of the Earth, A Story of St. Frances Xavier Cabrini	Greene, Brother Genard	In the Footsteps of the Saints	1955, 2009	NO	09-12
19	United States	Turquoise Rosary	Jacks, Leo Vincent	Catholic Treasury	1960	YES	10 and up
19	United States	Under Three Flags: The Story of Gabriel Richard	Abodaher, David J.	Hawthorn Junior Biography	1965	YES	11 and up
19	United States	Ursulines, Nuns of Adventure: The Story of the New Orleans Community	Kane, Harnett T.	Vision Books	1959	YES	09-15
19	United States	Web Begun, The (Civil War)	Betz, Eva K.	Similar to Catholic Treasury	1961	YES	10 and up
19	United States	William Gaston, Fighter for Justice	Betz, Eva K.	American Background	1964	YES	10-15
19	United States	Willy Finds Victory, A Blessed Francis Seelos Story	Stromberg, Joan	Glory of America series	2004	NO	07-12
19	United States	Wires West (telegraph)	Jacks, Leo Vincent	Catholic Treasury	1957	YES	10 and up
19	various	Journeys with Mary: Apparitions of Our Lady	de Santis, Zerlina	Encounter the Saints	2001, 2002	NO	09 and up
19	various	Journeys with Mary: Apparitions of the Blessed Mother	de Santis, Zerlina	Encounter Books	1981, 1982	YES	09 and up

19	various	Modern Crusaders	Moore, John & Rosemarian Staudacher	Vision Books	1957	YES	09-15
20	Africa (Sudan)	Saint Bakhita of Sudan: Forever Free	Wallace, Susan Helen	Encounter the Saints	2006	NO	09 and up
20	Albania	Blessed Teresa of Calcutta: Missionary of Charity	Glavich, Mary Kathleen	Encounter the Saints	2003	NO	09 and up
20	Albania	Mother Teresa	Winkler, Father Jude	St. Joseph Picture Books	2002	NO	05 and up
20	Austria	Father Flanagan, Builder of Boys	Stevens, Clifford J.	American Background	1967	YES	10-15
20	Bavaria	Johann of the Trembling Hand: A Story Set in Oberammergau (Passion Play)	Koob, Theodora	Similar to Catholic Treasury	1960	YES	10 and up
20	Belgium	Book of Saints, Part 11 (St. Mutien Marie Wiaux)	Lovasik, Fr. Lawrence	St. Joseph Picture	1997	NO	05 and up
20	Belgium	Our Lady of Banneux	Windeatt, Mary Fabyan	Windeatt Coloring	1954	NO	04 and up
20	Belgium	Our Lady of Beauraing	Windeatt, Mary Fabyan	Windeatt Coloring	1954	NO	04 and up
20	Brazil	Princess Isabel of Brazil and the Glittering Pen	Comfort, Mildred	American Background	1969	YES	10-15
20	Bulgaria	Dobry	Shannon, Monica	Newbery	1935	YES	10 and up
20	Canada	Brother Andre of Montreal	Clark, Ann Nolan	Vision Books	1967	YES	09-15
20	Canada	Champions in Sports and Spirit (Gil Hodges, Rocky Marciano, Maureen Connolly, Yogi Berra, Maurice Richard, Terry Brennan, and Bob Cousy)	Fitzgerald, Ed	Vision Books	1956	YES	09-15
20	Canada	More Champions in Sports and Spirit (Stan Musial, Carmen Basilio, Alex Olmedo, Juan Manuel Fangio, Ron Delany, Eddie Arcaro, Jean Beliveau, and Herb Score)	Fitzgerald, Ed	Vision Books	1959	YES	09-15
20	Canada	Mountain for St. Joseph (A): The Life of Brother Andre, Miracle Man of Montreal	Bond, Ian	Holy Cross Press	1965	YES	09 and up
20	Canada	My Eskimos: A Priest in the Arctic	Buliard, Roger P.	Vision Books	1956	YES	09-15

20	Canada	Saint Andre Bessett: Miracles in Montreal	Jablonski, Patricia	Encounter the Saints	2010	NO	09 and up
20	Chile	Prisoner of Lost Island (Catholic fiction)	Kolars, Frank	Similar to Catholic Treasury	1961	YES	10 and up
20	China	To Far Places: The Story of Francis X. Ford	Betz, Eva K.	Hawthorn Junior Bio.	1962	YES	11 and up
20	Ecuador	Book of Saints, Part 9 (St. Miguel Cordero)	Lovasik, Fr. Lawrence	St. Joseph Picture	1996	NO	05 and up
20	Ecuador	Saints of the Americas (St. Miguel Cordero)	Winkler, Rev. Jude	St. Joseph Picture	2006	NO	05 and up
20	England	Golden Basket, The [introduction of Madeleine]	Bemelmans, Ludwig	Newbery	1936	YES	08 and up
20	England	Ink in His Blood, A Story of Monsignor Ronald Knox	Overstreet, Brother Edward	In the Footsteps of the Saints	1960, 2013	NO	12-15
20	England	Lion of Poland: The Story of Paderewski	Hume, Ruth and Paul	Hawthorn Junior Bio.	1962, 2012	NO	11 and up
20	England	Master Mariner: The Adventurous Life of Joseph Conrad	Smaridge, Norah	Hawthorn Junior Biography	1966	YES	11 and up
20	England	You're Never Alone: The Story of Thomas Merton	Collins, David R.	Weaver Books	1996	YES	09-12
20	Europe	Fighting Irishman: The Story of "Wild Bill" Donovan"	Wilhelm, Maria	Hawthorn Junior Biography	1964	YES	11 and up
20	Europe	Lion of Poland: The Story of Paderewski	Hume, Ruth and Paul	Hawthorn Junior Bio.	1962, 2012	NO	11 and up
20	France	Fighting Father Duffy	Bishop, Jim & Virginia Lee	Vision Books	1956	YES	09-15
20	France	I Lay Down My Life, Biography of Joyce Kilmer	Cargas, Harry	Similar to Encounter Books	1964	YES	09 and up
20	France	Pancakes-Paris	Bishop, Claire Huchet	Newbery	1947	YES	08 and up
20	France	Pen and Bayonet: The Story of Joyce Kilmer	Smaridge, Norah	Hawthorn Junior Biography	1962	YES	11 and up
20	France	You're Never Alone: The Story of Thomas Merton	Collins, David R.	Weaver Books	1996	YES	09-12
20	Germany	Blessed by the Cross: St. Edith Stein	Hill, Mary Lea FSP	Encounter the Saints	1999	NO	09 and up
20	Germany	Book of Saints, Part 9 (Bl. Teresa - Edith Stein)	Lovasik, Fr. Lawrence	St. Joseph Picture	1996	NO	05 and up
20	Germany	Joseph from Germany	Mohan, Claire Jordan	Mohan Biographies	2007	YES	09 and up

20	Germany	Story of Pope Benedict XVI for Children, The	Mohan, Claire Jordan	Mohan Biographies	2007	NO	09 and up
20	Guatemala	Fire of Freedom: The Story of Colonel Carlos Castillo Armas	Steffan, Jack	Hawthorn Junior Biography	1963	YES	11 and up
20	Holland	Light Within: The Story of Maria Montessori	Smaridge, Norah	Hawthorn Junior Biography	1965	YES	11 and up
20	Holland	Winged Watchman, The	Van Stockum, Hilda	Favorite Catholic Books	1962, 1997	NO	10 and up
20	Hong Kong	Hong Kong Altar Boy	Hanson, Joseph E.	Similar to Catholic Treasury	1965	YES	10 and up
20	India	Bld. Teresa of Calcutta: Missionary of Charity	Glavich, Mary Kathleen	Encounter the Saints	2003	NO	09 and up
20	India	Light Within: The Story of Maria Montessori	Smaridge, Norah	Hawthorn Junior Bio.	1965	YES	11 and up
20	India	Mother Teresa	Winkler, Father Jude	St. Joseph Picture	2002	NO	05 and up
20	Ireland	Edel Quinn: Beneath the Southern Cross	Brown, Evelyn M.	Vision Books	1967	YES	09-15
20	Ireland	Father Flanagan, Builder of Boys	Stevens, Clifford J.	American Background	1967	YES	10-15
20	Ireland	Operation Escape: The Adventure of Father O'Flaherty	Madden, Daniel	Hawthorn Junior Biography	1962	YES	11 and up
20	Israel	Desert Fighter: The Story of General Yigael Yadin and the Dead Sea Scrolls	Miller, Shane	Hawthorn Junior Biography	1967	YES	11 and up
20	Israel	Monuments to Glory: The Story of Antonio Barluzzi, Architect of the Holy Land	Madden, Daniel M.	Hawthorn Junior Biography	1964	YES	11 and up
20	Italy	Apostle of Peace, The Story of Pope Pius XII	Hatch, Alden	Hawthorn Junior Biography	1965	YES	11 and up
20	Italy	Assignment to the Council	Lomask, Milton	Clarion Books	1966	YES	09 and up
20	Italy	Blessed John Paul II: Be Not Afraid	Wallace, Susan Helen	Encounter the Saints	2011	NO	09 and up
20	Italy	Blessed Pier Giorgio Frassati: Journey to the Summit	Vazquez, Ana Maria and Jennings Dean	Encounter the Saints	2004	NO	09 and up
20	Italy	Book of Saints, Part 1 (St. Pius X)	Lovasik, Fr. Lawrence	St. Joseph Picture	1981	NO	05 and up
20	Italy	Book of Saints, Part 2 (St. Maria Goretti)	Lovasik, Fr. Lawrence	St. Joseph Picture	1981	NO	05 and up

20	Italy	Book of Saints, Part 5 (St. Gemma Galgani)	Lovasik, Fr. Lawrence	St. Joseph Picture	1985	YES	05 and up
20	Italy	Boy Who Was, The	Hallock, Grace	Newbery	1928	YES	10/ up
20	Italy	Father Flanagan, Builder of Boys	Stevens, Clifford J.	American Background	1967	YES	10-15
20	Italy	Good Pope John (Pope John XXIII)	Sheehan, Elizabeth Odell	Vision Books	1966	YES	09-15
20	Italy	Light Within: The Story of Maria Montessori	Smaridge, Norah	Hawthorn Junior Bio.	1965	YES	11 and up
20	Italy	Lives of the Saints: Modern Saints (St. Pio of Pietrelcina)	Tesoriero, Bart	Aquinas Kids	2012	NO	05-09
20	Italy	Lucrezia Bori of the Metropolitan Opera	Marion, John Francis	American Background	1962	YES	10-15
20	Italy	More Saints of the Eucharist: A Gem of the Eucharist (St. Gemma)	Francis, Father	Father Francis Coloring	1959	NO	06 and up
20	Italy	Nino	Angelo, Valenti	Newbery	1938	YES	09 and up
20	Italy	Operation Escape: Adventure of Fr. O'Flaherty	Madden, Daniel	Hawthorn Junior Biography	1962	YES	11 and up
20	Italy	Padre Pio	Winkler, Father Jude	St. Joseph Picture	2004	NO	05 and up
20	Italy	Pope John Paul II	Winkler, Jude Rev.	St. Joseph Picture	2005	NO	05 and up
20	Italy	Pope Pius XII, The World's Shepherd	de Wohl, Louis	Vision Books	1961	YES	09-15
20	Italy	Pope St. Pius X	Forbes, F.A.	Forbes Biography	1918, 1987	NO	12 and up
20	Italy	Rich in Love: Story of Padre Pio of Pietrelcina	Bertanzetti, Eileen Dunn	Weaver Books	1999	YES	09-12
20	Italy	Saint Gianna Beretta Molla: The Gift of Life	Wallace, Susan Helen	Encounter the Saints	2012	NO	09 and up
20	Italy	Saint Maria Goretti	Windeatt, Mary Fabyan	Windeatt Coloring	1955	NO	04 and up
20	Italy	Saint Pio of Pietrelcina: Rich in Love	Bertanzetti, Eileen Dunn	Encounter the Saints	2002	NO	09 and up
20	Italy	Saint Pius X	Windeatt, Mary Fabyan	Windeatt Coloring	1955	NO	04 and up
20	Italy	Saint Pius X, The Farm Boy Who Became Pope	Diethelm, Walter	Junior Vision	1963	YES	09-11
20	Italy	Saint Pius X, The Farm Boy Who Became Pope	Diethelm, Walter	Vision Books	1956, 1994	NO	09-15
20	Italy	Saints of the Eucharist: A Lily in God's Garden (St. Maria Goretti)	Francis, Father	Father Francis Coloring	1958	NO	06 and up

20	Italy	Saints of the Eucharist: The Pope of Little Children (St. Pius X)	Francis, Father	Father Francis Coloring	1958	NO	06 and up
20	Italy	Story of Pope Benedict XVI for Children, The	Mohan, Claire Jordan	Mohan Biographies	2007	NO	09 and up
20	Italy	Story of St. Gemma, A	Ernest, Brother	Footsteps of the Saints	1957, 2010	NO	06-09
20	Italy	They Became Saints (St. Mary Goretti: "The Lily of the Marshes")	Francis, Father	Father Francis Coloring	1951	NO	07 and up
20	Italy	Way of the Cross (The), A Story of Padre Pio	Mohan, Claire Jordan	Mohan Biographies	2002	NO	09-12
20	Italy	Yes Is Forever! Mother Thecla Merlo, The First Daughter of St. Paul	Daughters of St. Paul	Encounter Books	1981	YES	09 and up
20	Japan	Dawn From the West: The Story of Genevieve Caulfield	Rau, Margaret	Hawthorn Junior Biography	1964	YES	11 and up
20	Laos	Doctor America: The Story of Tom Dooley	Morris, Terry	Hawthorn Junior Bio.	1963	YES	11 and up
20	Laos	I Charge Each of You: Story of Dr. Tom Dooley	O'Brien, Sr. Mary Celine	Holy Cross Press	1966	YES	09 and up
20	Lithuania	Kaze's True Home, The Young Life of a Modern Day Saint, Mother Maria Kaupas	Mohan, Claire Jordan	Mohan Biographies	1992	YES	09-12
20	Luxembourg	Mother Alfred and the Doctors Mayo	Richardson, James P.	Banner Books	1959	YES	09-15
20	Mexico	Dawn Brings Glory, A Story of Blessed Miguel Pro	Roberto, Brother	In the Footsteps of the Saints	1956, 2013	NO	12-15
20	Mexico	God's Secret Agent, The Life of Father Michael Augustine Pro, S.J.	Daughters of St. Paul	Encounter Books	1967	YES	09 and up
20	Mexico	Jose Finds the King, A Blessed Miguel Pro Story	Ball, Ann	Glory of America	2002	NO	7-12
20	Mexico	Nine Days to Christmas, A Story of Mexico	Ets, Marie and A. Labastida	Caldecott	1959	YES	04 and up
20	Mexico	Padre Pro, Mexican Hero	Royer, Fanchon	American Background	1963	YES	10-15
20	Mexico	Saints of the Americas (Blessed Miguel Agustin Pro)	Winkler, Rev. Jude	St. Joseph Picture Books	2006	NO	05 and up
20	Morocco	Charles de Foucauld, Adventurer of the Desert	Garnett, Emmeline	Vision Books	1962	YES	09-15
20	Netherlands	Book of Saints, Part 9 (Bl. Teresa - Edith Stein)	Lovasik, Fr. Lawrence	St. Joseph Picture	1996	NO	05 and up
20	Netherlands	Book of Saints, Part 9 (Bl. Titus Brandsma)	Lovasik, Fr. Lawrence	St. Joseph Picture	1996	NO	05 and up

20	Norway	Knute Rockne, Football Wizard of Notre Dame	Daley, Arthur	American Background	1960	YES	10-15
20	Peru	Trailblazer for the Sacred Heart, Fr. Mateo Crawley-Boevey (Globe-Trotter for the Sacred Heart)	Balskus, Pat	Encounter Books	1976	YES	09 and up
20	Philippines	Island Hero: The Story of Ramon Magsaysay	Gray, Marvin M.	Hawthorn Junior Bio.	1965	YES	11 and up
20	Poland	Blessed by the Cross: St. Edith Stein	Hill, Mary Lea FSP	Encounter the Saints	1999	NO	09 and up
20	Poland	Book of Saints, Part 6 (St. Maximilian Kolbe)	Lovasik, Fr. Lawrence	St. Joseph Picture	1985	YES	05 and up
20	Poland	Book of Saints, Part 9 (Bl. Teresa - Edith Stein)	Lovasik, Fr. Lawrence	St. Joseph Picture Books	1996	NO	05 and up
20	Poland	Lives of the Saints: Modern Saints (St. Maximilian Kolbe)	Tesoriero, Bart	Aquinas Kids	2012	NO	05-09
20	Poland	More Than a Knight, The True Story of St. Maximilian Kolbe	Daughters of St. Paul	Encounter Books	1982	YES	09 and up
20	Poland	Music from the Hunger Pit, A Story of St. Maximillian Kolbe	Roberto, Brother	In the Footsteps of the Saints	1954, 2008	NO	09-12
20	Poland	Pope John Paul II	Winkler, Jude Rev.	St. Joseph Picture	2005	NO	05 and up
20	Poland	Saint Maximilian Kolbe: Mary's Knight	Jablonski, Patricia	Encounter the Saints	2001	NO	09 and up
20	Poland	St. Faustina Kowalska: Messenger of Mercy	Wallace, Susan Helen	Encounter the Saints	2007	NO	09 and up
20	Poland	St. Maximiliam Kolbe, Story of the Two Crowns	Mohan, Claire Jordan	Mohan Biographies	1999	YES	09-12
20	Poland	Young Life of Pope John Paul II, The	Mohan, Claire Jordan	Mohan Biographies	1995, 2005	NO	09-12
20	Poland	Young Life of Saint Maria Faustina, The	Mohan, Claire Jordan	Mohan Biographies	2000	NO	09-12
20	Poland	Young Life of Sister Faustina, The	Mohan, Claire Jordan	Mohan Biographies	2000	YES	09-12
20	Portugal	Blessed Jacinta and Francisco Marto: Shepherds of Fatima	Heffernan, Anne & Patricia Jablonski	Encounter the Saints	2000	NO	09 and up
20	Portugal	Boy with a Mission, The Life of Francis Marto of Fatima	Daughters of St. Paul	Encounter Books	1967, 1981	YES	09 and up
20	Portugal	Children of Fatima and Our Lady's Message to the World, The	Windeatt, Mary Fabyan	Windeatt Saint Series	1991	NO	09 and up
20	Portugal	Our Lady Came to Fatima	Hume, Ruth Fox	Vision Books	1957, 2005	NO	09-15

20	Portugal	Our Lady of Fatima	Richomme, Agnes	Catholic Children's Library	1965, 2012	NO	10 and up
20	Portugal	Our Lady of Fatima	Windeatt, Mary Fabyan	Windeatt Coloring	1954	NO	04 and up
20	Portugal	Our Lady of Fatima	Lovasik, Fr. Lawrence	St. Joseph Picture	1984, 1991	NO	05 and up
20	Portugal	Story of Our Lady of Fatima, A	Ernest, Brother	Footsteps of the Saints	1957, 2010	NO	06-09
20	Russia	Lion of Poland: The Story of Paderewski	Hume, Ruth and Paul	Hawthorn Junior Bio.	1962, 2012	NO	11 and up
20	Spain	Book of Saints, Part 9 (St. Miguel Cordero)	Lovasik, Fr. Lawrence	St. Joseph Picture	1996	NO	05 and up
20	Spain	Book of Saints, Part 11 (Bl. Angela of the Cross Guerrero)	Lovasik, Father Lawrence	St. Joseph Picture Books	1997	NO	05 and up
20	Spain	Lucrezia Bori of the Metropolitan Opera	Marion, John Francis	American Background	1962	YES	10-15
20	Spain	Saints of the Americas (St. Miguel Cordero)	Winkler, Rev. Jude	St. Joseph Picture	2006	NO	05 and up
20	Thailand	Dawn From the West: The Story of Genevieve Caulfield	Rau, Margaret	Hawthorn Junior Biography	1964	YES	11 and up
20	United States	Amazing John Tabb (Civil War)	Betz, Eva K.	Catholic Treasury	1958	YES	10 and up
20	United States	Beyond the Clouds: The Story of Christa McAuliffe	Collins, David R.	Weaver Books	1996	YES	09-12
20	United States	Book of Saints, Part 3 (St. Frances Cabrini)	Lovasik, Fr. Lawrence	St. Joseph Picture	1982	NO	05 and up
20	United States	Brother Dutton of Molokai	Crouch, Howard E.	Catholic Treasury	1958	YES	10 and up
20	United States	Catholic Campuses, Stories of American Catholic Colleges	Staudacher, Rosemarian	Vision Books	1958	YES	09-15
20	United States	Champions in Sports and Spirit (Gil Hodges, Rocky Marciano, Maureen Connolly, Maurice Richard, Bob Cousy, Terry Brennan, and Yogi Berra)	Fitzgerald, Ed	Vision Books	1956	YES	09-15
20	United States	Dawn From the West: The Story of Genevieve Caulfield	Rau, Margaret	Hawthorn Junior Biography	1964	YES	11 and up
20	United States	Door of Hope: The Story of Katharine Drexel	Burton, Katherine	Hawthorn Junior Biography	1963	YES	11 and up
20	United States	Father Flanagan, Builder of Boys	Stevens, Clifford J.	American Background	1967	YES	10-15

20	United States	Fighting Father Duffy	Bishop, Jim & Virginia Lee	Vision Books	1956	YES	09-15
20	United States	Fighting Irishman: The Story of "Wild Bill" Donovan"	Wilhelm, Maria	Hawthorn Junior Biography	1964	YES	11 and up
20	United States	Forty-Ninth Star (The), Alaska	Savage, Alma	Banner Books	1959, 2011	NO	09-15
20	United States	Got a Penny? The Story of Dorothy Day	Collins, David R.	Weaver Books	1996	YES	09-12
20	United States	Governor Al Smith	Farley, James and James Conniff	Vision Books	1959	YES	09-15
20	United States	I Charge Each of You: The Story of Dr. Tom Dooley	O'Brien, Sister Mary Celine	Holy Cross Press	1966	YES	09 and up
20	United States	I Lay Down My Life, Biography of Joyce Kilmer	Cargas, Harry	Similar to Encounter Books	1964	YES	09 and up
20	United States	In American Vineyards: Religious Orders in the United States	Staudacher, Rosemarian	Vision Books	1966	YES	09-15
20	United States	John Fitzgerald Kennedy, Man of Courage	Strousse, Flora	American Background	1964	YES	10-15
20	United States	John LaFarge, Gentle Jesuit	Strousse, Flora	American Background	1968	YES	10-15
20	United States	Juanita	Politi, Leo	Caldecott	1948	NO	04 and up
20	United States	Katharine Drexel, Friend of the Neglected	Tarry, Ellen	Vision Books	1958, 2000	NO	09-15
20	United States	Katie, Young Life of Mother Katharine Drexel	Mohan, Claire Jordan	Mohan Biographies	2000	NO	09-12
20	United States	Kaze's True Home, The Young Life of a Modern Day Saint, Mother Maria Kaupas	Mohan, Claire Jordan	Mohan Biographies	1992	YES	09-12
20	United States	King of Song: The Story of John McCormack	Hume, Ruth and Paul	Hawthorn Junior Biography	1964	YES	11 and up
20	United States	Knute Rockne, Football Wizard of Notre Dame	Daley, Arthur	American Background	1960	YES	10-15
20	United States	Lion of Poland: The Story of Paderewski	Hume, Ruth and Paul	Hawthorn Junior Biography	1962, 2012	NO	11 and up
20	United States	Long Trail (The), The Story of Buffalo Bill	Kolars, Frank	Banner Books	1960, 2011	NO	09-15
20	United States	Lucrezia Bori of the Metropolitan Opera	Marion, John Francis	American Background	1962	YES	10-15
20	United States	Magnificent Failure: Story of Fr. Solanus Casey	Collins, David R.	Weaver Books	1999	YES	09-12

Saint Series Books in Chronological Order

20	United States	More Champions in Sports and Spirit (Stan Musial, Carmen Basilio, Alex Olmedo, Herb Score, Juan Manuel Fangio, Ron Delany, Eddie Arcaro, & Jean Beliveau)	Fitzgerald, Ed	Vision Books	1959	YES	09-15
20	United States	Mother Alfred and the Doctors Mayo	Richardson, James P.	Banner Books	1959	YES	09-15
20	United States	Mother Cabrini, Missionary to the World	Keyes, Frances	Vision Books	1959, 1997	NO	09-15
20	United States	My Eskimos: A Priest in the Arctic	Buliard, Roger P.	Vision Books	1956	YES	09-15
20	United States	Pedro, The Angel of Olvera Street	Politi, Leo	Caldecott	1946	NO	04 and up
20	United States	Pen and Bayonet: The Story of Joyce Kilmer	Smaridge, Norah	Hawthorn Junior Bio.	1962	YES	11 and up
20	United States	Prisoner of Lost Island (Catholic fiction)	Kolars, Frank	Similar to Catholic Treasury	1961	YES	10 and up
20	United States	Rose Hawthorne: The Pilgrimage of Nathaniel's Daughter	Sheehan, Arthur & Elizabeth	Vision Books	1959	YES	09-15
20	United States	Saint Frances Cabrini	Windeatt, Mary Fabyan	Windeatt Coloring	1956	NO	04 and up
20	United States	Saint Frances Xavier Cabrini: Cecchina's Dream	Dority, Victoria and Mary Andes	Encounter the Saints	2005	YES	09 and up
20	United States	Saint Katharine Drexel: The Total Gift	Wallace, Susan Helen	Encounter the Saints	2003	NO	09 and up
20	United States	Saints for Boys and Girls (St. Frances Xavier Cabrini)	Beebe, Catherine	Beebe Biography	1959	YES	09-14
20	United States	Saints for Girls (St. Frances Cabrini)	Muus, Solveig and Bart Tesoriero	Aquinas Kids	2012	NO	05-09
20	United States	Saints of the Americas (St. Katharine Drexel)	Winkler, Rev. Jude	St. Joseph Picture	2006	NO	05 and up
20	United States	Search for a Shepherd (A), A Story of Fr. Paul of Graymoor	Roberto, Brother	In the Footsteps of the Saints	1959, 2011	NO	09-12
20	United States	Sidewalk Statesman, Alfred E. Smith	Schofield, William G.	American Background	1958	YES	10-15
20	United States	Song of the Swallows	Politi, Leo	Caldecott	1949	NO	04 and up
20	United States	Submarine Pioneer: John Philip Holland	Morriss, Frank	Catholic Treasury	1961, 2012	NO	10 and up
20	United States	Tall American: The Story of Gary Cooper	Gehman, Richard	Hawthorn Junior Bio.	1963	YES	11 and up

20	United States	To Far Places: The Story of Francis X. Ford	Betz, Eva K.	Hawthorn Junior Bio.	1962	YES	11 and up
20	United States	To the Ends of the Earth, A Story of St. Frances Xavier Cabrini	Greene, Brother Genard	In the Footsteps of the Saints	1955, 2009	NO	09-12
20	United States	Ursulines, Nuns of Adventure: The Story of the New Orleans Community	Kane, Harnett T.	Vision Books	1959	YES	09-15
20	various	Chaplains in Action	Staudacher, Rosemarian	Vision Books	1962	YES	09-15
20	various	Children Welcome: Villages for Boys and Girls	Staudacher, Rosemarian	Vision Books	1963	YES	09-15
20	various	Journeys with Mary: Apparitions of Our Lady	de Santis, Zerlina	Encounter the Saints	2001, 2002	NO	09 and up
20	various	Journeys with Mary: Apparitions of the Blessed Mother	de Santis, Zerlina	Encounter Books	1981, 1982	YES	09 and up
20	various	Modern Crusaders	Moore, John & Rosemarian Staudacher	Vision Books	1957	YES	09-15
20	Vietnam	Doctor America: The Story of Tom Dooley	Morris, Terry	Hawthorn Junior Bio.	1963	YES	11 and up
20	Vietnam	I Charge Each of You: The Story of Dr. Tom Dooley	O'Brien, Sr. Mary Celine	Holy Cross Press	1966	YES	09 and up
20	world	King of Song: The Story of John McCormack	Hume, Ruth and Paul	Hawthorn Junior Bio.	1964	YES	11 and up
20	world	Trailblazer for the Sacred Heart, Fr. Mateo Crawley-Boevey (Globe-Trotter for the Sacred Heart)	Balskus, Pat	Encounter Books	1976	YES	09 and up
20	Yugoslavia	Mother Teresa's Someday, The Young Life of Mother Teresa of Calcutta	Mohan, Claire Jordan	Mohan Biographies	1990	NO	09-12
20	Yugoslavia	Young Life of Mother Teresa of Calcutta, The	Mohan, Claire Jordan	Mohan Biographies	1997	YES	09-12
21	Italy	Blessed John Paul II: Be Not Afraid	Wallace, Susan Helen	Encounter the Saints	2011	NO	09 and up
21	Italy	Pope John Paul II	Winkler, Jude Rev.	St. Joseph Picture	2005	NO	05 and up
21	Italy	Story of Pope Benedict XVI for Children, The	Mohan, Claire Jordan	Mohan Biographies	2007	NO	09 and up
various	Ireland	Big Tree of Bunlahy, Stories of My Own Countryside	Colum, Padraic	Newbery	1933	YES	09 and up
various	various	Athletes of God: Lives of the Saints for Every Day of the Year	Hughson, Shirley	Holy Cross Press	1930, 1940, 1957	YES	09 and up

A Bibliomaniac's Guide to Collecting Books
Books about Books

The word *bibliomania*, a term coined in the mid-eighteenth century, describes an obsesssion for books, a passion sometimes described as a "fatal disease." Bibliomaniacs are "gently mad" according to Nicholas Basbanes, author of several books about book lovers, book hunters, and books in general. However, if you feel you would not qualify as "mad" about books, perhaps the term *bibliophile* appeals more sensibly to you. This term defines "a book lover" or "a book collector." For many bibliophiles—and all true bibliomaniacs—no book ranks higher than a book about books.

The following lists include books with reading lists, books about collecting books, books that discuss books, and books about displaying book collections in whatever nook and cranny may yet be available in your home. Check them out from your library. Better yet, treat yourself and search your favorite used bookstore for them. Those marked with a cross (✞) may be ordered from Catholic homeschooling vendors such as Emmanuel Books.

> **The love of learning, the sequestered nooks, and all the sweet serenity of books.** —Longfellow

Books with Reading Lists
* *A Mother's List of Books* by Theresa Fagan (1999) ✞
* *All Through the Ages, History through Literature Guide* by Christine Miller (1997, 3rd edition 2008 available from Nothing New Press)
* *Book Lust, Recommended Reading for Every Mood, Moment, and Reason* by Nancy Pearl [See other books about books by this author/librarian.] (2001, 2003)
* *Books Children Love, A Guide to the Best Children's Literature* by Elizabeth Wilson (1987, 2002)
* *Books for Boys, Titles and Descriptions of Exciting and Compelling Books for All Ages* by Chris Roe (1999, now out of print)
* *Catholic Authors, 4-Sight Edition* [grades 7-9] (1949); and *Catholic Authors, Crown Edition* [grades 10-12] (1952, available from Neumann Press)
* *Catholic Lifetime Reading Plan* [for adults] by John A. Hardon (1989, 1998, available from Grotto Press)
* *Catholic Mosiac: Living the Liturgical Year with Children, An Illustrated Book Study for Catholic Children* by Cay Gibson (2006, available from Hillside Education)
* *Designing Your Own Classical Curriculum, A Guide to Catholic Home Education* by Laura M. Berquist (1994, 1995, 1998, 1999, 2010 as Kindle edition) ✞
* *For the Love of Literature, Teaching Core Subjects with Literature* by Maureen Wittmann (2007, also available as Kindle edition) ✞
* *Honey for a Child's Heart, The Imaginative Use of Books in Family Life* by Gladys Hunt (1969, 1978, 1989, 2002, 2010 as Kindle edition)

★ *Let the Authors Speak, Guide to Worthy Books Based on Historical Setting* by Carolyn Hatcher (1992, 1995, now out of print)
★ *Lifetime Reading Plan* [for adults] by Clifton Fadiman (1960, 1963, 1988, 1999)
★ *Read-Aloud Handbook, The* by Jim Trelease (6th edition 2006, with 7th edition available June 2013)
★ *Reading Magic, Why Reading Aloud to Our Children Will Change Their Lives Forever* by Mem Fox (2008)
★ *Reading Promise (The), My Father and the Books We Shared* by Alice Ozma (2011) [This is a story of a father and daughter who read aloud every night for over eight years. Note that this contains a secular list of books. Please be aware especially of those books by Judy Blume and J.K. Rowling.]
★ *Reading through the Ages, Reading Selections 3000 BC to Present* by Linda Thornhill and Sally Barnard (1995, 1997, now out of print)
★ *Who Should We Then Read? Authors of Good Books for Children and Young Adults* by Jan Bloom (Volume 1, 2001; Volume 2, 2008; available from BooksBloom)
★ *World's Great Catholic Literature, The* [for adults] by George N. Shuster (1942, etc.; now out of print)

Books about Collecting Books
- *ABC for Book Collectors* by John Carter and Nicolas Barker (2004)
- *Book Finds: How to Find, Buy, and Sell Used and Rare Books* by Ian Ellis (3rd edition, 2006)
- *Collector's Guide to Children's Books, 1850 to 1950: Identification and Values* (Volumes 1 and 2) by Diane McClure Jones and Rosemary Jones (1996, 1997, 1998, 1999)
- *Collector's Guide to Children's Books, 1950 to 1975: Identification and Values* (Volume 3) by Diane McClure Jones and Rosemary Jones (2000)
- *Pocket Guide to the Identification of First Editions* by Bill McBride, 7th edition (2012)

Books that Discuss Books
- *Among the Gently Mad, Strategies and Perspectives for the Book Hunter in the Twenty-First Century* by Nicholas Basbanes [and other titles by this author] (2002)
- *Bequest of Wings, A Family's Pleasures with Books* by Annis Duff (1966; now out of print; available POD or used)
- *How to Read a Book, The Classic Guide to Intelligent Reading* by Mortimer J. Adler and Charles Van Doren (1940, 1967, 1972) ✝
- *Landscape with Dragons (A), The Battle for Your Child's Mind* [fantasy books] by Michael D. O'Brien (1994, 1998)
- *Passion for Books, A Book Lover's Treasury of Stories, Essays, Humor, Lore, and Lists on Collecting, Reading, Borrowing, Lending, Caring for, and Appreciating Books* by [editors] Harold Rabinowitz and Rob Laplan (2001)

- *Shelf Life, How Books Have Changed the Destinies and Desires of Men and Nations* by George Grant and Karen Grant (1999)
- *What Should We Then Know? About Constructing, Furnishing, Maintaining, and Enjoying a Home Library* by Jan Bloom (2003, now out of print)

Books about Displaying Book Collections
- *At Home with Books, How Booklovers Live with and Care for Their Libraries* by Estelle Ellis, Caroline Seebohm, and Christopher Simon Sykes (1995, now out of print)
- *Books Make a Home, Elegant Ideas for Storing and Displaying Books* by Damian Thompson (2011)
- *Living with Books, The Book-Lover's Guide to Storing, Displaying, and Caring for Books* by Alan Powers (1999, 2006)

Much information is also available online. Using a search engine, look for book lists specific to your interests—such as "Catholic book list." Many homeschooling sites, especially Catholic curricula sites, have recommended reading lists. Searches for specific topics such as book repair or identifying first editions will produce a plethora of material especially on book collectors' websites. Hours can be spent happily browsing. Enjoy!

> **A wonderful thing about a book, in contrast to a computer screen, is that you can take it to bed with you.**
> —Daniel J. Boorstein

Book Collecting Basics

General Information

The hobby of book collecting is an affordable and delightful pastime for both individuals and families. Besides the sheer fun and excitement of the hunt itself, the fruits of book hunting can feed avid readers, enrich homeschooling curriculum, and—if desired—earn extra money (to buy more books?). All that is required is a little seed cash, some free time, a bit of book knowledge—and maybe space for your finds. Whether you are interested in adding to your current book collection, beginning a basic children's library, or earning some extra money, the following tips should be useful to you.

> **When I get a little money, I buy books; and if any is left, I buy food and clothes.**
> —Desiderius Erasmus

First, remember that just because a book is out-of-print does not mean that it is no longer available. Out-of-print merely means that printing of the book has ceased. However, used (and perhaps new) copies may still be readily available—and in fact may be less expensive than an edition of the book that is currently in print.

Secondly, remember to check with used vendors even for books recently published as this often results in new or almost new books at considerable savings. With Internet access, book hunting has become easier than ever before. Develop the habit of checking any book's availablity first in the used market as many books (especially recent publications) sold as used may be new or near new.

Shop for out-of-print books at thrift stores, garage (rummage) sales, library discard sales (including school libraries), and used bookstores. Several helpful online resources include booksalefinder.com (lists library book sales throughout the country), addall.com/used (which lists over 20,000 dealers), biblio.com, abebooks.com, alibris.com, and ebay.com. Additionally, searching for a book on amazon.com can help determine whether a book is out of print or has been republished. Both Amazon and Barnes & Noble carry used books that may not appear on other book search websites. For Amazon, use either their main website or their used book site at bibliofind.com. Valerie Jacobsen has a very useful website at valeries livingbooks.info. With lists of series books, links to home schooling booksellers, and tips and links for collecting, this website ranks as one of the most informative sites for collectors of children's books. Valerie's list of valuable books is especially helpful when attending book sales. (Be aware, however, that Valerie is not Catholic, and some of her curriculum recommendations are not appropriate for a solidly Catholic education.)

> **The pleasure of reading is doubled when one lives with another who shares the same books.** —Katherine Mansfield

Used Catholic Children's Books

Finding used titles specifically geared toward Catholic children requires only slightly more diligence than finding out-of-print secular books. Search at St. Vincent de Paul thrift stores and church rummage sales. If you hear of a Catholic high school or elementary school that is closing, contact them to find out what will happen to the books in their library. Although used bookstores that specialize in Catholic books are not common, many online sources exist to help you with your Catholic children's library. Try these sites: CatholicAuthors.org, kellerbooks.com, Loomebooks.com, Marys-books.com, and Immaculatabooks.com. Check for Catholic booksellers on ebay.

Additionally, Yahoo has many groups devoted to the discussion and sale or swap of used Catholic books. Try these two groups for starters: Catholic Curriculum Swap (over 6700 members) and Roman Catholic Book Buy and Trade (over 200 members). Check for used book links at Catholic curriculum websites, or conduct your own online search for whatever particular title or series you wish to find.

> **A home without books is a body without soul.** —Marcus Tullius Cicero

Library Discards

The purpose of your book collection will determine which volumes of books you will choose to purchase. If you are procuring a reading library for your children, library discards—as well as paperback editions—are acceptable options. However, if you hope to amass a library that will appreciate in value and be part (or all!) of your children's inheritance, be aware that library markings seriously undermine the value of a book. Many secondhand bookstores refuse to stock library discards. While the condition grade of any given book may vary from dealer to dealer, former library books are generally never graded better than "good"—the condition given to reading copies only.

However, library books have several advantages over more collectable editions. Many library books have been rebound, that is the boards removed from the book signatures and replaced. These books are smaller than the original edition with covers that may not be as decorative. Generally very sturdy, these books make excellent reading copies that withstand rough handling and ensure less worry about depreciation or destruction. Many books sold to libraries have been published with sturdier "library bindings" that withstand more general abuse. A description of "library binding" may apply to either of these conditions.

> **A wonderful thing about a book, in contrast to a computer screen, is that you can take it to bed with you.** —Daniel J. Boorstein

Aside from their durability, library books also have the advantage of being not only less expensive to obtain but also more readily available. Libraries often receive the first printed edition of many books; you will more readily find true first editions and first printings from libraries. Finally, the dustjackets of library books are generally encased in a protective cover. Considering that up to 80% of the value of a collectible book resides in the dust jacket, finding a reading copy edition with a near-perfect dust jacket can be a worthwhile purchase.

> **Book lovers will understand me, and they will know too that part of the pleasure of a library lies in its very existence.** —Jan Morris

Identification of First Editions

All serious book collectors eventually will deal with the issue of first editions, as this—along with condition—is *the* determining factor regarding a book's monetary value. First editions are significant as they indicate the first or primary state of the book. Additionally, the initial printing may be smaller in number and therefore more difficult to obtain—more collectible.

The term *first edition* is itself a misnomer and today is often used interchangeably with *first impression* or *first printing*. What book collectors refer to as a *first edition* (or just a *first*) is generally the first printing of the first edition. A book can be a first edition and not a first printing. Identification of a true first edition also needs to take into consideration the matters of *issue, points of issue,* and *state* —all of which highlight the various causes of confusion regarding true first editions and the complexity involved in determining them. To cover completely the issue of the identification of first editions requires a high level of expertise and more space than is available here.

However, several principles can help clarify matters. Since the late 1940's, many publishers have adopted a simple system for identifying first editions—a number or letter string on the copyright page which is used to indicate first and later printings. Generally the presence of the letter "a" or the number "1" that appears anywhere on this line indicates that the edition is a first printing. (Of course, exceptions do apply even to this simple rule—most notably with Random House publishers.) For publishers using this system, if the words *first edition* appear and not either the letter "a" or the number "1" on the copyright page, the book is probably not a true first.

Number or letter strings aside, throughout the years different publishers have had different methods of designating first editions. These methods not only vary from publisher to publisher but have also frequently changed within each individual publishing company. Some publishers admit that they have not always conformed to their own company's practice while some have no designation for determining firsts at all. Book club editions of a book may indicate a first edition but if the book was previously published as a trade edition, the book club edition is not a true first. Reprint publishers may indicate *first edition*, but again a reprint volume would not be a true first edition.

So now that the matter of identifying first editions has been totally muddled and complete confusion reigns, it is clear that the scope of this book cannot begin to do justice to this topic. However, assistance is not far away. Many good articles exist online to help alleviate confusion regarding the identification of first editions. Additionally, in *Book Finds*, Ian Ellis has added an appendix that lists many common publishers and their procedures throughout the years for identifying first editions. If you wish to delve into this subject more deeply, purchase Bill McBride's booklet, *A Pocket Guide to the Identification of First Editions*—a small but comprehensive reference that is indispensable to beginning book collectors interested in identifying first editions.

Book Club Editions

Knowledge about book club editions (BCE) will not only aid in the identification of first editions but also help determine the value of your book collection. Some BCE's are true first editions as they may represent the first time a title is in print. They sometimes also mark the first appearance of a book as a hardback.

Although exceptions do exist in children's literature, book club editions—especially those generated by The Weekly Reader Book Club—are generally valued only slightly higher than paperback editions. Commonly, book club publishers cut costs on paper and bindings in order to sell their books at 20-30% less than the original volume; for example, paper may not be acid-free and hence subject to degradation, yellowing, and crumbling. Book club editions can be identified not only by their lighter, less-substantial feel but also by the lack of a price on the inside dust jacket. "Book Club Edition" may be marked on the dust jacket. These books may also be identified by a small square or round indentation (called a *blind stamp*) on the bottom right corner of the outside back cover.

> **Good as it is to inherit a library, it is better to collect one.**
> —Augustine Birrell

If you are buying books only for content and are on a strict book budget, book club editions will serve your purposes well. However, if you are looking for volumes that will continue to increase in value as collectible editions, be cautious about spending much money on book club editions.

Reprint Publishers

Books printed by reprint publishers are, like book club editions, often misidentified as true first editions. Like BCE books, reprints generally offer cheaper paper and bindings. Several identifying characteristics of reprints include the presence of two publishers—perhaps one on the spine and a different publisher on the copyright page, or a publisher on the copyright page that does not match the publisher on the title page. Five of the most prominent reprint publishers of children's books include E.M. Hale, M.A. Donohue, Hurst & Company, A.L. Burt, and Grosset & Dunlap. With the exception of some series books (Nancy Drew, Hardy Boys, Bobbsey Twins, Tom Swift, Cherry Ames, Judy Bolton, and Rick Brandt series books by Grosset & Dunlap; and G.A. Henty, Horatio Alger, and Edgar Rice Burroughs [Tarzan series] by A.L. Burt), most books by these publishers are reprints and not true first editions. Again, these books are less expensive and easier to obtain but have less value as collectible editions.

> **How many a man has dated a new era in his life from the reading of a book.**
> —Henry David Thoreau

In recent years, with the advent of print-on-demand publishing, reprints of popular out-of-print books have bloosomed. These volumes are often produced from a scanned copy of the book. This technology has made many previously scarce (and therefore expensive) books more readily available to the general public. However, be aware of reprint companies who spend little time proofreading, editing, or creating an attractive cover. In many such books, numerous "typos"—and even missing pages—may detract from the reading quality of the book. Some reprint companies also charge relatively high prices for inexpensive paperback copies of the books they produce. These companies are becoming more numerous and can often be identified when they describe their books as "print on demand" or give disclaimers on the quality of the book itself. A very plain, generic cover may also be an indication of this type of book.

Remainders

Another class of less expensive books to consider is remainder books. These are the new books you find on the clearance tables of bookstores. As publishers' overstocks, remainder books can be purchased at a savings of up to 80%. Many fine first editions can be found as remainder books. However, in order to prevent these books from being returned at full price, these books are generally marked—usually with a black marker on the top or bottom edge. However, a clean remainder book can be an excellent bargain and even a marked edition will only lose about 20% of its full value. Stock up at Christmas time when these bargains are most frequently found.

> **It is not enough to simply teach children to read; we have to give them something worth reading. Something that will stretch their imaginations—something that will help them make sense of their own lives and encourage them to reach out toward people whose lives are quite different from their own.**
> —Katherine Paterson

Care and Storage of Books
Care of Used Books

Introduction

Older, used books—as well as their dust jackets—can become dirty and stained. Several simple care tips can help clean a book, make it more pleasing in appearance, and increase its value. Stickers and labels are often easy to remove. Musty odors can be eliminated. Books, as well as book jackets, can be protected with covers. True bibliomaniacs will handle their books carefully, store them safely, and enjoy them for years to come. For more detailed and varied information on the topics discussed below, please refer to *The Care and Feeding of Books Old and New, A Simple Repair Manual for Book Lovers* by Margot Rosenberg and Bern Marcowitz; *Book Repair for Booksellers* by J. Godsey (available from sicpress.com); or the repair section of *Book Finds: How to Find, Buy, and Sell Used and Rare Books* by Ian Ellis. *A Simple Book Repair Manual*, created by Dartmouth College librarians, is available as a free download at www.dartmouth.edu/~library/preservation/ repair. Every bibliophile should order a catalog from at least one of the following library supply companies: demco.com, brodart.com, and/or gaylord.com. Many inexpensive products are available to aid you in keeping your books in tip-top condition.

Several rules of care apply to all books regardless of condition. First, never use self-stick notes on books. A small amount of adhesive may remain on the book page. Use thin bookmarks (not metal or cardboard) or small pieces of paper instead. Secondly, never use tape on books unless it is the type of tape specifically designed for book repairs. (Check library supply companies for this tape.) Cellophane tape may discolor, leave adhesive marks, or otherwise damage books. Remember this basic rule when repairing any book: Make no repairs or alterations that are not reversible.

> **Old books that have ceased to be of service should no more be abandoned than should old friends who have ceased to give pleasure.**
> — Sir Peregrine Worsthorne

Remember that the following suggestions for care and repair are intended for ex-library books or other books that have little monetary or sentimental worth. Many easy repairs can be performed with simple equipment and a limited level of expertise, but if in doubt, wait until expert help can be consulted. All repairs or alterations to valuable books should always be relegated to professionals.

Cleaning Books

Clean the boards of books by rubbing soft gum erasers gently over stains and marks. Be careful not to remove any of the cover dye. Rubber cement can also be applied; wait until it is half-dry and then roll it off, removing stains with the glue. If these seem too risky or cumbersome, check a library supply company for other book cleaning products. Products specifically designed for book cleaning (Absorene, Groom Sticks, cleaning pads, and cleaning cloths) are available at reasonable prices. Vinyl or plastic erasers can also be purchased to remove pen and pencil marks.

Be sure to routinely remove dust from books as dust can accumulate, especially on the top edge of books, causing damage. Thoroughly vacuum your books, especially the top edges, at least twice a year. You may opt to dust your books with a dust cloth specifically designed for books (available from library supply companies). Be sure to include all bookshelves in this semi-annual cleaning.

> **Books are delightful society. If you go into a room and find it full of books, even without taking them from the shelves they seem to speak to you, to bid you welcome.**
> —William Ewart Gladstone

Removal of Stickers, Labels, and Tape Marks

Smooth, coated dust jackets may be cleaned using rubbing alcohol applied to a clean rag. Do not use this on rough papers—only glossy dust jackets. Tougher stains on jackets can be treated with rubber cement in the same manner as the boards of books.

Two techniques are generally successful in the removal of stickers, labels, and tape marks. If the offending item is on the board or on a glossy jacket, use an adhesive removal product such as Goo Gone or Un-Du. (Do not use these products on untreated, rough paper.) If the label, sticker or tape mark is on paper—or if the adhesive removal product is ineffective—use a hair dryer, *set on low heat*, and gently work the sticker off starting at one corner. This can be a slow process. Do not turn up the heat on the hair dryer and work carefully. While the hair dryer treatment is effective for many stickers, book plates are difficult to remove and may best be left alone. Check for additional supplies available from Demco, Gaylord, Brodart, or other library supply companies.

Rolled or Cocked Spines

Improperly shelved books may have edges that are no longer square, a condition referenced in various terms—rolled spine, cocked spine, or spine slant. These books may or may not be willing to return to their original state. Try placing a book with a rolled spine in a tightly packed shelf with books of similar size. Make sure the spine is straight with the front pressed against a solid ridge or object. Leave the book untouched for several months. If this treatment is unsuccessful, consider purchasing a book press from a library supply store. (To prevent this damage, see "Handling and Shelving Books" beginning on page 255 below.)

Broken and Loose Hinges

Do not neglect a cracked or loose hinge on a book. A book that has its cover separating from the text block needs attention to prevent further damage. This repair is easily made using either tape, book adhesive, or both. Remember that a little glue goes a long way. Protect the surrounding areas with wax paper before applying the glue. For a more detailed explanation on how to make hinge repairs, refer to either *The Care and Feeding of Books Old and New*, Brodart's free repair guide, *The Simple Book Repair Manual* available from the Dartmouth College website, or *Book Repair for Booksellers* by J. Godsey—as referenced above.

> **Just the knowledge that a good book is awaiting one at the end of a long day makes the day happier.** —Kathleen Norris

Elimination of Odors and Insects

Love the smell of old books? Research indicates that glue, mold, deteriorating paper, and silverfish droppings (a not-so-pleasant thought!) provide the magical combination that produces the delightful smell found in libraries, used bookstores, and within individual volumes of old books themselves—a smell not reproducible in "e-books"! Countering this addicting smell is the loathsome smell of books exposed to too much moisture or humidity. However, several easy and effective methods are available to eliminate the musty odor found in neglected and abused books.

Before choosing a method, make sure that the book is completely dry. Setting the opened book outside under direct sunlight will help dry the book and may be enough to eliminate the offending odor. If further action is required, try putting the book, along with an opened box of baking soda, in a closed container such as an ice cooler or plastic storage container for several days—or weeks if necessary. Charcoal (without lighter added), solid room air fresheners, or kitty litter can also be used. (Depending upon how persnickety your kitty is, you may or may not be able to recycle this litter into your cat's box.) Be careful that the books are not touching the odor-eliminating ingredient.

> **I know every book of mine by its smell, and I have but to put my nose between the pages to be reminded of all sorts of things.**
> —George Robert Gissing

Examine any newly acquired book for signs of insect infestation—silverfish, roaches, book lice, and beetles. Such signs include the appearance of small holes the size of a pencil dot in the spine, cover or text block; the appearance of insect excrement (frass), or of dead or living insects. (Frass can look like tiny grains of sand, small black pellets, or brown stains.) Place the dry book in a zipper-sealed plastic bag and keep it in the freezer for at least three weeks, then immediately refrigerate (to slow down thawing) in the unopened bag for several days. Leave the book wrapped in the bag for several weeks after removing from the refrigerator. This treatment takes some time but is simply done and will protect the other books in your collection as insect infestation can spread if not eliminated. (The freezer treatment is also effective in reducing some book odors.) Although I have never tried it, there are some who prefer a microwave treatment for book bugs. Research online for further information before you try this alternate procedure.

> **What is the most precious, the most exciting smell awaiting you in the house when you return to it after a dozen years or so? The smell of roses, you think? No, moldering books.**
> —Andre Sinyavsky

Book Covers

Protective covers for book boards, dust jackets, and paperback covers are readily available from library supply stores. These come in various styles, sizes, and shapes. (Are you beginning to understand why you need a catalog from Broadart, Gaylord, and/or Demco?)

For hardback books without jackets, choose vinyl covers of the appropriate size. These come in two clear pieces for each book that fit together to encase the book and protect against stains, dust, and liquids. Several types of protective materials to cover paperback covers are also available.

For dust jackets, the products are more varied. For books with heavy use, choose protectors with a paper backing attached to a clear, polyester cover—such as Mylar® or Melinex®. A more inexpensive product is the easy-to-apply cover that is simply a clear cover. These are available in rolls or precut single sheets of various heights. I keep on hand the precut nine-inch, ten-inch, and twelve-inch extra longs (for picture books), which cover almost every book in my collection. After the first application, these products will go on in less than ten seconds (no prior knowledge or skill required) to protect your jackets from dirt and rubbing—and to jazz up their looks. For several additional dollars, the "bone" tool used to apply these covers is a worthwhile purchase. As these clear sleeves are inexpensive (less than $15.00 for fifty), all of the dust jackets in your collection should be covered. Do not take your cue from library policy regarding dust jacket covers; please do not tape the jacket or the clear sleeve to the book. Sans tape and glue is the best application policy!

Yellowing, Toning, Browning, and Foxing

Yellowing is a term used to describe the discoloration of pages that have begun to decay due to aging and/or low-quality paper. A high acid content in the book's paper will cause the fibers in the paper to break down, resulting in discoloration. Good quality paper will resist this discoloration. However, many older books—most notably juvenile books—were printed on high-acid paper and are thus prone to yellowing.

Because high humidity and high temperature promote paper discoloration, yellowing usually can first be seen on the edges of pages. "Toning" is another word to describe this occurance, especially in its milder form. "Browning"—a more severe case of page discoloration—indicates a more brittle condition of the paper. Treatment for this paper deterioration consists in deacidification of the paper and is best left to the professionals.

Another condition for which there really is no home remedy is foxing. This refers to the splotchy, rusty-looking discoloration found on some books' pages. Caused again by impurities in the paper and facilitated by high temperature and humidity, foxing (so-named as it can resemble muddy fox prints on the pages) is an expensive defect to treat as it requires deacidification and bleaching of the paper. Put foxing in the same category as yellowing, water stains, bookplates, and remainder marks—permanent blemishes that individualize your books!

> **The greatest gift is a passion for reading. It is cheap, it consoles, it distracts, it excites, it gives you knowledge of the world and experience of a wide kind. It is a moral illumination.** —Elizabeth Hardwick

Handling and Shelving Books

Common sense reigns when handling books. Use clean hands. Do not turn over page corners. Never place an opened book face down. Do not lick your fingers when you turn pages. Do not put anything other than a bookmark inside a book (no flowers, newspaper clippings, paper clips, pens, etc.). Do not use books for beverage coasters. Perform all simple repairs—without using cellophane tape. Encase all dust jackets in clear Mylar® or Melinex® sleeves.

A few basic considerations also apply to the topic of shelving books. Ideally, all books should be shelved upright with books of like vertical height. (Uneven pressure can cause the spine to roll or the boards to warp.) Oversized books that cannot be stood upright should be shelved with fore-edges facing down. Piling books on top of each other puts stress on the hinges and causes rubbing of the jackets. Piles may topple damaging books. If books must be shelved this way, put the larger, heavier volumes on the bottom. Do not shelf books horizontally on top of a vertical stack of books as this may cause spines to loosen, creating a "shaken" book whose binding is slanted or loose.

> **Books to the ceiling,
> Books to the sky.
> My pile of books
> are a mile high.
> How I love them!
> How I need them!
> I'll have a long beard
> by the time I read them.**
> —Arnold Lobel

Shelving books with other books of like vertical size reduces the risk of the books' boards warping or spines rolling. Another cause of rolled or cocked spines—in which the book's straight vertical line is ruined—is arranging the books on the shelf either too loosely or too tightly. Books stored too loosely will lean and start to roll; books stored tightly exert too much pressure on the books and may cause the spines to roll. This also causes the dust jackets to rub, depreciating their value. Books should be stored so that they maintain a straight vertical position yet allow fingers to be placed on each side of the book for easy removal from the shelf.

To prevent books from leaning (and spines from rolling), use bookends. Be wary of the kind that has a section that inserts underneath the book as these can damage the boards, jackets, and book edges. Any heavy weight will suffice for a bookend. Be creative!

The preferred method of removing a book from a shelf is to gently ease books away from the selected book. Either slide them back a bit on the shelf (if space permits) or place your fingers between the book and the books on either side, grasping the book by both its front and back covers and removing it straight out from the shelf. If you cannot remove a book easily from its shelf with either of these methods, the books are too tight on the shelf. Try not to tip a book when removing. Do not pull with the index finger on the headband when removing a book from its shelf as this can damage the hinge, the spine, and/or the headband.

Badly shelved books can lose value. Books should be shelved so that they are touching but not leaning or rubbing. If it is hard to remove a book, the books are shelved too tightly. Spines should be squarely lined up so pressure is even. Examine your collection for proper shelving.

Books do furnish a room. —Anthony Powell

Book Storage and Retrieval

Shelves

Although wooden shelving for books seems most common, the best material for bookcases is metal. Metal is easy to clean, sturdy, and will not allow books to leach stain, paint, vapors, or moisture from its surface. If using wooden shelves, use unpainted, unstained wood, but beware as wood absorbs moisture—a true enemy of any book. Cheap particleboard can be used but only if it is first covered with shelf paper to reduce abrasion and moisture absorption. Cover not only the bottom of the shelf but also the sides. Glass-encased bookshelves—a more impressive look—prevent dust from accumulating so quickly; books stored in such cases still require dusting twice a year and will need periodic airing to reduce moisture absorption.

> **I would be most content if my children grew up to be the kind of people who think decorating consists mostly of building enough bookshelves.**
> —Anna Quindlen

Temperature, Humidity, and Sunlight

Locate bookshelves conveniently—inexpensive cookbooks in the kitchen, juvenile titles placed low on the shelves, etc. Keep in mind that books stored near the kitchen will absorb cooking odors, and books stored near moisture will absorb that moisture. If possible, keep shelving away from heat sources such as forced air vents and radiators. Ideal temperature for books is between 60-70° F.

Ideal humidity for books is between 45-60% and should remain relatively stable. (Remember ideal heat and humidity is 60-60 with neither exceeding 70.) High humidity will cause mold growth, insect attraction, and promote page yellowing. Low humidity will cause the glue to dry and lose its flexibility. Pages can become weak and crack. How much you are willing to pay—if anything—to maintain this ideal humidity is obviously a personal decision.

> **Treat books as you should your own children, who are sure to sicken if confined to an atmosphere which is impure, too hot, too cold, too damp, or too dry.** —William Blake

Another great enemy of your books is sunlight—a natural bleacher. If possible, do not shelve your books where direct sunlight will hit them. Sunlight can cause fading on both jackets and cloth spines ("sunning"), reducing not only their attractive appearance but also their value. Ideally, books should be stored in total darkness. Unless you have a "medicinal" reason for placing a book in the sunlight (to dry a soggy book or help kill mold spores), keep a healthy distance between sunshine and your books.

> **No man can be called friendless who has God and the companionship of good books.** —Elizabeth Barrett Browning

Creating a System for Retrieving Books in Your Library

Similar to having a great number of tools and never being able to find the right one when it is needed, having an extensive library of books is not helpful if the right book cannot be found when it is wanted. Entering your book collection onto a computer database lets you know not only what books you have but also where a specific book can be found. Although there are a number of book inventory programs available for reasonable prices, my own system consists of a database created on MicroSoft's Works program—I know, old school program—but Excel or a similar program will work equally well. Fields are created such as title, author, type of work (history, fiction, picture, etc.), time-period (if historical), condition, ex-library or not, price paid, and shelved location of the book. Any database program already installed on your computer that allows searches will probably work. Additionally, many commercial products expressly created to inventory books (or other media materials) are readily available. This software ranges in price from $30 to $400 or a monthly fee of $5.00 and up. Do an online search for book collectors or book inventory software.

> **It was clear that the books owned the shop rather than the other way about. Everywhere they had run wild and taken possession of their habitat, breeding and multiplying and clearly lacking any strong hand to keep them down.**
> —Agatha Christie

Summary

A love of books implies a concern for the care of books. Many online resources are available to aid in caring for your books; many libraries and binderies offer classes (either weekend or full credit) in book repair and bookbinding. If these general instructions regarding book restoration and maintenance have simply whetted your appetite for book preservation and conservation, check online for further instructions in book care. Treat your books with care and consideration, and enjoy them for years to come.

> **I like a project that never ends, and a library is that.**
> —David Hicks

Other Resources by Janet P. McKenzie

RACE for Heaven Study Guides for Mary Fabyan Windeatt's Saint Biography Series teach the Catholic faith to all members of your family. Written with your family's various learning levels in mind, these flexible study guides succeed as stand-alone unit studies or supplements to your regular curriculum. Thirty to sixty minutes per day will allow your family to experience:

- ☑ The spirituality and holy habits of the saints
- ☑ Lively family discussions on important faith topics
- ☑ Increased critical thinking and reading comprehension skills
- ☑ Quality read-aloud time with Catholic "living books"
- ☑ Enhanced knowledge of Catholic doctrine and the Bible
- ☑ History and geography incorporated into saintly literature
- ☑ Writing projects based on secular and Catholic historical events and characters

Purchase these guides individually or in the following grade-level packages. (Grade level is are determined solely on the length of each book in the series.)

Grades 3-4: *St. Thomas Aquinas, The Story of the "Dumb Ox"*; *St. Catherine of Siena, The Girl Who Saw Saints in the Sky*; *Patron Saint of First Communicants, The Story of Blessed Imelda Lambertini*; and *The Miraculous Medal, The Story of Our Lady's Appearances to St. Catherine Labouré*

Grade 5: *St. Rose, First Canonized Saint of the Americas*; *St. Martin de Porres, The Story of the Little Doctor of Lima, Peru*; *King David and His Songs, A Story of the Psalms*; and *Blessed Marie of New France, The Story of the First Missionary Sisters in Canada*

Grade 6: *St. Dominic, Preacher of the Rosary and Founder of the Dominicans*; *St. Benedict, The Story of the Father of the Western Monks*; *The Children of Fatima and Our Lady's Message to the World*; and *St. John Masias, Marvelous Dominican Gate-keeper of Lima, Peru*

Grade 7: *The Little Flower, The Story of St. Therese of the Child Jesus*; *St. Hyacinth, The Story of the Apostle of the North*; *The Curé of Ars, The Story of St. John Vianney, Patron Saint of Parish Priests*; and *St. Louis de Montfort, The Story of Our Lady's Slave*

Grade 8: *Pauline Jaricot, Foundress of the Living Rosary and the Society for the Propagation of Faith*; *St. Francis Solano, Wonder-Worker of the New World and Apostle of Argentina and Peru*; *St. Paul the Apostle, The Story of the Apostle to the Gentiles*; and *St. Margaret Mary, Apostle of the Sacred Heart*

The Windeatt Dictionary: Pre-Vatican II Terms and Catholic Words from Mary Fabyan Windeatt's Saint Biographies explains over 450 Catholic terms and expressions used in this popular saint biography series. Indispensable in expanding knowledge and practice of the Catholic faith, this book provides a ready access for the Catholic vocabulary words used in the RACE for Heaven Windeatt study guides. This dictionary also includes a Catholic book report resource that contains suggestions for forty-five Catholic book reports:

fourteen writing projects, ten book report activities, and twenty-one topics for saint biographies.

Graced Encounters with Mary Fabyan Windeatt's Saints: 344 Ways to Imitate the Holy Habits of the Saints is a compilation of the "Growing in Holiness" sections of RACE for Heaven's Catholic study guides for the Windeatt saint biography series and presents 344 examples of saintly behavior, one for nearly every chapter in each of these twenty biographies. Enhance your encounter with the saints by practicing the models of devotion, service, penance, prayer, and virtue offered in this guide.

Bedtime Bible Stories for Catholic Children: Loving Jesus through His Word contains twenty discussions of Bible stories that were originally published in serial form in a Catholic children's magazine. Their author stated, "The tales are extremely simple and unadorned. They are real conversations of a real child and her mother." Due to popular demand, the series was later (1910) published as a book, *Bible Stories Told to "Toddles."* The engaging conversational style of this book lends itself well as a bedtime read-aloud that allows Jesus to come alive in the Gospels. The study aids include discussion questions to help foster spiritual conversation, Bible excerpts relevant to the presented story, "Growing in Holiness" suggestions for living the Gospel message in our daily lives, and short catechism lessons for both children and adults.

I Talk with God: The Art of Prayer and Meditation for Catholic Children strives to instill in young Catholics a love of prayer and a practical knowledge of the art of meditation. This prayer book contains prayers to pray out loud (vocal prayer) or in the silence of your heart. It shows how you can talk with God, and more importantly, how you can love God. As you progress through this book—from discovering what prayer is to reading and reciting simple prayers to understanding meditation and then to helps for deeper meditation—you will see that prayer and meditation often go together. Meditation is described by the big *Catechism of the Catholic Church* as nothing more than "prayerful reflection" or *holy thinking*. You can use books, devotions, pictures, holy cards, and images (such as the stained glass windows in church) to help you think about holy people, events, and ideas. Learn how to talk with God each day to increase your love for Him and follow more closely His holy will.

Communion with the Saints: A Family Preparation Program for First Communion and Beyond in the Spirit of St. Therese imitates St. Therese of the Child Jesus and her family who studied and prayed for sixty-nine days in anticipation of Therese's First Holy Communion. Modeling this preparation, the *Communion with the Saints* program will help any family find renewed fervor in the reception of the Eucharist. This resource includes a chapter-by-chapter study of the following four books:

- *The Little Flower, The Story of Saint Therese of the Child Jesus*—to provide the foundation of God's love for us and to encourage a desire for holiness

- *The Children of Fatima and Our Lady's Message to the World*—to show the sinfulness of our world and the need to avoid sin

- *The Patron Saint of First Communicants, The Story of Blessed Imelda Lambertini*—to inspire devotion to the Sacrament of Holy Communion

- *The King of the Golden City* by Mother Mary Loyola —to illustrate Jesus' Presence as a source of grace necessary to live a holy life

Each of the sixty-nine days of preparation includes read-aloud selections with enrichment activities, meditational readings, catechism lessons, and plenty of practical application to promote a growth in holiness and sanctity. Weekend suggestions include a list of over thirty-five family projects. The use of *My First Communion Journal* is encouraged with this program.

My First Communion Journal in Imitation of Saint Therese, The Little Flower provides a lasting keepsake of a child's First Holy Communion. This journal has been constructed in imitation of the copybook made for Therese Martin by her older sister Pauline to help Therese prepare for her First Holy Communion. Although this book is not an exact replica of the copybook used by Therese, it does contain many of the same prayers and aspirations she used, the same idea of flowers inspiring virtue, and the same method of recording prayers recited and sacrifices made. It is up to you to decorate and complete this journal, replicating Therese's heroic efforts by raising your mind and heart to Jesus and by humbling yourself with small sacrifices. Learn as well to imitate St. Therese's love and knowledge of Scripture as you meditate on—or even memorize—the biblical passages that are provided for reflection. This journal may be completed in conjunction with the *Communion with the Saints* program or used separately.

My First Communion Journal in Imitation of St. Paul, Putting on the Armor of God was also inspired by St. Therese's copybook and uses the same method of encouraging—and recording—daily prayers and mortifications. However, instead of using flowers to illustrate virtues, this resource uses the battle model St. Paul describes in Ephesians 6:10-17. First communicants are encouraged to arm themselves with virtues and spiritual weapons in order to fight as soldiers of Christ. The scriptural words of Jesus and St. Paul are reflected on frequently to encourage the imitation of the actions and love of Jesus and to inspire a love and knowledge of Holy Scripture. This journal too may be completed in conjunction with the *Communion with the Saints* program or used separately.

The King of the Golden City Study Edition is a new edition of a book that was originally published in 1921. This treasure of a book was written in response to a student's appeal for instructions along with "little stories" to help her prepare for Holy Communion. To fulfill this request, Mother Loyola of the Bar Convent in York, England, wrote a simple story that illustrates Jesus' desire to share an intimate relationship with each one of His children. This new edition contains some updated language but, quite deliberately, does not contain any pictures. Readers, as they progress through this story, will form a mental image of their King, one as unique and personal as their own relationship with Him. The study sections assist with the allegory, connect to the Bible as well as to the catechism, and explore the art of prayer in the spirit of the three Carmelite Doctors of the Church. Although written over ninety years ago for a young child, this book remains a timeless masterpiece of Catholic literature suitable for all ages. (Also available as a study guide only)

The Good Shepherd and His Little Lambs Study Edition is a simply told Catholic tale of four children who meet with their beloved aunt for "First Communion talks." More than a story, it is a First Communion primer that takes the tenets of the catechism and, through naturally-flowing conversations, relates them in the language of little ones to authentic Christian living. As Mrs. Bosch explains, "We might learn the catechism all the way through beautifully, and at the end find ourselves still very stiff and clumsy about loving our Lord. When He comes to us, we don't want to welcome Him into our souls only with answers out of the catechism, do we?" Enriched by appropriate Biblical passages, points of doctrine, and prayers, this story-primer is an enjoyable and effective read-aloud that will prepare the Good Shepherd's little lambs to worthily receive Him in the Holy Eucharist.

A Reconciliation Reader-Retreat: Read-Aloud Lessons, Stories, and Poems for Young Catholics Preparing for Confession provides a basic doctrinal explanation and review of the Sacrament of Reconciliation as well as a Gospel examination of conscience—a seven-day read-aloud formation retreat. To help the lessons come alive and to enable young Catholics to more readily apply these doctrines to their own daily lives, the lessons have been supplemented with pertinent short stories and poems. Each lesson contains reflection questions, a family prayer, and a "Gospel Examination of Conscience" that is formulated according to the dictates of the *Catechism of the Catholic Church*. This reader-retreat will not only enrich and deepen the sacramental experience for each member of your family but it will also provide several tools to help you recommit to leading a virtuous life and to grow together in holiness.

Devotion to St. Joseph: Read-Aloud Stories, Poems, and Prayers for Catholic Children encourages children to love Jesus as St. Joseph did. As Scripture does not record a single word this great saint spoke; we must take our lessons of his life from his actions. In this compilation of stories and poems about our Savior's foster-father from renowned Catholics, children of all ages are encouraged to imitate the virtues the life of St. Joseph reveal to us in his loving dedication to Jesus and Mary. The discussion questions as well as the reflections on the virtues of St. Joseph lead children to apply the lessons of this saint's life to their own while the prayer section promotes a lasting devotion to the great St. Joseph. As St. Teresa of Avila declared, "I wish I could persuade everyone to be devoted to this glorious saint!"

The Month of St. Joseph: Prayers and Practices for Each Day of March in Imitation of the Virtues of St. Joseph was originally published in 1874. This book contains daily meditations on the life and virtues of St. Joseph for adults and high-school students. In addition, each day presents a prayer to St. Joseph, several resolutions, a short ejaculatory prayer, a relevant Scripture verse, and a brief consideration for reflection. The practices for each day are intended to assist the reader in acquiring the habits of prayer and interior recollection so necessary to living in the presence of God. Perfect for Lenten reading, this journey through the life of St. Joseph reveals his love of God and neighbor, humility, quiet action, and spirit of sacrifice. While the Bible tells so little about St. Joseph's life, here we discover the abundant virtues of this silent saint—and are challenged to imitate them.

Alternative Book Reports for Catholic Students contains forty-five book report ideas to encourage critical thinking for ages seven to fourteen. These ideas are intended to provoke a reflection on those themes and topics that support and encourage Catholic living as well as some that may conflict with our Faith. Many report topics require an examination of our personal faith life and prompt us to take lessons from the saints to strengthen our own faith in God. The suggested activities vary from written exercises to creative art projects and include twenty-one topics specifically designed for saint biographies. Other activities can be used within a group or family.

The Outlaws of Ravenhurst Study Edition contains a classic story of the persecution of Scottish Catholics that was first written in 1923 and was revised and reprinted in 1950. This 2009 edition of Sr. M. Imelda Wallace's *Outlaws of Ravenhurst* contains the revised story of 1950 plus chapter-by-chapter aids to assist readers in assimilating the book's strong Catholic elements into their own lives. The study section focuses on critical thinking, integration of biblical teachings, and the study of the virtuous life to which Christ calls us as mature Catholics. With its emphasis on virtues (theological and moral plus the gifts and fruits of the Holy Spirit), the spiritual and corporal works of mercy, and the Beatitudes, *Outlaws of Ravenhurst Study Edition* is a fun and effective catechetical tool for Catholics preparing for the Sacrament of Confirmation. (Also available as a study guide only)

The Family that Overtook Christ Study Edition: The Story of the Family of St. Bernard of Clairvaux is an excellent read for young adults who are preparing to receive the Sacrament of Confirmation. In this exciting chronicle of the life of twelfth-century knights, we have an entire family of nine saints who lay before us their individual means of achieving intimate union with Christ. Learn with the Fontaines family how to supernaturalize the natural, develop a God-consciousness, and attain sanctity by being yourself. Perfect for high-school read-aloud (or adult study), this new study edition has over 250 footnotes for increased comprehension and provides discussion/meditation points to promote the art of spiritual conversation. The appendix lists formulas of Catholic doctrine that are essential for confirmands not only to know but also to incorporate into their own spiritual lives.

A Confirmation Reader-Retreat: Read-Aloud Lessons, Stories and Poems for Young Catholics utilizes chapters from two excellent out-of-print Catholic books for children (*I Belong to God, Great Truths in Simple Stories for Children and Lovers of Children* by Lillian Clark; and *Children's Retreats in Preparation for First Confession, First Holy Communion, and Confirmation* by Rev. P.A. Halpin). This book provides a basic doctrinal review of the Sacrament of Confirmation as well as prayer experiences—a nine-day read-aloud retreat/novena. The reprinted material has been supplemented with short stories and poems that provide insights in applying catechetical doctrines to the daily life of young Catholics. Each lesson concludes with "I Talk with God"—a section that encourages readers (of all ages) to deepen their relationship with each of the Three Persons of the Blessed Trinity. Reflection questions promote the habit of spiritual conversation within your family—to encourage family members to discuss holy topics—and to help you grow together in holiness. Additionally, a traditional novena to the Holy Spirit is included.

By Cross and Anchor Study Edition: The Story of Frederic Baraga on Lake Superior relates the exciting, and often miraculous, missionary adventures of the "Snowshoe Priest"—Venerable Frederic Baraga, the first bishop of Michigan's Upper Peninsula. Declared "Venerable" by Pope Benedict XVI on May 10, 2012, this priest came to the United States from Slovenia in 1830 to undertake his mission as a "simple servant of God." For almost forty years, Fr. Frederic Baraga traveled across over 80,000 square miles of wilderness by snowshoe in winter and canoe in summer. In imitation of Christ, Bishop Baraga become poor so that he might bring the riches of the Catholic Faith to the Chippewa and immigrant residents of the beautiful peninsula he served. Although not strictly a biography, this book is a story based on historical facts drawn from Bishop Baraga's own journal and letters—a fascinating, easy-to-read history of Michigan's northern peninsula. While this exciting adventure is intended for youth who are interested in knowing more about this quiet, courageous priest, readers of all ages will be inspired by his life of humility, simplicity, and selfless virtue. This new study edition contains over 130 footnotes, defining less familiar vocabulary words and—gleaned from Venerable Baraga's *Journal* and other primary sources—details regarding the region's people and places. Also included are discussion questions, applicable Scripture passages, pertinent quotations of Venerable Baraga from the text, and—most importantly—a section illustrating how to imitate the various virtues of Venerable Frederic Baraga. Additionally, the complete text of Bishop Baraga's 1853 "Pastoral Letter to the Faithful" has been included with numerous references added in order that we may read this in light of Scripture and the *Compendium of the Catechism of the Catholic Church*. Learn more about the life, ministry, and heroic virtues of Venerable Frederic Baraga, the "Snowshoe Priest."

To Order: Email info@RACEforHeaven.com or place an order at RACEforHeaven.com. Discover, MasterCard, VISA, PayPal, American Express, checks, and money orders are accepted.

www.ingramcontent.com/pod-product-compliance
Lightning Source LLC
Chambersburg PA
CBHW082113230426
43671CB00015B/2688